The Economy of Recognition

Ethical Economy. Studies in Economic Ethics and Philosophy

For further volumes:
http://www.springer.com/series/2881

Carlos Hoevel

The Economy of Recognition

Person, Market and Society in Antonio Rosmini

Springer

Carlos Hoevel
Department of Economics
Pontifical Catholic University of Argentina
Buenos Aires
Argentina

ISSN 2211-2707 ISSN 2211-2723 (electronic)
ISBN 978-94-007-6057-8 ISBN 978-94-007-6058-5 (eBook)
DOI 10.1007/978-94-007-6058-5
Springer Dordrecht Heidelberg New York London

Library of Congress Control Number: 2013932877

Printed on acid-free paper

Springer is part of Springer Science+Business Media (www.springer.com)

Acknowledgements

A work as large and complex as this would not have been possible only with my own intellectual, emotional and material forces. Hence the need for a long list of acknowledgements. First, I would like to express my gratitude to Emilio Komar who, besides being my teacher in Philosophy, was the person through which I learned the existence and value of the works of Rosmini and the relevance of his economic thought. I also want to thank Leon Kass who, along with other professors at the University of Chicago, helped me to understand the main economic, political and ethical ideas of the Anglosaxon tradition, so important in Rosmini. Another person to whom I owe a special thanks is Francisco Leocata, who helped me with his extensive knowledge of Rosmini not only to find a way to order the enormous body of texts and ideas at hand, but gave me his generous support in moments of fatigue and discouragement.

I also want to thank Umberto Muratore, who always gave me invaluable guidance and support during all my research trips. I want to express a similar acknowledgement to Cirillo Bergamaschi, Pier Paolo Ottonello and all the other Rosminian Fathers, researchers and collaborators at the Centro Internazionale di Studi Rosminiani in Stresa, Italy. I want to acknowledge the support of the Istituto Trentino di Cultura, and especially of Antonio Autiero, for his generous help and invaluable support for my research in Trento. I owe a similar thanks to Michele Nicoletti, director of the Research Center "Antonio Rosmini" at the University of Trento, for his guidance, support and appreciation of my work. From my time in Trento, the friendship and help of Omar Brino, Lucia Galvagni and Pietrina Pellegrini were also invaluable. I would also like to mention Alberto Baggio, Michele Dossi, Francesco Ghia, Christiane Liermann, Paolo Marangon, and Francesco Traniello, who enthusiastically received the results of my work.

I am deeply indebted to the Catholic University of Milan and especially Daniela Parisi, who not only helped me with her vast knowledge of the history of Italian economic thought, but mostly with her friendship and support during my stays in Milan. I want to give a similar acknowledgement to Evandro Botto, who so generously opened to me the doors of the Center for the Study of the Social Doctrine of the Church at the Catholic University of Milan, to Simona Beretta, Alessandro

Ghisalberti and Andrea Villani, of the same university and to Marco Guidi of the University of Brescia, who were always willing to exchange ideas about Rosmini.

I also thank Markus Krienke, director of the Rosmini Chair at the School of Theology of Lugano, who from the beginning showed enthusiasm for my work and shared with me his thoughts, humor and friendship. My acknowledgement also to other Italian professors linked to that chair, Salvatore Muscolino, Giulio Nocerino, Silvio Spiri, Samuele Tadini, and Giovanni Ventimiglia, who showed interest in my research. Special thanks as well to Lorenzo Airoldi, director of the TV channel 6, dedicated to the promotion of the figure and thought of Rosmini. I also want to express my gratitude to Stefano Zamagni, from the University of Bologna, who was to me a central reference of contemporary economic thought and from whom I always received words of encouragement and interest in my work.

I also want to thank especially all the members of the European SPES Forum, particularly Luk Bouckaert, Rita Ghesquiere, Knut Ims, Hendrik Opdebeeck and Lazslo Zsolnai, who were interested in my work and gave me their support and friendship. I also appreciate the support and generosity of the Acton Institute, particularly of Samuel Gregg, with whom I share many ideas on the relationship between economics, philosophy and religion and also Kishore Jayabalan, Kris Mauren, Michael Severance and Robert Sirico. I do not want to forget mentioning also John Crosby, Severine Deneulin, Michael Naughton, Michael Novak, and Charles Wilber who guided me in the fields of personalist philosophy, the theory of human development and economic and business ethics. I also want to give special thanks to Miguel Alfonso Martínez Echevarría of the University of Navarra and to Felix Muñoz of the Francisco de Vitoria University for their interest and support to my work.

I want to express a particular recognition to the institution I belong to, the Faculty of Economics of the Pontifical Catholic University of Argentina (UCA), which for years has given me a space and an invaluable support for my research. From my colleagues at UCA, I want to give special thanks to Ludovico Videla, who opened me the world of Argentine economists and allowed me to know distinguished economists like Carlos Moyano Llerena, Felipe Tami, Francisco Valsecchi and Javier Villanueva, who were also inspiring figures for this work. I also want to thank Ricardo Crespo, Octavio Groppa, Gustavo Hasperué, Violeta Micheloni, Joaquín Migliore, Ernesto O'Connor, Alvaro Perpere, María Marta Preziosa, Marcelo Resico, Agustina Rosenfeld, Rafael Sassot, Camilo Tiscornia and Carlos Torrendell of the Journal of Economic Culture and the Centre for Studies in Economics and Culture of the Catholic University of Argentina with whom, since 1998, I share a rich intellectual environment, besides the joy of friendship. I am also indebted to Juan Francisco Franck, for his friendship and his deep metaphysical lessons on Rosmini. Moreover, also in the area of the UCA, I want to thank especially Carlos Ezcurra, Víctor M. Fernández, Carlos Garaventa, Manuel González Abad, Patricio Millán, Fernando Ortega and the other members of the Institute for the Integration of Knowledge; Eduardo Taussig and Alfredo Zecca for their constant support to my research. I also want to thank William Darós of the UCEL University in Rosario, Alberto Espezel and the other members of the Journal *Communio*, Hugo Ferullo of the National University of Tucumán, Cecilia Vázquez Ger and Gabriel Zanotti of the Acton Institute of Argentina and Mario Casalla, Santiago Kovadloff, and all the other members of the Canoa Group at the Association of Latin American Philosophy and Social Sciences.

Finally I want to thank Peter Koslowski, who opened me the doors of the Series *Studies in Economic Ethics and Philosophy* and was generously interested in my work in the months prior to his sudden and untimely death. I also want to give special thanks to the translators Laura Esteve, Lara Muscolini and María Sol Riscossa for their invaluable work in preparing the English version of this text, as well as Agostina Prigioni, for her precious work of proofreading and editing. My appreciation also to Diana Nijenhuijzen and Neil Olivier of Springer for their patience, efficiency, and sensitivity. In addition, I want to thank my parents, the insistence and support of Diego Rey and Neven Zivkovic, and the love of my wife Mare and of my daughters Clara and Inés, without which this work would surely have not seen the light.

Contents

Chapter 1
Introduction: From Autism to Recognition

1.1 The Autistic Economics

A few years ago, a group of French students of economics issued a surprising statement addressed to – in their own words – "professors and others responsible for the teaching of this discipline." They feverishly expressed a strong disapproval against an economics they found so distant from reality that it was considered an "autistic" science. "We wish to escape from imaginary worlds – they claimed. We no longer want to have this autistic science imposed on us" (Fullbrook 2000). Years later, in a milder tone though, a group of British students launched a similar petition in more precise terms: "As students at Cambridge University – they stated – we wish to encourage a debate on contemporary economics. As defined by its teaching and research practices, we believe that economics is monopolized by a single approach to the explanation and analysis of economic phenomena. At the heart of this approach lies a strong commitment to formal modes of reasoning that must be employed for research to be considered valid. The evidence for this is not hard to come by: the contents of the discipline's major journals, of its faculties and its courses all point in this direction" (The Cambridge 27, 2001).

It may well be argued that these are journalistic statements not to be taken seriously. However, – according to the Swiss economist Bruno Frey – similar views have also been advanced in the academic discourse. Actually, Frey illustrates, "Clower, former editor of the *American Economic Review*, states that "much of economics is so far removed from anything that remotely resembles the real world that it is often difficult for economists to take their subject seriously". Moreover, Frey adds, "Even Nobel Prize recipients in economics such as Leontief, Coase or Buchanan, criticize their field for its lack of involvement in real life issues". The most devastating judgment is, however, made by Blaug: "Modern economics is sick; economics has increasingly become an intellectual game played for its own sake and not for its practical consequences" (Frey 2006, 3). Now, what do these students and scholars refer to when they complain about this "single approach" that is so powerful as to monopolize a whole discipline? And, on the other hand,

C. Hoevel, *The Economy of Recognition: Person, Market and Society in Antonio Rosmini*, Ethical Economy 42, DOI 10.1007/978-94-007-6058-5_1,

what makes them maintain that "a general application of this viewpoint to the understanding of economic phenomena is debatable" to the point of considering it "imaginary," "autistic" and "a mere intellectual game" disconnected from reality?

1.2 The Neoclassical Paradigm

Undoubtedly, these critics make reference to the so called economic approach or "rational choice" model, also known as the "homo oeconomicus," "self-interest" or simply the "utilitarian" model (Kirchgässner 2008) which, held mainly by the supporters of the neoclassical economic theory, is based on three major methodological assumptions. Firstly, – as Gary Becker and George Stigler state – "the hypothesis that widespread and/or persistent human behavior can be explained by a generalized calculus of utility-maximizing behavior," a thesis that would not permit of direct proof because, according to its supporters, "it is an assertion about the world, not a proposition in logic" (Becker and Stigler 1977, 76). From this point of view, people are always "maximizing" means to achieve an end, that is, they seek the maximum benefit at the lowest cost, and render other people or values as means or instruments for their own ends. Besides, the most radical neoclassical economists believe that such a description would be valid not only for those who are involved in traditional economic activities but also for all human behavior: from the most ambitious stockbroker to Mother Teresa.[1]

A second axiom of the economic approach is the value-free principle. In terms of this assumption, it is irrelevant for an economic analysis to refer to other psychological motivations or moral and religious values to portrait the economic behavior, which explains why economists can do without these factors. Neoclassical economists maintain that these motivations are mere subjective "preferences" or "tastes" born out of culture or society's standard morals, which tend to be universal and constant throughout the years and, thus, do not modify in the least the maximizing orientation of human behavior. "Tastes neither change capriciously nor differ importantly between people (. . .) (They) will be there next year, too, and are the same to all men" (Becker and Stigler 1977, 76). Therefore, economic analysis can perfectly describe and foresee human behavior towards consumption, labor and exchange among millions of individuals as a group of activities governed by a maximization mechanism. This mechanism is homogenous for all human beings and measurable in terms of general standards, without involving complex psychological, moral and spiritual processes connected with subjectivity.

Finally, the neoclassical economic mainstream also relies on the "methodological individualism" assumption which states that an economic analysis can be carried out without taking into account the social or political dimension. Social entities are assumed to be, at least at a heuristic level, mere additions or "aggregates" of

[1]One of the best examples of this point of view is in Gary Becker (1978).

individual actions. According to this point of view, the interaction that takes place in social relationships among people does not modify the maximizing behavior of individuals, whose only fixed aim is still that of the utility that everyone seeks for themselves. This is the implied principle underlying the different Walrasian, Paretian or Arrow-Debreu's equilibrium theories. They describe the functioning of the macro-economy as a more or less mechanical and automatic adjustment process of a group of maximizing individual actions. When competing and accompanied by an appropriate policy of individual incentives, this adjustment results in a "rational" or highly efficient outcome, disregarding the political, social or cultural framework.

These three combined assumptions,[2] in addition to a process of extreme mathematical formalization, has turned economics into an increasingly "pure" discipline, separate from social and human sciences and isolated from praxis. Nevertheless, this "autism" did not imply a loss of the discipline's influential power. On the contrary, the analytical refinement of its models marveled supporters and lay as well, and paved the way for the so-called "economic imperialism," a term that uncovers the intention of making economics the epistemological model for all sciences and the single matrix for political and social praxis.

1.3 Besieging the Fortress: Objections and Alternatives to the Mainstream

From its first postulates, neoclassical economic theory has been the target of many critiques not only from Marxism but also from the Historical school (debate on method), the Institutional school or the Austrian school (Elster 1987). Even influential neoclassical economists such as Frank Knight, co-founder of the School of Chicago, and Keynes himself strongly opposed many of the anthropological foundations of the mainstream they took part in. Moreover, during the last decades, when the neoclassical model achieved its highest refinement and hegemony in and out of the discipline, a huge amount of internal critiques started to arise on the part of those who, even sharing some methodological principles, have begun to show inconsistencies and objections.

In 1957 the Nobel Prize winner, Herbert Simon (1957), had come up with the concept of bounded rationality, which explained our choice behavior not as optimizing nor maximizing but purely satisfactory, given the limitation of both the available information and the capacity to obtain it when having to make concrete decisions. In 1977, Amartya Sen, 1997 Nobel Prize recipient, described the utility-maximizing agents of the neoclassical economic theory as rational fools, since he believes that a maximizing behavior, which only takes into account the

[2] "The combined assumptions of maximizing behavior, market equilibrium, and stable preferences, used relentlessly and unflinchingly, form the heart of the economic approach as I see it" (Becker 1978, 5).

efficiency of means but is neutral when it comes to ends or values, derives in short-sighted, inefficient and self-destructive actions.[3] A few years later, another Nobel Prize winner, George Akerlof, outraged orthodox analysists in the field of labor by proposing a rational model for the efficiency wage hypothesis, which states that employers – driven by motivations different from maximization of utility – sometimes pay wages that exceed market-fixed prices, contrary to the neoclassical idea of maximization (Akerlof and Yellen 1986).[4] In the same decade, Vernon Smith and Daniel Kahneman (both 2002 Nobel Prize recipients) expanded the experimental economics field which opened the doors for many economists to start using the results of laboratory experiments and psychological studies (behavioral economics) to reveal that people's actual behavior is often different from that of the homo oeconomicus. Revaluing the role of spontaneous and intuitive thought, the aforementioned authors supported the heterodox idea of the variation of preferences – not always purely selfish nor stable – as well as the key role of fairness or reciprocity in economic relations.

Lately, authors like Bruno Frey have demonstrated the relevance of "intrinsic motivation" in the economic decision-making process as opposed to the neoclassical orthodox idea about the absolute priority given to monetary incentives (Frey 1997). Others have also highlighted the essential role of spiritual factors like the so-called "expressive rationality" and the importance of identity in economic decision-making (Akerlof and Kranton 2001; Hargreaves Heap 2001). Finally, the work of Richard Easterlin (1974) and Tibor Scitovsky (1976), later followed by other researchers like Alfred Hirsch (1978), Richard Layard (2005) and Robert Frank (2000), proved how people's decisions are strongly influenced by the pursuit of happiness, going far beyond economic profit or consumption satisfaction, as outlined by neoclassical economists.

Furthermore, similar objections have been addressed to the different Walrasian, Paretian and Arrow-Debreu's theories on market equilibrium which prevailed for several decades as the neoclassical assumptions in the social sphere. According to Ernesto Screpanti and Stefano Zamagni, since 1970, the neoclassical synthesis fortress in the macroeconomic field has been suffering a sort of decay, besieged by different theories: the New Classical Macroeconomic theories, the non-Walrasian equilibrium theory, the non-Keynesian theories, the different approaches of Institutional Economics (Hodgson 1998; North 1990), the neo-Austrian Schools of Economics, and the various neo or post- Marxisms (Sraffian, anti-Sraffian,

---

[3] "The economic theory of utility has too little structure. A person is given one preference ordering, and when the need arises this is supposed to reflect his interests, represent his welfare, summarize his idea of what should be done, and describe his actual choices and behavior. Can one preference ordering do all these things? A person thus described may be «rational» in the limited sense of revealing no inconsistencies in his choice behavior, but if he has no use for these distinctions between quite different concepts, he must be a bit of a fool" (Sen 1977, 335–336).

[4] The works of Ernst Fehr and Armin Falk have significantly weakened the neoclassical assumption of "perfect egoism" revealing how "fairness" and "altruist" reciprocity play a key role in labor relationships (Fehr and Gächter 2000).

Regulationists, neo-Schumpeterian, neo-Keynesian, etc.) (Screpanti and Zamagni 2005, 163). Despite marked differences among them, they all seem to reject an excessive rationalist and mechanicist model of market equilibrium, trying to explain the insertion of markets in the complex and entangled web of bonds, rules, habits and values rooted in society and culture. In this way, the new macroeconomic proposals made by authors such as James Buchanan, John Elster, Richard Hodgson or Douglas North seem to rely on more flexible modes of thinking proper of biology (developmental model), sociology, anthropology and law. In addition to these, new research in the field of economic development introduces social and cultural elements significant to economic development. Besides Albert O. Hirschman's developmental theory, in the last years highlighted Amartya Sen's hypothesis about the relation between economic development and political freedom (Sen 1999), Robert Putnam's theories on social capital (Putnam 2000) and Stefano Zamagni's civil economy (Bruni and Zamagni 2007).

1.4 Zenith and Collapse of the Modern Matrix

Certainly, the departure from the "autistic" model of human action, individually based on the idea of a rational subject that maximizes means for his or her self-preservation and socially based on a mechanical and homogeneous equilibrium among maximizing subjects who are indifferent and isolated from one another, is mainly an endogenous process that economics is going through. Nevertheless, this process is unquestionably part of a paradigm shift that is taking place in all disciplines, one of the symptoms of a colossal historical process involving the crack of modernity's matrix which has been witnessed in the past decades.

In fact, the neoclassical model of thought was only a part of the economic, political, social, cultural and scientific-technological organization matrix of modernity, which was shaped as a result of the vast process of development of modern States. Through the establishment of centralized political, administrative and educational systems, each State contributed to the emergence of important national political spaces, domestic markets and also to the development of a homogenized language, culture, race and religious profile of its population. The role of sciences, especially economics, was crucial to carry out this vast process of rationalization in society. Imbued with a mechanicist and utilitarian philosophy, social sciences tried to explain, predict and guide the behavior of the average citizen in the industrial society in order to make him follow a behavior pattern that would allow his efficient adaptation to the system requirements.

Undoubtly, this process of modern rationalization of society left back extreme particularism, unpredictability and fragmentation typical of the pre-modern world. It also made it easier for millions of people to become citizens granted with political and social rights. Finally, it made possible an unprecedented improvement in material-well being and gave way to new encounters, broadened horizons and shaped identities. Nevertheless, modern rationalization also showed its downside and extremely destructive potential. Actually, it also produced new ways of dominion, destruction of the social fabric, environmental devastation, and systematic exclusion or even disposal of individuals.

Nowadays, this modern matrix is bearing a rapid process of general crisis and transformation. In fact, after more than 400 years of constant evolution heading towards the same direction, national States are undergoing a unique process of reversion of their power concentration and capacity for rationalization. Due to the growing processes of opening up, interrelation and technological transformation of the economies, of capital mobility that weakens the State's taxing capacity, the ongoing increase of citizen's unsatisfied claims and the resulting crisis of governmental and political bureaucracies, States are no longer able to retain their political, educational and scientific monopoly. Therefore they cannot control their civil societies following the same one-way, homogenizing logic. Thus, this transformation is leading to a dramatic collapse of the old economic, social, education, racial, gender, linguistic and religious structures, and is giving rise to all kinds of new differences and identities.

In the epistemological level this process results in an increasingly evident inefficiency of modern rationalist sciences to explain and predict in a homogenous and mechanicist way such a complex world. Hence, there is a clear need for a new mode of thinking devoid of rationalist intentions that can give sense and guidance to a process which offers possibilities but is also creating new problems, just as serious as those aroused by the former modern matrix, or even worse. In this sense, the barrage of criticisms on neoclassical economics forms part of the turbulent shift from the modern rationalist-utilitarian paradigm to a new, although still uncertain, paradigm that can provide a framework for the transformation process that we are witnessing.

1.5 The Recognition Paradigm: The Hegelian Arguments

Together with this historical and epistemological transformation, during the last decades, we have also seen the last stages of decomposition of modern philosophy. However, despite extreme criticism and fragmentation – especially by post-modern authors – some philosophers have made the effort not to give in to the nihilist temptation of pure deconstruction by proposing a draft of what could turn into a novel paradigm of thought to replace the dying rationalist-utilitarian paradigm. In this sense, it is worth mentioning a series of works by authors who interpret our times as a transition from what they call the "Machiavellian and Hobbesian" paradigm of "self-conservation" to a new 'recognition' paradigm. While the first paradigm describes State, society and economy as an aggregate of utility or power maximizers subjects, closed to themselves and related to others in a mechanical way, the latter paradigm affirms that the former can only emerge from open subjects capable of recognizing others and establishing free and reciprocal bonds with them.

An example of this proposal is the one presented more than a decade ago by Axel Honneth, one of the new representatives of the Frankfurt School (Honneth 1996). Encouraged by his professor, Jurgen Habermas, to have a second reading of Hegel' s early works during his stay in Jena, Honneth claims that the concept of "recognition" (*Anerkennung*) formulated by the well-known German philosopher during the first stages of his thought, constitutes an alternative tradition to the modern philosophical model, focused on a self-interested and utilitarian subject, later inherited by our modern social sciences, especially by economics. In fact, in Honneth's opinion, Hegel's thought during the Jena period should not be confused with that reflected in the final version of the *Phenomenology of Spirit*. In this latter work, the autistic logic of interaction amongst self-interested subjects is ruled out by what Honneth calls the false idealist solution of a Reason and an Absolute Spirit that subsume individuals and intermediate institutions. On the contrary, the young Hegel proposed the pluralist and intersubjective road of recognition.

According to Honneth, the adoption of the Hegelian paradigm of recognition means not only the dismissal of the individualist paradigm of self-preservation but also of the classical statalist and socialist paradigms of "redistribution", based on Hegel's later thesis on master-slave dialectics (Fraser and Honneth 2003). Leaning not only on Hegel but also on post-Freudian psychologists such as Winnicott or sociologists like George Mead, Honneth argues about the possibility of giving these primitive Hegelian theories – never fully rounded off – an empirical support in order to enlighten the path of social sciences and of the complex social and cultural reality of our times. According to Honneth, the adoption of Hegel's early thought, enriched by the latter contributions, would put an end to today's instrumental rationality and a one-dimensional utilitarian vision of economy, politics and technology, and be able to reconstruct the latter based on the recognition of persons and their rights, identities, culture and lifestyles.

In addition to Honneth's proposal, the Canadian philosopher, Charles Taylor, puts forward another remarkable proposal regarding the recognition paradigm. Taylor (1994) grounds his argument in Wittgenstein and George Mead but mainly in Hegel, though not interpreted in the same way as Honneth. Taylor reduces the weight Honneth gives to struggle in the process of recognition, and essays a more romantic interpretation of Hegel's ideas when he links recognition to the search for "authenticity" and "expressiveness." According to Taylor, while in traditional societies recognition was almost non-existent owing to the fact that each individual or social group had fixed and pre-assigned roles and identities, modernity emerged when identity began to depend on reciprocal interaction and exchanges with what Taylor defines as "significant others." In fact, he states that the development of modern societies and economies started to derail when this process of recognition was stopped to be replaced by homogenizing tendencies. Precisely, in Taylor's view, the revival of the recognition paradigm would leave behind what he calls the "monological tendency proper to modern philosophy's mainstream," and would enable the recreation of a society, a culture and an economy based on dialogue, freedom and diversity.

One final example of the recognition paradigm in philosophy – strongly attached to current issues in social sciences and economics – are the works of the late Paul Ricoeur. The French philosopher criticizes the idea of recognition as identification – proper to modern rationalist philosophies – and proposes a concept of recognition based on "the ruin of representation" which Emmanuel Levinas describes as the result of Husserl's phenomenology and is taken to the extreme by Heidegger. Given this "ruin," recognition would not account for the result of the submission of things or others to the "objective" categories of a subject (Decartes, Kant) but for the outcome of relationality and pre-categorical circular reciprocity among subjectivities essentially opened to others. Informed by Axel Honneth's theses, Ricoeur also turns to Hegel as the connecting thread to understand what is happening nowadays regarding the social sciences. After a phenomenology of "self-recognition", Ricoeur takes the Hegelian concept of *Anerkennung* to analyze the transition from the self-preservation model to that of the recognition of rights and capacities (Amartya Sen), and to more radical phenomena of social recognition such as reciprocity, gift and agape (Ricoeur 2005).

Now, the question is what to do so that the development of a novel "recognition paradigm" is not thwarted by a new proliferation of forms of dominion, homogenization and concentration similar to those of modern times but in a global scale. In this sense, the "return to Hegel" movement as a philosophical cornerstone for a recognition paradigm might represent a risk. In fact, judging by Habermas and Honneth's proposal, the possibility of relying on the Hegelian approach is partial since it is restricted to Hegel's early Jena writings and, thus, it does not apply for the rest of his work. Certainly, there are some authors like Robert Williams (2000) and Robert Pippin (2000) who consider the recognition model to be transversal to all Hegel's works, even when he has grown out of his youth stage and seems to give priority to a totalizing Spirit that comprises all individualities. However, on the other hand, some authors like Michael Theunissen (1991) simply deny the idea of recognition being supported in any of Hegel works. Anyway, though it is not our intention of taking sides in this Hegelian debate, the already known classical arguments presented by Kierkegaard, Rozensweig, Adorno or Levinas on Hegel's limitations to ground a philosophy of recognition seem still hardly refutable.

1.6 Beyond Utilitarianism and Hegel: Rosmini's Contribution to a Recognition Theory

This book intends to introduce an alternative to the Hegelian foundation of a recognition paradigm in economics based on the viewpoint of the Italian philosopher Antonio Rosmini (1797–1855). Ignored by many in the world of philosophy even in our days, Rosmini was a thinker contemporary with Hegel who formulated a philosophical system as important and deep as the latter's. Moreover, Rosmini was seen for decades as a kind of "Italian Hegel" or "Italian Kant" due to the reception and interpretation of his work amongst the Italian idealists, Spaventa, Croce and Gentile during the first half of the twentieth century. Especially Giovanni Gentile – who was a great philosopher who gave his support to fascism as Mussolini's minister of education – tried to place Rosmini and also the Italian philosopher and Rosmini's contemporary Vincenzo Gioberti within a forced historiographical scheme. Through this scheme both listed as the followers of German idealism in Italy that would find its climax in pure "actualism," an extreme version of idealism represented by the same Gentile (1958). However, today's historiographical and philosophical critique considers that Rosmini borrows from Hegel not with the intention of assimilating his thought passively into an 'Italianized' version, but willing to go beyond him through a more profound and embracing speculative perspective (Ferroni 1987; Krienke 2008a; Donà 2001).

Like Hegel, Rosmini builds a general interpretation of modernity and particularly of economics upon an idea of a recognition that seeks to do away with the idea of a modern individualist subject. Rosmini argues that human action is not restricted to the individual's self-referential framework and to self-preservation natural needs; on the contrary, it involves a wider spiritual dynamics by which the individual self somehow "goes out of himself," meets the others and, only then, he is able to rediscover himself. Just like Hegel, Rosmini believes that the properly human dimension can be attained through a progressive recognition process which makes people realize that life is not just about following passively the course of their natural and individual impulses and needs, but it is necessary to "spiritualize" and "universalize" them so as to integrate them into a more comprehensive dimension. However, Rosmini departs from Hegel, or at least from his traditional interpretation, when Hegel understands recognition in terms of the disposal of the empirical individuality in favor of a supraindividual "we" (Objective and Absolute Spirit). On the contrary, Rosmini affirms that even though the dynamics of recognition limits our own individuality, it does not imply its denial.

Indeed, Rosmini's conception of recognition relies on a personalist idea of the human being far different from that held by Hegel and utilitarians. The Italian philosopher argues that the recognition phenomenon which characterizes human action is possible, in the first place, by virtue of what he calls the "idea of being." Indeed, the idea of being as objectively present in the human spirit is the central thesis of Rosmini's thought on which depend all other parts of his thinking from Metaphysics to Economics. In his *NewEssay on the Origin of Ideas* (1830), Rosmini presents an exhaustive critique of almost every epistemological system from Plato and Aristotle through Aquinas, Descartes, Locke and Hume to end in Kant and Hegel. In relation to Kant, Rosmini accepts and even deepens the critical problem posed by the German philosopher, but does not lapse into the immanentist conclusions of the latter. Indeed, according to Kant, our knowledge is conditioned by forms previous to experience inherent to what he calls transcendental subjectivity through which we construct the object and can never come to know reality itself. While Rosmini agrees with Kant that there is a form in our minds prior to experience through which we know reality, the Italian thinker does not conceive it as a subjective form, but as an objective idea that, although present in the subject, both transcends and surpasses it infinitely: this idea is precisely what Rosmini called the "idea of being." According to Rosmini, there is nothing we can think, feel or act without the idea of being. However, unlike what is claimed by Hegel, Rosmini believes that although the idea of being is discovered in thought, the latter is not the cause or the producer of the idea of being but, on the contrary, it is the idea of being the one produces and enables thought. By this argument Rosmini turns the turnabout made by Kant and deepened by Hegel, without falling on a naive realism previous to the emergence of the critical problem.

Moreover, according to Rosmini, it is due to the presence of the idea of being, that is the object and the form of our intelligence, that we can then illuminate our sensory experience, which is particular and subjective, transforming it into an objective knowledge of reality. Besides, it is also due to the same idea that we are also able to act morally going beyond our self- interest or subjective utility. Indeed, according to Rosmini, the human being, as a subjective individual, is a natural being (in Rosmini's language, a "real being") in search of his self-preservation. However, through intelligence, and also in virtue of freedom, he is capable of recognizing himself and others "objectively," taking thus part in a new form of being that Rosmini calls "moral being." Thus, through the involvement in what Rosmini defines as the "three modes of being" – real (subjective), ideal (objective), and moral (the bridge between subject and object) – the human being becomes this special kind of individual that Rosmini calls "person" (Franck 2006).

In fact, Rosmini defines the person as a real being (individual-material-subjective) that through the presence in his spirit of the ideal being (objective, universal, infinite, transcendent) can become a moral being (free, good, happy). Moreover, according to what Rosmini calls "transcendental thought," human beings must be also understood in relation to Infinite Real Being to which they are ultimately open through freedom and moral action. Yet, unlike Hegel, Rosmini does not reduce the individual to a dialectical movement of Infinite Being, but believes that the unity and infinity of being – that Rosmini defines as "synthetism of being"– is reflected in each particular person, who therefore exceeds any dialectics.[5] Thanks to this personalist approach, Rosmini departs from both extreme individualist subjectivism and extreme collectivist objectivism which have characterized modernity.

[5]"The limits of created beings do not come therefore from dialectics, as Hegel wants, but are previous to it. Nor it is true what this philosopher pretends that individual limits are fleety and mortal because they are lost dialectically in being. Nor dialectics can make finite beings get into infinite being, neither it can make them get out of it" (Rosmini 2001, 663).

1.7 Rosmini's View on Economics

In his detailed study *The Theory of the Individual in Economics*, John Davis (2003) points out that what could best characterize neoclassical economists' theses is the utilitarianism and individualism inherited from authors such as Hobbes, Locke and Bentham. Nonetheless, as Stefano Zamagni argues, besides this utilitarianism, there is another distinctive feature of neoclassical economics which the English economist Philip Wicksteed defines as non-tuism: the impersonality or indifference to the presence of a "you," typical of neoclassical descriptions of economic agents.[6] In this sense, the interest in bringing up Rosmini's economic thinking relies in the fact that it addresses a radical criticism of this depersonalizing utilitarianism that has dominated economics from Wicksteed and Robbins to Friedman and Becker. Moreover, Rosmini helps us to visualize an alternative to replace the utilitarian postulates by a recognition paradigm based on the idea of the human person.

Rosmini's critique of the utilitarianism inherent to the origins of economics, that we will present in Chap. 2 of this book, allows us to discover how micro-economic formulas which consacrate "maximization of utility" as the human behavior model do not derive from scientific principles or hypotheses, but from philosophical ideas acritically received: a combination of mathematizing rationalism and subjectivist empiricism that turns the subject into a utility function, devoid of spirit, free will and of the faculty of transcending towards the other. On the contrary, the Rosminian theories of human and economic action, developed in the light of the human capacity to freely recognize objective reality in accordance with its intrinsic structure – set out in Chaps. 3 and 4 – serve as a conceptual framework sufficiently deep and comprehensive so as to guide the valuable alternative attempts economics has made during the last few years.

In Chaps. 5 and 6 we shall attempt to portrait the way Rosmini, a visionary of what is occurring in today's debates, redefines from the perspective of truth recognition and the pursuit of happiness the meaning of many fundamental economic concepts such as utility, economic value, needs, wealth, poverty, work and consumption. Additionally, in these chapters we shall also try to show how, according to the Italian author, the lack of truth recognition, the absence of the pursuit of real happiness or ethical virtues in economic agents is the source of most economic problems with a highly destructive power, as we have seen in the 2008 financial crisis. Furthermore, Rosmini points out the need to take into account these factors in economic descriptions, predictions and prescriptions so that they do not end being partial, abstract and potentially erroneous.

---

[6]Zamagni cites Wicksteed: "A specific characteristic of any economic relation is not the egoism behind it, but non-tuism."(...) "The economic relation does not exclude everyone else except myself from my mind; it includes potentially everyone else except you." (...) "It is only when *tuism* guides my behaviour that it ceases to take on a fully economic form. It is therefore nonsense to think of selfishness as the characteristic feature of economic life" (Zamagni 2005, 311).

Rosmini also describes the deep transformation that the analysis of economic action goes through not only in virtue of the recognition of the order of being in general, but mainly of the recognition of the other as a person, at an individual and social level. In agreement with today's criticism on autistic economics, Rosmini finds economic action incomprehensible and destructive if not seen inside the confines of human relationships. From here comes the Rosminian conception of the market – analyzed in Chap. 6. According to Rosmini, the market should not be understood as a mere mechanism of collision of blind interests, but as an interpersonal network which encourages the mutual recognition of interests, rights and duties in the light of an objective idea of justice animated by the virtues of honesty, trust and charity.

Moreover, Rosmini thinks the market cannot be studied in isolation from the bonds, either material or spiritual, that build up society. Despite being partially expressed through the State, these bonds are not restricted to it. In this sense, Chap. 7 deals with Rosmini's sharp observations on market and State utilitarianism – patrimonial, populist, liberal, socialist or communitarian – which represent a valuable contribution to current debates on the new role of the market and the State in face of the crisis. Besides, Chaps. 8, 9 and 10 shall attempt to show how Rosmini's set of principles, instruments of social and economic policy and institutions – attuned to nowadays proposals of a transition from a welfare State to a welfare society – would harmoniously combine the market, the State, and civil society, without resulting in any Statism or economism that would distort economic rationality or ruin people's morality.

As we shall see in the conclusion, just like the eminent economic philosophers of all times – Smith, Hegel, Marx, Croce or Bulgakov – Rosmini has tried to elevate economic science to a wider sphere that, at the same time, could embrace and surpass its traditional form. While to some authors that wider sphere should be reached through the State, society or the market, Rosmini believes that what economics and the economy need is to acknowledge the human person, the key concept of his audacious attempt to give modernity a new and wider horizon of meaning.

Chapter 2
A Philosopher in Search for the Economy

2.1 Rosmini's Views on Economy Within the Framework of His Biographical and Intellectual Itinerary

2.1.1 Between Austria and Venice

Having developed a thought as comprehensive as that of Hegel or Kant's, Antonio Rosmini (1797–1855) is considered one of the most important philosophers of European modernity. He was also a practical thinker who, throughout a complex, personal and intellectual process, gave birth to a social and economic project that he found applicable to the Italy and the Europe of his time. He was born in Rovereto, a small town in the high mountains of the Adige Valley, a prelude to the Alps, in the contended borderline of the Italian Trentino. During the upheaval of Napoleonic Wars, Romanticism and the Industrial Revolution, Rosmini witnessed the first great social, political and material progress in Europe and the clash between two cultures undergoing a rapid change and cracking. Indeed, from a very young age, Rosmini felt a strong attachment to the Austrian Empire to which Rovereto used to belong. In his youth, he viewed the old Habsburg Empire – the Rosmini family having been ennobled by a special endowment of the Emperor Maximilian II in 1574 – as the great ideal of a vast political union built upon a rich social network that differed – as regards its solidity, organization and scope – from both the fragmentation and weakness of Italy and French centralist rationalism. According to Rosmini, the Empire's survival throughout the years implied that it was the last standing institution capable of safeguarding a politically and culturally Christian society from the attacks of the French Revolution, which Rosmini himself experienced during his childhood when the tranquil Rovereto was invaded by Napoleon's army for a short period of time.

After the first stage of his youth, though, Rosmini starts noticing the dark side of Austria, especially, its marked authoritarianism, its tendency towards immobility and the Machiavellism of its "reason of State" characteristic not only of Josephism

C. Hoevel, *The Economy of Recognition: Person, Market and Society in Antonio Rosmini*, Ethical Economy 42, DOI 10.1007/978-94-007-6058-5_2,

but also of Metternich's and the Holy Alliance's policies. Thus, he gradually transforms his political adherence to Austria into a generic adherence to the cultural ideal proposed by the Restoration. Inspired by the works of traditionalist French thinkers such as Charles De Bonald, the early Lamennais and, especially, Josef de Maistre, Rosmini took in the critiques against the utilitarian and individualistic aspects of the Enlightenment and the French Revolution. Thanks to the latter, the Roveretan incorporated the historical dimension to his thought attaching great value to the importance of tradition as the origin of societies. Nonetheless, not even in his youth did he completely follow French traditionalism that he always criticized due to its sacred conception of history. On the contrary, he plunged into the study of Karl Ludwig von Haller, a Swiss political philosopher of the Restoration, author of the *Restoration of Political Science* from which Rosmini draw his first patrimonialist conception of the political society and the State (Bulferetti 1942; Solari 1957).

Despite feeling a sense of political belonging to Austria, Rosmini was always culturally and spiritually Italian. Actually, besides being situated towards the end of the Alps, Rovereto is also at the beginning of the great plain of the Veneto, a natural entrance to the civil, humanistic, economic and commercial world of the Italian cities. Thus, being a native of this city – which had long belonged to the Venetian Republic – meant Rosmini's communion with the bourgeois, civil and humanistic spirit of the *città*. Besides, for years the Rosmini family had owned a silk factory in Rovereto which had almost 4,000 employees by the end of the eighteenth century. Even though during Rosmini's life the family business was already in decline, it infused him with direct knowledge and natural affinity with economic matters. The typical combination of literature, arts, religion and the civil and economic life, deeply rooted in the Italian bourgeois families, had a strong impact on Rosmini. This explains why he opened his mind to the so-called "Italian civil philosophers" with whom he had several differences – as we will see later on – but who also had a strong influence on his thought. Taking these facts into account, we can understand better his interest in the British civil and economic tradition that he will cultivate all his life.

Amidst this complex and significantly contradictory background of his double adherence, on the one hand, to the Austrian and Hallerian feudal patrimonialism and, on the other hand, to the Italian and British civil and bourgeois philosophy, between 1822 and 1823, at the age of 25 and recently ordained a priest and being a laureate in theology, Rosmini writes his first work on political philosophy – known as his *Politica Prima (First Politics)* or the *Politica Roveretana* (*Roveretan Politics*) – which contains his first essays on economic science. While a first series of essays displays the seed of Rosmini's theories on needs, on the relation between wealth and politics, and a first insight into his theory of development, the second series of the *Politica Prima* comprises another set of essays that make up *Book VI*, where Rosmini reveals many of his ideas on consumption, luxury, taxes and wealth spending. These texts reflect that Rosmini was probably one of the few philosophers in Continental Europe who, unlike many other thinkers, approved of the new economic capitalism. However, these early essays also attempt to redefine economic science from a humanistic, social and religious perspective.

In spite of his opening up to economic thought, even at the beginning of his career, Rosmini notices a central issue to be sorted out in the field of political economy: the impact of utilitarianism. This led him to a strong and bitter confrontation during his youth with followers of Helvetius, Maupertuis and Bentham in Italy, especially with the "civil economists" of the several Italian schools. But it is especially Melchiorre Gioia – a renowned Milanese economist – who Rosmini "chooses" as a target for his criticism arguing strongly with him until the Milanese's death. Actually, even when valuing Gioia's proposals on progress and well-being, Rosmini rejects the economist's utilitarian principles, which he finds denaturalizing and destructive for the economy. As a consequence, simultaneously to the essays in the *Politica Prima*, Rosmini published a series of controversial articles against Gioia – *Esame delle opinioni di Melchiorre Gioia in favore della moda, Galateo dei Letterati, Saggio sulla definizione della ricchezza* and *Breve esposizione della filosofia di Melchiorre Gioja*[1] – which the Roveretan originally intended to include in his *Philosophy of Politics* but later left aside to write his *Politica Seconda* or *Politica milanese*. Hence, together with the rest of the already mentioned texts, this set of early writings conform the matrix for Rosmini's future economic thought, a matrix that will be enriched and modified, though, as the great philosopher goes through new experiences – many of them controversial – and outdoes the limitations of his early thought to develop it in a new perspective and depth.

2.1.2 His Stay in Milan

Traditionalism, patrimonialism, Italian and British economic and civil culture, controversy with utilitarianism, are all apparently contradictory elements which build up Rosmini's thought and that will acquire a new meaning after his stay in Milan between 1826 and 1828. All the biographers agree that this period in Milan was a turning point in his philosophical thought and definitely also in his economic ideas. Though Rosmini had already been in touch with the thought and ideals of modernity while living in Rovereto and studying in Padua, his experience of the Risorgimento in Milan will substantially change his view on the conflict between traditionalists and reformists, in which he was quite involved. Even though part of the Risorgimento movement found inspiration in the reformist and liberal ideals of the Enlightenment, many Italians believed in the possibility of achieving the unity of their country holding onto the Christian faith they shared and, more precisely, onto the Church. Moreover, even Italian Catholics such as Rosmini, who realized that Austria gave a merely formal support to the Church while its real intention was to control and deprive it of its freedom, began to back up the Italian cause – as well as modern political constitutionalism – to free both their country and their Church.

[1]There are two classical works devoted to the topic: Benvenuto Donati (1949) and A. Giordano (1976).

This way, in the capital city of Lombardy, Rosmini joins this convergence group of Reformists and Catholics – led by Alessandro Manzoni, with whom Rosmini will forge a friendship that will last until his death – which will make him put aside the anti-modern remains of his juvenile thought and will let him re-elaborate his philosophical, political and economic ideas in the light of a fresher and definitely modern vision (Graziani 1972).

As a consequence of this revealing experience, Rosmini stops writing his *Politica Roveretana (Politica Prima)* in Milan to devote himself between 1826 and 1827 to three major pieces of writing: his treatise on *Natural Law*, later on released by Paoli as the *Frammenti di Filosofia del Diritto e della Politica* – which he used in 1841 to compose his remarkable work on the Philosophy of Right – the *Commentario a la Filosofia Politica* and finally the essay on *Della naturale Costituzione della società civile*, book that Rosmini resumed in 1848 to be published not until his death in 1887. Driven by the universalist ideas of the American and French Revolution and opposing the traditionalist arguments, Rosmini will introduce in these three texts – the core of what is usually called the *Politica Seconda* or *Politica Milanese* – the prolific topic of natural law into the economic issues of work, inequality, poverty, and the political representation of ownership, amongst others, that will deeply shape his subsequent philosophy of economics.

2.1.3 A Period of Philosophical Reflection and the Discovery of the Idea of Being

From 1828 to 1837, Rosmini partially walks off the political upheaval of his time and abandons his political and economic writing to lay the philosophical bases of his thought. This reflexive period will let him sharpen his view and consider economic issues in a depth and from a perspective he had not acquired before. From this point of view, the *Nuovo Saggio sull'Origine delle Idee* (1828–1830) constitutes the turning point after which the Roveretan leaves behind his early attempt to develop his philosophy by means of a basically empirical, historical and bottom-up method to adopt a top-down one. Although both the 'idea of being' and the three modes of being (ideal, moral and real) are partially sketched in his early works, the *Nuovo Saggio* will make an explicit reference to these theses which are central to Rosmini's philosophy. On account of his economic philosophy, the discovery of the idea of being will let Rosmini achieve of a novel understanding of utility within the framework of objectivity and universality unseen in his previous writings.

A similar phenomenon takes place in the *Principles of Ethics* (1830–1831), the *Anthropology as an Aid to Moral Science* (1831–1832) and the *Comparative and Critical History of Systems Dealing with the Principle of Morality* (1836), which apply the discoveries of the *Nuovo Saggio to anthropology and ethics* and, eventually, to economics. Moreover, in the *Anthropology as an Aid to Moral Science*, he develops, from the perspective of the idea of being, fundamental economic issues as the theory of needs, consumption, price and economic freedom.

As regards the *Principles of Ethics*, it contains key principles of the Rosminian economics such as the distinction between morality and eudaimonology, the relation between utility and happiness, the criticism and solution to the problem surrounding the role of self-interest in ethics, and the connection between moral good and economic growth. Finally, in the *Comparative and Critical History of Systems Dealing with the Principle of Morality* Rosmini issues a critique of all moral systems that serve as theoretical basis for economics – especially English utilitarianism and Scottish sentimentalism – and, at the same time, he presents his own ethical foundations of economics against these systems.

2.1.4 In the Eye of the Storm

From 1837 until the turmoil of 1848, having already set the most profound bases of his philosophy, Rosmini resumes his original project of writing a comprehensive economic, political, jural and social philosophy. In this period we find the most mature stage of his project, developed not only in the light of his great philosophical principles but also strengthened by his commitment with the dramatic events of the time. Although Rosmini had devoted most of his life to his philosophical writings and his religious activities, he had also always been involved in politics. But it was not until 1848 – when political and social conflicts reached a climax in Europe and Italy – that Rosmini became a central figure in the Italian political scenario. Aware of Rosmini's prestige at the Vatican, the King of Piamonte, Carlo Alberto de Savoia, asked the great philosopher to embark on a delicate diplomatic mission in Rome. He asked him to persuade the Pope to join his reign in a battle against Austria in order to achieve the independence and unity of Italy. Rosmini accepted the mission but he broadened its horizons. Once in Rome, he tried to convince Pius IX that the Church had to break free from Austria and also accept political constitutionalism to favor both the process of political unity in Italy and the Church's entrance into modernity.

As we know, this mission was a complete diplomatic failure. It meant an excruciating ecclesiastical conflict that sentenced Rosmini to an ostracism within the Church that lasted practically up to this death, and made him and his work suspicious for more than 150 years after he passed away. But despite this unsuccessful attempt in politics, his appearing before the Pope's Court highlighted the extraordinary set of his political and jural ideas and, to our concern, the economic thought that Rosmini had built up through the important writings of the previous 10 years. The most significant work of this period is the *Philosophy of Politics* (1837), a complete though not entirely different re-elaboration of the two early Politics we have already referred to. In the first book of the series, *Summary Cause for the Stability and Downfall of Human Societies*, Rosmini carries out a sort of philosophy of history, also applicable to the economy: there he describes the metaphysical and anthropological axioms of economic development, the connection between political and economic calculation, and some concepts on statistics that he will later enlarge in the works that followed. The second part of the *Philosophy of Politics*, entitled

Society and its Purpose, might be one of the most prolific resources for the study of Rosmini's philosophy of economy. This work offers an epistemological introduction referring to economic science, the relations between economy and society, economic science and right, and economy and happiness. It also goes into a theory of the common good and its connection with the concept of social utility, a theory of needs, the problem of consumerism, competition, labor and the role of political authorities in said issues.

The second great work of this period is the *Philosophy of Right* (1840–1841.) Its several volumes are loaded with philosophical-economic concepts and debates: it contains an epistemology opposing utilitarianism, a whole philosophy of ownership, a theory on jural freedom that lays the basis for economic freedom, a theory on price, commercial relationships, common good, economic functions of the government, taxes, economic competition, the distribution of goods and the relationships between economy and politics. In this book, thus, Rosmini unfolds almost all philosophical-economic topics, but puts them into play in the light of a more mature state of his thought.

Amongst other essential works of this period we can mention the *Saggio sulla Statistica* (1844) and the *Saggio sul Comunismo e il Socialismo* (1847). In the former, Rosmini criticizes the utilitarian-positivist concept of statistics and argues against the philosophical principles of empirical research in the social sciences and particularly in economics. In the latter, he makes an exhaustive criticism to all types of socialism which in those times were thought to be alternatives to market economy and shows the severe consequences that governmental control over the economy might cause in the economic, moral and spiritual spheres. Finally, it is worth mentioning two constitutional projects Rosmini writes in 1848 as the most practical and immediately applicable proposals to the crisis of his time. The first one is *La Costituzione secondo la giustizia sociale*, which consists in both a detailed portrait of the general jural framework of society and a series of jural and political instruments regarding economic policies proposed by the author for the Italy of that time – taxes, free commerce, State's functions in economic matters and economy regulatory institutions. On the other hand, the second text, entitled *La Costituente del regno dell'Alta Italia*, points out Rosmini's theses and politico-jural proposals regarding poverty and different kinds of social aid provided by the State, the Church and civil society.

2.1.5 The Economy Expressed in Metaphysical and Theological Terms

From 1848 until his death, partly forced by the Pope's request for silence and partly tired after such a great deal of conflict, Rosmini retreats to his house in Stresa, by the Maggiore Lake in the North of Milan, to complete his religious work in the Institute of Charity as well as his philosophical and theological work. As regards this last task, Rosmini will write the *Theosophy*, his outstanding and most important metaphysical work divided into several volumes, which he will not be able to round off due to his sudden death in 1855. As Pietro Piovani states, this metaphysical perspective was always a building block of Rosmini's economic philosophy. In the *Theodicy* (1845), he had already alluded to a series of economic issues expressed in metaphysical terms, such as inequality, the accumulation of goods, perfectism and antagonism. But it is in the *Theosophy* that Rosmini will demonstrate how socio-economic problems are governed by the laws of being. In this sense, the transcendental and dialectic aspect of the "synthetism of being" in the *Theosophy*, that harmoniously comprises the three modes of being (ideal, real and moral) is undoubtedly the milestone for the understanding of the true dimension of the Roveretan's philosophy of economy which spreads throughout his first writings, his more mature philosophical texts and the political essays of the 1940s.

Prior to this last stage of his life is the *Delle cinque piague della Santa Chiesa* (1832–1848), a key work to understand the ultimate horizon of Rosmini's economic thought. An ecclesiological text, the *Cinque piague* is much more than a theological-historical writing focused on the Church. Indeed, the theological approach it provides – so controversial for those times that it sentenced Rosmini to persecution and ostracism – and the fact that it might be his most visionary writing on society and modern history, brings about all the principles, institutions and instruments of the economy upon which Rosmini meditated and argued throughout his life. Therefore, it is in the religious dimension that his intellectual and vital itinerary reaches a zenith, which lays the basis for his philosophy of economy.

2.2 A Dialogue with Economic Thought[2]

2.2.1 Classical Economists

An outstanding feature of Rosmini's economic thought is its familiarity and dialogue with the most influential economists of his time, from which we can

[2] In writing this section we set out to make contact with the economic works read by Rosmini trying to discover the specific economic authors and issues that influenced his thinking. To do this we followed a research methodology based on a detailed tour through the primary and secondary sources which were mainly four:

- The catalog of Rosmini's personal library in Rovereto, his birthplace.
- The Library catalog in Stresa, the house where Rosmini spent his last years.
- The *Annali di Antonio Rosmini Serbati* by Gianfranco Radice (1991), which provides a fairly complete list of the works acquired by both the libraries of Rovereto and Stresa during Rosmini's life and the direct and indirect references in the works or in the correspondence of the Roveretan that with high probability formed part of its readings.
- Citations and references of economic works and authors present in the works of Rosmini.
- References of scholars and commentators of Rosmini's work taking into account unpublished manuscripts and letters by Rosmini.

deduce that our author possessed a true economic culture.[3] Actually, the Roveretan's philosophy of economy would be completely different if it were the work of a philosopher lacking this scientific and technically detailed economic knowledge. In addition, the fact that his philosophical-economic thought is attached to the economists' views not only allows him to have a place in the history of economic thought but mainly turns him into a thinker endowed with inter-disciplinary qualities hardly ever seen in intellectuals devoted to understand the philosophical problems of the economy.

Rosmini is, first and foremost, an enthusiastic reader and a true connoisseur of the first renowned classical economists such as Smith, Malthus and Say. As regards Adam Smith in particular, the Roveretan studies his texts since his youth – his economic writings as well as his work on morality and language (Rosmini 1976, 152, n 3, 1994a) – and participates of the Scottish economist's breakthrough in Italy.[4] In his *Politica Prima* Rosmini already makes reference to Adam Smith, placing him within the group of those he calls *politici avari*, who reduce the aim of politics to economy only (Rosmini 1933, 19). Nevertheless, in the same passage, Rosmini criticizes Smith's Italian critics like Gioia, who, according to him, had made much more severe mistakes than the Scottish economist, "an extremely praiseworthy man."[5] In fact, in his argument against Gioia, Rosmini partly leans on Smith's definition of economics as "a science of wealth" (Rosmini 1933, 19). He also distinguishes the *work value* theory as an undeniable achievement of the Scottish's economic theory[6]; he praises his conception about savings and capital accumulation as the basis of economy (Rosmini 1978a, 26, footnote 17; Smith 1843, 351); he agrees with the Smithean distinction between productive and unproductive labor (Rosmini 1978a, 21); and shares his critiques on excessive

---

In order not to bore the reader we do not present here a full bibliographical apparatus (see Hoevel 2009) but only the most significant data. The references at the end of the chapter include some of the original economic works read by Rosmini as a short illustration of his rich economic culture.

[3]By an author's *economic culture* I mean his knowledge about the outcomes of the economic science of his time. Inspired in Piero Barucci's research on Alessandro Manzoni's economic culture (Barucci 1977) and driven by the challenge posed by Giorgio Campanini, according to which "the features and origin of Rosmini's economic culture, not absolutely parallel to his political culture, have not been studied in-depth yet" (Campanini 1983, 99). I shall attempt to prove here the existence of an important economic culture in Rosmini.

[4]Smith's breakthrough in Italy has been studied by Guidi, Maccabelli and Morato from an interesting point of view (2000).

[5]"Il Gioia nel *Nuovo prospetto della scienza economica*, mi sembra però essere stato troppo acerbo in relevare questo errore dello Smith, uomo per altro degno di tanta lode. Il Gioia è rovesciato in due difetti maggiori . . . ". (Rosmini 1933, 19, n. 1).

[6]"Dopo Adam Smith nessuno più dubita, che il lavoro sia il fonte sommo della ricchezza e che abbia il lavoro ai capitali per usare un modo filosofico, ma ottimamente espressivo, come la forma alla materia" (Rosmini 1923, 92). See also Adam Smith (1843, 394).

profit and luxury, and his preference for frugality.[7] Against the new "industrialists" of his time, Rosmini sides with Smith in his physiocratic concept of the natural development of the economy.[8] Finally, Rosmini follows Smith – though keeping certain differences – in his defense of free commerce and competition and in his discontentment with monopolies, the State monopoly in particular (Rosmini 1952a, 143, 1993b, 2167–2168). Nonetheless, like most Italian economists, the Roveretan tends to assimilate Smith's thought in the context of the civil tradition of the Italian economy and its related topics of interest,[9] as well as in function of his own alternative synthesis.

As regards Thomas Malthus, Rosmini quotes him several times in his *Della naturale Costituzione della società civile* (Rosmini 1887, 340) and in *The Summary Cause for the Stability or Downfall of Human Societies*. Together with Machiavelli, Malthus is the main author who Rosmini relies on to elaborate the central argument of this last work, the one on the survival of societies. Somehow following Malthus's arguments against Condorcet and Godwin, Rosmini supports the idea of the existence of limits in the advancement of societies, beyond which they might perish. Besides, both in *The Summary Cause* and *Della naturale Costituzione,* the Roveretan agrees with the English economist's well-known arguments on the topic of population,[10] though he does it in a very different context of ideas and motivations than those of Malthus.

Another influential author of the classical economic school in Rosmini's thought is Jean-Baptiste Say. Rosmini reads Say from a very young age to quote him repeatedly in *Politica Prima* and in his essays against Gioia, mainly in the *Saggio sulla definizione della ricchezza*. The Roveretan borrows a great deal of material from Say to use it later on in his own theory of value and economic action: the critique on artificial needs, unlimited luxury and fashion postulated by the French economist, as well as his suggestions for slow consumption leading to real needs and favoring quality rather than quantity (Say 1854, 322–325). Following Say, Rosmini

---

[7]"Riguardo alla produzione della ricchezza, qualunque cosa si dica in contrario, la regola fondamentale è di seguire la natura, la quale chiede prima la coltivazione, dipoi l' industria manifattrice, finalmente il commercio." (Rosmini 1923, 133). See also Adam Smith (1843, 405).

[8]"Il buon senso di Smith . . . e di tanti altri scrittori delle cose economiche; i quali senza essere nemici dei piaceri, distinguono però accuratamente fra essi e la ricchezza, e predicano i risparmi, e la moderazione in tutte le cose di lusso e di diletto, perché questi diletti non li considerano come ricchezza, ma bensì come una distruzione della ricchezza . . . " (Rosmini 1978a, 37). See also Smith (1843, cap.1, 360, 362–371; cap.2, 127–128, 401–402, 442–443).

[9]Guidi, Maccabelli and Morato raise several topics for discussion regarding Adam Smith's thought in Italy: the discussion about statistics; the division of society (2000, 6); the debate on factors of production (2000, 7); the debates surrounding productive and unproductive labor, labor division, commercial and industrial protectionism, the countryside-city relationship, development, and the limits of the economic science (2000, 9–14), amongst others.

[10]"The fact is [that there is a] natural law according to which every population grows. The human race increases naturally by geometrical progression, whereas subsistence, the produce of the earth, can increase only by arithmetical progression. However, even this progression cannot continue, as that of population does." (Rosmini 1994a, 91–92). See also Thomas Malthus (1985, 71 and ss).

also criticizes the way in which Adam Smith classifies consumption and labor into productive and unproductive.[11] Say also provided Rosmini with a guide to depart from some of Adam Smith's thesis and get closer to the Italian-French conception of the economy centered in subjectivity, without disregarding the elements of the classical British school he finds praise-worthy.

In addition, Rosmini seems not to have taken an interest in other classical economists such as David Ricardo or John Stuart Mill. In relation to the former, it is highly probable that the Roveretan would share the negative opinions of the Italian economists who considered Ricardo an abstract, quite unclear author. When it comes to Stuart Mill, his writings were not circulating in the times of Rosmini's education and were probably not abundant later in Italy either, which would explain this notable absence in the Roveretan's economic culture.

2.2.2 *The Italian Civil Economists*

In his youth, Rosmini also gets in touch with texts produced by the so-called Italian civil economists. Through these authors Rosmini will get to know a conception of the economy based on the idea of happiness, which in the XVIII century reintroduces the traditions of Second Scholastics and of Renaissance humanism, in opposition to the conception of "security of power" which is present in Machiavelli and Giovanni Botero,[12] or to the more chrematistic vision of Anglo-Saxon authors. Another characteristic of the Italian economic philosophy which Rosmini incorporates is its "civil" character, a heritage he receives from Doria and mainly from Giambatista Vico (Bruni 2002, 106). Besides, it is possible to prove how the structure and topics of Rosmini's politico-economic works are much more similar to Ludovico Antonio Muratori's *Della Pubblica Felicità* or to Gaetano Filangieri's *La scienza della legislazione* – both Italian civil economists – than to Adam Smith's *Wealth of Nations*.

Using the well-known collection *Scrittori classici italiani di economia politica* by Custodi, which Rosmini will later consult throughout his life, he becomes acquainted, on the one hand, with the well-known Napolitan economists of the first part of the Settecento: Ludovico Antonio Muratori and Carlo Antonio Broggia, who will inspire him to incorporate "the moral and economic elements that rooted his reform plan" (Venturi 1969, 97). Amongst the civil economists of the second half of

---

[11]"(...) conviene risalire alla storia della celebre distinzione di cui parliamo fra'consumi produttori e improduttori. Lo Smith, che la rese celebre, certo non giunse a tirar fra essi la linea di separazione esattamente, giacché pose fra le classi consumatrici e improduttrici di quelle a cui non si può negare la facoltà di produrre. Il Say rettificò, in gran parte almeno, l'inesattezza dello Smith" (Rosmini 1978a: 29).

[12]"Nei secoli precedenti in Italia si parlava di 'felicità pubblica', ma in termini di 'sicurezza del potere'. Giovanni Botero *(La ragione di stato,* 1598), la definiva 'il modo di tener contenti e quieti i popoli'" (Parisi 1984, 96, n 128).

the Settecento, Rosmini will be especially inspired by Gaetano Filangieri,[13] Antonio Genovesi[14] and Giussepe Palmieri from the Napolitan School, by Pietro Verri and Cesare Beccaria from the Milanese School, by the Venetians Francesco Mengotti[15] and Giammaria Ortes,[16] and by Giambatista Vasco[17] from Turin. Rosmini will make a deep study and use of these authors' texts, included in the Modern Part of Custodi's collection, and will hold a dialogue with them about varied topics as the relationship between economy and happiness, consumption, labor, taxes, market freedom and poverty, amongst others (Hoevel 2009).

However, Rosmini's dialogue with the Italian civil economy reaches its peak when he gets in touch with the philosophers-economists of the Risorgimento, especially with the already mentioned Melchiorre Gioia and Giandomenico Romagnosi, both contemporary to Rosmini. In Gioia's project, the Roveretan notices an attempt to absorb ethics into economy, making consumption subjective and reducing right to pure interest.[18] However, despite the sharp tone of his criticism against Gioia's utilitarian propositions, one may notice the influence he had over him. Actually, Rosmini borrows from Gioia the idea of the humanistic-Campanellian origin which states that behind the production of wealth always lie human capacities – today we would say the "human capital" – synthesized in the triad *sapere, volere, potere* (knowledge, power and will).[19] Moreover, it was probably the reading of Gioia

[13]Rosmini cites Filangieri repeatedly especially in his *Politica Prima* and follows his teachings on many points. See Filangieri (1807, 158) and Rosmini (1923, 141).

[14]A direct reference to Genovesi (1768) can be found in Rosmini's famous letter to Maurizio Moschini (Epistolario, Lettera cccviii, 519) which refers to Chapter XIII , "Dell'impiego de'poveri e de'vagabondi" of the Parte Prima of the *Lezioni di economia civile*. Besides, multiple indirect references on the economic work of Genovesi can be found in Rosmini's criticisms to sentimentalists, especially with regard to their understanding of the concepts of benevolence and reciprocity, widely used by the Neapolitan economist.

[15]Rosmini follows Mengotti especially in developing a critical economic philosophy of mercantilism and in his reception of some major themes of the work of Adam Smith.

[16]From Ortes Rosmini seems to have received much of the Platonic and critical aspect of his economic philosophy especially in fields such as consumption, wealth and happiness, and the outline of the terms of relationship between wealth and political power. We should remember that Rosmini takes from Ortes his idea of the Political Tribunal that puts limits on the mere play of economic interests (Traniello 1970). Moreover Ortes influenced Rosmini's mind regarding the impossibility of completely remedying social ills but these elements are strongly compensated, in my opinion, by the influence of other authors like Gioia, Romagnosi and Sismondi.

[17]Vasco distinguishes two types of value, the subjective (arbitrary and capricious) and objective ("comune"). It does not seem unreasonable to think that Rosmini follows Vasco's line at this point – also very much in line with Ortes- when he makes his famous distinction between subjective and objective goods. Yet Rosmini cites Vasco specifically on social issues in his letter to Maurizio Moschini where he also mentions Palmieri, Muratori and Genovesi to address the topic.

[18]"(. . .) in Italia udimmo, alcuni anni sono, talun pretendere(n. 1 Il Gioia), che la morale fosse un ramo di economia" (Rosmini 1941, 161).

[19]The *Nuovo Prospetto delle scienze economiche* by Gioia deals with the matter of the *Potere* in the *Libro secondo*, *Classe Prima*, p.66–239; the subject of the *Cognizione* in the *Classe Seconda*, pp. 240–255 and the subject of the *Volontà* in the *Classe Terza*, pp. 256–275. In the rest of his work,

which warned Rosmini about the excessively chrematistic view of the British economists and helped him to confirm and make explicit the idea of the ethical and jural-civil organicity in which he considered that economy should be placed.

As regards Gian Domenico Romagnosi (1761–1835), Rosmini establishes with him a somewhat similar kind of troubled and at the same time assimilative relationship to the one he had with Gioia. Romagnosi's utilitarianism – though weaker than Gioia's – certainly represents to Rosmini the counter-model of his own intellectual project. Therefore, the Roveretan devotes long passages of his *Philosophy of Right,* of the *Principles of Ethics* and of the *Comparative and Critical History of Systems Dealing with the Principle of Morality*, amongst others, to a detailed refutation of Romagnosi's ethical, social and jural conceptions.[20] According to him, Romagnosi confuses "the subject with the object," (Rosmini 1988a, 106) virtue with utility (Rosmini 1941, 167), and, despite his intentions to reach a widened utilitarianism, he reduces every human motivation to mere interest.[21] Nonetheless, in spite of these general philosophical differences, Rosmini shares with Romagnosi the intention of achieving a more complete economic science,[22] neither "fragmentary" nor separated from the rest of the social philosophy (Romagnosi 1845, vol 6, 78–79).[23] He also takes from Romagnosi particular and not lesser elements such as the valuation of competition, labor division and market freedom, which Rosmini assimilates by reading Adam Smith's works, but also from Romagnosi, one of the many who introduced Smith in Italy.[24] Besides, Romagnosi and Rosmini show agreement not only in the valuation of the "mechanical" side of Smith[25] but also in their criticism on his work, probably inspired by Sismondi. In addition, Rosmini as well as Ramagnosi, recognizes the need of reintegrating the economy with the rest of sciences associating it with morality, politics and right.

Gioia applies these concepts to different particular subjects such as the human and cultural basis of credit, the value of money, consumption, labor, production, economic policy and commerce (Rosmini 2003, 369).

[20]"Come la falsa definizione che danno gli utilitarii del diritto confonda insieme le due scienze della politica e del diritto" (Rosmini 1995b, libro V, cap. III, 1251).

[21]"La parola *moralità* adunque usata così spesso del nostro publicista, come pure l'espressione *ordine morale di ragione, legge naturale, giusto ed onesto,* ecc. Non possono più ingannare nessuno... in questo sistema sensista ed utilitario, è manifesto, che la dottrina del giusto si riduce alla dottrina dell' utile" (Rosmini 1995b, n. 1740).

[22]"(...) Romagnosi has a more complex view than his predecessors, and feels the need to accept and take account of all elements (...)" (Rosmini 1994a, 140 n. 1).

[23]See especially "Preface to the Political Works" (Rosmini 1994a, 61).

[24]"In tempo della gioventù di Romagnosi arrideva generalmente agl' italiani la smithiana dottrina; e però non è a stupire che questo filosofo abbracciatala, la mantenesse colla solita sua costanza, e l' applicasse altresì ampiamente alle politiche cose" (Rosmini 1988a, 380). See also Rosmini's criticism against Romagnosi regarding the "invisible hand" (1994b, 395, footnote 5).

[25]"Lo studioso pertanto non abbisogna di molto affaticarsi su le opere straniere, tranne quella di Adam Smith, per la parte mecanica dell' economia" (Romagnosi 1845,79).

2.2.3 Haller, Sismondi, Utopian Socialists and Other Economists

Finally, other authors who have had a significant impact on Rosmini's economic philosophy are the Swiss Karl Ludwig von Haller, Simonde de Sismondi, the utopian socialists and a series of other thinkers. As regards Haller, author of the *Restauration des Staatswissenschaft*, even though Rosmini looked up to him, especially in his youth, he will eventually not adhere to his "macrobiotic" economic theory (a science that studies the means to boost the State's power to the maximum) due to the influence of the classical and Italian civil economists and his inclination towards constitutionalism. Nonetheless, Rosmini will discover very early in his career, surprisingly through Haller's patrimonialism, the importance of liberal principles like the respect for private property, industry and initiative, a moderate tax policy, free domestic and foreign trade and juridical security for investors, as well as other specific criteria about financial and social policies, amongst others[26] (Haller 1963, vol 2, 232ff).

When it comes to Sismondi, his influence is clearly present in the Roveretan's quotations, especially in the *Saggio sulla definizione della ricchezza*, where Rosmini seems to bear in mind the early Sismondi of the *De la richesse commerciale* (1803), a piece of writing in which its author adheres to the British classical economists almost without hesitation. Yet, Rosmini becomes acquainted and is influenced also by the Sismondi of the *Nuovi Principi di economia politica o della ricchezza nei suoi rapporti con la popolazione* (1819), written by the Swiss economist after his famous trip to England where he came face to face with the social evils of the industrial revolution and addressed his well-known critique against Adam Smith and the principles of classical economics (Rosmini 2003, 297, 350). Rosmini seems to follow closely Sismondi's opinions in favor of the integration of political economy with ethics and eudaimonology (Sismondi 1974, 9)[27] and against the reduction of politics to the production of material goods, to the population growth or the mere satisfaction of material needs.[28]

Rosmini also coincides with Sismondi in his critique against the reduction of the politico-economic problem to mere *laisser-faire* (Sismondi 1974, 8). In fact, they both believe that excessive competition tends to be harmful for the most

---

[26]However, Rosmini also seems to have shared with Haller the idea that a policy of economic liberalism does not eliminate the importance of a strong role of the State. In fact, Rosmini seems to follow Haller in assigning multiple functions to the State as legal assistance for any violation of rights, public safety, facilitate trade through public works, encourage and "abetting" industry with prizes and subsidies, provide pensions, founding hospitals and other institutions for public health and recreation of the people.

[27]See also Antonio Rosmini (1994b, 61).

[28]"Lo scopo del governo non è, astrattamente parlando, l'accumulazione delle ricchezze nello stato(...)" (Sismondi 1974, 23). See also "The Error of Those Who Tend to Materialise Society" (Rosmini 1994b, 265).

poor (Rosmini 1994b, 570, 1993b, n 2298, footnote). Rosmini also seems to follow the Swiss economist almost to the letter on his judgments about England's questionable prosperity (Sismondi 1974, 10–11; Rosmini 1901, 6). Nevertheless, they both criticize the temptation to sort out the problem of the unjust outcomes of the market by means of an abstract egalitarianism. This would do nothing but destroy the incentive to progress based not on society's distribution of material goods, but on each person's capacity to gradually achieve his or her own prosperity (Sismondi 1974, 24; Rosmini 1994b, 520). Remarkable similarities found in his works seem to point out that the Roveretan could have obtained from Sismondi part of the inspiration for his thesis on the "equilibrium" or "proportion" the legislator must "calculate" (Sismondi 1974, 47; Rosmini 1923, 177) in order to regulate the different factors of production, income, population and consumption,[29] even though they also agree that said regulation must be predominantly indirect.[30] Apart from that, there are also differences between Rosmini and Sismondi. Probably, the most substantial one is Rosmini's much more emphatic rejection to any 'socialist' or collectivist solution to the social problem or to any kind of proposal, outlined by Sismondi, to bring back some aspects of the system of medieval corporations. But it is mainly the tone employed in the judgment and the criticism of liberal economic principles that marks the difference between a much more radical Sismondi and a more moderate Rosmini.

As regards socialist economists, though Rosmini did not have contact with Marxism, he did study with great interest the utopian socialists like Morelly, Godwin, Enfantin, Babeuf, Owen, Fourier and Saint Simon, who provided him with an infinite list of inspiring topics he will always take into account as a permanent counterpoint in the formulation of his own theses. This can be easily seen in his *Philosophy of Politics* and the *Philosophy of Right,* but, above all, in the *Saggio sul Comunismo e il Socialismo*. By making use of primary sources like the *Doctrine de Saint-Simon,* or secondary sources like the *Études sur les Réformateurs ou socialistes modernes Saint-Simon, Charles Fourier, Robert Owen* by M. Louis Reybaud, Rosmini criticizes Sansimonians' State planning proposals, Robert Owen's cooperative movement, Fourier's harmonious association based on the total liberation of passions, and Babeuf's mandatory and socially planned work (Rosmini 1978c, 86, 88, 90, 95). The Roveretan states that these proposals violate basic rights such as the right to choose one's own way of life, of ownership, of free competition and work, and annihilate the incentives for individual initiative, family love, attachment to property, and free association, which will be fundamental

[29]"Mi sono proposto di dimostrare che è necesario, per la felicità generale, che il reddito cresca insieme al capitale, che la popolazione non superi il reddito che la debe far vivere, che il consumo cresca con la popolazione e che la riproduzione sia proporciónale al capitale che la produce e alla popolazione che lo consuma. Nello stesso tempo ho dimostrato che l'equilibrio di ognuno di questi rapporti può essere turbato indipendentemente da quello degli altri" (Sismondi 1974, 12). There are many similar texts in Rosmini, especially in his *Filosofia della politica.*

[30]"Ma, per condurre in porto queste riforme, suggerisco soltanto che si usino i mezzi lenti e indiretti della legislazione" (Sismondi 1974, 469).

principles in Rosmini's own economic philosophy. However, according to the Roveretan, the greatest damage caused by the socialist theses is the 'complete destruction of human freedom,' which leads to the destruction of man's moral and economic capacity because freedom 'is the root of all duties and, thus, of all human rights (...) the source of all individual and social goods' (Rosmini 1978c, 88). In addition, Rosmini will see in socialism the birth of a new secularized and deformed social religion (Rosmini 1994b, 446; Traniello 1997, 167).

On the other hand, it is worth mentioning the influence that Rosmini's economic culture received from classical authors like Aristotle, constantly quoted by Rosmini, especially in his renowned critique of the "unnatural chrematistics", (Rosmini 1994b, 608–609, footnote) and in matters regarding the relation among economy, ethics and politics. Besides, Rosmini draws on St. Thomas Aquinas and authors of the Second Scholastics like Suárez, Navarro, Lugo, Molina, Sánchez or Vázquez from whom he obtains key elements for his theory of contracts, of the just price, and of the right of ownership (Rosmini 1993a, n 1152, footnote 280). Finally, it is crucial to mention the constant dialogue about economic issues that Rosmini holds with Anglo-Saxon moralists and political philosophers like Mandeville, Hume, Ferguson, Stewart, Reid, Bentham or Benjamin Franklin; historians such as Blackstone, Robertson, Young, Raynal, Cobbet, Mably, Sidney, Squire and Wallace; political philosophers like Locke, Rousseau, Montesquieu, Harrington, Tocqueville, Constant, Hamilton, Madison and Jay; economists of German and French tradition like Sonnenfels, Dutot, Droz., G. F. L. Comte or Dunnoyer. Besides, one shall not ignore the decisive role played in his economic philosophy by the analysis of practical experiences, which he gathered from the works of ministers and officials of economic affairs like the Baron of Lichtenstern, Huskisson, Colbert, Sully, Necker or Guizot. Finally, it is essential to note the influence in Rosmini's economic thinking of a man of letters, his close friend Alessandro Manzoni. Rosmini argues with Manzoni over the years – as it can be seen through their rich epistolary – on issues such as the theory of economic value, the relation between ethics and economics, the problem of the latter being conceived from a utilitarian perspective, as well as the dramatic topics of poverty and social inequality that equally concerned both friends.

2.3 The Interpretations

2.3.1 Rosmini's Economic Philosophy as a Conservative Patrimonialism and a Classist Ideology

After having a glimpse at the framework of all these profound influences, there comes naturally the question concerning the position and the relative weight each of them has had on Rosmini's thought. Has Rosmini been a follower of classical economists, of Italian civil economists, of Haller, Sismondi or of the socialists? One might wonder if it is possible to establish a hierarchy according to their influence over the Roveretan. To even make an attempt at finding an answer to these questions leads us directly into the complex field of the existent interpretations of Rosmini's economic thought. In this sense, an early interpretation can be found in the works of the historian and essayist on philosophy of right, Gioele Solari (1872–1952). After Gentile's idealist interpretation of Rosmini's philosophy, Solari is considered one of the first authors to take interest in offering a more specific interpretation of Rosmini's political and juridical ideas (Solari 2000, 7–8). Solari's work is mainly a philological and historical study that recognizes and puts in chronological order Rosmini's early works in accordance with the evolution of his thought. In this work, for the first time, appears clearly a correlation between the *Politica Prima* and other philosophical-economic texts like the ones contained in Rosmini's controversial essays against Melchiorre Gioia. Solari's works have considerable importance in the reconstruction of Rosmini's philosophy of economy due to the unity of thought they show regarding this matter (Solari 2000, 65).

Still, Solari goes beyond this valuable and predominantly philological task to draw the first great interpretative map of Rosmini's early thought. Within the framework of this interpretation, Solari affirms that the first nucleus of the Roveretan's early economic texts, especially the one contained in the *Politica Prima*, written in Rovereto, would be completely determined by Rosmini's belonging to the *"aristocrazia fondiaria,"* his "aristocratic education" and von Haller's patrimonialist thought. In this way, although Rosmini "does not condemn the new capitalist activity and the science that studies it unless they are not informed and subordinated to ethical ends," (Solari 2000, 20) according to Solari, he suffers from a "radical incomprehension of those moral, social and economic forces that had issued the definite condemnation of feudal and patrimonial governments:"

> Following Haller's footsteps, Rosmini was a prisoner of nostalgia (...) He did not show (and the critiques to Smith and Gioia reveal it) sympathy nor understanding for the new industrial economy based on labor, capacity and personal initiative, nor for the new social lifestyles based on them which had found in revolution adequate political forms. (Solari 2000, 28)

In his work entitled *Il personalismo rosminiano* published in 1963, the political philosopher, Danilo Zolo, makes a deeper and more generalized application of Solari's thesis. Although Zolo shares Rosmini's personalist and Christian-oriented philosophy, he openly criticizes his economic philosophy. From a series of harsh judgments on Rosmini's early economic texts, Zolo will criticize Rosmini's philosophy of economy in general – including his mature period – which is a surprise if we take into account his methodological insistence to make a clear distinction between both periods. In fact, Zolo will highlight even more than Solari the historicist, empirical, traditionalist and patrimonialist character of the first phase of Rosmini's thought, and will erase the division line between the first phase and the iusnaturalist and constitutionalist phase that Solari had drawn from 1825 to 1828 (Zolo 1963, 26). Indeed, Zolo believes there is a profound gap in Rosmini's thought between his view of the economy and his personalist view of ethics, anthropology and theology or, in any case, he thinks this break evidences the internal contradictions present even in these aspects of his thought.[31] Finally, the harshest criticism made by Zolo is probably the accusation of "ideology". Indeed, Zolo considers Rosmini's economic thought being contaminated by the supposed defect of nineteenth-century Catholicism based upon a classist preconception which is reflected in its utter incomprehension of the meaning of the social-economic problem in relation to the ultimate truths of Christianity.[32]

2.3.2 Rosmini's Philosophy of Economy as Liberal Social Theodicy

Certainly, the most important work on Rosmini's philosophy of economy is the *Teodicea sociale di Rosmini* (1957) written by the Napolitan philosopher, Pietro Piovani. It is not a philological or historical work but a highly speculative vision of the Roveretan's economic thought within the framework of his social ideas, and in the light of his *Theodicy*. From Piovani's view, the key of the Rosminian social and economic philosophy lies in the *Theodicy*, a piece of work where many passages allude to Rosmini's social writings, especially the *Philosophy of Politics*.[33] Based on this ascertainment and on various parallelisms between both works, Piovani presents an extremely interesting and original thesis that is already expressed in its title. According to Piovani, the primary aim of Rosmini's social and economic thought was to defend the Christian-rooted classical theodicy by leaning on new socially-oriented arguments. Furthermore, in his opinion, Rosmini would have discovered that classical economic science acts as the key mediator between politics and theodicy.[34]

According to Piovani, although economic science has been founded as the science of restriction and scarcity, it has turned into a pretentious discipline that aims

[31]"Sul terreno etico-giuridico manca in Rosmini la consapevolezza del rapporto di complementarietà, di stretta reciproca inclusione fra economia e morale nella vita concreta della persona e della comunità: sarebbe agevole mostrare come il dualismo tra eudemonologia ed etica rappresenti una delle molte rifrazioni del radicale dualismo rosminano tra 'senso' e 'intelletto', tra ' individuo' e 'persona', tra ' bene soggettivo' e 'bene oggettivo'" (Zolo 1963, 305).

[32]"C'è in Rosmini una discriminazione psicologica fra la 'classe dei ricchi' e la 'classe dei poveri' che induce persino nel suo spirito di carità cristiana un acento paternalistico che sarebbe impossibile trovare in un padre della Chiesa... una conferma della crisi spirituale e religiosa della cristianità ottocentesca..." Danilo Zolo, *op. cit.*, p.253, n.46; "Di fronte a certe pagine rosminiane... non può che riflettere sulla crisi profonda che ha investito la coscienza católica nel primo 800 [...] Il liberalismo rosminiano mostra... la sua origine aristocratica e il suo horizonte classista..." (Zolo 1963, 309).

[33]"Alla luce di questo constante avvertimento rosminiano, assume particolare significato il rinvio, che è nella *Teodicea,* alla *Filosofia della Politica*..." (Piovani 1957, 10).

[34]"Senza l'aiuto dell'economia, non sarebbe possibile la collaborazione tra scienza politica e teodicea..." (Piovani 1957, 94).

to fulfill every need and find a solution to every evil. This negative transformation has been mainly the result of Rousseau's and the socialists' influence, as well as of the impact of the various types of Christian social thought (Piovani 1957, XXII). On the contrary, according to Piovani, Rosmini's philosophy of economy would represent, on the one hand, the first big attempt to assimilate and incorporate into Catholic Christianity the great findings of individualist economics – represented by authors like Adam Smith, Thomas Malthus or Jean-Baptiste Say – and, on the other hand, it would mean the most perfect philosophical critique and refutation of every kind of social Mesianism.

From all this, Piovani also deduces the "liberal consequences" of Rosmini's thought. In fact, according to him, it is evident that Rosmini believes that "the best government for civil society is that which wastes the least number of human actions" (Piovani 1957, 249) and, as the State's intervention renders an obstacle to the economization of actions, the logical consequence will be to guarantee that "all citizens exercise their freedom to its fullest" (Piovani 1957, 251). In this way, Piovani emphasizes, "beyond the fearful uncertainties of Catholic political reflection," the "accuracy of Rosminian thought" which is characterized by the "foundation of a liberal politics resulting from the need to respect the freedom that the universe's providential government guarantees to all individuals" (Piovani 1957, 247). In Piovani's words, Rosmini would be therefore the great critic of all kinds of "social Catholicism":

> Social Catholicism is the antithesis of this Rosminian hope; social reform is exactly the contrary to the reform supported by Rosmini. (Piovani 1957, 407)

Piovani holds that "the attempts to demonstrate that Rosmini's philosophy of politics contains 'a sociology that is the one and the same as that of Leon XIII' is bound to fail – due to the texts' refutation" (Piovani 1957, 408). On the contrary, in his opinion, Rosmini would be an "intransigent and coherent interpreter of the pessimism of the Catholic Church" (Piovani 1957, 408). Yet, this would not mean that the Roveretan is the representative of a *liberal Catholicism* understood as a "Catholicism that, with more or less conviction, recognizes some of the requirements of liberalism as its own," nor he would represent a *Catholic liberalism* understood as a "liberalism willing to adopt values proper to Catholicism." On the contrary, Piovani believes it is "Christianity, Catholic Christianity to be more precise, (...) which produces in itself fundamentally liberal requirements..." (Piovani 1957, 258).

2.3.3 Rosmini's Philosophy of Economy from the Perspective of Civil and Religious Humanism

A third interpretation emerges from the works of Luigi Bulferetti, a disciple of Solari, especially in *Antonio Rosmini nella Restaurazione* (Bulferetti 1942). According to Bulferetti's interpretation, even though Rosmini's political thought, in general, and his economic thought, in particular, suffer the influence of authors like Haller or the French traditionalists, they are interpreted within the framework of the Restoration project of the Christian culture that the Roveretan initiates from an Italian perspective. Even though Bulferetti shares with Solari the same views about Rosmini's patrimonialist and conservative ideas present in his first works, (Bulferetti 1942, 126–127) he places less emphasis than Solari on the most rigid aspects of the Roveretan's posture. Bulferetti even points out that Haller himself is much more open to the economic and bourgeois world than what Solari thinks, an opening which, by the way, would also be inherent to Rosmini from the very beginning.[35] Both Bulferetti and Solari will recognize the enormous importance of Rosmini's turning point that took place in Milan from 1826 onwards. However, the latter will lay special emphasis on the fact that Rosmini, already in his *Politica Prima,* analyzed political and economic matters from the perspective of the problem of "public happiness," which he draws not from Haller but from the eighteenth century Italian civil philosophy. Certainly, Bulferetti makes a partially critical description of the Rosminian institutional system of his constitutional period considering it too much inclined towards the political representation of economic interests. However he also values strongly the influence on Rosmini of Tocqueville and the American constitutional ideas (Bulferetti 1942, 231), which leads him to conclude that the Roveretan professes a "moderate Christian liberalism" (Bulferetti 1942, 233).

Another version of this third interpretation is the one proposed by Francesco Traniello, a historian from Turin, in his *Società religiosa e società civile.* In this work, Traniello analyses Rosmini's philosophy of economy from the original perspective of Christianity and, especially, of the Church.[36] Traniello also supports the thesis of the evolution of Rosmini's thought from Haller and De Maistre's traditionalism to liberal thought *latu senso*. Though this evolution line is important, he believes it is certainly not the only one. In fact, in Rosmini's *Politica Prima*, he detects elements of the Italian sensist Enlightenment,[37] of authors like Filangieri (Traniello 1997, 30, 35, 80, 166) and Muratori (Traniello 1997, 101, 154, 195, 196, 199, 211, 212), of thc physiocrats (Traniello 1997, 47) and of the British economists and constitutionalists.[38] According to Traniello, this would unveil Rosmini's internal struggle between the influence of traditionalist doctrines and

[35]"È da notare che così lo Haller come il Rosmini non considerano semplicemente il patrimonio fondiario ma pur quello mobiliare, e quindi hanno presente la reppresentanza d'interessi nella sua integralità, che dà loro modo d'interpretare, oltre che la storia feudale, quella comunale, e d'analizzare la struttura della monarchia borghese" (Bulferetti 1942, 79, footnote 1).

[36]"La sua *politica* vale piuttosto come sforzo di radicare una concezione della società in una più vasta antropologia religiosa d'ispirazione cristiana . . . " (Traniello 1997, 354).

[37]Traniello argues that in Rosmini exists "a long familiarity with the texts of the Italian Enlightenment and sensism (. . .)" (Traniello 1997, 129).

[38]"Accanto Haller paiano infatti ripresentarsi, sia pure in una forma e in un contesto mutato, istanze e suggestioni almeno parzialmente riconducibili alle fonti settecentesche della teoria rosminiana e, ancor più, allo studio degli economisti e dei costituzionalisti inglesi" (Traniello 1997, 49).

his strong interest in economic science.[39] Besides, Traniello seeks to demonstrate how the social conception developed by Rosmini springs from the illuminist and Christian ideas of "the universal society of mankind" and of "the ecclesiastical society" – that is, in Rosmini's terms, the idea of the Church. Though partly agreeing with Zolo's thesis on the existence of a certain inadequacy between Rosmini's social philosophy and Christian personalism, Traniello does not see a "dualistic" conception. In fact, he believes that Rosmini's partially insufficient of vision of politics and of the economy could be compensated by his utopian and moral conception of religious society.[40]

2.3.4 An Alternative Approach to These Interpretations

The approach to Rosmini's philosophy of economy introduced in this book contrasts, in the first place, with the thesis of Solari and Zolo, who are deeply influenced, in our opinion, by the historiographic interpretation of Rosmini that portrays him as a traditionalist thinker – basically a follower of Haller – whose acceptance of modernity is always partial and, hence, is incapable of dealing with the socio-economic issues of his time. To some extent, this is true. However, this approach could only be applied to some aspects of Rosmini's early texts – and surely not to all of them – but it disregards the evolution towards modernity that exists in most of Rosmini's social and economic proposals. For the rest, through the systematic exposition and interpretation of Rosmini's socio-economic texts, we will try to show that his philosophy of economy is not an inferior by-product of his thought or a mere ideological projection of his social class; on the contrary, it is organically and theoretically integrated into the whole of his philosophy.

Moreover, in this book we will differ from Pietro Piovani's view of a simple identification of Rosmini's Christian personalism with individualist economic liberalism, as well as from Zolo's arguments which reduce Rosminian economic thought to a "Catholic-liberal dualism". We will make an attempt to show that these arguments suffer both from historico-philological and theoretical flaws. In regard to the first one, we have already seen in the first part of this chapter how Rosmini assimilates the ideas of the economic classical school but criticizing them from the humanistic perspective of the Italian civil economists and even from that of authors

[39]"Ma sin dalla *Política I* le soluzioni offerte al problema della autorità dalla retorica rica di fascino del de Maistre e dalle brillanti formule dei tradizionalisti non possono bastare al Rosmini, più sensibile, anche in conseguenza dei suoi interessi economici, alla dinamica delle forze sociali" (Traniello 1997, 45).

[40]"...il Rosmini è riuscito a sottrarsi finché ha intravisto nella dimensione ecclesiale della religione il massimo compimento della naturale sociabilità umana ..." (Traniello 1997, 55).

like Sismondi.[41] As a matter of fact, an in-depth analysis of the Roveretan's works leads to the conclusion that, in his opinion, the problem of economic science does not stem only from socializing and statists economists like Gioia, Bentham or the utopian socialists, as it is argued by Piovani, but also from individualist and liberal economists such as Mandeville, Malthus, Say and Smith himself. A deeper reading of Rosmini's philosophy of economy also shows that his project did not consist, in "resuming the original individualism of economic science" in order to go back to "its cultural origins," just as Piovani assures, but, on the contrary, in rescuing liberal political economy by reconstructing its philosophical foundations from the root.

In this sense, and following the line of argument put forward by previously mentioned authors like Bulferetti or Traniello, and others such as Marco Minghetti (1868), Anton Ferrari (1954), Clemente Riva (1958), Felice Battaglia (1987), Paolo De Lucia (1995), or Mario D'Addio (2000), we will try to show how Rosmini's central approach to economic science is not grounded on classist or political assumptions, but on sound criticism of the subjectivist and utilitarian conception of the economic science, and on a proposal for the latter replacement by a broad theoretical-practical personalist approach.[42]

[41]However, we certainly do not agree with Luigi Bulferetti's thesis about a *rosso*, Sismondian or Christian- socialist Rosmini included in his work *Socialismo Resorgimentale* (1949), which was, at the time, widely debated by Pietro Piovani.

[42]In this sense our opinion will also be that of an essential compatibility between Rosmini's economic thought and the rest of his personalist philosophy, also compatible with the mainstream of Christian social thought.

Chapter 3
The Utilitarian Paradigm

3.1 The Anthropological Assumptions and Their Arguments

3.1.1 The Utilitarian Point of View of Human Action

One of the main inspirational motives of Rosminian philosophy has probably been his criticism against utilitarianism in itself and as a philosophy underlying different sciences, and amongst them, political economy. As we have discussed, Rosmini is an admirer and an enthusiastic student of economics, which, in his own words, is a "*bellisima ed utilissima*" science (Rosmini 1934, 26). Nevertheless, he also thinks it is necessary to undertake an extensive revision of the utilitarian assumptions that are implicit in economic science – in the socializing and statist version as well as in the liberal and individualist one. According to Rosmini, this implicit utilitarian conception is not due to a defect of political economy as a science (Rosmini 1933, 19) but to a defect of those economists who are *influenced by the utilitarian philosophy* (Rosmini 1933, 19). In other words, it is not the internal logic of the science that converts it into a utilitarian science but the extrinsic influence exerted by philosophical utilitarianism to which many of the first economists adhere owing to historical and cultural circumstances.

The heart of the utilitarian influence in modern economic science lies, according to Rosmini, in the conception of human action as a behavior always oriented towards "maximization of utility or interest":

> Isn't it true – argues Romagnosi, quoted by Rosmini – that no one can act according to any previously known norm other than that of his own advantage? Can individuals go outside themselves and act for motives other than those which determine their own will? In a word, is it possible for anyone to act except for self-love? Self-love is taken here as the general will to remain in a satisfactory a state as possible. The law of self-interest is as absorbing and imperative for human beings as the law of gravity is absorbing and imperative for bodies. (Rosmini 1996, n 1740)

The utilitarian point of view affirms that whatever the decision a human being makes, he or she will always be driven by the idea of a reward, benefit or advantage

C. Hoevel, *The Economy of Recognition: Person, Market and Society in Antonio Rosmini*, Ethical Economy 42, DOI 10.1007/978-94-007-6058-5_3,

for himself because "the only possible rational order is that which makes each of us act according to our own maximum utility" (Rosmini: 1996, 66). But, while the most traditionalist utilitarians understand the term "utility" as the maximization of profits or as the satisfaction of certain needs and desires, a more radical utilitarianism widens the concept of utility as if it were equivalent to "happiness," that is, comparing it with the utmost satisfaction of all human desires. Furthermore, happiness identified with sheer utility breaks all connection with the intrinsic values that can measure the hierarchy or mutual relationship between preferences and desires. In a coherent utilitarianism, human actions and economic activities are not connected to the true qualities of the goods and services consumed, produced or exchanged. The rational use of the latter depends on the arbitrary will of the individual, which is only limited by time and money:

> It makes no difference to production if the owner of a net product, as hungry as an *Erastus*, consumes his goods, reduces them to ashes, throws them to the sea, gives them away to his servants or distributes them amongst singers.... (Rosmini 1978a, 29, footnote 24)

Besides, similarly to the contemporary economist Gary Becker who states that "all human behavior implies participants who maximize their utility" (Becker 1978, 14), the utilitarians of Rosmini's time argued that even the actions that seem to have a different logic from self-interest, like moral commitment, love or abnegation, can be explained through the same utility calculus practiced by an average consumer.[1]

3.1.2 Sensists

Rosmini claims that this utilitarianism introduced in his discipline by economists is grounded on the subjectivist gnoseological assumption that man is unable to know anything beyond himself:

> Just as it is absolutely impossible for a person to go outside himself and to feel outside himself, it is absolutely impossible for him to act for anything but self-love. (Rosmini 1991, n 141)

An extremely simplistic first version of this subjectivism introduced in economics is the type of extreme empiricism of those who Rosmini calls sensists.[2]

---

[1] "Gli asceti stessi, così il filosofo, che sembrano odiare la vita e i comodi che l'accompagnano, hanno il loro fondo di sensazioni aggradevoli e dolorose, da cui solo traggono i motivi d'agire. Indipendentemente dai piaceri mondani, uniti alla fama di santità, questi *pii atrabilarî* si lusingano che ciascuno istante di dolor volontario sarà ricevuto per un secolo di felicità alla banca del paradiso, e loro calcolo è affatto simile a quello dell' usurajo che presta cinque per ottener cento, o del ghiottone che lascia crescer l' appetito per soddisfarlo con maggior golosità" (Rosmini 1976, 169).

[2] Amongst the "pure or organic" sensists, Rosmini mentions Gioia, Bentham, Verri and others of very similar style to the one of the first neoclassical economists such as Stanley Jevons and some contemporary neuroeconomists.

According to the latter, "the existence of human being is reduced to sensations" and "so do the stimuli of his acts" (Rosmini 1976, 98). In this way, human needs and desires are no more than "an uneasy and painful state of the organs that ceases with the removal or addition of a thing or action" (Rosmini 1976, 99) so "the moment during which the pleasant sensation lasts is called happy and unhappy if the sensation is painful" (Rosmini 1976, 99). On the other hand, sensists describe the moral dimension of human beings as a mere calculation of pleasures and pains that leads the subject to act "choosing carefully the most effective means to attain his ends, but, at the same time, carrying it out with precaution so as not to be exposed to problems (...) Setting an end is enough to have the right to use all the means that lead to it" (Rosmini 1976, 110, footnote 2). In conclusion, morality is not different from economy. The moral man does no other thing than "economize" his human resources or capacities – pleasures and pains – by gaining the utmost advantage at the lowest cost.

3.1.3 *Sentimentalists*

A more refined version of utilitarianism is brought up, according to Rosmini, by sentimentalists.[3] He thinks that sentimentalism coincides with sensism in that the only kind of human knowledge is the sensitive one. However, sentimentalism provides a wider interpretation of human sensitivity introducing in the subject a certain psychological complexity. This is the reason why sentimentalists conceive sensations as "ideas" and the combination of sensations as "intelligence". Furthermore, in their opinion, the dynamics of human action is not governed solely by a mechanism of maximization of pleasures but also by the operation of a sensitive affectivity that is able to transcend self-interest. Sentimentalists admit the existence of a "superior" affectivity generated by the so-called "moral sentiments" such as sociability, reciprocity, benevolence towards others and even disinterested virtue, understood as sensitive tendencies or instincts that are able to transcend one's own subjectivity and interest:

> It is true that pleasure, totally individual and subjective in the first place, can be caused by reasons that are not subjective and individual. Grounded on this fact, many philosophers that rendered pleasure a moral principle thought they could break free from the accusation of being selfish by showing that in their moral philosophy they also included benevolent tendencies towards other men and even included disinterested virtue (as they call it) as a source of exquisite pleasures. (Rosmini 1941, 163)

As an illustration of this applied to economics, Rosmini quotes Adam Smith and his thesis on "sympathy" as a moral principle,[4] through which there would be an

---

[3]As Anglo-Saxon representatives of this tendency, Rosmini mentions Joseph Butler, Francis Hutcheson, Dugald Stewart, Thomas Brown, J. Mackintosh, Anthony Shaftesbury, Thomas Reid and, of course, Adam Smith. Amongst the Italian authors, the Roveretan mentions Genovesi, Filangieri and Palmieri.

[4]"Nell' ubidire adunque a questa simpatia collocò Adamo Smith il principio della morale" (Rosmini 1941, 160).

opening up "of one man to another" (Rosmini 1941, 160). Rosmini points out that Smith's sympathy as well as Shaftesbury and Hutcheson's moral sense, or Reid and Stewart's moral faculty (Rosmini 1941, 159–190), would imply the existence of a sort of moral reasoning in human beings, but not in the sense of a conscious, rational calculation but rather as an instinct (Rosmini 1941, 160).

3.1.4 Social Utilitarians

A third type of justification of the utilitarian conception of human action springs from social utilitarians according to whom, in Rosmini's opinion, human action and "morality is contained in utility calculation." However, it is a utility calculation in which they "involve society" considering it "something useful for each of them because of the mutual advantages gained by the associates that compose it" (Rosmini 1941, 164) and a font of "profit that individuals aspire to make over others and a game or, furthermore, a secret fight in which the associates seek to win or acquire most goods for themselves, or for the benefit of the social body but considered as a means for himself" (Rosmini 1941, 164).[5]

In this way, in Rosmini's view, social utilitarians maintain that the principle of *sociality* "can be understood in two ways: either as the instinct which human beings have for associating with their like, or as a *calculation* of reason by which they understand they can obtain their own individual utility by promoting the common utility" (Rosmini 1993a, 88, n. 153). "In this system, if one associate does not harm another or if an associate benefits another is due to *reciprocity*, that is, the expectation to achieve a utility equivalent to others or even a better one" (Rosmini 1941, 164–165).[6] Therefore, "society, as a universal means to all the goods that individuals can enjoy, acquires the maximum value and becomes the source of all morality" (Rosmini 1941, 378).

3.1.5 Eudemonists

Finally, in Rosmini's view, there is a much more refined, fourth type of utilitarian argument formulated by eudemonists, who "full of truths and errors" (Rosmini 1941, 161) reduced human action to the *tendency towards self perfection or*

---

[5]As we have already said, Rosmini quotes, amongst the social utilitarians, many economists influenced mainly by La Rochefoucauld and Bentham (Rosmini 1941, 165). Rosmini also mentions Machiavelli, Grotius and even Cicero amongst those 'who deduced the duties of men from *sociality*' (Rosmini 1993a, 87, n.151).

[6]The concept of 'reciprocity' as a 'social' motive of human action is present in many economists that Rosmini studies, especially in Italians such as Genovesi or Romagnosi.

happiness; in other words, "they assumed that eudaimonology was equivalent to morality" (Rosmini 1941, 161). The Roveretan draws a first distinction between those who reduce human action to the pursuit of happiness without determining its nature, and those who try to determine the nature of happiness in some way. As regards the former, Rosmini makes reference to those who claim that human action is always a purely rational maximization, that is, an effective disposition of means to ends; the content of this maximization could be a subjective or objective good (Rosmini 1941, 159). On the contrary, other authors – whom the Roveretan relates to *Aristotelian eudemonism*[7] – maintain that "we can act only through the principle of self-perfection and can never act beyond this motivation" and that "a natural inclination to self-fulfillment and perfection spurs us to use our faculties to overcome our inertia whatever the cost to ourselves" (Rosmini 1993a, 98, n. 174). Therefore, they conclude that "if we are required to tend to our own *perfection*, we must implicitly propose some good for ourselves" (Rosmini 1993a, 98, n. 173).

However, even though Rosmini carefully shows the existing differences and nuances of all these versions, he thinks that "all these systems are subjectivist because they all begin and finish in the subject, they are all bounded to the subject's excitement that satisfies himself and seeks the good for himself and nothing more; his principles and conclusions are bounded by selfishness" (Rosmini 1941, 167).

3.2 Social, Jural and Economic Consequences

3.2.1 Society as a Market

As we have already discussed, in Rosmini's description of utilitarianism, society is perceived as an extension of individual utility,[8] a mere exchange of benefits or mutual interests:

> Self-love is the only possible virtue in the morality of pleasure because even when we act for someone else's good, this is not done and cannot be done unless there is self-interest involved: 'in any system, says our author [Gioia], one gives to receive.' (Rosmini 1976, 117, footnote 1)

[7]Rosmini links directly or indiretly the eudemonism of self-perfection to Ficino, Leibniz, Spinoza and even Socrates and Plato: "Platone pone il principio della felicità ad un tempo e della virtù, nella *perfezione della natura umana*, cioè in questo, che l'uomo sia come dee essere, tanto rispetto a sè, quanto rispetto alla società. Aristotele non muta che le parole a questo concetto del suo maestro" (Rosmini 1941, 162).

[8]"Quindi -writes Rosmini- in altro modo non si può raccomandare la subordinazione sociale, che col mostrare che ciò richiede, almeno *hic et nunc*, il proprio interesse" (Rosmini 1976, 146). "...il solo *piacere* e il *dolore*: quello che forma, mantiene e termina qualunque convenzione fra gli uomini. Nessuno è obbligato a stare alle convenzioni con proprio danno, se non fosse per evitare un danno maggiore" (Rosmini 1976, 147).

As an illustration, Rosmini quotes the economist Gioia, who supports this thesis after analyzing the nature of family, whose foundations, according to him, are exclusively the utilitarian psychic needs of its members, starting by the parents' love for their children.[9] The latter is never true love, understood as the recognition of the other as another (which is impossible in utilitarianism), but merely an internal fantasy, a projection of the parents' illusions on their children whose aim is not the children's good in itself, but rather the psychic satisfaction of parents:

> The illusion is that which supports parents' duties regarding their children. Throughout his life, the father – argues Gioia – tries to provide his children with all the best leisure activities and pleasures he can; he plans thousands of projects for their progress and fortune. These innocent pleasures in the mature and senior stages come very much alive as they are embellished by illusion. (Rosmini 1976, 120)

Although it might sound paradoxical, utilitarians try to show that these needs and illusory sentiments projected on others replace *moral virtue* by moderating and deceiving self-interest and, at the same time, taking it to its maximum satisfaction. Also expressed in this way is the advancement of civilization, which evolves from the coarse passions of primeval times to the *intelligent interests* of refined societies (Rosmini 1977a, 120, footnote 1).[10] In this sense, utilitarians deem society a product of virtue, not understood from the classical point of view of a disinterested pursuit of the common good, but of a tactical exchange between "intelligent" interests. In conclusion, according to the utilitarians quoted by Rosmini, "society is not, was not and will never be any other than a general market in which individuals sell and offer their goods and services so as to receive other individuals' goods and services. In this exchange, each individual gives what he values less to get something he values more; as a result, everyone benefits from association. Even when men provide services that seem to be for free, it can be said that they make a good deal; they cede part of their ownership and time to gain a nicer and more genuine pleasure: the pleasure of helping other people; or else to get rid of a deep sorrow: other people's misery. They make an exchange in the exact same way as the person who gives away money to procure a firework that entertains him or to chase away anything disturbing" (Rosmini 1976, 135–136).[11]

3.2.2 The Utilitarian Conception of the Law

Utilitarianism conceives the jural system as a sort of artificial superstructure that organizes the multiple spontaneous and individual ways of pursuing utility by giving

---

[9]It is amazing how Gioia is almost 200 years ahead of his time regarding the modern economic theories on family formulated by Gary Becker which are contained in his works *A Treatise on the Family* (1991) and *The Economic Approach to Human Behaviour* (1978).

[10]See also Melchiorre Gioia (1815–1819, 345).

[11]Rosmini quotes Gioia (1815–1819, I).

them a maximum stability and guaranteeing a useful outcome for the whole social body. As a matter of fact, utilitarians believe that "punishments and rewards are necessary to direct the private interest in order to be useful to the public, as the description of the advantages of civil society in general, as stated above, is not enough reason to make men respect it: in fact, it is more convenient for men to be restricted by civil society through the constant presence of constraint and fictional pleasure" (Rosmini 1976, 155).

According to Rosmini, it is evident that there is no difference between utility and right in the utilitarian approach. As utility is the sole principle of human action, right is also reduced to economic utility, the only difference being that it is a renowned utility supported and enforced by the law of the State. The law has one function only: support, strengthen and establish certain positions of power that individual interests have *in fact* achieved providing them with stability. Then, the law will be reduced to the utmost social utility calculated according to the type of political utilitarianism adopted (statist-oriented or individualist-oriented):

> If man has no other duty than pursuing his own utility and his own pleasure, if everyone can make the calculation that believes is best for his utility and his own tastes, these multiple *moral calculus*, through which everyone takes into account only his or her own selves, putting into practice the whole of moral philosophy, would put in danger the existence of mankind. Therefore, a force is required by means of which all tastes become subjected to one taste and a person's calculation is obliged to submit to one single calculation made by one or more persons. If the prevailing force is in the hands of one person or more, they must eliminate themselves until one taste prevails over the rest or until each of them sacrifices a taste so that from everyone's taste emerges one that turns into *law*... in a word, right is born out of force. (Rosmini 1976, 138)

According to utilitarians, right does not have an internal content that includes objective and invariable principles in some of its parts; on the contrary, it is reduced to a set of purely conventional norms that fluctuate according to the interests -mainly economic ones- involved in a specific society. Gioia expresses it as follows:

> What are laws if not norms, orders, wills of that who governs society, calculated upon the physical, moral and political interests guaranteed by the threat of inflicting pain on the recalcitrant wills? What are rights if not advantages, goods, conveniences, that is, real or possible pleasures whose possession is guaranteed by the law as well as the punishment for those who violate it? What else can obligations and duties be but offenses, evils, uneasiness, that is, real pains, limitations to the undetermined power to act that becomes a pain the law enforces by threatening those who transgress it with a more severe punishment? Contracts are no more than an exchange of little pleasures for bigger pleasures... Laws, rights, duties, contracts, crimes, virtues are additions, subtractions, multiplications, divisions of pleasures and pains, and the civil and criminal legislation is no other than the arithmetic of sensitivity. (Rosmini 1976, 137, footnote 2)[12]

In addition, Rosmini makes a distinction between a statist jural rationalism according to which laws are the product of an artificial intervention of the State or of a group of ruling people, and the other variant represented by the Scottish

[12]Quoted by Rosmini from Gioia (1841, 6).

and English economic philosophy (Mandeville, Hume, Smith, Burke),[13] French traditionalism and German and Italian historicism, according to which positive law is the product of a factual interaction between interests that takes place throughout history (Rosmini 1941, 381).

3.2.3 The Political Forms of Utilitarianism

With regard to politics, Rosmini describes a first type of utilitarianism that seems to be related to individualist liberalism, Adam Smith being an example – although he also mentions other Italian and French authors, provided the nuances among all of them are rightly considered –[14] who, in his opinion, try "to demonstrate that private interest is that which shapes public good (Rosmini 1941, 379)".

> Some pretend that private interest agrees and identifies itself by nature with public interest, and also say that men are so sagacious when it comes to their private interest that they naturally tend towards public good, and there is nothing better than giving private interest as much freedom as possible because alone it will produce public good. So, if we try to direct private interest, both will cease to exist: a similar system is followed *partly* by Beccaria, Smith, Condorcet, etc. (Rosmini 1976, 154, footnote 1)

Besides, the supporters of this approach think that nothing can be expected from governments' intervention since individuals that compose them are also driven by their particular interests with the difference that they are not subjected to competition but possess the monopoly of power. This type of liberal utilitarians "proclaims the need for free competition as the most favorable to all interests" (Rosmini 1941, 380). In addition, according to Rosmini, in the extreme of this approach would be Bernard de Mandeville's renowned thesis on private vices as public virtues, according to which "there is no human vice that is not useful to anyone who knows how to make a profit out of it" (Rosmini 1977a, 104, footnote 2).

A second type of political utilitarianism is supported by the representatives of the also renowned doctrine of the *enlightened self-interest:*

> Others also claim that because of its nature private interest coincides and identifies with public good but they do not believe that individuals know this interest by themselves: private interest does not coincide with public interest unless it is rightly understood, and it is not so easy for everybody to fully understand it. In this sense, men must be taught about their private interest because, if directed with real skill, it becomes one along with common interest. (Rosmini 1976, 154, footnote 1)

Even when Rosmini does not name specifically any representative of this thesis, he seems to refer to the one supported by many authors and, probably, amongst

---

[13]This type of jural historicism has been brought back in the twentieth century by Friedrich Hayek.

[14]In fact, we have to bear in mind that even though Rosmini disagrees with Smith's individualist and utilitarian theses, he admires him in many other aspects he always procures to highlight.

the economists he wanted to allude, it was Romagnosi, who promoted the idea of educating interests as a way to make them coincide with the common good.[15]

Finally, Rosmini distinguishes a last version of political utilitarianism supported by those in favor of a permanent action of the State, which, through external incentives, intervenes in the 'natural' exchanges amongst individual interests, and introduces an *artificial interest* amongst them that tips the balance in favor of what the government considers more useful to society. Though this *statist utilitarianism* does not fully eliminate the power of individual interests (like communism does), it practices a sort of social engineering by which it subjects the calculation of interests made by each individual to the "social" calculation made by the government:

> Others state that even if privates knew how to perfectly calculate their own interest and, therefore, understood it well, not even in this case would private and public interest coincide. On the contrary, in many cases they would be opposites: and this is our author's [Gioia] point of view; though he is not always coherent with himself and sometimes talks in a way that makes one believe that private interest, as long as it is well understood, conforms the public good itself. Now, being private and public interest opposite in nature, our author says it is necessary for the *government* to create an *artificial interest* through punishments and rewards: this interest will help private interest find pain when it distances public interest and a prevalent pleasure when it approaches it; in such a way, private interest will artificially become the public good of a quality that will always be of private interest. (Rosmini 1976, 154, footnote 1)

This last political approach derived from utilitarianism goes back, according to Rosmini, to Helvetius' French tradition of rationalism and sensism; it continues mainly with Jeremy Bentham's English radical trend; and it could be ultimately be related to utopian socialism and communism – based partly on Hegel's "statolatry" – in which individual needs and interests are scientifically organized by the State.[16]

3.3 The Impact on Economics

3.3.1 Chrematistics

In addition, Rosmini states that utilitarianism has also had a significant impact on economic science itself. He distinguishes two modes or two different degrees of utilitarianism in economics. The first one is supported by the economists

[15]Rosmini himself, like Romagnosi, is an enthusiastic supporter of the education of interests and of the subordination of their freedom to the people's culture (Rosmini 1923, 138–139). Nonetheless, as will be seen later on, the Roveretan considers that neither the social nor the economic order can be based only on interests, not even if they are "well understood."

[16]"Collocato al centro di tutte le opinioni, il governo debe prestar a tutte la stessa protezione, perché in materia di opinioni, l'errore ha gli stessi diritti della verità [...] Si trova però sempre la soluzione di questo problema in un esatto catalogo dei piaceri e dei dolori privati e pubblici" (Rosmini 1976, 150).

belonging to the classical school, to whom, as we already know, Rosmini truly respects and values[17] but considers that they are also influenced by an utilitarianism which he defines as "avaricious" or "chrematistic."[18] In this sense, Rosmini refers to Adam Smith[19] and Say relating them to a wealth-centered and self-interest conception of the economy which has no sufficient connection with the doctrine of "eudaimonology" or *happiness* (Rosmini 1933, 19, 1994b, 81–82).

In Rosmini's view, the characteristics of a chrematistic economic science would make it tend towards a "meticulously economic spirit" (Rosmini 1923, 56) that always considers necessary to "spend little" and not "spend wisely" (Rosmini 1923, 59); sees poverty and need as the primary incentives to promote work and diligence (Rosmini 1977a, 103, footnote 1); worships saving in detriment of consumption (Rosmini 1923, 153 and following) and has an excessively limited vision of the latter's productive dimension (Rosmini 1978a, 29). On the other side, in Rosmini's opinion, this "avaricious" utilitarianism also tends to "materialize society" (Rosmini 1994b, 81) reducing the right of ownership to the possession of an "external property" (Rosmini 1994b, 89, footnote 67), and common good to a "mere game of interests"[20] and to "free economic competition."[21] This type of utilitarianism leads many economists to have an extremely particularistic idea of society's general wealth, identifying too easily social utility with the sum of individual patrimonies (Rosmini 1923, 68–69); to have excessive confidence with the natural regulation of economic interests amongst countries which are solely moved by the love for wealth (Rosmini 1978a, 26, footnote 18) and to reduce politics to economy depriving the latter of a superior regulation and direction.

3.3.2 Subjectivism

Nevertheless, Rosmini argues that classical economists' characteristic 'avarice' does not pose so many problems as the subjective utilitarianism shown by the economists who support sensism. They represent, in his opinion, the most extreme utilitarianism in political economy.[22] In effect, as regards chrematistic utilitarianism,

[17]Indeed, he praises them constantly, and claims that "it would be advisable for Italians to study English (sic) political scientists and economists (...) Vi hanno delle verità positive negli scrittori di questa nazione pensatrice" (Rosmini 1952a, 237).

[18]As a reference, Rosmini quotes Aristotle in the passages where he reflects on the issue of avarice in the economy (Rosmini 1994b, 370, footnote 1).

[19]"Alla prima classe si accosta lo Smith" (Rosmini 1933, 18).

[20]"Adamo Smith parlando d´interessi materiali sostenne (...) che l'interesse privato è quello che forma il bene publico" (Rosmini 1941, 379–381).

[21]As an example, Rosmini quotes Romagnosi when he claims that " the apex of the true civilization of human associations consists in free and guaranteed *economic* competition' (Romagnosi 1839)" (Rosmini 1994a, 90, n.2 –Appendix).

[22]"L' errore di Smith è certo il meno colpevole e sarebbe utile alla società, se potesse esser utile un errore" (Rosmini 1933, 19).

the Roveretan argues that in it there is still a certain distance between desire and its object: utility understood as a desire to accumulate wealth requires a certain 'economy' and momentary limitation of other desires. On the contrary, when it comes to sensist utilitarianism, political economy becomes the science of happiness, interpreted in the hedonist sense of sensism, that is, the search for the biggest amount of pleasures or satisfactions not only monetary but of any kind and without boundaries (Rosmini 1978a, 15).

On the other hand, according to Rosmini, in this type of subjectivist economicism, consumption – prototype of subjective satisfaction – becomes the economic action *par excellence*. Hence, according to them, the distinction between productive and unproductive consumption (Rosmini 1978a, 29) will make no sense and nor will the recommendations on expenditures in proportion to savings that is still present in classical economists.[23] On the contrary, in this type of utilitarianism, consumerism and fashion – interpreted as the process of permanent changes in tastes and needs without any objective quality of goods and services but as the product of imagination and of mimetic relations amongst consumers – are the key for a dynamic economy.[24] Indeed, sensist utilitarians claim – contrary to what chrematistic economists did – that consumerism, luxury, and fashion induce work and diligence (Rosmini 1977a, 101–102)[25]; are a means to fight corruption[26]; and even have a redistributive effect in the economy as "they dissolve the enormous wealth of the minority and distribute it more evenly amongst the majority".[27] Rosmini argues that said theses come to the conclusions that "vanity and absence of real qualities are useful economically" (Rosmini 1977a, 126) entrepreneurs must procure to carry out their activities free of moral urges (Rosmini 1976, 131), and fruitful economic policies must set free and arouse all kinds of artificial needs and desires in consumers so as to obtain more prolonged growth cycles.[28]

---

[23]"Gioia is against Smith and other authors who recommend *economy*, that is, annual savings as a means to help the accumulation of wealth by increasing the necessary capital for its production, stating that it means a desire to 'work without pleasure'"(...) "to accumulate capital every year without being any happier, similarly to an avaricious man who contemplates his treasures..." (Rosmini 1978a, 26–27).

[24]"As social bonds increase, so does the need for quick consumption (...) This need for *variable appearances* in society's current state must *grow in proportion to the lack of real qualities*." Quoted by Rosmini from Gioia (1815, T. IV, II, in Rosmini 1977a, 125–126).

[25]"The hope of, one day, procuring the pleasures of luxury for oneself is a powerful incentive for the mass: as that incentive diminishes, the mass gets closer to a state of inertia, leisure, numbness, and so the well-known vices that go along with it arise" (Rosmini 1933, 55).

[26]"Ora il capitale disponibile per la corruzione è maggiore in tempi di rozzezza, che in tempi di mode... Dunque... la moda diminuisce il capitale disponibile per la corruzione" (Rosmini 1977a, 107).

[27]Quoted Rosmini (1977a, 113) from Gioia.

[28]Melchiore Gioia: "The basic means to enhance a country's civilization consist in the increment of the intensity and number of needs, and in the acknowledgement of the objects that satisfy them. Since the amount of desires is always higher than the amount of desired objects, by raising the

3.3.3 Economism

According to Rosmini, the main consequence of subjective utilitarianism applied to the economy is the reduction of every human action to pure subjective pleasure. In fact, "reducing all – Rosmini affirms – even the very notion of wealth to pleasures, having nothing outside to regulate them . . . this supreme art of pleasure remains alone with an absolute empire, unable to find other norm above itself" (Rosmini 1978a, 29).

Yet, apart from consumption's empire and limitless subjective satisfaction, another consequence of utilitarianism, at an epistemological level, is the reduction of all human sciences, especially social sciences, to the economic approach. As a matter of fact, Rosmini states that although utilitarians still call the different sciences by their names, and even propose political economy "widening" and "opening up" to other fields, the truth is that the intrinsic logic of an approach which reduces morality, society, right and politics to the principle of utility[29] leads naturally to a generalized expansion of the economic science over the different knowledge fields[30] reducing, in Rosmini's words, "all human knowledge to economic speculations" (Rosmini 1978a, 116, footnote) and turning political economy into an "usurping science" (Rosmini 1870, 183).

---

amount of the former, men are consequently in a constant state of hunger, a state that becomes the cause of a perpetual movement." (Rosmini 1994b, 317, 1933, 55).

[29]Rosmini introduces with great dramatism the triumph of utilitarianism in all the sciences: "Dalla sovversione anzi dall' annientamiento della Filosofia operato nel secolo scorso dagli autori del sensismo, guazzabuglio di negazioni e d' ignoranze, che sotto il nome assunto di filosofia invase tutta l' Europa con più detrimento del vero sapere, che non vi avesse recato giammai alcuna invasione barbarica, derivò quella corruzione profonda della Morale, del Diritto, della Politica, della Pedagogia, della Medicina, della Letteratura, e più o meno di tutte l' altre discipline, della quale noi siamo testimoni e vittime (. . .) le passioni e l' ignobile calcolo degli interessi materiali sono divenuti l' unico consigliere, l' unico maestro delle menti . . . " (Rosmini 1934, 19).

[30]"Nè vogliamo qui perscrutare quale istinto inducesse i sensisti a conservare con tanta sollecitudine questo nome di Morale, quando parea dovere loro bastar quello d' Economia politica, giacchè, non dovendo rimanere più che questa sola scienza, pare che per una scienza sola non ci sia bisogno di due nomi" (Rosmini, *IF*, 26). See also Rosmini (1976,134, footnote 4; 1933,19; 1934, 26).

Chapter 4
Recognizing the Truth: Human Action Beyond Utilitarianism

4.1 A Phenomenology of Human Action: From the Subject to the Object

4.1.1 The Starting Point: Physical Need and Vital Spontaneity

After having made explicit and analyzed the utilitarian assumptions present in economic science, Rosmini criticizes them and, at the same time, presents his own positive formulation. Rosmini's main criticism points at the anthropological core of utilitarianism, which conceives human action as a behavior always oriented towards some kind of "maximization of utility." According to our author, the problem of this utilitarian formulation lies on it being based on a partial and distorted observation of human condition. In order to refute it, Rosmini adopts a fundamentally phenomenological point of view[1] that leads him to carry out a meticulous observation of human phenomena.

As regards sensory-oriented utilitarian theories supported by "those writers who became accustomed to considering men as a sensation complex or as a subject endowed with sheer sensory powers from which they intended to deduce and explain the whole of human development," and, hence, to describe human acts and ethics as "the satisfaction of all animal tendencies" (Rosmini 1941, 154), it is clear, from Rosmini's viewpoint, that these certainly account for some human observable phenomena. From the perspective of developmental psychology, during the first stages of a person's life, there is an outstanding predominance of those animal needs that make the human soul "determine itself to those movements which give it most natural pleasure" (Rosmini 1991, n.446). In fact, Rosmini claims that at the level

[1] "We live in a century in which the only scientific method worth-considering is that recognized by Galileo, a method principally aimed at firmly establishing observed facts. Any hypothesis whose avowed aim is to destroy undeniable facts is out of place" (Rosmini 1991, n. 242).

C. Hoevel, *The Economy of Recognition: Person, Market and Society in Antonio Rosmini*, Ethical Economy 42, DOI 10.1007/978-94-007-6058-5_4,

of "vital, animal and human instinct," human beings tend to follow a physical need strongly associated with our animal condition, which is analogically involved with the inevitable nature of *physical need* of the material world.[2] This kind of natural spontaneity is part of us even in adulthood.

Nevertheless, it should be considered that, during infancy stage, instincts can never be fully explained in terms of pure physical need. Even though they are closely related to the laws of matter – especially the one of inertia – they show a sort of drive that the author defines as *vital spontaneity*, which lessens and modifies the mentioned laws "from the inside" of the subject. Rosmini supports his thesis with a significant amount of documents based on all kinds of observations – especially those in the medical field – which show the existence of a series of phenomena in human beings that would prove wrong the most materialistic utilitarian model of a human behaviour governed by a pure physical self-preservation economy. Rosmini presents as evidences the phenomena of non-equivalence between an external stimulus and an inner reaction, the lack of a strict parallelism between the body's physical-mechanical movement and profound organic reactions or unpredictable variations in vital behavior (Rosmini 1991, 537). Nonetheless, according to Rosmini, despite its greater independence and flexibility regarding the strict laws of matter, vital spontaneity is an essentially subjective tendency which does not go beyond the self-preservation logic of animal needs.

4.1.2 Rational Spontaneity, Subjective Value Judgments and Psychological Needs

If one goes deeper into human action it is clear, according to Rosmini, that there exists a second type of spontaneity that the Roveretan calls *rational spontaneity* which, though still connected to animal instinct, transcends the strictly vital level. In fact, Rosmini shows how a little child starts to manifest what he calls *affective volitions*. These are ways of behaving through which an imperative act and a certain "choice" of goods (Rosmini 1991, 537) are developed, though instinct is still prevailing and there is no capacity to go beyond the sheer sensitive satisfaction. Moreover, as the abstraction capacity arises stimulated by the use of language, the child – and later on the adult person – is able to build general and universal ideas, and therefore the rules of action which enable him not only to *desire* something but also to *judge* that desire as good or bad:

> For example, how can I judge that a loaf seen by me is something good? Note that I am not asking how I can *desire* the loaf, but how I can *judge* it to be good. Abstract ideas are not needed to desire it; the animal appetite, whose act or desire can be perceived and willed immediately by the rational principle, suffices for this. But desiring the bread is not of itself

[2] "We understand physical necessity as a real force, which we are unable to conquer and overcome" (Rosmini 1993a, 80, n. 134).

> sufficient for judging that what I see with my eyes is good. In addition I need at least the specific idea of nutrition as good, and I must also know beforehand that bread is something to eat, something nourishing. Then I can judge. (Rosmini 1991, 544)

This way, there is a transition from the already mentioned affective volitions, by which the human being simply follows what he instinctively feels pleasant, to *evaluative volitions*, *evaluative judgments* or *subjective value judgments*. Certainly, the latter do not abruptly replace affective volitions but coexist peacefully with them for some time.[3] However, the progressive emergence of value judgments modifies the original precarious harmony existing in the child, who can not attain all the physical good he would like to and is pushed to "choose" the good he judges better to satisfy his instincts. It is clear that, at this stage, the choice is made amongst goods the child can "evaluate" only subjectively, that is, according to his desires; it is necessary to reach the stage of freedom to find a type of essentially different choice (Rosmini 1991, 547–549). Observation shows, though, that in this developmental stage it starts to flourish a capacity of choice not just amongst physical goods strictly attached to the satisfaction of instincts but amongst the latter and psychological goods. In virtue of these subjective value judgments, argues Rosmini, the child and the adult human being are not only able to desire physical goods as they are directed by animal instinct, but also as a means to satisfy their own *self* (Rosmini 1991, 553), their idea of *property* (Rosmini 1991, 551), or their idea of *one's own greatness* (Rosmini 1991, 552). This way the first inner psychological conflicts are born, which start to reveal the motivational complexity of human action, not reflected in the simplified descriptions made by sensist utilitarians (Rosmini 1991, 554).

4.1.3 The Experience of Freedom, Objective Value Judgments and the Idea of Being

As we have already said, according to Rosmini, at the stage of subjective value judgments there is not yet a truly free choice: "It is possible, therefore, that in the whole sphere of subjective good surrounding and affecting the human being no sufficient reason is to be found capable of arousing an act of pure, *free choice*" (Rosmini 1991, n. 656). Only at a higher level, Rosmini states, "a completely new extension of human activity is revealed" (Rosmini 1991, 560). In effect, "through introspection, we have discovered that there exists an act of will which is prior to feelings and independent from them" (Rosmini 1941, 181). Rosmini describes it as a *force* which is, to some extend, independent from our animal and psychological needs and also from all external stimuli which "added by the subject, (it) tips the balance by determining the mode of activity. This force is, properly

[3] "At this level of development, the baby's *evaluative volitions completely agree with his affective volitions*, just as these harmonize perfectly with his *animal instincts*, which they strengthen and assist. At this age, the baby's powers are in complete peace and concord" (Rosmini 1991, 546).

speaking, *freedom* [which] has no constant, determined relationship with the stimuli or impulses given to the will. On the contrary, it disturbs the stimuli which oppose it, sustains the weak against the strong, and determines the hesitant subject to a decision. Its opposites are both violence and necessity, to neither of which it can be subject" (Rosmini 1991, n. 610–611).

Now, how can we account for the existence of human beings' freedom? According to Rosmini, free acts are possible by means of man's "faculty for esteeming and evaluating all things objectively, that is, as they are, rather than as related to him" (Rosmini 1991, 561). The ultimate origin of our free actions is the spiritual capacity of formulating *objective value judgments* essentially different from affective evaluations and subjective value judgments, which are driven by instinct or the already described subjective needs.[4] Unlike the previous stages, when the child can only esteem things and others in a more or less compulsive way "relative to himself," during adulthood the human being develops the capacity to evaluate them freely, "relative to human nature in general" and "weighing the degree of entity they posses in themselves" (Rosmini 1991, 561). Then, "if we ask, therefore, how the human being can act according to the objective esteem of things without regard to their subjective esteem, we have to reply that he draws the strength to do so from the objective and absolute world itself in which he exists and lives as an intellectual being" (Rosmini 1991, n. 562).

According to Rosmini, this is possible, firstly, because the capacity of intellectual knowledge present in human beings is essentially different – and not just in degree – from sensitive knowledge, contrary to the arguments held by utilitarians of every kind:

> If we observe our acts of knowledge – Rosmini adds – we see that the intellect, in contradistinction to feeling, perceives objectively, that is, focuses its attention on an object different from itself. In its very act of understanding, the intelligent spirit posits something different from itself, abandoning itself in order to concentrate on what is present to it. Indeed, it is a condition of the intellectual activity that the term of the operation is perceived as different from the one who perceives, or better yet, excludes the perceiver. (Rosmini 1988a, n. 13)

A multiplicity of Rosmini's texts reveals the key role of the intellect to get out of the self-interested logic of our subjectivity and to reach the freedom to recognize the objective value of things. Then:

> It is the nature of our knowledge-faculty to judge things disinterestedly, that is, as they are, not as they are of use to us. In this way we esteem them according to truth, not according to the passion proper to self-love (. . .) We also possess the gift of intelligence through

[4] "Dynamic is the word I have used to describe the connection between the judgement (first effect of the volitive force) and the affections of the spirit, between the affections of the spirit (second effect) and the corporeal feelings, between the corporeal feelings (third effect) and external operations (fourth effect of the same volitive force). This connection is, in fact, a real force by means of which the volitive judgement effectively arouses the power of spiritual affections. These in turn move to corporeal feelings which then generates instincts, movements and actions" (Rosmini 1993a, 70, n. 110).

> which we know the value of things that are neither pleasurable nor advantageous to us. We are able to consider these things as pleasurable and good for others or for themselves. This value, which our understanding enables us to know in things, is not measured by their relationship to us. We do not reflect on our own interest but on objective good. (Rosmini 1994b, n. 73–74)

Even more emphatically:

> Intelligence (...) is not limited to subjective good, as we have seen. It conceives every good impartially, considering each good in itself, measuring its degree of goodness disinterestedly. (Rosmini 1988a, 84)

In addition, Rosmini argues that this capacity of disinterested and objective knowledge of the intellect is possible due to the existence in human beings of what he calls "the idea of being".[5] According to the Roveretan, all that we think, experiment and do implies this idea,[6] which does not derive from sensitive experiences (Rosmini 1987, 400, 414) nor is an outcome of the "feeling of one's own self" or of the "idea of self" (Rosmini 1987, 442) but is the subjective manifestation or presence in the form of an idea of the whole objective order of reality.[7] Therefore, the "faculty of objective evaluation, the essentially objective and absolute faculty, is a consequence of the first and most sublime of his powers, which intuits being and constitutes his intelligence" (Rosmini 1991, 561). Indeed – Rosmini states – as the idea of being is "the font of *objectivity of all human knowledge*" (Rosmini 1987, 408–409) since it enables us to "perceive things as they really are in themselves, independently of any relationship with anything else" (Rosmini 1987, 415) "those who reject the theory of being I have set out, are forced (even against their will) to make moral actions impossible" (Rosmini 1988a, 8).[8]

---

[5] "The foundations of all certainty are built on a tiny and discrete part of the knowledge which, despite its size and it being almost imperceptible, is firm and solid as a rock and it is the place where all the operations of reason rest. This is the *idea of being* from which the source and being of all human ideas originate" (Rosmini 1987, 1068).

[6] "The analysis of any knowledge we may have will always result in the same conclusion: 'Nothing can be conceived without the idea of being.' In fact, our knowledge or thoughts cannot be dissociated from the idea of being. Existence is the most common and universal of all qualities" (Rosmini 1987, 411).

[7] "The intimate nature of every intellective being is formed, as we said so often, by the idea of universal being which enables us to know every being and every good" (Rosmini 1988a, n. 63). We shall remember that the idea of being makes us participate, according to Rosmini, only in the *idea* of being but not in its reality. However, it is precisely the idea of being which enables us to grasp any reality objectively, independently from our subjective interests.

[8] In effect, according to the Roveretan, the *idea of being* is "the notion we use to produce all moral judgments" (Rosmini 1988a, n. 4) "We can know, through possession of such a faculty, everything to which the notion of good extends (...) Because our understanding conceives every species of good, every good can be considered by us objectively" (Rosmini 1988a, n. 74).

4.1.4 Recognition, Law and Moral Good

However, objective value judgments and, therefore, free acts cannot be explained, according to Rosmini, through the mere capacity of objective knowledge of the intelligence, but mainly through the subject's active voluntary and free capacity of "recognizing" what the intelligence "knows."[9] In effect, according to Rosmini, most of our acts of knowledge are those which allow us to establish a first contact with things "as they present themselves," without "valuing or judging" them; making a value judgment about them implies some direct knowledge of the thing to be judged which, obviously, one does not possess before that first contact (Rosmini 1988a, n. 140). These acts of knowledge, which Rosmini calls "direct," "passive" and "instinctive," take place "necessarily" in ourselves, that is, without the intervention of any act of will on our part. On the contrary, objective value judgments are *secondary* acts of knowledge by means of which we "re-cognize," that is, we actively and freely "know again" the being of things, which we had only known in a passive way and without the mediation of any free act or reflection. Rosmini maintains that "the exercise of human choice begins, therefore, in the faculty by means of which we acknowledge things. Prior to this faculty there exist in us only first, non-deliberate, spontaneous movements which are proper to the faculty of basic knowledge" (Rosmini 1993a, 66, n. 103).[10]

Besides, according to Rosmini, the free nature of the acts of recognition is a consequence of their not responding to the subject's natural tendency to satisfy his physical or vital needs, but to what he calls, with different names, "moral 'needs', 'obligations' or 'laws'." In contrast with the other needs or laws ruling human nature, moral "need," "obligation" or "law" is not rooted in the subject but in the object. Indeed, according to the Roveretan, once our intelligence knows the objective truth about a thing or situation, the latter gives us the certainty, by its own

[9]"The moral system that I have proposed requires first of all the existence in the human being of a faculty of judgment which can be exercised freely" (Rosmini 1993a, 49).

[10]There is a multiplicity of texts and places in which Rosmini reassures the thesis on value judgments or voluntary intellectual recognition as the key to moral life: "The will then prompts reflection on what is known. This reflection is either morally good or bad in so far as the worth of these things are impartially acknowledged, or disavowed and distorted" (Rosmini 1988a, n. 144). "Our free will is evil if, seduced by self-love, it lays siege to our knowledge with the aim of falsifying it, or attempts to corrupt the natural judgments of our understanding" (Rosmini 1994b, 74). "The will, if it remains firm and unassailable against the attractions of subjective love, is good. It lends the practical support of its power to the law of our understanding by permitting our intelligence to judge according to the truth it perceives, and by taking pleasure in the understanding's right judgments" (Rosmini 1994b, 74). "If the will is good, that is, free from self-interest, secondary end and perverse instinct, its sole end is to acknowledge known things for what they actually are (. . .) In this case, the will moves naturally towards the *truth* (. . .) What is known is loved in all its parts, as it is; no wrong is done to it because all the being found in it is loved without exaggeration or diminution" (Rosmini 1988a, n. 145). In this way, "the will, harmonizing with the law by an act of *voluntary reflection*, acknowledges things exactly as they are in direct knowledge" (Rosmini 1988a, n. 193).

intrinsic logic, that "we cannot change anything in it, no matter the pain or pleasure it may provide us with" (Rosmini 1993a, 85, n. 148) and thus it creates in ourselves the imperative need – not physical or psychological but moral – of "acknowledging and judging it as it is; there is no doubt that unchangeableness of the essence that represents the thing to us has a kind of eternal force and absolute necessity inherent in its own simple nature" (Rosmini 1993a, 79, n. 130).[11]

Thus, according to Rosmini, in virtue of our faculty of voluntary recognition of truth, and therefore of the moral need, obligation or law contained in the being of things, the realization of moral good is also possible. As a matter of fact, even though someone may know intellectually the objective good contained in the moral need or law, "a being is not morally good in so far as its instinct moves it towards its own pleasure and good" (Rosmini 1988a, n. 87). "Our essentially disinterested knowledge of things becomes the basis of morality" only when "it is considered in relationship to the will" (Rosmini 1994b, 74) and "only when the subject *wills* the good which he *knows* does good as willed begin to be moral good" (Rosmini 1988a, n. 89).[12] "Moral good, therefore, consists in the relationship between objective good and the will" (Rosmini 1988a, n. 90). In other words:

> Morality consists in a bridge between the act of knowing one thing by *nature* and the act of recognizing it by the *will*; the thing is *true* as far as it is known, and its recognition is an act of *will*: so the moral essence rests on a relationship between will and truth. However, the truth or direct knowledge of things pertains to the objective order; the will, on the other hand, to the real subject. In conclusion, morality is neither in the subject nor in the object exclusively (...) but in the good resulting from the complete adherence of the subject to the object. (Rosmini 1941, 152)

---

[11]Rosmini uses similar formulations several times: "The first law, therefore, is made by *the being itself of things*, independently of us, and is promulgated by the simple presence of beings to our understanding. In presenting themselves to us they show us that it is not within our power to destroy, change or alter them in accordance with what is useful or pleasurable to us" (Rosmini 1993a, 79, n.131). "Truth, as we have already pointed out, demands our assent with a force totally independent of ourselves. This force is eternal, proper to truth itself, and we in our insignificance are nothing compared with it. We cannot change anything in it, no matter how much pleasure or pain urges us to do so. We can know what is painful, but things do not cease to be true simply because they are painful, nor do they diminish our obligation to acknowledge them for what they are" (Rosmini 1993a, 85, n. 148). Rosmini believes that "moral necessity exists in the objective, absolute world; the human being shares in moral necessity in so far as he shares in this objective, absolute world. Such necessity is of its nature invincible and insuperable precisely because the nature of beings which form the objective, absolute world is invincible and insuperable" (Rosmini 1991, n. 562).

[12]"Objective good, therefore, is moral good, but becomes such only when desired by will." (Rosmini 1988a, n. 89).

4.1.5 Happiness

Though the moral dimension Rosmini finds in human action outdoes the naturalist and subjectivist interpretation of utilitarianism, the Roveretan does not disregard the subjective and natural dimension of man. Certainly, the nucleus of moral action lies in the intellective-volitive recognition of truth and objective good. Nonetheless, such recognition always leads to subjective consequences, that is, to the real union between the subject and the object, which enables the achievement not only of moral but also of eudaimonogical perfections. Therefore, according to Rosmini, "moral good has an intimate relationship with eudaimonological good" (Rosmini 1994b, 268).[13]

However, the Rosminian conception of happiness is essentially different to the utilitarians'. In effect, the latter's mistake has been, according to Rosmini, to misunderstand the essential difference between the dynamics of physical and psychological subjective capacities and needs, and a wider subjective dynamics that Rosmini calls human capacity or desire, which is not born in the senses but in the intellect:

> What the sensists cannot understand or accept is the distinction between physical feeling and human capacity. They systematically reduce all human powers to corporeal feelings and so cannot possibly form a correct concept of human desire, which does not stem from feeling but from understanding. (Rosmini 1994b, 308)

Actually, what human desire ultimately aims at is not a partial material or psychological satisfaction but a kind of complete satisfaction of human nature which Rosmini calls appagamento and could be translated as happiness, or "contentment":

> Pleasure and contentment are different things, just as pain and unhappiness are different things. Human beings can enjoy things, yet still be discontent; they can suffer and be happy. The contradiction is only apparent; the truth of what we are saying is seen every day. (Rosmini 1994b, 392–393)

This can be explained, in Rosmini's opinion, by the fact that happiness is not a purely physical or psychological state but primarily an intellectual state:

> The feeling principle will be in a pleasant state thanks to a pleasant sensation; the state of the intelligent principle will be pleasant only as a result of the knowledge of good, that is,

[13]The ultimate anthropological foundation of the possibility of these eudaimonological goods consists in the relative autonomy inherent to the natural or subjective faculties in which they lie. In effect, "the fact that we cannot move our lower powers directly, and indeed are obliged to move and control them by means of their link with the neighbouring powers, reveals a related truth: the lower powers are not, properly speaking, ourselves (our person) although they are so closely bound with us that they form a single individual" (Rosmini 1991, n. 840). In this way, "different principles of action can be joined together in one individual, as in the case of the human being. But, although joined together and subordinated to a supreme activity, they do not cease to have an activity of their own" (Rosmini 1991, n. 841).

> by means of the judgment with which it declares itself content. I, as an intelligent being, can be content only by judging myself content. (Rosmini 1994b, 253)[14]

In fact, Rosmini explains that human happiness is based ultimately on virtue, which – as we have seen – consists of the act by which good will "feels truth's authoritative demand for *adherence* and surrenders to it" (Rosmini 1994b, 75).[15] In other words, according to Rosmini, contentment and virtuous recognition of the objective order of being go together.[16] Hence, the importance that Rosmini attaches to the "eudaimonological sciences", which study the way of achieving natural perfectioning in order to open the way to the legitimate aspirations of happiness, but integrating it to the dynamics of personal and moral perfecting.

4.2 Critique of Utilitarian Theories

4.2.1 Utilitarianism Is Based on Incomplete Observations

Rosmini argues that the problem of utilitarian theories is mainly that they overlook the capacities for objective knowledge and for free recognition of human intelligence and will, reducing human capacities to one of its subordinated functions: instrumental calculation at the service of self-preservation or satisfaction of subjective needs. Rosmini maintains that utilitarians are centered "not in the *objects* of reason but in man's *forces* and *rational* operations and their products. Therefore, they confuse the *moral order* with the *order of forces*" (Rosmini 1941, 155). Besides, Rosmini states that the reduction of human action to some form of search for pleasure or psychological utility comes as a result of an incomplete observation of man's developmental process, which is limited to the level of *affective volitions*

---

[14]This need to make a eudaimonological judgment of oneself has its ultimate anthropological cause in the fact that "in any particular act whatsoever, person always uses the noblest activity it can dispose of at the time (. . .) Because the faculty of judgment is more noble than that of sense, he is forced to judge himself and his own well-being" (Rosmini 1994b, 254).

[15]Indeed, according to Rosmini, besides the acts of adherence and approval of the objective truth "the other two elements are eudaimonological, that is, components of happiness necessarily joined with virtue" (Rosmini 1994b, 75), as their subjective effects. These are, on the one hand, "*delight* [or pleasure] from its adherence" and, on the other hand, "the approval [made] by the intellect" (Rosmini 1994b, 76). Therefore, for Rosmini, "happiness must result from two elements, *delight* and *approval*" (Rosmini 1994b, 75).

[16]"The very origin of virtue, therefore, contains an intimate bond joining it with happiness"(Rosmini 1994b, 75–76). This affirmation, repeatedly stated by Rosmini in several of his texts (See especially Rosmini 1991, ns. 890–895), reveals his essential discrepancy with Kantian moral rigorism. Besides, according to the Roveretan, full coincidence between virtue and happiness does not take place until the next life, since virtue attains an extremely imperfect adherence to good and truth in this life and, consequently, the degree of enjoyment and internal approval are also imperfect. This is also why, when referring to happiness attainable in this life, Rosmini prefers call it "appagamento" or "contentment" rather than happiness.

amongst material goods (search for maximum pleasure and minimum pain) or to the level of *subjective evaluative volitions or subjective value judgments* (satisfaction of oneself at the minimum cost). In other words, Rosmini shows that the utilitarians' problem lies in considering only inferior childhood stages of human development disregarding superior capacities which appear later in the individual's psychology. Utilitarians seem to put adult's capacities, of choice and evaluation at the same level as children's capacities of choice and evaluation.[17]

4.2.2 Feelings Do Not Account for the Moral Dimension

As regards the arguments posed by *sentimentalism*, the Roveretan deems them superior to those offered by sensist utilitarians. Rosmini considers a merit of sentimentalists to have tried to understand moral action as an opening of the subject in order to meet the others. He shares the sentimentalist thesis which states that "human being soon realizes that he cannot be content and happy at the cost of making others miserable. On the contrary, he must seek the happiness of others as though it were his own" (Rosmini 1991, 560). In effect, in the Rosminian ethical conception, the human being attains moral plenitude not just by means of acts of recognition of things in general but mainly through the recognition of others as "other selves" whom he sympathizes and finally joins with.

Now, "what inner light shines (in man), asks Rosmini, enlightening him in this sublime way, leading him to limit his own enjoyment by ordering it in harmony with the enjoyment of others?" (Rosmini 1991, 560). This "light," in Rosmini's opinion, is neither our "self-interest," nor even our "intelligent" self-interest which would lead us to seek the happiness of others as a means to obtain our own, nor a moral sentiment or sense which would allow us to "sympathize" with others and, thus, extend the subjective love we feel for ourselves through a "benevolent" love for others. According to Rosmini, the sentimentalists' mistake lies precisely in identifying the act of recognition of others with a "disinterested" feeling, which implies, in his opinion, a contradiction in terms (Rosmini 1941, 163). Indeed, "the feeling (as long as it does not derive from reason, in which case it would share in its nobility)... is neither *interested nor disinterested* since to be one way or the other it would be necessary for it to anticipate the things which happen after itself; but the feeling ends up in itself and does not anticipate anything. In one word, feeling is blind and, thus, it cannot show interest or disinterest" (Rosmini 1941, 165).[18]

---

[17]It does not follow, though, that to Rosmini a purely childish use of the will cannot be *actually* observed in the actions of one or more adults.

[18]Rosmini makes a distinction between actions which are driven by feeling and those driven by *interest*, which he defines as "la disposizione dell'uomo, che pone le sue azioni colla mira agli effetti delle medesime."

However, in the act of recognition of "other human beings" (Rosmini 1991, 561) "an order of things (...) far more sublime than anything already encountered" (Rosmini 1991, 560) is revealed that Rosmini calls "moral inobjectivation." Such special form of recognition is not originated in feeling but in the extension of the volitive intellectual act of recognition of things into an act of recognition of others as ends in themselves, as "other selves," which allows us to "transport ourselves into others." Certainly, Rosmini takes into account the role of feelings of benevolence and sympathy in these acts of "moral inobjectivation." He argues, though, that these feelings are merely concomitant to these actions and do not constitute their essential nucleus. To illustrate this, Rosmini explains that the mistake in Adam Smith's moral theory lies not in having valued the role of sympathy but mainly in not having perceived that what is moral in this feeling does not come from its sentimental nature but from its intellectual element.[19] Rosmini states, therefore, that the problem of sentimentalists was that "they lacked of sufficient analysis of sympathy and volition" for they restricted both of them to their sentimental element, disregarding their intellectual character and, thus, confusing "moral feeling aroused by good or bad actions" with "the *judgment* man pronounces about moral value".[20]

Finally, Rosmini asks himself if "the sentimentalists' system is really superior to the one of [sensist] utilitarians" (Rosmini 1941, 165). In his opinion, it is evident that "neither *utility* nor *feeling* can constitute moral obligation, which is essentially attached to disinterest" (Rosmini 1941, 165). Hence, "*feeling* as well as *utility*, even if the latter is considered at its maximum extension, can only be involved in [moral action] as *principia cognoscendi*, nothing more" (Rosmini 1941, 311). Nonetheless, Rosmini holds that we shall distinguish sentimentalism from crudest utilitarianism as "it can be seen that of these two non-moral doctrines, that of utility can be considered much more inferior without comparison to that of sentiments, because the former reduces action to mere interest – and this is essentially evil and immoral in itself – while the latter doctrine is just amoral, in the same way as physiological laws, without implying in themselves a moral evil" (Rosmini 1941, 165–166).

[19]"Adamo Smith si è fermato a considerare esclusivamente la tendenza simpatica di un uomo verso l'altro. Sebbene nel fenomeno della *simpatia* vi abbia l'intervento, e non in picciola parte, delle leggi dell'animalità; tuttavia, com'egli si manifesta nell'uomo, non si può dubitare, che nello stesso fenomeno giuchino assai le potenze intellettive..." (Rosmini 1941, 160).

[20]Besides, Rosmini also develops an extended argument to criticize other sentimentalists' appeal to a special moral faculty (Rosmini 1941, 171). Rosmini recognizes in sentimentalists such as Douglas Stewart or James Mackintosch the merit of being "rings" of communication between sentimentalist "material ethical theories" and "formal" ones, and gives them credit for trying to overcome pure feeling as the principle of action; still, he criticizes them for "focusing their attention on the *matter* of virtue without expressing its *form* (...) which takes place only when *intelligence* gets involved in morality" (Rosmini 1941, 188).

4.2.3 The Absurdity of Social Utilitarianism

As regards social utilitarians, Rosmini states that their introduction of the principle of sociality or social utility to explain the logic of human action makes no sense as far as it either keeps sensists' or sentimentalists' utilitarianism as it is or leads it to insoluble contradictions. In effect, according to the Roveretan, once the principle of social utility has been introduced, only two options remain. In the first option, society is understood as a pure means to get one's own utility, which implies that the consideration of other members of society is pure fiction. In the second option, society is seen as a means used by the instinct or utilitarian calculation of each individual to get others' utility, which implies that "between our own utility and another's utility, we would put another's utility before our own" what would be simply absurd if at the same time we propose the principle of utility as the ultimate motive of all human actions (Rosmini 1993a, 87, n. 152). Consequently, "if we grant that human beings must follow what is useful, then there is no longer any reason why we should place another's utility before our own, or, in cases of conflict, place what is useful to the group before what is useful to us individually. When the only value of social utility is what is useful to oneself, the former is a means, and the latter an end" (Rosmini 1993a, 88, n. 153).

In one word, as in social utilitarianism "every good is relative, everything is reduced to calculus, there is nothing that man should keep unconditionally: even society's good is taken into account in the calculation" (Rosmini 1941, 378). According to Rosmini, the only way out of this labyrinth would be to acknowledge the existence of "a superior reason that could make the others' goods respectable and sacred": only in this way "I do not need to make any calculation to know whether I have to respect them or not; I will just respect them disregarding my own utility" (Rosmini 1941, 378).

4.2.4 The Limitations of Eudemonism

Finally, in relation to eudemonists, the Roveretan will agree with many of their observations about the existence of "a human instinct tending to perfection which draws us into action" (Rosmini 1993a, 98, n. 175) and "a double tendency towards preservation and perfect development" (Rosmini 1988a, 37). Actually, in Rosmini's opinion, "the observation of the strict connection between *actions* and *affections*" shows an "important truth": "we always act in dependence upon our predominant love. It would be absurd to think of abandoning something we love more for the sake of something we love less" (Rosmini 1988a, n. 128). Moreover, Rosmini holds that exists in human beings a calculation of happiness by which "we balance present and future good with the intention of gaining the best available subjective good. We avoid sacrificing a greater to a lesser good, which is in accord with the laws of natural spontaneity" (Rosmini 1991, n. 655). Nevertheless, even though "it is necessary to attribute this instinct [for the search for happiness] all that it deserves," Rosmini warns, in a critical tone, that "we must be careful not to exaggerate its power" (Rosmini 1993a, 98, n. 175). In that sense, he will develop a series of arguments against eudemonists to show that human action cannot be explained in terms of a mere search or tendency of man towards happiness.

A first argument is centered in the critique to the eudaimonological confusion between the "tendency towards happiness" and "moral action." In fact, in Rosmini's view, "this *power* [of search of happiness] urges us to action rather than inaction" (Rosmini 1993a, 98, n. 175). But moral action cannot be explained, argues Rosmini, simply in terms of a merely effective "action" because it always means "acting in a *certain way*" driven, as we have seen, by the moral need or obligation contained in the objectivity of things, essentially different from the rest of the subjective needs, physical or psychological. In this sense, according to Rosmini, the tendency towards one's own perfection as a "power moving man to act" is clearly different from the moral need or obligation that directs "*the mode of action*" (Rosmini 1993a, 98, n. 175). In fact, "instinct certainly moves us, but it does not oblige us to move. Sometimes, it will direct us to carrying out what we are in any case obliged to do. But even if it opposed the carrying out of our obligation, we would still remain obliged. The obligation, therefore, does not depend on our inclination or aversion to carrying out the obligation" (Rosmini 1993a, 86, n. 151). The Roveretan concludes that "if this is true, the principle of perfection cannot be moral principle, which must leave us free, binding us only morally" (Rosmini 1993a, 98, n. 174).

A second argument by Rosmini attacks the eudemonist theory which tries to demonstrate the predominance of the tendency towards happiness in human action, due to the fact that moral action always produces contentment or satisfaction. Certainly – argues Rosmini – "troublesome things can indeed cause us pain in so far as they are troublesome; at the same time they give us a certain peace in so far as they are fully acknowledged by us as true" (Rosmini 1993a, 85, n. 148). It is also true that when we acknowledge the truth, we "obtain harmony and peace by freely adapting ourselves to and delighting in truth, as though it were a special friend. It is also true that in failing to acknowledge or love truth, we find ourselves at odds with ourselves and with truth" (Rosmini 1993a, 84, n. 145). Now, "I have said that we feel pleasure when we follow the truth. But the question consists in knowing whether *pleasure* is the object to which we must direct our attention when acting" (Rosmini 1993a, 85, n. 148). In that sense, Rosmini´s response is clearly negative. In his opinion, when we perform an act of moral recognition of things, "we feel an obligation to acknowledge them not because individually or collectively they bring us peace, but because each carries the message: 'I am true. Behold me, and acknowledge me'" (Rosmini 1993a, 85, n. 148). The force to answer affirmatively to the moral obligation or law does not stem, according to Rosmini, "from one's subjective good or evil" but from "necessarily assenting to truth independently of any other subjective good or evil. The necessity intimated to the human being of acknowledging the truth is independent of him; it is a force that obligates from outside himself" (Rosmini 1993a, 84, n. 145). There comes how "this echo of good or evil is the effect of having followed, or not followed, the prior obligating force" rather than its cause. Therefore, "the force of the moral law obliging the personal human will precedes good and evil without depending on them." On the contrary, "the good or evil of the subject is related to and dependent upon this force [moral law or need]" (Rosmini 1993a, 84, n. 145). Therefore, Rosmini believes that the presence of happiness in moral action is just a *sign* or "simply an *indication* for discovering the source of the obligation and cannot constitute the obligation itself" (Rosmini 1993a, 86, n. 151).

Thirdly, Rosmini makes a critique of the eudemonist argument which states that moral actions, always coinciding with the choice of our greatest eudaimonological good, would be determined by our subjective tendency towards happiness. On the contrary, even though Rosmini affirms that our actions follow the bottom-up hierarchical structure of our volitions or preferences, this hierarchy does not result from the necessary tendency towards happiness, but from a free act of moral valuation that is independent from it. In other words, Rosmini explains that "with our free will we must make our greater eudaimonological good consist in the acquisition of moral good and its consequences" (Rosmini 1993b, 121, n. 427). So, the actions that the subject finally carries out will certainly obey the rationality (reason or sufficient cause) of the predominance of the greatest good or pursuit of happiness, though this rationality will be the outcome of a free act rather than its effect.[21]

Fourthly, Rosmini goes against those who intend to reduce human and moral action to the pursuit of happiness but leave aside any determination of its *objective* contentment appealing to the maximization principle of a purely instrumental rationality by which man always struggles to "... get the means to attain an end." Contrarily, Rosmini agrees that "man manages to be virtuous (...) by the use of his faculties and mainly by his reason." However – he wonders – "will it be enough to say that it is necessary to use these faculties to state the way in which man becomes more virtuous?" (Rosmini 1941, 159). Though it is true that moral behavior implies a rational action in which means are efficiently displayed to attain certain ends, it does not mean, according to Rosmini, that this effective disposition, regarded in abstract terms, can solely explain moral action, since "though moral good consists of an efficient operation, it does not mean that every efficient action is moral" (Rosmini 1941, 179).

---

[21] "Whichever kind the will chooses, therefore, its *volition* always has a cause, or better, a reason. It depends on the opinative good present to the spirit, and upon the spontaneity aroused by this good. The act of volition does not lack a suitable reason; the problem lies in knowing how the spirit determines itself to choose one of the volitions rather than the other (...) We have to distinguish that which moves a person to make a choice from the choice itself. Although the human being is moved spontaneously to choose, this spontaneity does not determine the way in which he must choose. (...) It is this act of choice which determines one of the possible volitions, and which therefore must precede all.(...) This act, therefore, does not lack a cause; its cause is a special activity of the spirit, aroused to operation by the presence of several different kinds of opinative good" (Rosmini 1991, n. 639).

Consequently – our author states – "the principle 'Be perfect' can under a certain aspect be classified with those principles which make utility the norm for human beings" (Rosmini 1993a, 97, n. 171). Actually, Rosmini believes that the nucleus of the problem with the utilitarian approach is its inability to distinguish the personal and moral rationality, which enables us to define the justice or injustice of actions, (Rosmini 1988a, n. 184) from the eudaimonological rationality, which helps us to reflect upon our happiness and our own subjective good (Rosmini 1988a, n. 185). In opposition to the utilitarian interpretation in which eudaimonological rationality is the only one, to which moral rationality is reduced as well, in Rosmini´s interpretation, eudaimonological actions perfect our natural dimension but only moral action "perfects human beings as persons" (Rosmini 1991, n. 853).[22] "Such a difficult concept to understand!" – Rosmini claims, and he is right. However, Rosmini holds that it is precisely in the idea of person and moral perfecting – essentially different from natural perfecting – in which "it is necessary to meditate in deep" to try to find the key to a full and not reductionist comprehension of human action.

4.2.5 The Double Dimension of Human Action

These critiques of the different utilitarian theories can be synthesized in Rosmini's distinction between a *personal* dimension in the human being whose developmental logic is essentially different from the *natural* dimension that is the only one taken into account by utilitarians. Indeed, "all the powers forming part of an individual constitute the individual's *nature,* but the individual's *person* is constituted by the most noble power and highest active principle, that is, the rational power" (Rosmini 1991, n. 851). In this way, out of "the five principles of action observable in the human being (. . .) the three instincts, life, sensuous and human," belong to nature, while the two superior powers of "will and freedom" belong to person (Rosmini 1991, n. 845). Now, given that "every action either begins spontaneously from the subject, or is aroused by the object" (Rosmini 1991, n. 845), it could be argued that the former are the "principle of subjective actions" while the latter are the "principle of objective actions." Therefore, "(human) nature could be said to increase in perfection every time the powers it contains are perfected. But we cannot say that person is perfected unless the highest and noblest of the active principles present in the individual where person resides is increased and perfected. It is this difference between the perfecting of nature and the perfecting of person that makes many err in their judgments and speculation about movement towards human perfection.

[22]However, Rosmini explains that even though every act of *moral perfection* is *personal*, since only the faculties coming from the personal principle enable it to happen, not every personal action is moral. This is the case of, for instance, the non-active aspects of personal life such as the field of *personal experiences,* which do not imply morality (see Rosmini 1991, n. 854–864).

People sometimes show enthusiasm for things which perfect human nature but do not improve the human person" (Rosmini 1991, n. 852–853).[23]

According to the Roveretan, the font of the perfecting of the *person* is the act of *recognition,* which "consists in adhering to objective entity taken in its fullness, and therefore, in its order. The good proper to the human person does not originate therefore from the human person. Rather, persons find it in the *object* to which they unite themselves by means of a willed act of intelligence. This fact takes persons outside themselves in order to find the object which when found provides their perfection. The act of bringing person to perfection is simply their sharing in the goodness of the object, their coupling with being" (Rosmini 1993a, 81–82, n. 140). Indeed, the Rosminian conception of moral perfection is based on the apparently paradoxical fact that "it is not the human person who produces the object; it is rather the object which produces the human person" (Rosmini 1993a, 82, n. 142). Certainly, "moral good and moral evil is personal good and evil, an [that] persons are subjects" (Rosmini 1993a, 81, n. 139). Nevertheless, the person "is not any subject," so "it is not enough for this good to be subjective if it to be moral; it must also be *personal*" (Rosmini 1993a, 81, n. 139). This way, in the process of alternation of subjective and objective powers implied in all human perfecting, objective or "personal" powers should always be given priority over those which are subjective or "natural."[24]

[23]In Rosmini's opinion, happiness is a personal phenomenon: "A pleasant state pertains to nature; contentment properly speaking concerns person." "The human person, when judging internally that he is content, is different from the proximate principle of simple feeling." "If the proximate principle of feeling is in a pleasant state, it does not follow that the other, higher principle, which understands, judges, and properly speaking, constitutes human personship and 'myself' (the word usually expresses a person aware of himself) is content and happy" (Rosmini 1994b, 253).

[24]"Objective powers [however] always precede subjective powers in their development so that the human spirit always puts forth some new kind of activity after new kinds of objects have been revealed to it" (Rosmini 1991, n. 566).

Chapter 5
Economic Action, Happiness and Personalized Self-Interest

5.1 The Nature of Economic Action

5.1.1 The Role of Eudaimonology and Economics

Upon his personalist doctrine of human action, based on the idea of recognition of personal truth and happiness or contentment as its subjective consequence, Rosmini will make an interpretation about the whole dynamics of the eudaimonological actions tending to the satisfaction of other subjective needs of man, including the economic ones. In effect, apart from moral happiness or contentment, Rosmini maintains that there are other subjective goods which are not concomitant to moral virtue and thus require, besides it, a type of *actions different from moral actions* for said goods to be obtained. Rosmini will also refer to these subjective goods as "relatively necessary," to differentiate them from the "absolutely necessary" ones. The latter are those which necessarily result from moral virtue and the human being cannot cease to search without renouncing to his human destiny. However, although virtue and happiness are the only necessary goods absolutely speaking, economic goods can become in many cases "absolutely necessary" goods because without them moral life and eudaimonological fulfillment becomes practically impossible (as for example when basic needs of food, shelter or cloth are not fulfilled). In other words, economic goods are relatively or absolutely necessary depending on the specific circumstances the person is going through.

In addition, according to Rosmini, these two types of eudaimonological goods require two different eudaimonological sciences. On the one hand, "eudaimonology properly speaking," which studies the possibilities for happiness brought by moral virtue itself as a consequence of its union with the objective good; on the other hand, the eudaimonological sciences which study the goods that result not only from moral virtue,but also from the adequate exercise of subjective capacities. Rosmini argues that it is precisely this second type of sciences, which are in charge of studying the role played by the economic dimension in the human being.

C. Hoevel, *The Economy of Recognition: Person, Market and Society in Antonio Rosmini*, Ethical Economy 42, DOI 10.1007/978-94-007-6058-5_5,

5.1.2 Objective and Subjective Dimension of Economic Action and Value

In his theory of economic action and value, Rosmini draws the best principles from the economists of his time. On the one hand, he assimilates the objective conception of value taught by classical economists centered in the material dimension of the economic phenomenon as the result of actions such as labor, saving and capital accumulation. Actually, according to Rosmini, economic value demands an important degree of solidity or "objective materiality," in the sense that it should be able to subsist with a certain degree of entity of its own, regardless of the subject who produces or consumes it. Indeed, there is already economic value and utility in goods and services from the moment that they are "available" and suitable to satisfy someone's potential needs.[1]

However, in spite of this considerably quantifiable physical and material dimension of economic value reflected in a country's total production, commercial balance, savings rate, levels of consumption and income, and in the quantitative relationships amongst all these factors, this objective quantitative aspect is in fact, according to Rosmini, just the external aspect of economic value: it reflects a deeper phenomenon which takes place in the subjectivity of the people who are behind those quantifiable forces. In Rosmini's opinion, economic valuations and actions depend on personal judgment. That is to say, the level of poverty or wealth, of material well-being or discomfort, is defined by means of a valuation the subject carries out in accordance to the degree of personal satisfaction.[2] In this sense, Rosmini's conception of economic value leans on the Italian civil economists' subjective conception – that later on will be that of the neoclassicals' – whose

[1]Actually, among economic goods defined in this way, Rosmini mentions "the produce of the earth, the crops, grapes, white mulberry leaves, sugar, coffee, flax, hemp, cattle and other products of agriculture and stockbreeding" as far as "they are *suitable* for satisfying needs and pleasures." Under a second category he mentions "the technical work, by means of which raw materials are reshaped and become suitable for satisfying the same needs more efficiently or for satisfying new needs and obtain new pleasures and comforts. This increase of suitability means an increase of value and wealth." Under a third category are "commercial transport which, by distributing the agricultural and manufacturing products in more appropriate places to be consumed, that is, by distributing them according to the needs and desires, makes them more suitable for satisfying both (. . .) This greater aptitude or easiness for satisfying needs and originate pleasures is a value or an added and created wealth." Finally, there are "*personal abilities* which can satisfy a need, generate pleasure or be exchanged for things that are suitable as well or that can somehow generate satisfaction" (Rosmini 1978a, 16).

[2]To illustrate his opinion, Rosmini addresses Cicero: "Cicero recognises that material benefits which do not content the human spirit are not good: Who do we take to be rich? In my opinion the person whose possessions are such that he is easily content with a free life in which he neither looks not longs for further desires. If we are content and consider the money we have sufficient, we are, without doubt, rich. It is the human spirit that must be called rich, not the strong-box; as long as I see you empty, I will not consider you rich, no matter how full the safe is" (Rosmini 1994b, 322, footnote 300).

synthesis Rosmini sees in the definition of wealth proposed by Gioia in his *Nuovo prospetto delle scienze economiche*:

> This is the first definition of our author which now I draw upon to support my own reasoning. The term *wealth* is applied to anything that can satisfy a need, bring us some comfort or pleasure. (Rosmini 1978a, 15)

According to Rosmini, wealth is certainly a value emerging from some objective qualities of a thing, but these qualities do not have a meaning in themselves unless they are related to the subject's capacity to experiment some kind of satisfaction or pleasure through them. That is why economic value is not something fixed and unchangeable, but it is each person who "at every instant determines and fixes the value of things" (Rosmini 1994b, 414):

> We know through the science of political economy – affirms Rosmini – that it is necessary to make a subtle distinction between the value which persists and the changing shapes under which value hides. (Rosmini 1977a, 115)

Consequently, it is essential for economic valuation what Rosmini calls the "faculty of abstraction" of reason, which allows us to "see relationships and qualities in isolation from things" (Rosmini 1994b, 402) and, thus, allows us to value it not in accordance with its essence or complete nature, but only in relation to the end or ends we aim at in a specific moment. Hence, economic action is always characterized by a sort of instrumentalization of a group of goods aiming at a certain end.

Besides, according to Rosmini, being able to satisfy needs or desires is not enough for a thing to have economic value: it needs to be a scarce, limited good, which, therefore, demands the sacrifice or refusal of other goods to be obtained. In short, economic value is also defined by the thing's capacity to be exchanged for other goods or by the amount of goods one needs to use, consume or exchange to get it. In a word, a thing has economic value as long as one can assign a market price to it:

> There may be material objects such as the air, the sun, etc., which satisfy needs and produce pleasure but still cannot be considered objects of the economy. They do become objects of economy only when they demand expenditure or labor to be maintained or when it is necessary to protect them from too many consumers; in that case, they can be sold and purchased. However, when they abound for everyone without the need of any expenditure or effort, nobody is willing to exchange them for any other thing, no matter how insignificant it is; though they satisfy the greatest needs of life, they do not have a price. In this sense, they are excluded from the number of things which can be given a price, those which economy is concerned about. (Rosmini 1978a, 16–17, footnote)

Therefore, according to Rosmini, there is economic value when three requirements are met: *availability, possession or existence of a good or service*; *immediate or mediate capacity of this good or service to satisfy a need; and scarcity* of this good or service, which is expressed in the *possibility of exchanging it in the market* for a certain *price*. These three characteristics will derive in the characteristics of economic action which, according to Rosmini, will consist in a set of economic operations such as the production, consumption and exchange of goods or services, which allow us to keep or raise the available economic value to the maximum, or at least to lose as less as possible of it. In order to achieve this, it will be necessary to "economize" or "optimize" our decisions, that is, to spend as less as possible of the available means (cost) and try to keep to the maximum their capacity to satisfy needs (benefit or economic utility.) It is all about what Rosmini defines as the *legge del minimo mezzo* [*law of the minimum means*] the golden rule of every wise economic decision.[3]

Now, is the economic value of a good properly defined if referring only to its availability, capacity to satisfy needs and scarcity? Besides, in relation to economic action, is it enough to characterize it as the maximization of economic value understood in that way? In other words, is it sufficient a formal definition of economic action characterized as the pursuit of the maximization of any good or service provided it can be exchanged?

5.2 Economic Action and Happiness

5.2.1 Economic Action and Dynamic of Human Desire and Its Contentment

According to Rosmini, a purely formal definition of economic activity is not enough. In effect, the Roveretan believes that it is also fundamental to answer other questions: which are the needs to be satisfied? What do we need to "economize" – that is, to use in accordance with the *law of the minimum means* – in order to keep economic value and manage to extend this satisfaction throughout time? And finally, up to what limit is it necessary to economize and who should be the subject of economization?

Rosmini states that both the objectivist and subjectivist answers given by economists are incomplete. In his opinion, the utilitarian quest for a certain *quantum* of "utility" necessary for man does not have a univocal answer. In fact, how would it be possible to define this quantum? Economic utility understood as subjective satisfaction is not equal to the measurement of a certain amount of external stimuli on our physical organs. According to the Roveretan, quantitative and material forces always operate "inside" of what he calls the "fundamental feeling" which is

[3]"Of all the means a wise man can think of in order to obtain the effect he has set in his mind, he will clearly choose the simplest and easiest so that it gives him the desired effect with equal perfection. If the desired effect is what sets him to act and he desires nothing but that effect, he will not be interested in using other means but precisely that which is enough to attain the desired effect. He will choose, then, the minimum cause to produce it, the minimum quantity of action, the minimum means. This is what we call the 'law of minimum means'" (Rosmini 1977b, n. 433).

in its turn integrated to human being's spiritual "feeling" or subjectivity. Therefore, Rosmini explains, "the maximum excitement [sensuous pleasures] depends [in human beings] on the amount of external stimuli" which result not only from external material goods, but also from the "internal stimuli" of instinctive and physical nature which these material goods arouse in the subject and, mainly, from what Rosmini calls "the state of the soul, that is, from the action of the rational principle" (Rosmini 1988b, n. 2077). In fact, the dynamics of the satisfaction of "the appetite of (man's) individual powers or capacities" is involved in what Rosmini calls contentment or happiness, understood as "the whole appetite of human nature" (Rosmini 1994b, 73), and also in *human good or human being's true good*, "a good which is definitely good for human nature and in harmony with all its needs, so that human nature entirely approves and desires it" (Rosmini 1994b, 72).

Thus, given that contentment always depends on the intellectual inner judgment – which declares the human being content or unhappy, as we have seen – any economic action implies an intellectual valuation of material or sensitive means:

> Whether they use material or spiritual means to make themselves content, they [human beings] are fully satisfied only when they have made an interior judgment. We must conclude therefore, as we have said, that 'contentment is always intellective whatever we use, even something crass and material, to acquire it.' (Rosmini 1994b, 254)

In this sense, according to Rosmini, any economic satisfaction or "utility" is always enlightened by the personal faculties of reasoning and freedom, which include them in a wider framework constituted by "human desire or capacity." Eventually, this can be explained by the predominance of the personal principle that governs human beings and integrates the subjective faculties, without them losing their nature, to the personal faculties, which results in the economic action being a type of complex action both natural and personal.[4] This is how, according to Rosmini, economic action loses its sense if satisfied needs or economized goods are not incorporated into the dynamics of contentment:

> Clearly, every time an external good does not satisfy [non appagano,] it is not a good (. . .). (Rosmini 1994b, 322)

Definitively, according to Rosmini, one should only consider "external goods and the pleasures they provide after having reflected on *contentment*" (Rosmini 1923, 133).

[4] "[Consequently,] the different principles of actions united in one individual operate in two ways: of themselves, according to the laws of their own nature, as moved by the supreme principle. If they act themselves without the intervention of the supreme principle, their acts are simply natural. But if they are moved by the supreme principle, their acts are called *personal.* Hence, in the human being, acts are natural and personal" (Rosmini 1991, n. 842).

5.2.2 *How Economic Value Depends on Objective and Moral Good*

As a consequence, economic goods, which are primarily subjective and relative, turn into objective and absolute moral goods through the dynamics of contentment.[5] In effect, although in the economic valuation a certain set of goods are considered subjectively – that is, disregarding their intrinsic value to concentrate on the way they relate to the satisfaction of one or more subjects – they also take part in a eudaimonological valuation and thus in the capacity of recognition of objective and moral good. Therefore, a subjective state (material, sensitive satisfaction,) a eudaimonological judgment (inner intellectual judgment) and an objective moral valuation (perception of the intrinsic structure of the good in itself) combine into a sole economic action.[6] According to Rosmini, then, economic action always implies the subjection to a more or less stable objective structure of "real good(s) given to us by the nature of things as objects of our legitimate desires" (Rosmini 1994b, 265), and it is vital for it to "exclude every desire that cannot be fulfilled (. . .) and to limit its desires proportionately to objects it can attain" (Rosmini 1994b, 393) all this because of its intrinsic integration to contentment, and, through the latter, to virtue:

> Contentment of spirit is not therefore the task of human beings alone. They certainly contribute to it with acts of their understanding and will, which make them conscious of their well-being. They first contribute by determining their practical reason to direct their desires to real rather than imaginary good, and finally by their efforts to actually possess the real good. Nevertheless, they have to seek this real good from the nature of things as from a generous benefactor, and are obliged to accept them as they are from the hands of this provident mother. We must submit to the ontological laws which bind real good to the constitution of the human being, and which must be faithfully obeyed. (Rosmini 1994b, 264–265)

Rosmini thus anticipates neoclassical economists' subjective theories of value, yet his understanding of the concept of subjectivity is much more elaborated than theirs. Economic value is certainly neither a "thing" nor the result of a mere subjective satisfaction or of a formal rationality, but a subjective good capable of

---

[5]This is possible, Rosmini argues, because the nature of the human person consists in such a sharing of the sensitive dimension in the intellectual dimension, of the natural in the personal, which enables "corporal sense, necessarily enclosed as it is in its own proper particular and material affections" (Rosmini 1994b, 255) to open up to its involvement with the objective world.

[6]"To clarify the notion we must first say something about objective good, that is, every good in so far as it is perceived objectively or becomes an object of knowledge. As we have seen, the absolute notion of good consists in that which benefits the intrinsic order of being in every nature and to which all the forces of a given nature tend. The relative notion of good, on the other hand, consists in something desirable to another and as such the term and aim of the forces natural to this other nature, which move towards and tend to unite possessively with what is desirable. These notions provide us with knowledge of two kinds of good, the good of things in themselves and the good of things relative to other things. Both kinds of goods become *objects* of our intelligence, and thus *objective* (. . .) every good can be considered by us objectively" (Rosmini 1988a, n. 73–74).

being appreciated in the light of personal faculties which connect it to the objective order of reality. According to Rosmini, economic action implies a minimum recognition of the objective good, and therefore, a minimum of moral virtue. An economic process reduced to the purely subjective satisfaction of needs, and thus disconnected from the personal and ethical dimension, would destroy itself since "whenever good of any kind is incompatible with virtue, it ceases to be human good" (Rosmini 1994b, 75).[7]

In Rosmini's opinion, then, economic action is not a mere technical action of means coordination which seeks to attain a subjectively determined end but an action ruled by "practical reason," the mediator between "one's own utility" and "the force of truth and justice" (Rosmini 1993a, 84, n.147). That is how in economic actions such practical reason "acts as a kind of arbiter between the *utility* and the *probity* of actions, it judges what is better for us to do here and now, and is based on moral as well as eudaimonological reasons" (Rosmini 1988a, n. 187). This is the core of Rosmini's principal thesis on economic action which differentiates him from other economic thinkers.

5.3 Economic Action and Personalized Self-Interest

5.3.1 The Role of Individual Interest

Which is then the role of individual interest? One might wonder if this approach subordinates economic action to a disembodied and depersonalized moral objectivism. The truth is that it all depends on how the expression "individual interest" is interpreted. For sure, Rosmini argues that individual interest, understood as a purely subjective interest, can never be the ultimate motive of economic actions. If this were so, then utilitarians would be right when they claim that economic activity is reduced to a technique of means maximization to gain satisfaction or an end determined by the subject's pure arbitrariness. On the contrary, according to Rosmini, "if I make a practical judgment based on eudaimonological, non-moral motives, I sin, and certain affections and immoral actions follow" (Rosmini 1988a, n. 190). Therefore, the motive of economic action should always have a minimum involvement with the objective demands of human nature and cannot be based on subjective interest alone.

Nonetheless, if individual interest is understood as the search for one's own happiness or contentment, which, as we have seen, depends on objective moral valuations, it is certain, then, that Rosmini considers the pursuit of this interest to

[7]"Mankind would have never reached the flourishing state by which it possesses so many suitable means to lead a content and honest life if (...) it had never tempered the bad habits and the corruption of its passions by igniting the light of truth in the spirits" (Rosmini 1887, 98). "Nothing is truly useful except for truth" (Rosmini 1977b, 124).

be at the core of economic action. Actually, in his opinion, if the instinct or the subjective interest impelling us to satisfy our own or others' needs is imbued with the pursuit of true happiness brought by moral recognition, it will also be penetrated, in some way, by the force of human nature with its objective demands, which urge us to make this interest "reasonable:"

> The reasonableness of the instinct means the need reason has to acknowledge human nature, which we mentally conceive, for what it is, and as much as, meriting love – if we respect human nature, we desire for it all possible good. (Rosmini 1988a, n. 222)

Moreover, according to Rosmini, in ordinary circumstances, an economic valuation integrated into an objective ethical valuation would imply the satisfaction of, firstly, our own needs or the ones of our closest, and only afterwards, of the needs of those who are not directly related to our "interests." In fact, the Roveretan maintains that "the good of human nature is indicated by natural human instincts and inclinations, directed by the [natural] law towards certain persons rather than others, according to the persons' circumstances" (Rosmini 1988a, n. 226).

In addition, understood in this way, the subject's own interest is a powerful and necessary means for economic action since it points us our needs as well as others', with the accuracy only experience – and not statistics – can provide:

I cannot know from others, but know only from myself, by the feeling I have of "myself." All the different sensations (pleasure, pain, needs, instincts, etc.) that modify myself are experiences indicating to me what takes place in my fellow human beings (Rosmini 1988a, n.218).

In short, even though Rosmini finds economic actions subordinated to the recognition of objective good and its resulting moral contentment, such integration does not mean either a disregard for individual interests or the impossibility that the former and the latter, in normal circumstances, could be harmonically balanced.[8]

5.3.2 *Incentives, Capacities and Contentment*

On the other hand, Rosmini argues that material economic incentives that act upon individual interests are also perfectly legitimate "when they present themselves as an aid to the conscience of one's own duties, that is, as an additional stimuli to the main one which is *moral obligation*" (Rosmini 1976, 131, footnote). Certainly, though he affirms the indestructibility and independence of freedom, even with all the

---

[8]Indeed, the Roveretan believes that the Gospel's commandment "you shall love your neighbor as yourself" implies the idea of giving priority to self-love as the natural basis of our love for our fellow men, who we shall love just for being "subjectively" the closest to us. In this sense, according to Rosmini, ethical valuation does not oppose individual interest but rather elevates and objectivizes it. See also, Rosmini (1988a, n. 226–227).

conditioning factors against,[9] the Roveretan never stops highlighting the importance of incentives or external stimuli that condition instinctive and spontaneous forces and, through the latter, the practical force of will. Now, because "we want a *state*; we are inclined to *stabilize* everything round us" (Rosmini 1994b, 261, footnote 254). Thus, specific economic incentives do not act, according to the Roveretan, in isolation; on the contrary, they are integrated to the more or less permanent successive 'states' of contentment – or discontentment – in which we find ourselves, and only through them can they exert influence over our actions. As a result, an incentive "can contribute to contentment only if it finds the human spirit well disposed and conditioned to receive its good effect of contentment. But it can do nothing about contentment if the spirit of the person who possesses the good lacks the necessary interior dispositions for it" (Rosmini 1994b, 304).

That is the reason why Rosmini believes that utilitarianism is committing a fatal error in conceiving economic incentives as a mere addition of consecutive stimuli directed to generating specific states of dissatisfaction and satisfaction submitted to a purely quantitative dynamics in which current satisfaction depends solely on the addition of immediately previous satisfactions gained by the subject (decreasing marginal utility,) or of what he expects to attain in the future (expectations.) "We see in this system – Rosmini argues – how contentment of spirit counts for nothing; only transitory sensations are considered valuable" (Rosmini 1994b, 317). Despite the fact that this quantitative dynamics exists, what should be taken into account are the more or less permanent states that the use of incentives can produce in our capacities and desires in a period of time:

> We must therefore pay careful attention to the relationship between our actions and the improvement of our habits and faculties. Philosophers who neglected this, who restricted their considerations to ephemeral acts of pleasure without linking this to the effect they leave in our habits and faculties, who above all posited human happiness in acts alone, were led into innumerable disastrous errors about virtue and the eudaimonological good of humankind. (Rosmini 1994b, 261)

In fact, according to Rosmini, economic incentives must, above all, aim at ensuring that the progress of the satisfaction of subjective needs is not made at the expense of the person's moral contentment:

> It cannot be denied that I have benefited an individual, if I succeed in leading him from one of these two states to the other. While keeping his spirit fully contented, I have provided with him eighty degrees of greater enjoyment which he previously lacked. This passage from contentment containing fewer degrees of good to contentment containing more degrees of good is a kind of natural, legitimate movement for mankind and for society. (Rosmini 1994b, 395)

On the contrary, economic incentives lose their meaning when they induce the passage from a state of little wealth, yet of contentment, to a state of greater wealth, but of unhappiness:

---

[9]This thesis will gain importance, as we shall see, when studying the kind of influence that social and economic forces may exert on the individual.

> Let us suppose now that we have an individual who has a capacity for twenty and possesses twenty. I stimulate his capacity and succeed in enlarging it to one hundred. Made restless and active by his new desire, he succeeds in obtaining for himself sixty, let us say, of the desired objects. Forty degrees of his capacity are still unsatisfied; he now experiences forty degrees of unrest although his enjoyment, which has now reached sixty, has increased threefold. But is the increase in enjoyment of any help, granted the loss of contentment of spirit and consequent unhappiness? His enjoyment, increased by two-thirds, has not bettered but worsened his state. My mistaken benefice has rendered him very bad service. (Rosmini 1994b, 395)

5.3.3 The Psychological and Moral Problem of the Economy

Rosmini maintains that the central problem of the economy is not just technical or political. It is a problem of internal eudaimonological and ethical balance of the economic agents; a problem that has always been overlooked by utilitarianism, which, based on a naturalist and subjectivist anthropology, considers production, accumulation, satisfaction of needs and exchange of goods and services as a uniform and predictable dynamics, generally with positive results or, at least, adjustable to a correct disposition of external incentives. On the contrary, the Roveretan tries to show how the desires for consumption and accumulation, given his freedom, go hand in hand with plenty of problems. There are many unreasonable economic behaviors which, according to Rosmini, must not be perceived as the normal result of human nature, but rather as manifestations of a moral problem whose origin is related to the search for security (Rosmini 1994b, 371), avidity for domination (Rosmini 1994b, 371) or an abstract instrumentalism (Rosmini 1994b, 371–372).[10] Now, in Rosmini's view, the ultimate cause of these phenomena lies on the tendency within individuals to deceive themselves by arbitrarily creating a chimera about the characteristics of the goods desired:

> We cannot exclude from the activity of the human spirit – argues Rosmini – a notable action on the objects of its desires, on the increase and reduction of the objects, and, on their destruction and creation. Undoubtedly, our spirit, making special use of the help offered by the imagination, creates everyday countless beings which do not exist in nature, and counterfeits those that do exist. We cannot deny that these chimerical, false creations become not only the object of affections and desires but often do so to a greater extent than if they were real and true. (Rosmini 1994b, 473–474)

At the same time, Rosmini argues that this false evaluation is the result of trying to find an absolute and infinite good such as happiness within finite and limited goods:

> The enumeration of longings through which we hope to uncover the infinite in the finite, that is, make possible what is intrinsically impossible (. . . .) (is the) result of conceiving

[10] However, though this is originally a moral problem, given that freedom is the one to make the wrong choice, it turns into a psychological-eudaimonological problem because, once self-deceit has started to operate, all the forces of passion begin to act.

these things ideally, that is, without limits (. . .) (Rosmini 1994b, 607–608) In persuading ourselves internally that we must find the happiness we seek in this given good, we put in this real object something that it does not contain. (Rosmini 1994b, 366)

Thus, this non-recognition of the true objective structure of goods is not, however, the result of an instinct, a need or natural physical desire[11] but of a willed and personal value judgment:

In contradiction to animals, only human beings change bodily pleasure into a spiritual object, that is, into a means for containing the general capacity of their spirit. (. . .) 374 This explains the unrestrained libido proper to human beings alone, and unknown in animals. Human desire for ever-increasing pleasure is never satisfied; people often prefer to die rather than renounce it. This also explains the infinite longings and perpetual deceits of physical love, as well as all the arts of seduction. (. . .) It is the rational, personal will which, although it requires satisfaction, cannot be satisfied with anything limited and seeks within bodily enjoyment something infinite which cannot be present, and which therefore we never find there. (Rosmini 1994b, 368)

This is how Rosmini describes, for instance, the tendency to accumulate wealth as the fruit of an intellective self-deceit[12] that identifies it with status and power,[13] and which opens a series of desires ending in an unlimited and insatiable search.[14] Hence, it all results in a dynamics of a "false infinity" and frustration ingrained in the nucleus of human capacities and in the related economic actions.

Clearly, Rosmini admits that behavior of this kind could be grounded on an order of preferences of a very strong internal stability and coherence. Yet, this will never

[11]"The passion for sumptuousness is itself as unlimited as other capacities; an individual can eat at a banquet fit for a king but still not be content precisely because *in sumptuousness he seeks something other than sumptuousness*" (Rosmini 1994b, 375).

[12]"Cupidity for artificial wealth is more noticeably intellectual than the result of sensual gratification" (Rosmini 1994b, 370–371).

[13]"Another kind of experience impels individuals to find their happiness in exterior good by means of the idea they form of wealth. (. . .) The practical reason can therefore deceive itself in two ways relative to the possession of external things. First, it begins by trusting in its power to find *status* in the possession of wealth considered as a kind of extension of the person's own existence. This is an abstract idea, posited in a material, finite object. Then it hopes by means of wealth to obtain any pleasure it wants. Wealth, it seems, can secure for individuals the enjoyment of all their desires, and make them enjoy all pleasures simultaneously through the hope and assurance it gives them" (Rosmini 1994b, 369).

[14]"This explains the origins of disgusting, twofold avarice – avarice whose end is money, as though money made human beings great, and avarice which sees in money the means for obtaining comfort and enjoyment (. . .) However, because it is really impossible for people to find in wealth either *status* or complete *dominion* over enjoyment, it is also impossible for them to find contentment and happiness. Human capacity, aggravated by this, grows; the heart attributes lack of fulfillment solely to the small quantity of wealth possessed and acquired. People press on to riches with greater cupidity which, as it increases, feeds like a starving wolf on all their desires. It is no surprise therefore to see in misers an increase in their longing and need for wealth as their riches grow. (. . .) Moreover, this capacity does not increase by arithmetical progression; like every capacity, it increases by geometrical progression, because what people gain in this way, unceasingly intensifies their previous capacity" (Rosmini 1994b, 369–370).

lead to the utilitarian conclusion that these are normal ways of behaving which can serve as a parameter to build a whole economic order. Therefore, according to Rosmini, the "restless search for gain and self-interest," which can be seen in economy, is not a "natural" manifestation of human behavior to be encouraged – as utilitarian economists claim – but "a clear symptom of their unhappiness" (Rosmini 1994b, 370), potentially destructive for persons and the economy as well.

5.3.4 Person: Beginning and End of the Economy

To conclude, Rosmini defines economic action as the outcome of a *circular process that begins and ends in the human person.* In fact, it is in the personal spirit where valuation and economic action originate because the presence or absence of internal happiness or contentment is the driving force behind the different types of valuation, disposition or use of goods. From that on, these goods acquire an objective economic value which extends beyond the person with certain stability. Finally, the circle closes up when the goods, endowed with economic value, reenter the sphere of the person who makes a new valuation and reinitiates the process:

> The spirit (. . .) and things modify one another respectively (. . .) The love or passion that the spirit has towards things is that which at every instant determines and fixes the value of things. [On the other hand] the abundance of things present to the spirit has a persuasive force which modifies the spirit and stimulates its movement towards them. (Rosmini 1994b, 414)[15]

In this sense, it is in the concrete and living person rather than in any other generic entity (market, State, enterprise, etc.) where the economic action attains its sense, limits and its ultimate end.[16] If there is no personal principle, it is impossible to reach an ultimate norm of the economic actions and, therefore, they become irrational and senseless. Certainly, according to Rosmini, economic rationality implies an instrumental dimension – "faculty of abstraction" or "faculty of means" as he calls them – of great importance as it enables the "accidental perfection" of human beings (Rosmini 1994b, 402). Nevertheless, said "accidental perfection (. . .) has no value unless it harmonizes with substantial perfection" which is ruled by what the Roveretan defines as "faculty of thought" or "faculty of ends." In fact, "any attempt to obtain accidental perfection will result only in *apparent*, artificial *refinement*"

---

[15]"Arts, sciences and projects of every kind are produced by human activity, which has its hidden origin and, as it were, its home in our spirit. Moreover, this activity returns with its effects to the spirit from which it sprang. In the last analysis, the products of human activity have no other natural tendency than to satisfy human desire" (Rosmini 1994a, 7).

[16]From a metaphysical point of view, only the person is a reality in a proper sense; the rest of the living and material things are somehow incomplete realities whose end is to serve the person. Thus, addressing Kant in this point, Rosmini centers the sense of all moral action in the respect for the person as an end in itself: "The principle of moral virtue, simple stated, is: 'Respect person as end; do not use person as a means for yourself'" (Rosmini 1994b, 12).

(Rosmini 1994b, 402) as individuals "run a risk of neglecting substance through fallacious love of accidents" (Rosmini 1994a, 61):

> All these things are useful if they have a solid end previously established for human beings by the faculty of thought. It is always true that "the applications of the faculty of abstraction bring true utility when, and only when, they are subordinate to the ends established by the faculty of thought" (Rosmini 1994b, 404)

Then, an economy based on wealth, utility or interest, abstractly speaking, without a responsible subject who undertakes them is always a false economy. Due to this, Rosmini places at the core of the economy the concept of *ownership,* which, long before being applied to the jural ownership of external goods, he discovers in the property or self-possession that the person has over his or her own nature. The original concept of ownership is founded on an "entirely *personal* principle involving *consciousness* and therefore presupposing an intelligent principle capable of reflecting upon itself and seeing itself objectively" (Rosmini 1993a, 178, n. 338). Upon this capacity, human beings become able to value and possess economic goods as well:

> The human person incorporates to himself some things by means of his nature and others through an act proper to him, a physical-moral act. (Rosmini 1993a, 178, n. 338)

In fact, the relationship between the person and economic goods does not come down to a "simple appropriation or physical juncture such as that between beasts and their own body, their food, their nests, etc.," (Rosmini 1993b, n. 394) that derives solely from "the nature of the subject which seeks in the juncture the subject's own good" (Rosmini 1993b, n. 399) but it also stems from a "moral juncture" which "comes from the nature of the object" (Rosmini 1993b, n. 400). In this sense, when the link between the person and economic actions is not recognized, "we use a thing *unlimitedly*, without any regard for the thing itself." On the contrary, when acknowledging the relationship with the person, we feel that "we have to impose some limit" (Rosmini 1994b, 19).[17] This does not mean that the relationship with the person sets an arbitrary limit to the process of economic efficiency taking it possibilities. In fact, it is the person who shapes and gives meaning to the whole economization process. Therefore, economic efficiency understood in a personalist sense consists, above all, in the economic means being at the service of the greatest possible objective good of human nature involved in each particular circumstance:

[17]Rosmini has this view because only free and virtuous moral act transforms purely material needs and goods into true economic means and needs as it makes them suitable to perfect human personship: "The will is the power with which the intelligent subject works to become author of his own actions. Without the subject's will, a long series of phenomena, of which he is not the cause, can take place in him, as though he were a spectator of what occurs; not everything that happens in us is done by us. If our will is not engaged in what is happening, other powers and forces work in us but without our active intervention. Only the will provides actions that we characterize as our own, and use to fulfill our human personality" (Rosmini 1988a, n. 90).

> Such efficacy [of means] consists solely in the good influence by which political means satisfy the desires of human nature. As a result this philosophy teaches us to know when, which and how such means are efficacious or inefficacious. (Rosmini 1994a, 8)

In a word, according to Rosmini, the highest value of an economy does not lie in the natural resources or in the "utilities" and technical capacities, but in personal capacities, which are the result of freedom and moral virtues. Indeed, because "the greatest activity of nature, and the sole activity of person, consists in the use of freedom," "the natural, appropriate use of freedom [moral virtue] is, therefore, the greatest subjective human good and the sole good of the human person" (Rosmini 1994b, 275). Therefore, according to Rosmini, virtue is "the most important utility of all."[18]

[18]"La virtùè la suprema delle utilità" (Rosmini 1978a, 25). However, in Rosmini's opinion, the person's virtuous freedom is attained only if one condition is met: that it is desired in itself and not as a pure means for the economy: "It won't be difficult to show, as others have already done, that virtue is the mother of wealth and vice the mother of poverty. But we prefer, and it is more adequate in relation to the value of virtue, to demand from men that they consider virtue itself as an addition of all pleasures and that they prefer nothing over it, that they put it before everything, even if it were found in poverty." *OIP*, p. 157. This seems to be other of Rosmini's warnings for "the economic writers, always more concentrated on immediate utility than on the indirect one" (Rosmini 1923, 103).

Chapter 6
Rethinking Labor, Wealth and Consumption

6.1 Labor

6.1.1 Beyond Adam Smith

In order to analyze the different economic activities and labor in particular, Rosmini will draw many elements from the objective theory of value, either through reading directly the work of the Anglo-Saxon classical economists or through the indirect influence of the Italian, French and Swiss economists. In *Politica Prima,* Rosmini first mentions his agreement with Adam Smith's criticism on accumulation of wealth by predatory methods, as in the case of the Roman conquest, feudal Lords, Spanish conquerors and mercantilism,[1] which make it potentially destructive for people's moral and economic life.[2] Rosmini also appreciates the Smithian *labor theory of value,*[3] and joins the economist's praising of frugality,[4] saving (Rosmini

[1]The Roveretan criticizes mercantilism's conception of economic value understood as an external object, radically material, disconnected from human labor, reduced to a loot obtained as a residual by-product of the exercise of power.

[2]"Il che però più impetuosamente e anche disordinadamente avviene in quella gente che si fa ricca col vigile e faticoso amore dell' acquistare, ma a cui toccò una ricchezza non principalmente desiderata siccome una schiava venuta dietro alla potenza e alla fortuna. Non cercavano i romani l' oro: volevano solo la signoria dei signori dell' oro: non cercavano gli Spagnuoli le miniere americane, ma da prima la novità di un altro mondo. Però non avendo costoro, come fu già molte fiaro osservato, il cuore apposto alla ricchezza, e questa essendo tuttavia in sequela della potenza venuta lor nelle mani incontanente grandissima non seppero nè pregiarla, nè usarla, nè conservarla: nè altro pensiero s' ebbero che di profonderla e gittarla" (Rosmini 1923, 176–177).

[3]"Dopo Adam Smith nessuno più dubita, che il lavoro sia il fonte sommo della ricchezza e che abbia il lavoro ai capitali per usare un modo filosofico, ma ottimamente espressivo, come la forma alla materia" (Rosmini 1923, 92). See also Adam Smith (1976).

[4]"Il buon senso di Smith... e di tanti altri scrittori delle cose economiche; i quali senza essere nemici dei piaceri, distinguono però accuratamente fra essi e la ricchezza, e predicano i risparmi, e la moderazione in tutte le cose di lusso e di diletto, perché questi diletti non li considerano come

C. Hoevel, *The Economy of Recognition: Person, Market and Society in Antonio Rosmini*, Ethical Economy 42, DOI 10.1007/978-94-007-6058-5_6,

1978a, 26, footnote 17),[5] productivity (Rosmini 1978a, 21) and a moderate lifestyle as the bases for a labor culture.[6]

Nevertheless, Rosmini borrows from another classical economist like Say in order to depart from some of Smith's theses,[7] and goes even deeper when he approaches the Italian-French conception of labor, centered in subjectivity. Rosmini borrows from economists like Genovesi, Sismondi and Droz a limited valuation of Smith and the need to integrate his theory of labor as a source of wealth creation into a wider anthropological theory (Rosmini 1994a, appendix 2, 121)[8] which links it to the idea of happiness.[9] Yet, it was mainly Gioia and Romagnosi who warned Rosmini about the mechanical nature of Adam Smith's theory of labor[10] and helped him to confirm and make explicit the idea of an ethical-anthropological organicity in which, in their opinion, the labor theory of value must be framed to avoid its "isolation" from the rest of social philosophy.[11]

---

ricchezza, ma bensì come una distruzione della ricchezza . . . " (Rosmini 1978a, 37). See also Adam Smith (1976, 1, p. 360/pp. 362–371; 2, pp. 127–128, pp. 401–402/pp. 442–443).

[5]See Adam Smith (1976, I, 351) Chap. III, "Of the Accumulation of Capital, or of Productive and Unproductive Labour."

[6]"Quelli all' opposto che acquiserano tali cose colle industrie e coi commerci, poniamo gli inglesi, hanno pur colle lunghe cure e sollecitudini nutricato in sè stessi l' effetto dell' oro e però nol gittano sì agevolmente. Dall' abondanza dunque della pecunia che sovverchia le necessità e dalla disposizione dei ricchi popoli riguardo alle industrie ed ai calcoli dei guadagni, si fa ragione a quello che dispone la nazione di porre nei suoi piaceri." (Rosmini 1923, 176–177).

[7]In fact, in line with Say's thought, Rosmini criticises the way in which Adam Smith divides productive and improductive labor and consumption. "(. . .) conviene risalire alla storia della celebre distinzione di cui parliamo fra'consumi produttori e improduttori. Lo Smith, che la rese celebre, certo non giunse a tirar fra essi la linea di separazione esattamente, giacché pose fra le classi consumatrici e improduttrici di quelle a cui non si può negare la facoltà di produrre. Il Say rettificò, in gran parte almeno, l'inesattezza dello Smith" (Rosmini 1978a, 29).

[8]Romagnosi takes a more complex view than his predecessors and feels the need to accept and take account of all elements (. . .)" Rosmini shares Genovesi's idea that the economy seeks the satisfaction of human needs, which he distinguishes from pure animal needs. The former certainly rest on animal needs, but they are modified by the "needs of opinion" – those of a greater well-being and, mainly, the need for approval – coming from society, which modifies instinct through reason and allows reaching the true human level (Genovesi 1768, T. VIII, 271 and ff).

[9]According to Sismondi, "wealth increase is not the end of political economy but the means it employs to procure individuals' happiness" (Sismondi 1974, 9). "Lo scopo del goberno non è, astrattamente parlando, l'accumulazione delle ricchezze nello stato" (Sismondi 1974, 23). See also, Rosmini 1994b, Book II, Chap. VIII, . In Sismondi's opinion, this happens because "man is a mixed being who possesses both moral and physical needs" (Sismondi 1974, 22). According to Droz, quoted several times by Rosmini, "quando si studia la scienza delle ricchezze, è essenziale di non peredere mai di vista le sue relazione col miglioramento e colla felicità degli uomini. Si santura questa scienza, se non si considerano le ricchezze che in se medesime e per se medesime" (Droz 1854, Vol. VI, II, 1077). Rosmini will show practically identical ideas throughout his work.

[10]"Lo studioso pertanto non abbisogna di molto affaticarsi su le opere straniere, tranne quella di Adam Smith, per la parte mecanica dell' economia" (Romagnosi 1845, 79).

[11]"(. . .) è riconusciuto che se fino dal secolo decimosesto fu in Italia iniziato lo studio della politica economia, viene pur anche confessato che li argomenti di essa non vengono trattati in Italia con le

6.1.2 Incentives and Intrinsic Motivation

Although the Roveretan supports the Smithian thesis on labor division, he does not agree with the idea that productivity is only the result of purely material incentives, as classical economists were thought to have supported, especially in Italy. Rosmini differs from the utilitarian conceptions in which the incentive of *pain*, provoked by the fear of material privation proper to poverty, was the key to productivity. Despite conceding that clearly man will not put his efforts on work if he is in a position of abundance and satisfaction – because all efforts "suppose an inferior state which human nature desires to move from into a better one" (Rosmini 1977b, n. 584), – he considers that pain is not always nor necessarily a good labor incentive:

> Man does not always act according to his beliefs. The fact that a person is unwilling to tolerate poverty does not mean that he will work harder to alleviate it (Rosmini 1977a, 103). If one wishes to persuade a man to work, it is not enough to increase the weight of privations that idleness subjects him to: it is highly probably that one will make him more unhappy and less active. (Rosmini 1977a, 103, footnote 1)

Neither will material benefits guarantee greater productivity at work:

> The fact that fashion makes man more eager to get the fruits of his labor does not mean he will become industrious (Rosmini 1977a, 103) (. . .). To induce man to love external things that express and fuel, at the same time, vanity and banality does not constitute a means that will necessarily increase honest labor and the good industries which serve society, as it may seem at first sight. All altered and false feeling in man is an error or a vice; error and vice are only useful for a short time and in appearance. (Rosmini 1977a, 104)

This way, Rosmini also deploys the conception that reduces the entrepreneur's labor capacity, innovation and enterprise to sole skills, action capacity and search for self-interest in business, in disregard of any moral virtue. According to the Roveretan, it is clear that the principle of subjective utility alone cannot form the basis for the entrepreneur's action; Rosmini believes that the truly competitive entrepreneur is the one who is mainly endowed with a minimum of moral values that make him trustworthy:

> Is being active enough for a man to obtain these advantages? Can they be obtained by an active man deprived of morality? What will happen if someone found out that this man does not recognize any moral obligation beyond pleasure and the calculation of self-interest? (Rosmini 1976, 131, footnote 2)

---

vedute sbranate, specialmente odierne, di certi paesi, ma bensì come problemi di sociale filosofía. 'Il metodo seguito dagl'Italiani è affatto differente dall'inglese, perchè essi trattano la scienza sotto tutti i loro rapporti. Essi cercano non solo la ricchezza, ma anche il benessere del maggior numero possibile. Questo secondo oggetto è per loro tanto importante quanto il primo'" (Romagnosi 1845, vol. VI, 78–79). This seems to coincide with Rosmini's criticism of the "abstractism" of certain economists and their attempt to reach an economic wisdom. See especially Rosmini 1994a, "Preface to the Political Works," 1.

Moreover, he also rejects the socialist proposal of increasing productivity by turning labor into an activity exclusively imposed by the State:

> We believe that governments cannot force any man to work: they can just persuade him. (Rosmini 1923, 91)

Rosmini argues that the entire structure of labor and business collapses if the motivation to work falls outside the scope of moral contentment and ethics, and if it is based on pure subjective utility as its only principle. In that case it will be impossible to set a limit to the professionals' excessive search for profit (Rosmini 1976, 132, footnote 2) or to convince the poor that work is the key to progress.[12] Though material benefits, regarded as an ordered "love of comforts, of well-being, of the natural means of life, can be reasonable and honest," and "as such they can also be a labor incentive because they are attached to intelligence and virtue" (Rosmini 1977a, 107, footnote 1), anyway, the core of work is interior freedom enlightened by truth. Only when personal freedom comes into play, will the other incentives have a productive effect: being not only a utilitarian but also a moral activity, "labor cannot be increased – Rosmini maintains – unless it is through the development of morality:" (Rosmini 1977a, 106–107)

> It is necessary to enlighten man's intelligence, showing him that the cause of all his evils is no other than his laziness; otherwise, he will blame everybody except himself and will lose all capacity to reflect. It is necessary to employ moral means which are suitable for fighting his inertia and the bad habits turned into a terrible need to do nothing. Then, he must be lead through the path of labor, shinning a light for him to find a remedy to all his problems – which he does not have a practical and efficient idea about. In a word, he will be granted the possibility of improving his condition when he is able to see the means that guarantee a less miserable position; he will feel an urgent moral duty to make use of them and will start to think about a solution; he will try to move forward defying the immobility that kept him in pain, which he lacked the virtue to resign. In a word, the more a man is helped to increase his morality, the more conscious he will be about his own activity and, because of this conscience, he will become an industrious person. (Rosmini 1977a, 103, n. 1)

6.1.3 Intellectual Capacities and Ethical Virtues

The moral and eudaimonological dimensions have a key role in the encouragement of a human and economically productive labor. Rosmini claims that capital is only raised if there exists in people some degree of "love of wealth and social influence" (Rosmini 1994b, 342), "desire for new needs" (Rosmini 1887, 205), "the dominion over himself to defer the satisfaction of his desires" (Rosmini 1994b, 327), the use of "intelligence" (Rosmini 1887, 205), the "increase of reflections" (Rosmini 1887, 205), a deeper "attention capacity" (Rosmini 1887, 205) and capacity of "foresight" (Rosmini 1994b, 327), amongst others. Economic growth is, thus, the result of "a full knowledge of the use of wealth" and of a "hierarchical development of ideas"

[12] "Né pure i poveri vorrano lasciare per questo il *merito* dell'arricchire usando i mezzi più comodi al fine loro," (Rosmini 1976, 132, footnote 3).

(Rosmini 1887, 206) rather than the result of an accumulation driven by external material incentives or by a mere abundance of natural resources: "when civil society is culturally developed, wealth prevails" (Rosmini 1887, 206, n. 1). In a word, the progress in capital accumulation implies "the same degree of progress in man's spirit" (Rosmini 1887, 204).

But above all capacities there stand the moral capacities as the ultimate source which enriches and organizes, according to our author, the other motivations, leading to a truly productive accumulation. As an example, Rosmini mentions the case of the head of a family, who saves and accumulates not to satisfy his individual, temporary selfishness, but to meet the needs of his family and the community in which he lives, in view of present and future generations: "The most sacred moral stimulus of one's own duty, which foresees and provides for the future necessities of domestic and civil society [is] in a way more helpful than any other duty" (Rosmini 1994b, 342).

6.2 Wealth

6.2.1 Accumulation and Saving

Rosmini closely relates accumulation and saving to the concept of labor as the proximate means for wealth creation; yet, the Roveretan does not support any type of accumulation but the one which corresponds to the ultimate ends of economy. In fact, on the one hand, Rosmini supports a type of accumulation oriented towards productive investment, which is attainable, in his opinion, following the advice of "economic authors [who] recommend the accumulation of capital which can serve the production of more capital (...) not for our use but for commerce, in which they become the source of new wealth" (Rosmini 1978a, 24). Any other kind of accumulation is a "meaningless, unproductive and wasted capital" (Rosmini 1978a, 24).[13]

In this sense, on the other hand, Rosmini spots the dangers of money accumulation following the teachings of Aristotle:

> Aristotle's observation that avarice properly speaking entered the world with the invention of money, seems to be both true and philosophical. "Wealth – he continues – dependant on such a method of gain is infinite. Every art seeks its end without limits; only the means employed are limited as a result of the end. Thus, this art of making money has no term; wealth like this, and such a method of achieving it, is itself the end" (Politics, Book I, 1257 b 23–30). (Rosmini 1994b, 370, footnote 376)

[13]This positive accumulation starts in the family itself under the shape of simple saving: "Saving is praise-worthy for the family as well; it makes it stronger and more capable; and it should be praised in middle-class families to whom any small unforeseen event can result in a serious misfortune such as an unexpected accident, the extension of the family, or any other reason that implies a larger or extra spending" (Rosmini 1923, 154).

The unlimited search for the accumulation of money leads to destruction since "avaricious persons can never be induced to throw away money on pleasure because they are continually afraid of losing it all" (Rosmini 1994b, 369). Given this, "even wealth could be sacrificed in an infrequent contradiction by which the power of attaining wealth is more sought after than wealth itself" (Rosmini 1994b, 372). Hence, the accumulation within the framework of a chrematistic mentality of this kind "finally produces blind men and women who sell their all – their tranquility, health, chastity, blood, life itself – for the sake of money." Given the ethico-psychological problem of human being, Rosmini believes that "we should not marvel that the human heart behaves like this" (Rosmini 1994b, 370), but what does not make sense to him is the encouragement of this unlimited accumulation outside all ethical framework as if it were a good for the economy:

> There is greater reason to wonder at the attitude of certain economists crazy enough to maintain that the wealth of nations may be increased by the sale of virtue, and that vice should be encouraged if the State would otherwise lose some of its wealth. (Rosmini 1994b, 370)

The saving and accumulation spirit is only meaningful in so far as, because of a foolish avarice, it closes its relationship with consumption and, through the latter, to the development of spiritual and moral capacities:

> Generosity is preferable to mean saving, either in benefice of others or in benefice of oneself, since the price of the things we get through spending is higher than the degree of power we obtain through saving. Then, all spending is praiseworthy and deserves to be encouraged as long as it increases the person's merit, the soul's virtue or mind's wisdom. (Rosmini 1923, 155)[14]

Hence, the mistake modern economists have repeatedly made is to take the economy for a constant adjustment of spending and consumption. In this sense, Rosmini criticizes Adam Smith classifying him within the group of those he calls *politici avari*: (Rosmini 1933, 19)

> It should not be forgotten the significant damage that an excessively economic spirit may cause to the enterprises directed to great goals. The economy always has a short-term view and does not understand the meaning of greatness. That is why greatness spirit and economic spirit are often opposites and exclude each other. (Rosmini 1923, 56–57)

In Rosmini's opinion, then, "the economy does not only consist in spending a little but in doing it wisely" (Rosmini 1923, 59).

6.2.2 *Wealth Creation and Consumption*

Although Rosmini conceives consumption as an essential stage in the economic cycle, he also criticizes the opposite tendency of the Italian and French utilitarians,

---

[14]"Man has many higher goods: apart from his body, he possesses a spirit that aspires to happiness and virtue, two ends to which everything, even wealth, must be subjected" (Rosmini 1978a, 22).

who are more inclined to consider any type of consumption economically useful. In fact, many utilitarians think that "wealth is not the set of things capable of producing pleasant sensations; it is sensations themselves that constitute wealth. This means that whoever enjoys the most, whoever experiences more pleasant sensations will be the richest (. . .) For instance, according to Gioia, the dissolute man who multiplies his pleasures to the extreme, the prodigal one who spends all to enjoy pleasant sensations, will be the rich man" (Rosmini 1978a, 23).[15] On the contrary, backed up by the classical economists, Rosmini maintains that "other economists affirm that removing the wealth from pleasures in order to devote it to profit, one becomes richer, and that this is the way to get rich, since wealth does not imply the abundance of pleasant sensations but the abundance of objects capable of producing those pleasant sensations and of satisfying needs" (Rosmini 1978a, 24).

Indeed, Rosmini develops a sort of basic grammar of consumption, in which he states the idea that not any use of an object, no matter the subjective utility it may provide, implies the creation of economic value or wealth increase (Rosmini 1978a, 19). In his opinion, "there is undoubtedly a way of consuming wealth that is disadvantageous for its reproduction; as it is also clear that there are other ways of consuming that bring about a reproduction of wealth . . . " (Rosmini 1978a, 21). Rosmini reaffirms the distinction made by classical economists between productive and unproductive consumption, yet he highlights that the boundaries between them have been badly drawn, especially by Adam Smith.[16] However, some economists claim that such distinction is not so, owing to the fact that the apparently unproductive use of wealth produces economic utility – understood as the subjective utility of the satisfied need or of the pleasure gained – ; in Rosmini's view, they confuse economy with eudaimonology or the science of happiness:

> This discourse does not pertain to economic science but it would be appropriate for a book about the art of enjoyment or happiness and even for a treaty on morality. (Rosmini 1978a, 21)

In effect, this arbitrary identification of all consumption with economic utility implicitly derives in the reduction of the latter to subjective pleasure, which, in his opinion, leads the economy to destruction:

> Reducing everything, even the notion of wealth itself, to pleasures, and without anything to regulate and direct these pleasures beyond themselves, political economy is destroyed, left to hang on its absolute empire, where there is no rule above itself and its pure caprice. (Rosmini 1976, 29)

[15] Rosmini argues that this confusion of concepts – present in the first definition of wealth given by Gioia is self – evident in his second definition: "A nation's wealth – affirms Gioia in another passage quoted by Rosmini – consists in the addition of pleasant sensations the people experience."

[16] "Even though the boundaries between them have been badly drawn, it is out of question that the distinction usually made by economic writers between productive and unproductive consumptions has its foundation in nature" (Rosmini 1978a, 21).

6.2.3 Economic Consequences of Consumerism

Rosmini shows, with bitter irony, how Gioia and the utilitarians' intention to achieve the creation of wealth through an economy motivated by an unceasingly and unlimited promotion of consumption ends up having exactly the opposite effect:

> All pleasure sought in itself is destroyed (. . .) Pleasure taken as the only supreme law can never bring happiness to human beings (. . .) When we desire everything, we lose everything: the existence of pleasure in itself becomes absurd for men if it is not associated with virtue (. . .) If you wish to give human beings a maximum utility and to show them the way to get maximum pleasure, you must hide or, better yet, you must dismantle your system [utilitarianism]. Do not attempt to convince men that pleasure is the only motivation behind their actions and the only principle of morality (. . .) The philosophy of pleasure and utility (. . .) is precisely the one that makes utility and pleasure impossible. (Rosmini 1976, 116)

In effect, according to Rosmini, to parallel all satisfaction of a need or the gain of pleasure to the creation of economic value supposes the confusion between the end, that is, the satisfaction, and the means, that is, the capacity to gain that satisfaction. Where the absolutization of consumption prevails, subjectivity reigns and, therefore, all the means to attain satisfaction itself are eliminated. These means, that is, productive labor, effort, a certain degree of minimum privation and mainly ethical virtue which provides a framework of objectivity to all the process, become useless in a consumerist context where only immediate satisfaction is compulsively sought:

> [Productivity incentives] turn out to be ridiculous and are ruled out in a system in which duty does not exist (. . .) Who has the right to condemn me if I chose to hold on to a privation which depends completely on my arbitrariness? Who will be the judge? The pleasure I experience is a thing of mine and as such it is at my disposal. (Rosmini 1976, 131, footnote 1)

Therefore, Rosmini reassures the need to follow the golden rule on the balance between expenditure and income[17] and criticizes the constant promotion of desires and needs proper of consumerist societies:

> The supposition that human beings are always stimulated to industrious activity by the pressure of increased needs is false. In certain circumstances the pleasure only produces impoverishment and even extreme misery of peoples, who give up what is necessary for their existence in order to satisfy the irresistible urgency of their needs (. . .). Why do people who have already applied themselves to agriculture sell their agricultural tools? And finally, why do those on the verge of civilized life sell their cultivated lands? The answer is always: the need for drink, fine clothing, useless ornaments, and other necessities and longings aroused in them. (Rosmini 1994b, 324–339)

[17]"Shouldn't consumption be proportional to profits?" (Rosmini 1923, 94).

6.2.4 Luxury and Fashion

According to Rosmini the destructive consequences of consumerism on wealth are illustrated by luxury and fashion. Firstly, Rosmini defines both of them as *disordered* uses of wealth, the result of a 'reckless' and 'vain' kind of consumption in which "wealth is not spent but wasted." This way of consuming leads to "the perversion of men and along with the loss of dignity and virtue, it destroys what the effort of industrious men has harvested and produced" (Rosmini 1923, 156). Considering it sophistic, Rosmini rejects the utilitarian argument which states that, given that luxury and fashion often take place in highly industrious, cultured and rich societies, the former are the propelling forces behind labor, culture and wealth. Actually, excessive luxury and fashion are evils that feed from the good they depend on but, eventually, end up destroying it:

> Despite constituting an evil, excessive luxury and capricious fashion spring from a good: like parasitic plants which get their food from others to end up drying them and extracting their sap. Thus, when man's reason gets stronger, when culture expands, when the abundance of external things grows, (...) evils begin to swarm around these goods (...) It is the strong reason that can attack the truth; it is culture that can organize crime in the same way as it organizes charity; finally, it is abundance that comes from culture that makes luxury and fashion possible. However, luxury and fashion tend to waste the abundance of external goods, as crime tends to poison and kill culture, and sophistics to darken the truth. (Rosmini 1977a, 110)

Moreover, when ethical foundations are weak and power is strong, luxury and fashion destroy not only the economy and society, but also the capacity of enjoyment aimed at:

> In a corrupt and powerful community, luxury and fashion increase the dominion of idleness rather than work effort; the members of the community only make an effort to feed themselves by drying up the sources of wealth from which they fuel. Then, the community ends up getting its fuel blindly and destroying itself similarly to the disordered man who, being a slave to his pleasures and desiring them viciously, makes his life shorter and also deprives himself of the capacity of enjoyment. (Rosmini 1977a, 106)

Nevertheless, in spite of this criticism, Rosmini does not condemn all kinds of luxury. Though he rejects luxury when it is part of the disordered ambition of the individual interest, he defends it when it springs from the citizen's civil virtue to enhance, through a sensitive means, the nation's greatness:

> Luxury will be the epidemic of society when it is the sign of selfishness and individual ambition, but if it empowers the law, the prince or the magistrates, it will be useful by nature, unless in excess. (Rosmini 1923, 174)

Rosmini praises luxury in relation to public architecture, that is, the "public use" of luxury in contrast with its private use. But he also accepts private luxury as long as it is "innocent," that is, if the person who consumes it possesses an economic, cultural and ethical capacity to enjoy it in a proper way:

> The noble luxury we approve and that seems useful and desirable is the one which is not lost in the private triviality; it is rather created to radiate splendor and for common use. If riches

are more abundant than needs, then, it is reasonable for the former to be spent, but it is yet more reasonable if they are spent not on a caprice but on a real utility for the individual and for the community. (Rosmini 1923, 176)

6.2.5 Wealth Creation and Corruption

Rosmini also refutes the utilitarian thesis which looks at economic corruption as either a less important and inevitable evil which goes together with any economy of wealth creation, or even as a beneficial phenomenon. In words of those times, this idea was represented by the thesis of "private vices, public virtues" stated by Bernard de Mandeville, who favored the productive character of vices proper to modern corruption, which were refined if compared to the great disordered passions of the past. On the contrary, Rosmini states that modern sophisticated corruption does not create but destroys wealth, even more than the less sophisticated ways of corruption of other times:

> It could be said that refined, domesticated vice, gracefully ornamented, has led to a much greater level of corruption, on the one hand, and that the latter easily slips through everywhere and sticks as a tough plague, since it hides its evil – as pure vice overtly accuses the vicious – because it allows for excuses and justifications originated in the triviality around it. It could be said that the people's vices in feudal times were coarser; however, it would not be absurd to think that corruption in those times was not really greater than that of some highly educated gentlemen of our time. (...) [Today] these vices are masked with gallantry, yet they do not inflict a less mortal wound on individuals and society. (Rosmini 1977a, 121)

Thus, Rosmini suggests "closing our ears to the seduction of these miserable economists, who overtly teach how the State is enriched through the increase of all vices and denial of the only true nobility of mankind" (Rosmini 1923, 156).[18] Opposing Hume,[19] Mandeville and Gioia, he maintains that "public vices are not

[18]Rosmini rejects the Scottish idea that morality is acquired through the mutual control that vices exert upon one another. The fact that consumerism could diminish the evil of corruption in some cases does not mean that it is a good in itself: "In fatti il lusso e la moda che accresce la corruzione dov'ella non è giunta ancora all'estremo, la diminuirebbe forse in quei luoghi dove ha toccato il suo colmo: come se s'introduce un minor male dove c'è un vizio maggiore, questo disminuisce: e se spirerà in un'atmosfera bollente un vento caldo bensì, ma meno della temperatura generale, quel vento che sarebbe stato soffocante in tutt'altri momenti, allora vi ristorerà e raffredderà l'aria. È il medesimo nelle cose morali: se un uomo che metteva tutti i suoi sollazzi ne'lupanari, prenderà diletto de'giuochi d'azzardo, consumerà in questi quell'ore che logorava in quelli, e avrà forse guadagnato qualche cosa se in vece di stemperarsi la salute e la vita, fa il gitto solo delle sostanze. È a dir vero un bel modo di far l'apologia della moda e del lusso, quello di paragonar questi mali a dei mali maggiori, e mostrare così che in paragone di quelli si possono chiamar beni!" (Rosmini 1977a, 108–109).

[19]Although Rosmini was an avid reader and admirer of Hume as a historian especially, he disagrees with his superficiality in the valuation of vices: "(...) the English philosopher [sic] remains under the spell of the seducing covering extended over these vices during the philosophical and gallant

full of pleasures as many believe; way more than virtue, vices are always cruel to men, while virtues are beneficial" (Rosmini 1923, 156).

Besides, Rosmini also refuses the idea that the mere creation of wealth in a society will make corruption decrease. In his opinion, this proposal is based on an erroneous understanding of human nature, which does not consider that if the spirit is sick of avarice or consumerism it will not be satisfied with the attainment of more goods. On the contrary, in the latter case, the spirit will find a much broader field of action where to increase its violent ambition and its desire to get those goods by all means:

> In this case, the error of superficial moralists is similar to that of superficial hydrologists. When a river overflows and causes damage, they immediately suggest dividing it into more channels hoping that the waters will thus abate. Yet, things happen contrarily to their poor prediction: waters fill the new channel unexpectedly without much success in the decrease of the waters flowing in the former. The superficial moralists think alike; give new objects to passions and you will thus weaken their strength in relation to each of them. Nonetheless, when passion is disordered, it does nothing but reinforce itself in proportion to the number of objects, and not only does it jump onto the different objects it comes across as energetically as before but it desires them even more. (Rosmini 1977a, 116)

There is no external or material solution for corruption,[20] for it is caused not by the abundance or scarcity of goods but by a "never-ending rage" originated by "the torment and unhappiness that come as people see themselves subjected to long awaited but perpetually frustrated satisfaction" (Rosmini 1994b, 368). Such a subjective state is thus the ultimate cause of "all injustice which will make man envious, dishonest, thief, assassin, full of all those vices which may lead him to obtain others' goods illegally" (Rosmini 1977a, 106.107). In that sense, "corruption is measured not in terms of what man spends but in terms of what he would like to spend and purchase" (Rosmini 1977a, 117). Therefore, the only true solution for corruption and thus for true economic progress consists in the education of freedom and the culture of spirit:

> A man is not a machine. In men, wealth and corruption are not two fluids that must always be leveled like in a bifurcated tube: beyond instincts lies the moral and free force that presides in man in the use of wealth. (. . .) In this sense, the encouragement of luxury and capricious fashion would not avoid this evil [corruption], on the contrary, the culture of the spirit and the heart are required (. . .) Excessive luxury and fashion only increase corruption and become its fuel and means of growth (. . .) If human beings are educated, they will abandon the vanity and extravagance of fashion and luxury and pursue a moderate life and run a wise

century he lived in: once again, it is shown that, during cultured centuries, vices – without being any less evil – become capable of seducing men who display a penetrating spirit for other things. These vices are still ugly, though enveloped in soft wrappings; they are still poisonous, though mixed with honey so that one swallows the liquor but in longer sips" (Rosmini 1977a, 121).

[20]"I think that Gioia does not know any other kind of corruption different from the external one, and ignores that man's corruption lies on the dispositions of his spirit. He calls himself an economist and believes that corruption can be measured as if it were wheat" (Rosmini 1977a, 114). "The desire for corruption itself is already corruption, in moral terms, because corruption lives in the spirit and does not come from the outside."

economy, without this implying a reduction in wealth or a deprivation of these means, which are not necessarily means of corruption. (Rosmini 1977a, 111–112)

6.2.6 Wealth and Poverty, Relative Concepts

Rosmini borrows from Gioia the humanistic-Campanellian idea that behind wealth creation there always lie human faculties, synthesized in the triad "sapere, volere, potere" (knowledge, will and power), today known as "human capital." This triad implies, both for Gioia and for Rosmini, that economic value is not the result of a mere material dynamics (technology, labor division, natural agents, spontaneous order of material interests, as in Adam Smith's theory); they state that it is intimately related to human factors such as moral power (trust, valuations,) the level of culture (knowledge of one's own interests, education, culture, level of instruction in public opinion) and the way in which behavior and affections work (interests, affections, will, customs, and social habits).

In a word, according to Rosmini, "honesty, virtuous moderation and truth are always useful for human beings' happiness: this is also the appropriate argument for a wise economist who never forgets that he is a moral being who also recognizes in material things, and in wealth as well, a sanction of the law by which the creator of nature obliges him to be ordered and virtuous" (Rosmini 1978a, 22, footnote 11). Such a view will also imply that the sense of economic policy will have to be broadened to account for the ethical, cultural and social aspects of the economy (Rosmini 2003, 369).[21]

Besides, in Rosmini's words, both poverty and wealth are relative concepts since they depend on the varied valuations which can be done on a certain level of income, in different places and at a particular time, by different people and in diverse social classes. Rosmini makes a clear distinction between relative poverty, which might be a legitimate expression of the existing life styles and vocations, and absolute poverty which implies the incapacity to satisfy basic needs that any human being objectively has. In that sense, Rosmini describes this abject poverty, degrading and forced by the circumstances, as a negative reality which will never aid the moral fulfillment of the person in any way, but will rather constitute an obstacle or a source of oppression.

According to Rosmini, this kind of poverty mainly consists in a permanent disproportion or imbalance between the expenditure and income of a certain

[21]Gioia (1815–1819, 66–239) deals with the topic of *Potere* in Book II, Classe Prima; the topic of *Cognizione* in the Classe Seconda (240–255), and the subject of *Volontà* in the Classe Terza (256–275); in the rest of the book, Gioia applies these concepts to different particular subjects such as the human and cultural basis of credit, of the value of money, of consumption, of labor, of production, of economic policy, of commerce, etc.

number of persons or even of a country.[22] This phenomenon is clearly a symptom of an imbalance amongst a variety of factors such as investment, employment, consumption, production, commerce, currency, and taxes, amongst others. However, according to Rosmini, behind of these unbalances, poverty should be analyzed from the perspective of other kinds of unbalances such as the demographic, political and, above all, the cultural, psychological and moral imbalance affecting a country and its inhabitants.

In effect, Rosmini defines extreme and structural poverty as a critical cultural, psychological and moral imbalance that consists in a state of permanent incapacity resulting from a constant and urgent proliferation of needs combined with the inability to develop one's own means to satisfy them, which condemn the individual to a state of material and moral incapacity (Rosmini 1994b, 324ff). Consequently, Rosmini states that the true solutions for poverty certainly do not lie in a mere material distributism but in the recovery of the human capacities which enable the individual to become a wealth creator and the architect of his own destiny.

6.3 Consumption

6.3.1 Modern Economy and Artificial Needs

Rosmini argues that one of the key problems of modern economy lies in the increasingly sophisticated and accelerated character of needs and desires by which these desires tend to replace spiritual needs. This was not a problem for primitive economies, where material and intellectual development was not significant and, thus, a natural realism of economic needs used to take place:

> The further back we go into the ancient memories of humanity (...) we have to note carefully that in this period people do not give an ideal value to physical objects. Increasing the value of physical objects by adding ideal values to them requires the prior formation of many abstractions. Physical objects are considered for what they are, and nothing more; people do not go searching madly to satisfy the spiritual needs by bodily good, as they would later. Bodily good has the power to really satisfy corporal needs; nothing more is claimed for it during this early period when it satisfies people. This explains the nature of extremely simple golden ages during which there was no artificial wealth; everything was natural. People, I have to repeat, did not want to satiate with physical good the voracity of spirit aspiring to things outside the confines of reality. The memory of this first contentment, formed of few, simple objects, and the latter experience of something similar by temperate persons, suggested the following philosophical teaching: '*nature contents itself with little; true wealth is poverty adjusted in accord to natural laws.*' (Rosmini 1994b, 352)

[22] We have already discussed how the problem of economic balance manifests itself at an individual and social level, according to Rosmini, owing to the equilibrium between the growth rate of needs and income. See Rosmini, (1994b, 340).

On the contrary, in modern economies, in which a wide range of consumption possibilities unfolds in the context of an insufficient moral disposition in people, a new phenomenon takes place: the constant creation of what Rosmini calls, in broad terms, "artificial needs,"[23] characterized by their lack of realism and its alienating compulsiveness:

> The words 'artificial needs' imply something immoral. 'Need' implies necessity. Thus, those with unnatural, artificial needs are subject to a kind of slavery, and do not have the time and calm necessary for calculating the effects of their actions. It should come at no surprise therefore that the virtue of prudence in human beings, so necessary for procuring a state of satisfied existence for themselves and their dependence, diminishes in the measure that imaginary needs grow. (Rosmini 1994b, 343)

Artificial needs understood in this broad sense have devastating consequences on the ethical, intellectual and material basis of the economy, such as the birth of "strong, impetuous passions" (Rosmini 1994b, 326–327), "confused intellect" (Rosmini 1994b, 327) and the destruction of "the ability to choose the best means to satisfy them" (Rosmini 1994b, 327). In effect, these needs result from the combination of the increment of the consumption possibilities, characteristic of a sophisticated economy, with the weakening or underdevelopment of intellectual, psychological and moral capacities of people. In fact, they are a consequence of not *knowing* (how), not *being able* and not *wanting* "to satisfy (one's) needs by upright, useful means" (Rosmini 1994b, 327), as in the case of people or communities which lack the capacity of "foresight" to choose the right means, "self-dominion" to defer the satisfaction of one's own desires, so that "any delay would be unbearable" for them or the sufficient moral virtue to look for lawful means to satisfy them (Rosmini 1994b, 327).

Under any of the said conditions, the multiplication of goods will propel the creation of destructive artificial needs. The Roveretan sees the devastating consequences of these needs reflected on many different kinds of people, especially on primitive communities, poor families, offspring who are not yet prepared to work, or craftsmen, who sacrifice everything they possess to satisfy those needs. However, he also sees such consequences in the upper classes, which are affected by consumerism and the insatiable ambition for satisfaction, and the subsequent indifference for the others' needs (Rosmini 1994b, 322–342). This way:

Nothing could be more disastrous or indeed more evil (...) than this system of politics which requires that artificial needs of the members of a society be increased, but does not indicate the quality or limit of these needs, or the classes in which these artificial needs can usefully increase, or the social circumstances which make the increase desirable (Rosmini 1994b, 334).

[23]However, Rosmini will make a distinction between artificial needs which are destructive and those which are honest and useful.

6.3.2 *Responsible Consumption*

The Roveretan starts an analysis of consumption from a new anthropological foundation, as the counterpart of consumerist economism. It is certainly not about "defending consumption in general," which can only be "a sophist's argument of mere declamations, though not a useful argument for humanity to learn to reason and to arrive at a practical conclusion." "The same must be said when it comes to condemning them in general (...) Gioia would have been right (...) if, instead of favoring consumption (...) he had plunged into distinguishing useful from harmful consumptions, without diverting his attention into general and abstract propositions (...)" (Rosmini 1978a, 22, footnote 11). Rosmini believes that consumption is productive provided that it is involved in the dynamics of recognition of human beings' economic, eudaimonological and ethical order. Indeed, when referring to consumption, "that which is accidental" must be told apart from "that which is substantial" since "the disorder in consumption" is not the same as "consumption itself:" there is an "arbitrary and disordered consumption" as well as a "necessary" one (Rosmini 1923, 93).

> When reasoning about wealth consumption, we should note first that those who condemn it in general foolishly fall into repugnant avarice (Rosmini 1923, 153) [Thus] wealth consumption is human when illuminated by the light of reason, which brightens up only within an upright order. (Rosmini 1923, 153)

In fact, ordered consumption is useful, in the first place, for wealth creation itself:

> Honest and moderate pleasures help to reintegrate bodily and spiritual forces. However, this does not occur with dishonest and immoderate pleasures: in the first case, the profits obtained from those forces fully compensate for the wealth lost since bodily and spiritual forces are necessary for the growth of wealth. (Rosmini 1978a, 22, footnote 11)

Above all, consumption is mainly useful when it is an aid for the attainment of higher spiritual and moral goods:

> Well-ordered consumption not only produces wealth increase and infuses greater dynamism and life into society, but also enriches men with true goods. (Rosmini 1923, 155)

It is, therefore, necessary to formulate a balanced idea of consumption which does not imply a rigorist stance but an integration of consumption and pleasure into the whole dynamics of human happiness:

> Nobody shall distort this speech with pharisaic terms nor repeat the mistake of attributing us the intention of depriving human beings of the pleasures made for them, nor claim that our reasoning is sad and melancholic. On the contrary, sacrificing some pleasures, illuminated by reason and in the previously described way, opens up the path for greater pleasures, though unknown by those who are far from reaching spiritual nobility (...) To quit vanity, triviality and a dissolute and unlimited luxury does not mean that we will be unhappy; instead, it implies getting rid of many miseries, giving our spirit a sweet rest and the chance to enjoy pleasures which are more true, real and firm. (Rosmini 1923, 156–157)

6.3.3 Relativity and Realism of Needs

Despite one might think, Rosmini does not encourage a naturalism of needs by means of which only basic physical needs will be legitimate in contrast to all the other needs and desires, seen as unnatural and deceiving. On the contrary, the Roveretan accepts the possibility of satisfying artificial needs within the parameters of an ethical and economically constructive order. In fact, Rosmini strongly rejects the "perfectism" which states that an unlimited satisfaction of needs is possible, in the same way he criticizes economic immobilism or conservatism that intends to fix people's possibilities of economic growth forever. According to Rosmini, the concept of need is always relative to the valuation of the person, who is constantly changing and evolving as time goes by and different circumstances emerge, just like his or her needs. The problem is not the complexity and spring of new needs, but rather their quality and their relationship to the parallel evolution of moral and economic capacities to satisfy them.

In addition, in Rosmini's view, a strong *realism* is required as the fundamental principle to avoid the dynamics of a person's economic needs deriving into destructive artificial needs. Rosmini affirms that this realism manifests itself following two central criteria. The first and most important criterion consists in the person developing economic needs for *real objects or goods* rather than for intellectual fictions. In effect, the core of the psychological and moral problem of economic needs, as it has already been described, is the attempt to satisfy spiritual needs with economic goods, which makes these needs insatiable and unlimited, and results in hopeless discontentment. In this way, all economic need and desire will be productive, in the first place, if it is a *determined* need or desire, that is, if it is directed to limited objects which are not transformed into impossible substitutes for objects providing unlimited satisfaction. Actually, even when this determined artificial need or desire is not satisfied and, thus, does not contribute to the person's contentment, it will not be as potentially destructive as the undetermined artificial need:

> [On the one hand] As I have said so often, unsatisfiable capacities are those by which individuals seek an object proportioned to some good, abstractly contemplated, which lacks an adequate object. Such capacities constitute states of absolute unhappiness. On the other hand, capacities, if determined, may or may not be satisfied. If they remain unsatisfied, individuals lack contentment, but are not necessarily unhappy as a result. The disquiet and penalty they suffer is limited, just as the capacity to which it refers is limited. (Rosmini 1994b, 396)

Anyway, this is not enough even when referring to the needs for real objects. According to Rosmini, a second condition is also necessary for a realist dynamics of needs; it consists in that "those who open these capacities must really posses the means for attaining the real object" (Rosmini 1994b, 398). In this sense, Rosmini finds it essential to consider the potential of our own natural and technological resources and the human capacities available to estimate the degree of impact new needs and desires will produce. Given these conditions, Rosmini wonders whether it will always be beneficial to introduce new needs and desires into society. In his opinion, it will turn out beneficial as long as those desires are "highly likely to be satisfied" and are accompanied by "a highly virtuous spirit which tempers the desire in such a way that it is in complete conformity with the reality of things," which "does not impede the spirit's state of contentment," and consequently "increases human energy and activity" (Rosmini 1994b, 399). On the other hand, it will not be beneficial if those desires "are indeed projected towards a real object proportioned to the means available," but "are accompanied by a probable hope only" and also "lack the virtuous moderation of which we have spoken," which "impedes full contentment of spirit" (Rosmini 1994b, 399). Nonetheless, though it is convenient to favor and encourage the first type of desires, the latter are significantly different from the insatiable ones that Rosmini fully rejects and believes to be tolerable only as previous steps to the creation of the former.[24]

6.3.4 Developing a Scale of Needs

Finally, as a synthesis for the whole theory, Rosmini introduces a sort of "scale" of economic needs. Though such a scale can neither be constructed disregarding people's concrete situations, nor made permanent, it lays out some general objective limits or criteria which, according to the Roveretan, derive from the intrinsic structure of human nature that economic agents should recognize and respect. At the top of the scale, Rosmini places what he considers a priority obligation: the provision of economic means must always be directed in view of "the acquirement of virtue." This implies that even basic needs can never be satisfied as ends in themselves but as means to the realization of man as a person.[25] Upon that priority, an order is established for the rest of the needs, that is, health,[26] housing, basic material well-being, and secondly, the other "luxury" needs, as far as they are structured, especially in the family sphere, taking into account vital needs, the production and saving capacity, as well as the capacity of human, social and religious fulfillment of all its members.[27]

---

[24]Following Tocqueville's reflections, the Roveretan sees how the realist economic desires are fulfilled in the America of his times (Rosmini 1994b, 397–398). "Two causes already mentioned account for this singular phenomenon in the United States, where great desires for wealth produce activity which is not harmful in the present conditions of society: 1) American desires are determined. The object of this people is not an abstract idea, but real things. 2) Americans have abundant means for satisfying promptly such *determined* desires." We wonder if Rosmini would think the same of contemporary United States.

[25]"The expenditure on the acquirement of virtue comes in the first place" (Rosmini 1923, 155).

[26]"The expenditure on bodily health or strength comes in the second place." (Rosmini 1923, 155).

[27]"As regards the family, luxury consumption can be carried out if the following conditions are met: first, that the basic needs of the family must be satisfied; second, that the fund must be preserved intact, otherwise the family would deacy, and such a downfall must be considered as a misfortune

Thus, by means of the doctrine of human needs, Rosmini fully integrates the totality of human being's economic activities into his personalist thesis on recognition and moral contentment:

> In Book I we had distinguished three degrees in which external goods related to our spirit produce some kind of satisfaction. Firstly, the attainment of goods; secondly, the pleasure obtained by using these goods; and thirdly, the contentment these pleasures are destined to produce in us. (Rosmini 1923, 133)

---

which becomes a really serious matter for the family (...); third, that a part of the fund must be set aside for family maintenance in case of unforeseen events; fourth, that it must be set apart all that which demands the necessary cultivation of the spirit, the means of virtue, the help of charity and the offerings of mercy. Now, the nobler the objects on which the rest of the wealth is spent, the better and more generous the expenditure will be. The rest of uses beyond the ones mentioned will imply better and more generous spending only when it is devoted to the noblest objects. Nonetheless, over and above these duties, there is still something left which can be used to satisfy honest pleasures, and here is where expenditure derives from comfort or pleasure habits and everything understood as luxury." (Rosmini 1923, 158). "If the head of the family, loved by all the members of the household, spends a fair share of his income on making life more enjoyable for them, organizing spending in a proper way, this family, a harmonious nest, becomes a worth-seeing show." (Rosmini 1923, 159)

Chapter 7
Recognizing the Other: Rights and Ethics in Market Relations

7.1 Rights and Ethics as Recognition of the Other

7.1.1 The Economy in the Context of Interpersonal Relationships

So far, we have seen how – according to Rosmini – economic actions may only be understood within the framework of human action, which in turn implies an objective-moral dimension, as well as a subjective-eudaimonological dimension. Economic utility is to be understood within the context of this interplay between both dimensions: there can be no true economic perfection unless within human action, taken in its integrality. However, so far, we have only dealt with the economic action of a person as an individual, making little reference to the human being's interpersonal and social dimension. Clearly, this has been just a methodological strategy, since it is evident that, in real conditions, economic action not only takes place within personal, individual action, but with relation to other persons. Moreover, through the analysis of the integral dimension of human action – especially as regards the possibility it has of objectivizing the person's own subjectivity – we have already seen that, to Rosmini, human action entails a reference to other persons, so that personal and interpersonal become non-contradictory terms, but the expression of the human being's essential dimension.

In fact, to Rosmini, the opening of economic action to the moral dimension, implies the depart not only from one's own subjectivity through the recognition of an objective order, but also through what Rosmini calls "inobjectivation," i.e., the human being's capacity to acknowledge otherness in the form of an object – as when we perceive things "objectively," but through the "intersubjective" form that permits to "transport oneself into the other" (Rosmini 1938, vol. III, n. 867; 2001, 2, 678). Thus, by means of inobjectivation, the human being acquires its moral plenitude reached through the encounter and mutual recognition amongst persons for being, in the context of Rosminian philosophy, the only realities in the full

C. Hoevel, *The Economy of Recognition: Person, Market and Society in Antonio Rosmini*, Ethical Economy 42, DOI 10.1007/978-94-007-6058-5_7,

sense of the term. Therefore, in Rosmini's thought, the formulation of moral virtue as "acknowledgment of objective good" is completed by "moral inobjectivation," which obliges us to recognize the person as an end in himself, not only forbidding his instrumentalization, but obliging us even to love him as "another I." Now, the interpersonal and intersubjective character of the person will lead Rosmini to unfold several levels of analysis of economic actions.

The first level of economic relationships that Rosmini tackles from this new perspective has to do with the relationships amongst the individuals involved in a market; these, on the one hand, are regulated by Right, as the ultimate, predominantly negative and most basic manifestation of ethics. Rosmini will attempt to show a first aspect of the jural dimension of market, especially through the analysis of the natural rights of the individuals – or "rational rights" as he prefers to call them – the rights of economic freedom, of ownership, and through the considerations of the nature of contracts. Yet, apart from this analysis of individual rights, the Roveretan will also incorporate to this first approach a consideration of other non-jural moral duties, and even other moral virtues which are not strictly obligatory – they are part of what Rosmini defines as the "supererogatory" aspect of ethics – but are essential to the functioning of the markets.

7.1.2 Critique of Jural Utilitarianism

Rosmini's first concern in the analysis of individual rights in play in the market economy will be the critique of the different forms of jural utilitarianism and their replacement by what he considers a true conception of these same rights. For this task, he engaged in a strong debate developed in Italy on *Diritto ed Economia*, especially with Melchiorre Gioia and Giandomenico Romagnosi, in a nineteenth century Italian version of our contemporary debate on "Law and Economics." But Rosmini's stand on this issue transcends Italy and should be understood within the wider framework of the juridical debate that took place at the end of the eighteenth century and the beginning of the nineteenth century and includes French juridical rationalism of Rousseaunian and Napoleonic origin, the German juridical philosophy of authors such as Kant and Hegel, and also the English and Scottish philosophy in its individualistic (Locke, Smith), social-constructivist (Bentham) or historicist versions (Mandeville, Hume, Blackstone, Burke).[1]

To Rosmini, most of the juridical stands of his time confuse right and justice with some form of utility. For example, the principle of "co-existence" upheld by the social utilitarians in general and supported also by Kant, who defines right as the "faculty of carrying out all those actions whose execution, although universal, does not impede the co-existence of other persons" (Rosmini 1993a, n. 270), presents serious deficiencies in Rosmini's view. In fact, "there could be some other action,

[1]This type of juridical historicism is taken over in the twentieth century by Hayek, for example.

unlawful according to a law of nature, which nevertheless does not exclude the co-existence of others who also commit it. But no one would have the right to such an action. The right to do evil does not exist" (Rosmini 1993a, n. 270). Besides, "the whole force of the argument is found (...) in the supposition that the "co-existence of persons is necessary." But we could ask why the co-existence of persons is *necessary*. Are we speaking about moral necessity, or some necessity arising from the interest each human being has in his own existence?" (Rosmini 1993a, n. 270). If this is so, as Rosmini believes, we are no longer referring to a "state of right, but of a state of fact, useful to all" (Rosmini 1993a, n. 270), which "*could not be sustained for long without some moral sanction. It is impossible for individuals, guided by principles of self-interest, to persuade themselves that their own personal interest would always gain some advantage from the respect shown to the personal interest of others*" (Rosmini 1993a, n. 343, footnote 195).

The same applies to the principle of self-preservation, sustained by Romagnosi, for example. According to Rosmini, "I cannot affirm my right to preserve my life in such a general manner," as "it is certain that there are a number of unlawful things I can do to preserve my life (which as unlawful, are not part of my right)" (Rosmini 1993a, n. 330). For example, we believe it is not lawful to "kill an innocent being to save our life, although we could do so, if we had an absolute right to our preservation" (Rosmini 1993b, n. 272).[2] The same argument might be applied if we attempted to establish rights on the urgency to satisfy our own needs or on the "instinct for happiness (which is) a kind of physical impulse insufficient to form a right."[3]

As we will see in detail further on, the same happens with freedom. According to Rosmini, freedom, as the mere faculty to act without restriction, does not constitute a true right because it might be used in an unlawful manner; besides, "what is wrong cannot be right." Thus, Rosmini will make a distinction between a purely "physical," "*de facto*" freedom, and a "*de jure*" freedom (Rosmini 1993a, n. 236). Likewise, he will make a clear distinction between "ownership in fact" of external things, and "ownership by right" or right of ownership proper (Rosmini 1993b, n. 951–952).

Thus, to Rosmini, founding a right on utility or self-interest amounts to opening the door for eventually reducing right to the mere force of facts, the latter being collectively grouped or presented in the form of individual interests. Besides, Rosmini will also reject the idea that this very interplay of forces may generate *per se* an order of mutual respect amongst persons; he argues that any "force can be overcome only by a greater force" (Rosmini 1993b, n. 155) and, consequently, will end up by restraining itself in order to remain more or less within its own limits. To Rosmini, although this might be factually possible – "which is not true" – there will

[2]Further on, we will see how and under which conditions the self-preservation instinct becomes a right.

[3]In chapter V on human action, we have already seen how Rosmini refutes eudaemonist Utilitarianism by sustaining that the possibility of moral action cannot be limited to tendency to happiness alone. Likewise, for Rosmini, it is also not possible to found a right on such tendency.

always be a "superior force exercised by someone. In this case, there is no one to prevent injury by this force or check its exercise (. . .)" (Rosmini 1993b, n. 423). Thus, "[if] we grant that human beings must follow what is useful, then there is no longer any reason why we should place another's usefulness before our own, or, in cases of conflict, place what is useful to the group before what is useful to us individually" (Rosmini 1993a, n. 153).

Therefore, according to Rosmini, principles of social utility, such as "peaceful co-existence," "greatest happiness for the majority," "public wealth," or of individual utility, such as "self-preservation," "freedom," "ownership," "needs," "own happiness" or "self-interests," taken in isolation, are certainly real or potential subjective advantages, or benefits for one or more persons, but do not imply true rights *per se* on which to found economic relations.

7.1.3 Confusion Between Justice and Utility

Thus Rosmini discards founding rights on a purely subjective, eudemonological or utilitarian bases that he believes are related to the modern confusion between justice and utility. Against utilitarians, Rosmini states that, neither rights in general nor economic rights in particular, may be rooted in utility as a *fact*, this being either social or individual; instead, they should be based on that superior reason which he calls "the *idea* of justice":

> In applying these considerations to positive laws, I became convinced that the most simple, basic, and therefore most noble idea is the idea of justice. All solid attempts at reasoning about positive laws must begin here. Ever other value possessed by positive law appeared accidental, accessory and derivative; the essence of the perfection of laws consisted in justice alone (. . .) (Rosmini 1993a, n. 8)

This idea of justice does not differ, in the last resort, from the one arising from the very objective order of being, which – as we have seen – is the source not of subjective or natural necessity but of the moral obligation or necessity that transcends every finite subject:

> These obligations arise (. . .) from the law as their first source. Rights are such only in relation to the moral law. (Rosmini 1993b, n. 415, footnote 128)

In this sense, subjective utility is just the indirect consequence of respect to the objective requirements of justice:

> Some of them would certainly want to tell me that justice is simple what is useful, and is nothing more than self-interest properly understood (. . .) Justice is a principle; utility is a consequence. While utility as a consequence is considered in its connection with the principle of justice, thought remains sound; when utility alone attracts the spirit's attention, sophistry reigns in minds and anarchy in society. (Rosmini 1993a, n. 9–10)

Neither is it valid the argument posed by those who sustain that justice is only a "deferred utility" or a utility "in the long run," as if it were just a temporal matter.

In Rosmini's opinion, justice cannot be deduced from any purely subjective or relative instance, and demands considering human nature from an integral point of view, not along time but beyond time as far as its objectivity is concerned, an objectivity which transcends the positive or negative consequences it may bring about at any time in the present or in the future:

> It is false to say that those who recognize this distinction fail to consider that one thing is what is momentarily useful and another thing is what is useful in the future. [In fact] everything that is momentarily useful and everything that is useful in the future, even if useful along all this life, does not entitle anyone to fail to fulfill his duty. Such duty can exist independently from one's own pleasure, because duty arises from a law that human beings receive from outside, which is different from their sensitivity. (Rosmini 1976, n. 112, footnote 1)

Therefore, "justice and utility are different things; they demand different calculations and depend on different principles" (Rosmini 1976, 113). Thus, to Rosmini, it is also false that justice always prevails in this life, or that it is always linked to utility. On the contrary, since "justice is *essentially* different from utility," it happens that "many times in this life justice remains oppressed by those who violate all sacred things in the name of utility" (Rosmini 1976, 114). Besides, although Rosmini believes – as we have already seen – that true utility can only be achieved as a consequence of the idea of justice, it is also false that by following justice we may obtain all possible utility:

> Moreover, not only utility is different from justice: we cannot even assume that, by knowing the principle of justice, we will reach all utility. This is so because, as we have already said, in order to know what will be truly useful in the future we should be a kind of divinity capable of foreseeing the future. (Rosmini 1976, 113)

This is so due to the very limitation of human intelligence, which will never succeed in obtaining all the potential benefits even if considering things in a just and complete manner:

> The gratuitous assertion that justice always brings about the greatest utility is essentially impossible to prove, as it happens with all the general facts that cannot be reasonably induced unless from all the innumerable particular facts included in them. (Rosmini 1976, 114)

This shows the ultimately transcendental and superhuman nature of justice, which – as to Rosmini – only achieves complete realization in divine justice, beyond any human calculation:

> This life is not the place where justice is always linked to utility (...) Those who are fair, very often overrun by the prepotent ones, must raise their eyes to a more sublime remunerator who, after this life, may inform human matters with a fairer measure and compensate the upright man with a utility that cannot be subjected to humankind's ridiculous, perverse and presumptuous calculations. (Rosmini 1976, 114)[4]

[4]"Bentham's sophism claiming that justice is nothing but utility calculated for the future is supported by the gratuitous assumption that justice is always accompanied by the greatest utility. If this were true, utility could not be confused with justice" (Rosmini 1976, 114).

7.1.4 *Moral Relationality of the Human Being Against Jural Individualism and Positivism*

Human nature – considered not from the subjective and eudaimonological point of view but from the objective and universal one, as part of the source of moral obligation – is also the source of the idea of justice. According to Rosmini, objective good, which is the basis of every right, is the good that reason can perceive as suitable to the human nature of a person, considering the latter not from the subjective point of view, that is, as a source of subjective satisfaction or happiness, but from the objective point of view, that is, understood and valued for what a person is – not for the utility he may bring – through the reason and free will of another human being or even of the one who is the very subject of such right. Rosmini calls this objective good "the true human good." Thus, to him, right is indeed founded on this human nature, which demands being known and respected not because of its utility but for what it is in itself. In this sense, Rosmini's jural conception carries within itself a restoration of the integral dimension of Man.[5]

For this reason, Rosmini will prefer to give natural Right the name of "rational" Right, so as to exclude any chance of falling into the naturalistic reductionisms present in the classical iusnaturalistic tradition as well as in sensism and contemporary utilitarianism, which tended to identify the idea of "nature" with the human being's purely physical and individual aspects, and considered his moral or social dimension as something "artificial."[6] From this reductionism of human nature proceeds, on the one hand, the individualistic conception of rights that sees "the individual human being surrounded by beasts and material things, but cut off from his fellows" and leaving aside its relational and moral dimension:

> In this system, the human being taken in isolation is granted (...) strict, inflexible rights, simply because these rights are established without the least regard for other co-existent human beings. Rights conceived in this fashion are inevitably false because they are not derived from human beings as human beings are and must be. These are not true human rights, which are moral relationships between several individuals, not simply qualities inherent to the nature of the individual. True human rights spring from common human nature existent in each human being. (Rosmini 1993b, n. 907)

[5]Rosmini believes it is essential to go back to the true iusnaturalistic tradition, leaving aside all the distortions it experienced along time through authors such as Machiavelli, Hobbes, Spinoza, Locke, Hume, Blackstone, Rousseau, Kant or Bentham, and returning to the Greco-Roman, medieval, and Germanic sources, to the Spanish Scholastics' iusnaturalism, and to some modern iusnaturalists such as Puffendorf, Grotius, Leibniz, Zeiller, as well as to the iusnaturalist elements present in the Italian, Austrian, and British traditions, and in the American and French constitutions.

[6]Rosmini sees the synthesis of this modern error in Rousseau's conception, which "excluded [from the concept of human nature] the effect or requirement of reason and morality," as well as "his relationship with other people precisely because they are not contained in the simple concept of the humanity of an individual." To Rosmini, this conception of natural right is rather that of "an animal, not a human right". Actually, it is "a Right that was no Right" (Rosmini 1993b, n. 902–903).

According to Rosmini, in opposition to and as a consequence of this juridical individualism, it appears the modern current of *social positivism* (Rosmini 1994b, n. 139) which sustains that only positive or civil laws established by society and enforced through the State's coercive power can impose limits to "human nature," understood as pure individual force, and, thus, can complete the constitution of rights.[7] On the contrary, Rosmini assures that rights precede the sanction of any positive law and coercion, as they find their source in natural Right understood as rational right, arising from the very human nature, understood as *person*,[8] that is to say, a physical, individual and subjective subject, who is nevertheless *naturally* open to moral relationships with others because of intelligence and free will:

> The basis of our natural Right is not a hypothesis concerned with isolated individuals, but supposes that human beings are already in full communication with one another. (Rosmini 1993b, n. 913)

7.1.5 Rights as Eudaimonologico-Moral Faculties

Now, founding rights on the idea of justice beyond any subjective utility does not mean suppressing the idea of utility. On the contrary, although rights rest on the idea of justice, they do not constitute themselves as such unless the idea of justice is connected to some subjective utility. Therefore, according to Rosmini, "the word 'right' defines 'a faculty which human beings have for doing or experiencing anything useful' " (Rosmini 1993a, n. 29). Consequently, right has to do with a subjective benefit a physical or legal person may obtain from the exercise thereof. If this were not the case, what would a right mean if it did not benefit its holder? Without actual utility there are no possible rights. We cannot have right to something that brings no benefit of any kind, or that harms the subject of such right. Then, right implies in the first place the existence of some subjective utility, but it is evident that it is a utility which, according to Rosmini, always implies an "eudaimonological good," that is, not any subjective good but – as we have already seen – a "human good" resulting from considering human nature objectively. In this sense, "rights pertain, properly speaking, to eudaimonology" and "an evident proof of this is found in the fact that a person with more right than another is said to be more fortunate, nor morally better" (Rosmini 1993a, n. 29). "On the other hand, right is not simply a mere eudaimonological faculty. The faculty could never be called 'right' unless it were protected and defended by the moral law (. . .) Consequently, the protection afforded by the moral law is properly speaking the *form* by which the

---

[7]Rosmini sees this position in Spinoza and Hobbes, but not in Kant, as the latter admits the existence of rights resulting from the "law of reason." Anyhow, to Rosmini, the problem with Kant is that his "law of reason" eventually falls into naturalism and even utilitarianism, because it is not based on a complete idea of *person* (Rosmini 1993a, n. 345).

[8]"I myself take the dignity of person, or rather the element which gives person its dignity, as the universal reason for rights and prior to that, even as the source of duties" (Rosmini 1993a, n. 350).

merely *eudaimonological* by nature takes on *jural* dignity" (Rosmini 1993a, n. 29). Rosmini then concludes that "right consists in a 'eudaimonological faculty protected by the moral law" (Rosmini 1993a, n. 53).

Moreover, in this point, we can see how solidly founding rights on the objective idea of justice towards nature or human objective good does not imply in any way falling into a juridical rationalism that denies economic utility. In opposition, such utility is part of the intrinsic nature of rights, as far as it is jural economic utility, that is to say, utility protected by moral law, not taken as an abstract generalization – as in jural rationalism – but as a concrete universality, i.e. shared in the subject of right in question.

7.1.6 Rights as Personal Activities

Besides, this conception of rights implies that they must always be the result of the *personal* activity of the rights' holder. In effect, Rosmini says that there can be no rights as a result of merely material or physical activities. For a right to exist, the subject of right must be a person, endowed with intelligence and free will. Thus, Rosmini thinks it is not possible to speak of rights in the case of animals (Rosmini 1993a, n. 242). In this point, we can also notice the marked differences – we have already mentioned them – between Rosmini and the sensist-utilitarian conception of rights upon the basis of purely material acts or faculties, understood even as mere forces (Rosmini 1993a, n. 243). Unless those acts are related to the free and personal principle ruling all human nature, they cannot constitute a right. Therefore, although right may be accompanied by a material force that defends it (jural coercion), in Rosmini's view, right is in itself a moral entity that springs from the relationship between personal freedom and moral law (moral freedom), and consequently, it is the opposite of a force (Rosmini 1993a, n. 224). Indeed, the right over a faculty or good arises from a type of relationship with the personal principle in first act, which Rosmini will call "ownership." In his words, "ownership" should not be understood in the sense of external or economic ownership alone, but in the sense of any union of the free personal principle with a faculty, activity or good, so that it becomes of the subject's *own*, that is to say, "forms part of his *ownership* by natural law."

Anyhow, the Roveretan does not support an extreme personalism that would consider as rights only those actions or facts that are under the permanent and continuous performance of personal acts. As a matter of fact, Rosmini believes that "the personal, free activity of which we are speaking (. . .) is necessary as a constitutive element of right [but] does not always have to be in second act, as they say in the schools" (Rosmini 1993a, n. 245). Thus, this characteristic of union or *personal ownership* allows the person to enjoy his rights, even if they are not constantly exercised, as it grants him the power to "take up once more the exercise of his power over the activity as soon as the accidental circumstances impeding or suspending it had changed" (Rosmini 1993a, n. 245). Besides, if this power of personal exercise of a right does not exist in a more or less proximate potentiality, it may be said that the activity has ceased to be personal and, consequently, it can no longer constitute a right.

This would have a very relevant application in the field of economy, for those who, having ceased in the *exercise* of their personal and free acts, or having morally corrupted such exercise, still keep the rights over their economic freedom or ownership over their goods, provided these rights were constituted by means of a connatural or acquired union with the personal principle of moral freedom, which is the first foundation of right. However, we will also see how a right also perishes, once all union with the personal principle has ceased, either because of corruption or complete abandonment by the subject himself, or for other causes.

7.1.7 Rights and Duties

Finally, we must mention the essential difference Rosmini establishes between a merely "lawful" or "morally good" activity, and a right. Differently from what has been sustained by so many philosophers of right, Rosmini argues that right's dependence on the idea of justice requires that actions susceptible of rights be lawful and moral. I have no right to do wrong, as I have no right not to do the greatest possible moral good to others. But the moral prohibition not to do wrong, or the moral duty of doing well that every person has with relation to another person does not always constitute a right the latter may demand from the former. Likewise, the lawful actions or facts that may lead a person to his physical, intellectual or even moral improvement do not always constitute rights which other persons must respect jurally.

This is supported by Rosmini through two fundamental theses. The first one consists in affirming that rights are such not by themselves but because of "the duty others have to respect them," thus, "the idea of duty precedes that of right." The second thesis consists in the difference Rosmini makes between "jural duties" and "moral duties." While the former are the source of rights, the latter only imply an obligation for the ones who exert them, not a right for those to whom they are addressed. Further on, we will discuss the huge consequences of such a conception, especially when we come to the limitations to the claim of economic rights by individuals between themselves, as well as in their relationship with the State.

7.1.8 Derivation, Alteration, Modification and Modality of Rights

Upon the basis of all the aforementioned elements, which make up "the essence of right" (Rosmini 1993a, n. 318), Rosmini will establish the rules to follow when "applying the notion of right to different human activities in order to verify which activities acquire the moral dignity that makes them rights" (Rosmini 1993a, n. 321). Amongst the rules that Rosmini also calls rules of "derivation of rights," the main one, as we have seen, is that of ownership, by which every right is indeed the union of a faculty or a good to the "essential right," that is to say, the free personal principle, where such union acquires the dignity and inviolability of that same principle:

> Jurists use the word 'ownership' exactly, therefore, when they imply it to express 'the dominion that a person has over something.' This is ownership in the genuine meaning of the word which truly expresses 'the strict union of a thing with a person by means of which that thing is reserved totally and exclusively to the person as if it were part of him.' Mine does in fact express a part of 'self,' something that belongs to 'self.' But in this intimate connection, SELF, the person, does not and cannot lose personal dignity. (Rosmini 1993a, n. 339)

Thus, in order to determine if an activity is a right, it is necessary to determine if it has an ownership union with the personal principle of moral freedom. In that way, according to Rosmini, they will constitute rights as absolute and inviolable as the personal principle, in the first place, the very human nature of person – "the first, proper seat of *ownership*, if we consider human nature as pertaining to and subordinated to person, that is, as something *proper* to person" (Rosmini 1993b, n. 60), and upon the basis of it, all the so called "connatural" and "acquired" rights of the person amongst which we can find economic rights.

Besides, Rosmini adds two further rules which, as we will see, are important for our subject of discussion. For example, he mentions the rule of the distinction between "simple and complex rights" (Rosmini 1993a, n. 322–323). This rule demands that it be verified, in any activity, the complexity of other simple activities that the former may include, so that it is possible to determine which of these activities imply rights and which of them do not. This prevents that certain activity or complex action potentially containing unlawful actions within itself, or at least actions susceptible of not constituting true rights, be considered a right in a general manner. Another derivation rule is the "distinction between *complete* rights and rights *relative* to certain human beings" (Rosmini 1993a, n. 326–327), which prevents the generalization of rights which are not valid in general but with relation to certain persons.

Moreover, when dealing with the application or derivation of rights, Rosmini believes it is a key question to realize that although rights have their universal source in the personal dignity of human nature, "it is unjust and false to claim that person alone is the *principle of the derivation or determination of rights*" (Rosmini 1993a, n. 350).[9] We will see the importance of this in the economic debate in which rights

---

[9] "If it were true that people living on earth possessed only the essence of human nature, without any accidental additions, this principle might be useful in deducing the rights existing between living, human essences. But it is not true. In fact, we possess infinite particulars that do not form part of our human essence but which, nevertheless, serve as the basis of varying relationships between us, and of varying rights. In other words, the principle in question, when it considers us as naked essences devoid of all particulars, could at most lead us to hypothetical, abstract rights, but

easily derive from the simple human condition without taking into account their dependence on other conditions.

Apart from these derivation rules, Rosmini also claims the importance of considering the "alterations" rights may experience as such, like those derived from the transfer of rights to others through "contracts," "abandonment" or "succession." Likewise, rights also experience "modifications," either by virtue of "innocuous acts" on the part of others, which limit the exercise of a right but do not violate it, or because of "injurious acts," in the face of which the rights of "defense" and "satisfaction" arise.

Finally, Rosmini poses the fundamental question of the "modality" of rights:

> The expression "modality of rights," which I use in opposition to right, value or good of right, is defined precisely as "everything that can be done with or about a right without diminishing the good contained in it; this good must pertain inviolably to the subject or owner of the right and either remain equal or be increased." (Rosmini 1996, n. 2131)

The modality of rights includes acts such as commutative exchanges, where "a person's goods lose nothing of their value" since "the change is only in their modality" (Rosmini 1996, n. 1616), or the case "one person tries to save another from imminent harm by removing some good or right inferior to the damage to which he would otherwise be inevitably subject": there we "have a change in modality, not the subtraction of a right" (Rosmini 1996, n. 1616). The same happens, as we will see later on, when the political society is in charge of regulating the modality of the rights of its members, modifying the mode in which those rights are exercised without diminishing their value, with the aim of attaining a higher degree of common good. It should also be pointed out that, although the change in modality is indifferent for the one who possesses the right, it may not be indifferent for other persons. In such case, "the former has the obligation to permit the variation of the modality of his right, and others to whom this is of assistance have the right to demand it" (Rosmini 1996, n. 1617). This obligation to allow changes in the modality of rights, in Rosmini's view, does not arise as a consequence of the positive laws of the State but from natural law (Rosmini 1996, n. 1618).

7.1.9 *Morality as Limit and Fullness of Rights*

Another characteristic necessary to understand economy's jural bases in Rosmini is that of the essential function *morality* has as a means to temper and reconcile the exercise of rights. In fact, Rosmini rejects the extrinsic conception of right that reduces it to the consideration of external actions, or the jural acts or facts protected by a law sanctioned by a State. According to Rosmini, although rights have an external dimension, they are intimately linked to the subjective aspect of

---

not to true, real rights that bind people together. And it is these rights for which we are searching" (Rosmini 1993a, n. 346).

persons, who are the subjects of rights. Therefore, for the good exercise of rights, abidance by external acts does not suffice: it is essential that external acts are imbued with a strong internal morality. According to Rosmini, as far as morality is absent, the exercise of rights will inevitably be marked by stiff selfishness, which will eventually turn own rights into absolute rights, and lead to a struggle of everyone against everyone:

> We need more than knowledge of our rights if we are to learn to act as we should. We must at the same time be fully cognizant of the limits of our rights, and the way in which they are to be employed. Only morality teaches this (. . .) It is immediately obvious that there can be no mutual confidence, harmony, peace and collective security between individuals in society and its government and administration unless such extended, undetermined rights are given precise, determined limits by good faith, equity and goodness – in other words, by duty and moral virtues. The intervention of morality is absolutely necessary; its authoritative veto has to forbid various parties the use, or rather abuse, of their cold, coarse rights. (Rosmini 1996, n. 1617)

Upon the basis of this fundamental thesis, Rosmini rejects the idea of absolute use or exercise of our own rights, and dictates a maxim that should preside over any exercise of a right:

> Morality first establishes the supreme safeguard: "No one has the right to make bad use of his own right." It is not sufficient for individuals or even governments to vaunt a precautionary right as an excuse for doing what they please, without limit or supervision. Both individuals and government must always use their precautionary right "well, and as little as possible." Every unnecessary enactment or restriction entails overstepping one's limits; it is a real injustice and brings into being that summum jus which is indeed summa injuria. (Rosmini 1994b, n. 144)

Therefore, the exercise of rights demands to be completed and enriched by the exercise of moral virtues. Amongst them, the virtue of *reciprocity* is a key one. By virtue of it, "the limit of our right to use the means for our happiness is determined by the equal right of all others" (Rosmini 1994b, n. 223). However, to reciprocity, it should be added the permanent inclination to adequate external jural acts to the spirit of justice, and of *humanity*, *benignity* and even *charity*, which allow for the necessary self-sacrifice when, in cases of doubt, they oblige subjects "to renounce their own right generously and prefer not to offend others' right rather than exercise their own" (Rosmini 1994b, n. 146). Hence, "only virtue, that is, equity and benignity, can temper such a *summum jus*, and limit the unjust pretensions of subjects" (Rosmini 1994b, n. 146).

In sum, all these observations made by Rosmini show the limitation of the jural dimension, which occupies "the lowest place in the order of moral matters." So, given that "human nature, according to the great designs of the Creator, must be borne up to meritorious, generous and *perfect* matters, which occupy the highest places in the moral order," it is necessary that "what is *lawful*, such as rights, must whenever required give way to the cause of virtue and of the moral perfection of the world" (Rosmini 1993b, n. 1741).

7.2 The Right of Ownership

7.2.1 *Critique of the Individualist Arguments*

Having considered all these principles, we may now see more accurately how they apply, according to Rosmini, to the jural dimension of economy. Rosmini believes that the main joint articulating the jural dimension of economy is the right of ownership. As we have seen, to him ownership is the principle from which all rights are derived, because of their relationship with the principle of personal moral freedom, which is the first of all rights. However, on speaking of the right of acquired ownership, we are no longer referring to this general principle of derivation of rights, but to a specific right that arises from the connection between the person and external goods. In this sense, Rosmini also calls it "right of external ownership" to distinguish it from the right of ownership we possess over our own nature and its faculties, as we have already explained.

Now, Rosmini will develop his theory on the right of ownership, engaging in a controversy especially with utilitarians and socialists, and will attempt to reach a vision that takes into account the legitimate concerns in these two positions, but surpasses them in terms of Rosmini's personalist conception. Indeed, on the one hand, he makes the criticism of individualistic utilitarians, who – in his view – tend to conceive the right of ownership as "a force" "regulated by reason, in such a way that reason directs the operator to obtain *maximum satisfaction*" (Rosmini 1993b, n. 347), or utility, in such a way that our dominion extends to "all that reason finds to be an opportune means for reaching this end" (Rosmini 1993b, n. 414). In Rosmini's opinion, although this stand sees the right of ownership as a natural right, it conceives it as a right "not determined by sound reason but by desire and capacity. Consequently, the individual, considered under the rule of nature alone, lawfully desires whatever he judges useful for himself, either on the basis of sound reasoning or as a result of stimulus from his desires" (Rosmini 1993b, n. 416). Another argument of individualist utilitarianism is that which sustains that the right of ownership is based on the capacity of occupancy of a good, this capacity extending to "what is necessary for the preservation of their lives" (Rosmini 1993b, n. 476), or to "everything an individual is capable of defending" (Rosmini 1993b, n. 478). According to Rosmini these two arguments are absurd because, if being followed, "no one can prevent an individual (. . .) from desiring the whole world if he believes its possession to be useful for his own perfection" (Rosmini 1993b, n. 418). Thus, "affirming that human beings have the forces needed to use things proves nothing relative to right" (Rosmini 1993b, n. 434).

A third argument of individualist utilitarianism is that by Locke, who maintains that the right of ownership is the result of the "principle of corporal labor," based on the idea that "because a person's labour on a thing makes the thing the work of that person's hands, the thing therefore is the person's property" (Rosmini 1993b, n. 365). According to Rosmini "this is a contrived solution. First of all, not all labor on a thing makes the thing the property of the laborer" (Rosmini 1993b, n. 336).

Besides, "accepting labor as the universal source of the right of ownership means failing to see that the essence of right is moral, and that its moral essence is found solely in a corresponding jural duty" (Rosmini 1993b, n. 368). In fact, according to Rosmini, founding the right of ownership on labor, only takes into consideration a physical-psychological fact, but fails to go deep into the moral essence of said right.

7.2.2 *Refutation of the Social Foundation of the Right of Ownership*

Rosmini also criticizes the theses by authors such as Blackstone, Bentham, Kant or Genovesi, who maintain that the right of ownership is based either on a mandatory *reciprocity* of respect for others' ownership so that our ownership is also respected, on *social consensus* – by which we collectively agree to establish said right – or on a *force of social coercion* applied with a view to some kind of "social utility." In any case, these authors have in common the fact that they "do not recognize rights to ownership outside civil society" (Rosmini 1993b, n. 351).

According to Rosmini, such arguments lack solidity, in the first place, because "early human beings lived for a long time in a state of domestic society," that is to say, in pre-political societies, but it is evident that the right of ownership existed amongst them. Besides, it is also evident that "if ownership did not exist and could not exist before civil society, the founders themselves, before establishing civil society, did not own anything. Therefore, how could they have made laws without an arbitrary decision about something to which they themselves had no right?" (Rosmini 1993b, n. 333). Thus, although it is true that the principle of reciprocity is "necessary to give binding force to the duty of respecting others' ownership" (Rosmini 1993b, n. 355), it would be ineffective "if those amongst whom we lived lacked all feeling of justice and were always intent on doing us harm" (Rosmini 1993b, n. 355).

Besides "it may be objected that the law of ownership was established by the consent of all in the civil society." In the first place, because "it is impossible to explain how present consent could bind future consent" (Rosmini 1993b, n. 355); in the second place, because both tacit and explicit consent are absurd since "a large of the section of the human race has never reflected on the extent of the law of ownership, and has not made any internal judgment on its utility. People have simply adapted to the fact and submitted to circumstances as they found them." Moreover, "in this system, where the justice of ownership depends not on ownership itself, but on the common consent of those who judge it useful for themselves, theft would be a protest against this so-called unanimous consent" (Rosmini 1993b, n. 339). Moreover, to found ownership on society's coercive power is unsustainable because "we have seen that right is a moral, not a physical power" (Rosmini 1993b, n. 349).

Finally, Rosmini rejects the solutions to the question of ownership provided by "Saint-Simonists, Chartists, Communists" and other socialist utilitarians, who found the right of ownership on "arithmetic equality, merit or need" (Rosmini 1993b, n. 430). Rosmini criticizes the purely ideological conception of ownership of these "ultra radicals", which fully ignores its historical and factual dimension, because "presupposing that for a thing to be mine, it is sufficient that I judge on the basis of certain speculative reasons that it belongs to me" would imply that "I do not need to take possession of it, nor is it relevant that others have already done so" (Rosmini 1993b, n. 431). According to Rosmini, instead, "the human race has never understood the word 'ownership' in this manner" (Rosmini 1993b, n. 432). In fact, if an attempt were made to distribute ownership in "arithmetically equal parts," "it is clear that if substances are divided in this way, some people will have plenty and others insufficient" (Rosmini 1993b, n. 442). Besides, "it would be absurd to imagine that the whole of mankind should divide all available substances," because "if responsibility is given to a few, will they be judged by the multitude in cases of injustice? In this case, the whole of mankind would again have to intervene either as distributors or as judges of the distribution" (Rosmini 1993b, n. 443), something which is evidently absurd.

Moreover, "similar comments may be made about the other system which would share out substances according to merit," to which we should add the additional difficulty to "search for a human tribunal capable of infallibly judging true merit" and even in the case such thing were possible, it could not be the foundation of stable ownership since "the merit of each person ebbs and flows from moment to moment." He also points out that "if merit can claim what is available, demerit (which is something over and above merit) requires deprivation of what is available," the consequence of this being that "a good number of people are going to die of hunger" (Rosmini 1993b, n. 444). In the same sense, Rosmini criticizes the socialist argument of needs: "saying that human beings need to use things (. . .) proves nothing. Having a need for things does not form a right" (Rosmini 1993b, n. 435). Besides, "there would be no one to judge the needs of individuals" and "each person would claim, with apparent reason, that he should measure his own needs," which would result in the fact that "agreement in these cases would be impossible." To this it should be added the evident fact that "needs are of many kinds" and "are also subject to continual, rapid change," which would mean that "strife and war would be necessary because of every possibility of discussion would be impossible" (Rosmini 1993b, n. 445–446). Hence, Rosmini concludes that all these conceptions of ownership "are *gratuitous* relative to their first fundamental propositions and *impossible* relative to their execution" (Rosmini 1993b, n. 447). Let's see now the solution Rosmini himself gives to the question.

7.2.3 The Personalist Conception of the Right of Ownership

As we have just seen, Rosmini criticizes the various utilitarian conceptions of the right of ownership; however, he does not reject all elements present in them but inserts such elements within his personalist and ethical conception of Right.

To him, the mistake made by individualist utilitarians was that of founding the right of ownership on the fact of pure utility, occupancy or labor of a subjective nature, without any relationship whatsoever with moral opening to others; social utilitiarians, on their part, made the mistake of founding it on the abstract idea of objective utility, need or merit, collectively determined without any relationship with each person's subjective dimension. In spite of the divergence in this respect, both conceptions agree in detaching the right of ownership from the unity of person's physical, spiritual, eudaimonological and moral elements which, as we have seen, grant said right its jural nature. Consequently, following the path of either individualist subjectivism or social objectivism, the right of ownership is reduced to a mere utilitarian relationship. According to Rosmini, in both cases the result will be no other than the violation of the true right of ownership, the instauration of a basic injustice in economic relationships, and the injury and degrading of the human person.

Rosmini will attempt to find a way out of this utilitarian conception of ownership by re-integrating the elements of utility, occupancy, labor, need or merit, which utilitarianism disaggregates. He will incorporate them around the idea of the "juncture of goods with person," upon which ownership is based. In effect, since Rosmini claims that ownership is the result of the juncture of some goods not with a mere individual but with person, this relationship will be threefold: "physical," "intellectual" and "moral." None of these three dimensions can be neglected. Indeed, upon them, Rosmini will demonstrate how the right of ownership itself determines not only the just space for each person's economic self-accomplishment but also the limits to it that result from the physically and intellectually limited nature of the human being, as well as from the necessary moral relationship between a person's economic self-accomplishment and the respect for the self-accomplishment of others. In a few words, the right of ownership is neither individualistic nor socialist: it is personal, interpersonal and social at the same time.

As a matter of fact, in the first place, the right of ownership implies utility understood as the actual possibility of a "physical juncture" of person with some external goods, that is to say, "a real relationship of utility between something and a person." On this point, Rosmini agrees with utilititarians in that for the right of ownership to exist, the first requirement is that something be "physically" suitable for some kind of use by the person. However, said utility is not a purely physical relationship with the thing, but implies an "intellectual juncture" with it: "an act of intelligence with which the thing is mentally conceived and conceived as good for oneself" (Rosmini 1993b, n. 386). Finally, it also implies a "moral juncture" that springs precisely from an "act of will which uprightly desires the thing," that is to say, it honestly evaluates whether the thing is going to be useful or not, so that "if the thing were altogether useless to us, we could not acquire a right to it as a result of what has been said" (Rosmini 1993b, n. 389).

The second requirement for the right of ownership to exist is to "take possession of the thing", that is, to occupy it. This is an extremely important question since, according to Rosmini, occupancy is the foundational (though not sufficient) fact of the right of ownership. Without physical occupancy there can be no possession and, therefore, no ownership. Here the first factual limit to ownership appears as occupancy by others: "the thing in question is, therefore, not yet open to occupancy" (Rosmini 1993b, n. 474). Then, the socialist error that attempts to ignore the fact of prior occupancy as an essential factor to take into account in order to establish ownership – although not all prior occupancy is necessarily just. Occupancy to be really such from the factual point of view also implies that "the thing [is] taken and retained with one's own *real* forces" (Rosmini 1993b, n. 385). This means that it is not enough to "territorially" occupy things or to be "capable of defending" them: it is necessary to have "the power to administer or turn them to some advantage" (Rosmini 1993b, n. 469). It is clear that it does not concern the original utility of a thing we mentioned above, but the utility we may derive from it through *labor*.

Here, Rosmini adheres to the conception that puts labor as the source of ownership, but denies ownership an unconditional and absolute nature by placing it within a limited context. In fact, "neither *effort* nor *expense* constitutes the matter of the right to occupancy, but 'the effort involved in its use.' Mere effort or heedless expense which is not directed to utility has no power to bind anything to a person in such a way as to make it the person's own" (Rosmini 1993b, n. 492). Thus, Rosmini will consider as grounds for occupancy of a good only certain kinds of work. In this sense, he points to labor that is "preparatory," "productive," that "uses or consumes," that is "formative or inventive" (Rosmini 1993b, n. 494), which either immediately or in a certain future may make said good give some utility. There will be no true capacity of occupancy if labor is just "simple hope" (Rosmini 1993b, n. 472). Thus, labor required to attain "jural occupancy" evidently implies not only physical or material force but an intellectual and moral act that "moves real forces for the purpose of taking possession for the sake of occupancy" (Rosmini 1993a, n. 388).

7.2.4 *Limits to the Right of Ownership*

In Rosmini's words, the concept of ownership is certainly based on the *fact* of appropriation: "*appropriation* consists in the act with which the *person* makes things part of himself, in his feeling and persuasion." Consequently, "we should not be surprised if *ownership* shares in the very characteristics of person." Such characteristics are "exclusiveness," "perpetuity," "unity," "simplicity" and "unlimitedness" (Rosmini 1993b, n. 946–952). Now, Rosmini makes it clear that these characteristics belong to "ownership in fact" but not to "ownership by right." This is a fundamental distinction since, precisely by neglecting it, many authors "maintain that the human being can do what he likes with what is his: he can abuse it, prevent others' from using it harmlessly, destroy it without any motive other than caprice, make it harmful to others and even to himself. It is certainly true that person has the physical faculty to do this (...) But this, according to me, is only the *fact* of ownership, not the *right*" (Rosmini 1993b, n. 953).

Being Rosmini's conception of the human being not *individualistic* but *personalist,* for him the right of ownership can never be that of "the isolated individual who appropriates things without regard for his fellow human beings," but of the person who "coexists with other human beings to whom he is related through his intelligence and moral status" (Rosmini 1993b, n. 879). In this way, the right of ownership as subordinated to the idea of justice and to objective moral law, implies, from its origin, transcendence with regard to the subject of right and *includes others*. So, the right of ownership is exclusive but non-excluding:

> When [he] makes things his own, therefore, he has to take others into consideration. Mere caprice can no longer provide a good foundation for the right of ownership. (Rosmini 1993b, n. 879)

Hence, Rosmini harshly criticizes those who "go on to propose the crudest and most inexorable right of ownership which they declare lawful even while admitting its essentially immoral character" (Rosmini 1993b, n. 908).[10] Yet, this unlimited conception of the right of ownership based on an individualism that alienates person from its essential relationship with others disappears when these relationships are again considered as an essential dimension of person:

> Ownership which remains intact even when detrimental to other people can be derived only from the suppression of intellectual and moral relationships between the individual to whom ownership is attributed and his fellows. Ownership of this kind can only be understood without reference to these relationships. It vanishes, considered as right, when the relationships emanating from human nature are reinstated as part of the calculation from which they had been unlawfully excluded. (Rosmini 1993b, n. 909)

From this, it follows that "the right of ownership is one;" it is a *relative* and *complex* right with multiple "*modes*, actions, applications, *functions*." So, Rosmini says: "The subject, one and simple as it is, produces ownership as a unique, 'almost compact' thing. When ownership is then considered in relationship with other people, it is multiplied and transformed into as many different rights as there are special relationships with these people" (Rosmini 1993b, n. 970). In his view, from this relative and manifold nature of the right of ownership, there arise the *limits* to the right of ownership:

> According to this rational Right, therefore, limits are placed to private ownership. (...) First it is limited when there is a right to exercise some, but not all the acts of ownership; second, it is limited when the right to exercise acts of ownership is relative to some persons, but not to others. (Rosmini 1993b, n. 934–935)

In the first place, we have the limit of the act of *acquisition* of ownership, which is only jurally valid if it takes place as a consequence of "morally free or lawful

---

[10]To Rosmini, individualists who support an absolute and unlimited dominion over property are also unaware of the moral problem affecting the human being with regard to economic goods – with which we have dealt in the former chapter – by which "personship delights in its dominion over things not for the benefit and justice accruing from dominion, but solely for the sake of naked dominion and the pleasure of feeling its own superiority" (Rosmini 1993b, n. 877).

actions" (Rosmini 1993b, n. 314), that is, when there exists a "relative freedom of action" over a good, made possible by the fact that the good is not already jurally occupied by others. Obviously, all occupancy or acquisition is limited by this right of freedom towards the thing, which is always *relative* to its state of occupancy regarding others.

In the second place, although a good may be jurally occupied, according to Rosmini, the right of ownership is limited in time and subjected to numerous conditions. For example, there is a limitation arising from the utility of the good so that "it seems clear that if an object becomes evidently and perpetually useless to me and mine, rational Right requires that it be considered no longer as occupied by me, but free" (Rosmini 1993b, n. 869). The immediate consequence is that such good is then considered unoccupied and open to jural occupancy by others. In these cases, Rosmini admits the possibility of adverse possession or prescription provided the new occupier is not moved by exclusive zeal for his pure right alone but, following the principle of moral moderation of rights we have previously referred to, due moral consideration is shown for the former occupier:

> This object could therefore be occupied by another provided that the new occupier shows the necessary moral regard due to the person who wrongly wishes to continue his occupation. In other words, the new owner must provide a clear explanation of what he is doing so that the other person does not suffer reasonable displeasure. (…) It could even be removed from the unreasonable occupier by force if he tried to retain it by force. (Rosmini 1993b, n. 870)

In the third place, in the event of a "temporary non-use of anything," it would not be right "to conclude that its owner has no intention of ever using it again." In fact, it cannot be admitted that "another person's ownership be disturbed if he makes little use of what he owns and draws less benefit from it than he could" since "an owner has to be granted full power of decision about the quantity and quality of the use of the things he owns, provided that he makes some use of them" (Rosmini 1993b, n. 883). Nevertheless, according to Rosmini, "lack of understanding, power or will in the use of some given thing authorizes others to complain to the owner, according to rational Right, if they suffer harm from the privation of some good that might accrue to all from better use of the thing." Moreover, others "may come to some agreement with him about better use of what he owns, even put pressure on him with due moderation if he evades the agreement, and resultant harm is serious, evident and common" (Rosmini 1993b, n. 884). Therefore, it is evident that the very productive use required by the right of ownership involves others who do not share in the right of ownership over the good but have a right not to be deprived of the potential advantages the use of said good might bring to them. This is the foundation of natural Right that allows appealing to a proprietor in favor of "the public, or even of private good," and making "laws with which civil society places wastrels under supervision" (Rosmini 1993b, n. 885). In this sense, the jural obligation of putting at stake a good of one's own through productive investment as required by the right of ownership prevents said right from becoming an individual's protective shield and turns it, instead, in a vehicle for personal donation to his fellows.

In the fourth place, Rosmini also points to another limit to the right of ownership consisting in what he calls the possibility of "innocuous use" by others. Thus, "occupancy does not completely destroy in other people the faculty for an *innocuous* use of the things taken possession of." This innocuous use must be understood in its strict sense, that is to say, "the use made of the thing must be incapable of causing any reasonable trouble to the owner. It must not cause him the least discomfort nor take from him the least amount of present or future advantage, use or pleasure that he can have from what he owns" (Rosmini 1993b, n. 498–499). Besides, said use should be agreed on with the owner, who has the right to refuse only in case he has reasons to show that such use would be harmful for him (Rosmini 1993b, n. 505–506).

Even beyond the previous cases, there also exist limitations to the right of ownership that arise from its relationship with other rights. As an example, Rosmini mentions limitations to the right of ownership with regard to jural freedom – which we will consider next – as well as the limitations relative to the right to defense and to an unavoidable necessity concerning the common good of the civil or political society – which will be dealt with as we refer to Rosminian economic policy. Likewise, there are those imposed on private ownership on account of the right of self-preservation, in which case Rosmini maintains that the owner has "the *jural* obligation to allow others to use what is his when this is necessary for the preservation of their existence, provided it is not necessary for his own existence" (Rosmini 1993b, n. 879). Below, we will also see how Rosmini funds his social assistance policy on this last principle.

In the fifth place, even in the absence of strictly jural duties as the ones already mentioned, "private ownership must observe certain responsibilities of equity and benevolence towards others if it is to be just and moral" (Rosmini 1993b, n. 934). In other words, there exists on the part of the owner the moral duty to exercise his just right taking into consideration his ethical obligations with respect to persons, be them either individuals or collective bodies.

In this sense, we could say that the right of ownership means in Rosmini a solid and quite stable exclusive dominion by the person, but the very person is always obliged to legitimate, enlarge and publicize said dominion beyond the strictly individual sphere because of its essential limitation and its relationship with others. Any good whatsoever which cannot be *jurally* occupied – that is to say, occupied on the abovementioned conditions – opens up the way to the right of other people to dispose of its use. Additionally, it is always implicit a *universal* disposal even in the jural use of ownership, where the other is ever present in some way or another. Probably because of this, Rosmini's conception of the right of ownership does not require much amendment on account of his social philosophy since it seems to contain many of the great principles to be considered below, when dealing with the social question.

7.3 Economic Freedom

7.3.1 *Characteristics*

In Rosmini's way of thinking, the second axis on which the jural dimension of economy is built is the concept of jural economic freedom. In effect, the dynamics of economic relations presupposes not only the possibility of ownership over things – there could be no productive use without it – but the possibility of freely performing the acts allowing such use. The exercise of freedom is, in the first place, the act that allows us to develop our capabilities and makes the fact of ownership possible. Therefore, the development of freedom is essential to take the first steps in any economic life, which lies in access to ownership:

> It is clear that by exercising our freedom we both develop our powers and create external ownership for ourselves. (Rosmini 1993b, n. 302)

Moreover, it is also by virtue of freedom that we can turn ownership productive by means of acts of actual occupancy of the goods, which imply labor capacity to derive profit from what is owned. Without economic freedom, the right of ownership turns ownership into something sterile:

> This ownership is then pervaded by freedom, because, as we said, ownership is only a kind of extra instrument acquired by persons, in order to operate according to their ends. (Rosmini 1993b, n. 302)

However, thanks to the right of ownership, the exercise of personal freedom is also made possible. Although personal freedom is a principle inherent to the nucleus of person and is the fundamental right from which all the other rights derive, if ownership did not exist, freedom would have no room to exert its actions. In this sense, "the idea of *ownership* essentially embraces and contains that of *freedom* (of free use)" (Rosmini 1993a, n. 340).

So, in Rosmini's economic philosophy, freedom is understood as a co-principle that is completed and fed-back by ownership, this allowing jurally just and economically productive development within economic relationships. Whenever freedom is not sufficiently developed, there is no capacity to acquire property, the latter remaining always in the same hands. At the same time, without freedom, it is not possible to attain full productivity from what is owned, since there is neither enough labor capacity on the part of the owner, nor any need for improvement, which appears in the presence of free competition from others. Thus, according to Rosmini, an economy very much centered on the defense of ownership but neglectful of the development of freedom tends to be static, scarcely productive, and unjustly distributed. Freedom is the dynamic element in economy that makes ownership circulate, be produced and be distributed.

Now, Rosmini's conception of economic freedom must be carefully analyzed to avoid inaccurate appreciations. In the same way he distinguishes between the *fact* and the *right of ownership*, similarly, when Rosmini advocates economic freedom, he is referring not to a simple factual freedom but to what he calls "jural freedom," that is not a simple useful freedom but a freedom based on justice:

> The question of free trade has scarcely been considered under this aspect of justice, although it is the principal point of view from which it should be examined if indeed it is true that justice precedes every other question and interest. (Rosmini 1993b, n. 1676)

Thus, Rosmini shows several differences between the idea of freedom in general and freedom as an economic right. In the first place, jural economic freedom differs from "pure, simply personal freedom" because the latter "cannot by its very nature be increased or diminished. It does not have *quantity*; it is a *quality*, an essence (. . .)" (Rosmini 1993b, n. 299).[11] On the contrary, jural economic freedom or economic freedom as right is not personal freedom itself but only a "sphere in which *personal* freedom can act" (Rosmini 1993b, n. 300). In this sense, such sphere is not pure and absolute but "can certainly be extended and diminished" (Rosmini 1993b, n. 300). In other words, economic freedom is not an absolute or connatural right that springs from the very nature of person, but a *relative acquired right* deriving from a certain type of actions the person must perform in certain conditions and within certain limits in order to possess it. The first general condition for economic freedom to become a right is that its exercise "does not harm the rights of others" (Rosmini 1993b, n. 304). But, what type of actions are those which allow the fulfillment of this first general condition that turns economic freedom into a true jural freedom? Moreover, what type of limits does this freedom have?

Rosmini establishes two essential conditions for jural economic freedom to exist. The first of them is that there should be no prior occupancy of the goods intended for use, consumption or enjoyment: "nor can we perform actions which disturb or obstruct the rights they have taken possession of" (Rosmini 1993b, n. 305). If prior occupancy does not exist or is only partial, there would be – in principle – jural economic freedom to compete for the occupancy of such good.

As regards the second condition, "the only acquired rights to be classified amongst rights of freedom are those which come into being through the abilities and skills we learn with the use of our powers. (. . .) All other human beings must respect activity which has increased in this way" (Rosmini 1993b, n. 304). In other words, the second condition for economic freedom to be jural is that it should be the result of greater talent, harder work and higher skills, that is, of comparatively greater competitiveness to occupy a formerly non-occupied good:

> The natural right of a craftsman extends only to the possibility of depriving competitors of their earnings by means of the superiority of his own output and marketing. Such excellence provides him with the lawful fact enabling him to occupy available earnings before anyone else. No one has any cause for complaint against him because every person is master of

---

[11] Rosmini also distinguishes the concept of "jural freedom" from that of "natural freedom:" "La naturale libertà può considerarsi siccome una general potenza di fare ciò che si vuole, senza coazione e necessità. La quale potenza si risolve in facoltà, funzioni, ed atti speciali che considerati in relazione alla legge etica che li tutela, prendono natura e nome di diritti: diritti naturali, civili, politici" (Rosmini 1978c, 96).

> what his ability enables him to occupy before others. (. . .) This explains why a government which makes some means of income exclusive to a person or family is usually the object of animosity. The people's good sense wants to know why the freedom of many craftsmen should be restricted for the sake of a single worker who might be worthy of the privilege but would have had no need of it if his own predominance had enabled him to capture business from others. (Rosmini 1993b, n. 1675)

7.3.2 The Limits to Economic Freedom

Rosmini is undoubtedly a supporter of market economic freedom not only as the most efficient means to reach the highest productivity and the best distribution of property in the economy but as a natural right of the ones who demonstrate the capacity to reach those goals better than others. Now, what would happen if a great part of economic agents who are part of a market economy have the said capabilities, talent and hard work to exercise this economic freedom whereas others are partially or completely lacking these qualities?

In that sense, according to Rosmini, the right to economic freedom should be analyzed under the light of the problem of ignorance, lack of education or "incomplete information" that most people involved in a market economy suffer. Indeed, "the quantity of right (that is, jural freedom) is equal to the amount of knowledge we have of the *consequences of our actions*" and since "none of us can claim to know all the consequences of our actions," then "absolutely speaking, no one has full and absolute jural freedom" (Rosmini 1993b, n. 660–661). Thus, "according to natural right, human beings are mutually free only in so far as we have an approximately equal amount of knowledge and of foresight of the consequences of our actions, or at least in so far as we must *presume* these equality of knowledge of consequences in each other (unless the opposite is evident)" (Rosmini 1993b, n. 665). Certainly, "generally speaking, we must judge that we all have equal knowledge of the consequences of our actions," a presumption on which civil laws must be based (Rosmini 1993b, n. 667–668). However, "the equality of knowledge of the consequences of our actions cannot always be supposed," and civil laws must take into account exceptions, such those who are incapable of "*sufficiently* maintain our individual self, our freedom, family and external property, and acquire what is necessary for our own and our family's preservation" (Rosmini 1993b, n. 668).

Consequently, in certain cases, the need arises to "allow ourselves to be guided by those who see and weigh the consequences carefully" (Rosmini 1993b, n. 679), that is to say, although "in natural right each of us is the competent judge of our own evil and good" it is possible "an appeal against a competent judge is possible when there is moral certainty" (Rosmini 1993b, n. 713). According to Rosmini, when in society predominates "malice, ignorance or incompetence, others are going to act without regard for their rights, which they put at risk" (Rosmini 1993b, n. 306).

> Under these circumstances, not knowing how to use our freedom competently, we cannot use it to the full extent to which we would otherwise have a right. (Rosmini 1993b, n. 308)

In this case, economic freedom clashes with the "right to defense and security." In such cases, "removing material freedom in the case under discussion does no harm to our subject; this freedom ceases to be his of right;" however, "in no case are we concerned with unlimited coercion, or any kind of violence which may do initial harm to others under the pretext of doing them good afterwards" (Rosmini 1993b, n. 307). Besides, such limit to freedom imposed by ignorance may only occur in case of actual harm, but not in the event the consequences of a free action are "simply a lack of an unnecessary good" (Rosmini 1993b, n. 714). This "feeling of the *need of defense* explains the varying rigor and strictness of State laws. It also explains different forms of government or political constitutions of varying benignity, which allow their citizens various degrees of exercise of freedom" (Rosmini 1993b, n. 310).

In this sense, for Rosmini, market freedom cannot be supported or opposed in the abstract or by means of pure utility argumentations, but requires that an economic policy informed by a jural sense determines what must be done in each case, taking into account both the characteristics and the limits of jural economic freedom. Likewise, as in any other right, just exercise of economic freedom always demands a strong dose of morality by which "in certain circumstances individuals have to sacrifice a small part of their natural rights for the sake of peace and mutual respect" (Rosmini 1993b, n. 731).

7.4 Market Relationships Under the Light of Ownership and Freedom Rights

7.4.1 Contracts

Upon the basis of this personalist reformulation of the right of ownership and jural economic freedom, Rosmini will develop his conception of interpersonal economic relationships within the framework of Right through his theory of contracts.

> When I free something of my own free in favor of someone else who, under certain conditions or without conditions, accepts and takes it immediately as his own; this is called "contract." (Rosmini 1993b, n. 1045)

Now, he will construe the contractual relationships that lie under economic relationships, especially those of a commutative nature between individuals within a market, in the light of his personalist theses and in opposition to utilitarianism. In fact, contracts do not express a mere "negative relationship with our fellows," which would consist in their "duty not to encroach on the sphere of our acquired rights," but reveal "the moral need to understand each other's rights" (Rosmini 1993b, n. 1053–1054). Contracts ruling a market relationship are not, thus, the outcome of a mere clash of interests or of the State's legal coercion, as utilitarians and positivists maintain. Instead, they are the result of "the moral-jural law written on the hearts of us all," which leads us to make peaceful agreements through personal mutual consent in order to solve our disputes (Rosmini 1993b, n. 1054).

Therefore, for contracts to be jurally effective, it is not sufficient for them to be "useful" and "lawful;" they must be made upon the basis of a type of consent between the parties which, according to Rosmini, must fulfill the following conditions: (1) "concern a thing capable of being the matter of a contract," so "no action that is substantially and without exception evil can be the object of a contract" (Rosmini 1993b, n. 1115); (2) "be given by persons jurally able to give it" since "no one can give valid consent unless he is able to use his understanding and free will" (Rosmini 1993b, n. 1119), consequently "some are capable of giving their consent in simple matters but not in more complex matters" (Rosmini 1993b, n. 1121); (3) "not be produced by an injustice of one contracting party to the other," and (4) "be expressed in such a way that it must and can be considered a true, certain consent" (Rosmini 1993b, n. 1112).

7.4.2 Just Price and Market Price

Rosmini deals with the application of these theses on contracts in the field of interpersonal economic relationships in his theory of sales contract and just price. In this point, he evidently recovers all the great medieval Greco-roman tradition and that of the Spanish scholasticism, and incorporates it as a key factor in the jural nucleus of economy, while bringing it into play in his debate with the jural and economic utilitarianism of his time. According to Rosmini, exchange relationships within the market are the most common cases of "commutative contracts." In fact, a sales contract "presupposes and requires equality between what is given and what is received, between the thing sold and its price. When this equality is present, the price of the thing is said to be just" (Rosmini 1993b, n. 1212).

Rosmini describes the formation of a just price as a process of rational, free debate, where the key lies in the possibility of "persuading the other to accept his estimation of the just price," and since "no norm exists to establish the just price for the thing, both parties are able to range between two extreme just prices" and "within this range they finally find a price they agree to, a price which can vary between the lowest and the highest" (Rosmini 1993b, n. 1214). Now, Rosmini will refute those who relieve that said freedom in the determination of a just price thwarts the possibility of establishing a just price.

> It is true that some deny the existence of a just price, because, in their opinion, a just price cannot be rigorously determined. (Rosmini 1993b, n. 1215)

However, such freedom is not of an absolute nature since the just price is not any price at which a thing may be sold, but one that "oscillates between two extremes, outside of which we can certainly declare the price is unjust" (Rosmini 1993b, n. 1216). Nevertheless, as his scholastic predecessors said, this jural-moral dimension of price does not imply a moralist conception of market relationships but an integration of quantitative relationships with ethic-jural relationships in the formation of prices. Indeed, after Spanish scholasticism, Rosmini considers that price certainly results from clear quantitative elements such as "the quantity of goods being traded in a particular city, province or region," the "quantity of money in circulation" and "the desire for goods, which in varying degrees hill be stronger than the affection for money" (Rosmini 1993b, n. 1218). These elements are combined through the competition process where "vendors therefore by reducing their prices compete for customers" until "the reduction however finally reaches a limit (. . .) determined by a relation of equality between the saleable quantity of goods and the quantity of desire purchasers have for it," as "the vendors have no reason for reducing the price below this limit because, once this price is arrived at, they are able to sell all their saleable merchandise" and, on the other hand, "if one of them wanted to keep a higher price, he would alienate the buyers and be left with his goods unsold." Therefore, "a uniform price emerges, called the *current* price, which is the *just price*" (Rosmini 1993b, n. 1221).

As we can see, Rosmini seems to draw a parallelism between market price and just price. However, what would happen if the market formed extremely high or extremely low prices? Could we call these prices also just prices?

7.4.3 Beyond the Equivalence Principle

According to Rosmini, the "just price" is equivalent to "market price," so long the latter is formed "within jural and ethical limits." In fact, to the Roveretan, there exist different circumstances when prices resulting from the merely factual exchange between buyers and sellers are unjust. For instance, a price that is high in relation to the current price would be unjust in the event of "the monopoly or some other action depended upon fraud or violence" (Rosmini 1993b, n. 1229). In the latter case, fraud would affect not only the seller but the buyer: although the latter is "rarely forced to buy because of necessity, his passions and the clever seductions of others lead him to buy" (Rosmini 1993b, n. 1244).

> The excess above the just price comes about: one of the parties has the chance of a better bargain because of the competition possible at the time, but he is made to accept (or does so because he is foolish or deceived) a worst bargain. He does this either by selling to someone who offers too little or by buying from someone who demands too much compared with the price which the wills of the other buyers would have determined. Hence, legalists correctly apply to cases of injury the dictum: "Consent given to someone mistaken or deceived is null and void" and Roman laws call the injury "fraud in the act itself". (Rosmini 1993b, n. 1249–1250)

Moreover, it would also be unjust if "the price of the goods [were] so high that it exceeded the balance between all the goods and all the existing wealth" so that "a quantity of useless, unsold merchandise would be left" (Rosmini 1993b, n. 1232). Another case of unjust price would occur when "the price increase did not reach this balance but was high enough to leave some goods unsold because few people had sufficient resources to buy them" (Rosmini 1993b, n. 1233). Besides, "if a price in a private sale is excessively low, an obvious injury is done because it is not known whether it was determined by all the buyers available at the time, o rather by the greed of one of them, who by his purchase profited from the simplicity or shame of the needy" (Rosmini 1993b, n. 1245).

Finally, a price higher than the current one would also be unjust in the event "the owners' capricious refusal to sell necessary goods meant that people would die of hunger:" (Rosmini 1993b, n. 1231) this would be against the right of self-preservation, which is above any other right. A similar injustice would take place in case an extreme price resulted either from excessive consumption or excessive saving on the part of the more wealthy that would deprive the poorer ones of the goods essential for life:

> Moreover, the law of humanity and of charity would oblige a dealer not to sell the rich more than they needed. In this way, goods necessary for the existence of other human beings would not be uselessly removed either by excessive consumption on the part of the rich or by an excessive fear of future needs which could persuade the rich to lay up a superfluous quantity of goods. The injury to right resulting from this failure to case for humanity would depend more on the rich who had removed goods necessary for others but superfluous to their own needs. (Rosmini 1993b, n. 1236)

For this reason, Rosmini believes that, for the formation of just prices, it is essential that markets have certain general characteristics: they should involve the greatest possible number of competitors,[12] they should be as stable in time as possible, and they should be as transparent as possible (Rosmini 1993b, n. 1245). To this general conditions, which most economists share with reference to the idea of an efficient market, Rosmini adds the need of a civil law capable of regulating cases of possible injury, such as the aforementioned ones, which might occur "in the case of private sales arising from the great needs of sellers and buyers" (Rosmini 1993b, n. 1244).

Besides, the exercise of equity in the fulfillment of contracts is fundamental for attaining a just price and for the existence of morally acceptable markets:

> A commutative agreement or contract is just if the agreed price is just. But an unforeseen accident which puts the price beyond just limits can occur between the formation of the contract and its complete execution by both parties. (Rosmini 1993b, n. 1253)

In fact, "although a contract may be formed on a sound basis, unforeseen accidents can be such that its execution would be impossible without harm to the rational laws which govern just contracts" (Rosmini 1993b, n. 1203). In this case equity will consist in modifying the terms of the contract in the event it is susceptible of amendment:

> Equity modifies the execution of contracts when, because of some accident, their strict execution would deviate from natural justice and, more properly speaking, from

[12] "Reduction in the number of contracting parties leaves the price more undetermined and open to fluctuation" (Rosmini 1993b, n. 1242).

> commutative justice (...) We see therefore how the law of equality between giving and possessing in commutative contracts is that which forms the natural justice of these contracts (...) We see how equity must be applied to restore and strengthen the lost balance whenever equality is upset by some accident independent of the acts of the contracting parties. (Rosmini 1993b, 1209–1211)

In fact "the thing sold must be paid for at the just price current when the contract was made. If in the meantime the just price has been altered, there would be no occasion for exercising equity." On the contrary, equity must be exercised "1) if the means used for calculating the price at the moment of the contract were still valid, but the present value of the article were now known to be different from its earlier value; 2) if the article were to suffer some unforeseen and uncalculated modification which, if foreseen, would have been calculated by both parties as part of the agreement and would have influenced the price; 3) if anything else occurred which would be recognized as having seriously influenced, relative to the value justly put upon the article when the contract was made" (Rosmini 1993b, n. 1254).

This way, Rosmini does not absolutize the letter of contracts as the basis of market relationships jurally understood, but subordinates it to the sense of justice, which can only be achieved through equity. Besides, to the jural logic that rules market relationships, Rosmini adds the ethical dimension, which dominates his vision, where the end of transactions is the attainment of the greatest possible economic utility for the parties but always within the framework of the mutual recognition of persons as ends themselves.

Chapter 8
A Critique of Political Utilitarianism

8.1 Economy and Society

8.1.1 Society as Mutual Recognition Amongst Persons

Once Rosmini tackles the dimension of interpersonal economic relationships governed by ethics and rational right, he finally arrives at the crucial issue of the social and political dimension of the economy. In fact, economic relationships do not take place solely between individual persons, but also between them and different types of societies (family enterprises, commercial, civil, political and religious organizations), which Rosmini calls by different names, such as collective "bodies" or "persons." Rosmini conceives society as the result of bonds between persons, which transcend the mere search for individual interest and utility. According to Rosmini, there is an essential difference between the "bonds of utility" by which "we join to ourselves *things* which are useful to us" and the "bonds of society" "by which we join *persons* to ourselves and, at the same time, we join them":

> [...] This union, proper to persons, differs entirely from our union with things: we do not consider persons as advantageous to ourselves (in this case they would be the same as things), but as people in whose company we can enjoy the advantages offered by things. Persons united in this way acquire a communion in good, and together form a single end; things are only a means to the end which all persons have in common. This is a bond of society. (Rosmini 1994b, n. 34)

Because of this, the social bond is for Rosmini an essentially moral bond: "Associated persons, therefore, together form a moral person." Besides, "each of the associated persons by the very nature of society, desires the good of all, because each desires the social end, which is common to all." Now, for Rosmini, every society is an essentially ethical reality for the simple reason that moral virtue consists precisely in considering the human being as an end in itself, a condition which characterizes all true social bonds:

C. Hoevel, *The Economy of Recognition: Person, Market and Society in Antonio Rosmini*, Ethical Economy 42, DOI 10.1007/978-94-007-6058-5_8,

> One important consequence of this, which does honor to human society, is that a moral element is present in the very essence of society, because the constitutive principle of moral virtue is also, generally speaking, the constitutive principle of society. The principle of moral virtue, simply stated, is: 'Respect person as end; do not use person as a means for yourself.' The object of virtue therefore is always the dignity of the person, and here precisely lies the origin of human association. (Rosmini 1994b, n. 38–39)

Obviously, according to Rosmini, this does not mean that the societies formed by men do not also have utilitarian ends and do not provide subjective goods to their members. In fact, according to Rosmini, the original sentiment which moves men to the formation of human societies is that of "benevolence," in which "human beings do not forget themselves (. . .)" but "attach themselves to the society, loving it and its common good only for their own good, that is, for love of themselves" (Rosmini 1994b, n. 93). This is the reason why, Rosmini considers that "the bonds of *society* and *seigniory* are generally found as mixed in various actual human societies" (Rosmini 1994b, n. 62). However, societies can only subsist if this utilitarian element is limited by a basic recognition of the dignity of persons. Furthermore, society has its origin in the subjective source of social benevolence, as "it is a subjective love generating an objective love" (Rosmini 1994b, n. 93) that grows in nobility until it becomes true, disinterested "friendship." But in Rosmini's view, this ennoblement is achieved by the growth of society which, through the increase in the "number of persons who come together" and the "growth in the good which forms the end for which the union was formed," slowly converts the sentiment of benevolence, originally limited to a few persons and partially selfish, into a benevolence "which is purely a love of virtue, an essentially objective, unselfish love" open to the universality of all the good for all possible persons (Rosmini 1994b, n. 98).

It is clear that this description of the ethical nature of society is never fully realized within the limited societies of the family, the associations with particular ends, or even the very political or civil society as characterized by Rosmini, which we will deal with further on. Society reaches its fullness as a moral and spiritual union amongst persons only at the supernatural level of the society of men with God, which Rosmini identifies with the Church.[1] The "religious" or supernatural society is the only one that can fully attain "the constitutive law of society," which consists in "many individual persons being joined in such a way so as to form a single moral person" (Rosmini 1993a, 182).

---

[1] In God, the individual aspect and social aspect are identified. In human beings, there is an original social unconscious tendency (unity of the human race), but its realization takes place from an individual personal nucleus that "becomes wider" and incorporates the others. The point of arrival is also the person, who is both individual and social, which is found in Christ and in the Church (universal society). The error of individualists would be that they failed to take into account that human being, as person, achieves his realization in the encounter with the other and, above all, with the Other. On the other hand, the mistake on the part of the socialists would be that of assuming this encounter as something fully realized, ignoring the finiteness of human nature and the wounds of sin. For Rosmini, instead, the human being becomes social only based on his individual and finite dimension.

8.1.2 Beyond the Market and the State

From this ethical conception of society as a "moral person," it is clear that Rosmini could never admit the individualistic and utilitarian ideas that reduce human society to market relationships, much less if these are understood in the utilitarian way, as relationships between individuals exclusively moved by their own self-interest. But even if we understand the economic interpersonal relationships characterizing a market ruled by contractual ethical and jural relationships, these do not create by themselves a bond of social union as we have described (Rosmini 1994a, n. 121, appendix 2).

> Whatever importance is given to economic matters, it will never be true that the apex of human associations consists in economy. (Rosmini 1994a, n. 121, appendix 2)

For Rosmini, society implies something in common *(comunione)* amongst the individual contracting parties which is the moral and jural person.[2] Therefore, society also has its own rights, which are as inviolate as those of individuals.[3] In this sense, "in relationship to right, a collective body is only a jural person equal to any other individual. Between the collective body and its members, and between it and all other jural persons not its members, jural relationships exist and jural questions can arise, just as they do between individual persons" (Rosmini 1993b, n. 1657).

Furthermore, Rosmini forcefully underlines the opposite danger of "social" utilitarianism "in those who think that right, when connected with a social body, or in general with a more powerful subject, must prevail over the same right when it is connected with an individual or weaker subject" (Rosmini 1993b, n. 1648). Rosmini maintains that this utilitarianism should be rejected for two reasons. On the one hand, owing to the fact that even though "*individual persons*, when they become part of a social person, acquire only an additional relationship," this relationship does not "destroy them [as individuals] in any way" (Rosmini 1993b, 1649); in fact, according to Rosmini, there exist "extra-social" rights each individual person possesses beyond that of forming part of any society, which demand to be respected. On the other hand, "properly speaking, society is the *means* and individuals are the *end*" (Rosmini 1993b, 1660) so that, although society has rights, these do not have any other meaning but that of being the instrument to better conserve and perfect the rights of the individual persons that form it. Indeed, "if all the citizens are sacrificed to the few who are masters, not citizens, and hold the reins of the State in the name of society, what remains of society?" (Rosmini 1993b, 1652).

---

[2]"The concept of society requires that the individuals forming society have, with an act of their will, posited something in communion. It is this communion which binds and unifies their wills, all of which want this communion and conjunction. The cause of society, therefore, are wills which posit something in communion" (Rosmini 1995a, 37).

[3]Both individual and social subjects are capable of rights" (Rosmini 1993b, n. 1647).

8.1.3 Overcoming a False Dialectics

Thus, Rosmini rejects the false dialectic between the individual and society proper to utilitarianism, be it either individualist or socialist. To him, society has its rights (Rosmini calls them "social rights"), which must be respected by the individual but, in turn, these rights can never reach the point of being maintained at the cost of the rights of the individual ("extra-social rights"). However, this does not mean that society cannot, at some point, request "the sacrifice imposed upon one member at a moment of urgent, sudden need" (Rosmini 1993b, n. 1656). However, this sacrifice of private good in favor of public good can never signify, according to Rosmini, the sacrifice of private good of "*a single member of the society*," but the "*good of all the individual members of the society*" (Rosmini 1993b, n. 1656) in such a way that the effort is socially shared and an individual or a group of individuals is not used as a means to the ends of all the others. Rosmini is, therefore, as far away from individualism as from socialism:

> The mistake of those who exaggerate social right to the destruction of extra-social right inevitably produces absolutism; just as the mistake of those who exaggerate extra-social right to the destruction of social right inevitably produces ultra-liberalism and anarchy (Rosmini 1994b, n. 138).

In both cases, Rosmini sees the negation of the person who, considered in an integral fashion, is at the same time individual and social. Rosmini develops a social philosophy based on the idea of the individual without this signifying individualism or a negation of the social aspect.[4] According to Rosmini, the social dimension is based on what has a concrete existence and not on the generic. The social dimension is not an abstract "whole" constructed beyond the parts, but precisely from the parts, that is, the whole takes place within the individuals. Rosmini's original version is precisely that of considering society, in the last instance, as an extension of the person, as a moral person in which the affirmation of the self implies and cannot be separated from the affirmation of society and vice-versa:

> Thus society itself becomes end for every human being, not because our end must serve society, but because society and human beings become a single thing, just as the spirit and the body surrounding it become a single thing. This explains why the father feels he is defending himself when he defends his own family. In its members he does not see beings distinct from himself, but vital parts of his own existence. His reason and his heart carry him into all those parts and make him live in them. In the same way, every member of more extended societies forms with his fellows (in so far as he is united with them – the work of his intelligence) a single existence, a single moral person, for whom he desires and obtains all that he desires for himself, and from which he distances all that he distances from himself. (Rosmini 1994b, n. 168)

[4]"Fatto è l' uomo per la società, e per questo è che il genere umano più si perfeziona quanto più si consocia" (Rosmini 1923, 221).

8.1.4 The Regulation of the Modality of Rights

Now, Rosmini will place his social vision of the economy especially in the framework of a special type of society as is the case of "civil"[5] or political society. But in Rosmini's view, what specifically characterizes civil society beyond its being a "moral person," a feature which, according to him, is common to all types of societies? How does his conception of civil society differ from the conceptions held by those economists he sees as so influenced by utilitarianism?

Rosmini explains the main characteristics of civil society in two of his works: *Philosophy of Right* – where he especially develops the jural aspects of said society – and *Society and its Purpose* – where he focuses mainly on specifically political aspects. According to Rosmini, civil society is clearly distinct from other two types of societies such as the family society and the theocratic (religious) society. This is so because, in the first place, civil society is an "artificial" society, not due to a lack in human nature of a natural tendency to form it, but because its end "is not given by nature but found as a result of human genius and art" (Rosmini 1996, n. 1585).

However, we are interested in highlighting here another distinctive characteristic of civil society, that is, the "proximate end of civil society," as Rosmini puts it. This end consists in what he calls – by his already quoted famous expression – the "regulation of the modality of rights" (Rosmini 1996, n. 1591). By this he establishes one of the most important bases of his political philosophy, which will have important consequences for his economic policies, as we will see further on.

In fact, the idea that civil society must regulate the modality of rights implies that society cannot modify any right, either natural or acquired by individuals, both extra-social and social, but "the *mode* of a right can be changed without the possessor of the right losing any of his goods, his pleasures or his reasonable contentment" (Rosmini 1996, n. 1616). In this sense, civil society is above all a union of individual persons, families, the Church and all other intermediate societies which agree to regulate the manner in which the rights administered by said civil society are preserved and, furthermore, reach their fullest and most satisfactory use. Civil society has as its proximate end the production of means – such as institutions, laws and political actions – which enable the best possible way to regulate the exercise of all rights involved, both individual and social, so that these rights may be preserved and deployed to provide the associates with the greatest possible good.

8.1.5 Without Economy There Is No Civil Society

Rosmini deeply values the economy as an important aspect of the bases of a civil or political society. In fact, in his work *Della naturale costituzione della società civile,*

[5] We should remember that "civil society" is a synonym to "political society," both in Rosmini and all authors until the beginning of the nineteenth century.

Rosmini describes the transformation of a "family" society having a non-market, subsistence and closed economy, based on the strength of *personal* influence, into a "civil" or political society with a market economy, open, with sophisticated production and consumption, where both the *right of ownership and jural economic freedom* become key factors. Rosmini goes back to Roman times to show this movement from family society to civil society and the crucial importance of the economic factor in said movement. Thus, he marks the passing from the division of the Roman people originally performed by Romulus according to a family-based conception of society dependent on the war force of the people[6] to that of Servio Tullius, who "distributed into six classes the entire Roman people, according to degrees of wealth" (Rosmini 1887, 210). Furthermore, this last was, according to Rosmini, "the wisest institution that the Romans had" and "the nucleus of Roman politics" (Rosmini 1887, 212).

Rosmini sees a repetition of this same process in the origin of modern civil or political society he traces back to the medieval times of the bourgeois *communes* (Rosmini 1887, 229–230), which were, to great extent, the civil and social expression of a new economic reality based on money, on a monetary economy and on their jural protection upon the basis of the right of ownership.[7] Faced with this reality, Rosmini mentions the ever-present tendency – like a dead weight on civil societies – towards the "lack of economy", that is, the government of society's contempt for the economic factor. In his view, this contempt is a remainder of feudal times by which wealth is considered a resource obtained by force and plunder and not by productive work, distributed not according to productivity and individual effort, but to the discretion and generosity of the lord (Rosmini 1923, 176–177). There, Rosmini sees the origin of the providentialist and moralistic mentality of the government of society, and believes that it must be inevitably replaced by an administrative-economic conception of said government (Rosmini 1887, 263).

According to Rosmini, the economy is, therefore, the external accidental condition which allows, at the stage of civil society, that there be something to be shared, something in common to be contributed, in a word, something *social.* Furthermore, only if certain economic development exists, the material bases appear for the establishment of a truly civil society in which it is no longer a question of subordination of a number of vassals to a lord, but of the agreement on rights in the form of an association of peers. Thus, the right to free access to capital and to the ownership of capital made possible by a monetary market economy is an external and accidental condition, but a very necessary one during the civil or

[6]"La division che fece Romolo del popolo romano fu un' istituzione famigliare; poichè essa ebbe riguardo alle persone, o sia alla forza militare, e non alle ricchezze" (Rosmini 1887, 207).

[7]"La società civile non può esistere se non mediante il danaro: ella paga gl' impiegati e la milizia, *come abbiam detto,* fa eseguire opere pubbliche, ecc; nulla fa senza danaro" (Rosmini 1952a, 198). "Il danaro nella società sviluppata è il rappresentante di tutto: nella società non sviluppata nè venuta a civiltà è ancora la proprietà quella condizione a cui l' uomo può vivere, educarsi, operare." See Rosmini (1952a, 197).

political stage in the history of societies, which is quite different to that of family or feudal societies:

> Domestic society subsists comfortably on natural wealth, but it is almost impossible for civil society to subsist comfortably without money. Natural wealth contributes goods which are perishable, and they have no other price than the natural price, that is, the one consisting in the advantage obtained by consuming them, while money is preserved, easily accumulated, and produces more money, which is also accumulated. Natural wealth, furthermore, is not as easily transported as money, neither as useful as money for exchange purposes, and it is not suitable for representing the common measure of valuables. For all these reasons, natural wealth may suffice for a small society such as the family society, but for a very extensive one such as civil society, money is almost indispensable. It is, therefore, reasonable that civil society rapidly moves to give great importance to money as the most powerful force, the force that has the most extensive, most rapid and most multiple activity of all other forces. This is the modification suffered by passing from the narrow, domestic stage to the extensive, civil stage. (Rosmini 1887, 203–204)

For this reason, Rosmini will add the economic dimension to the idea of the regulation of the modality of rights as a proximate end of civil society. In Rosmini's way of thinking, the weight of the economic aspect in civil society does not answer to ideological reasons but to what he considers an absolutely factual reason arising from the nature of things and not from abstract theory.[8] This factual reason would be rooted in the fact that the growth of society in extensiveness and number of members necessarily implies the multiplication of ownership, division of labor, greater creation and circulation of wealth, sophistication and intensification of needs, and the existence of an inevitable inequality of results for the different individuals implicated in all this process.[9] Thus, the natural consequence is that civil society, as the regulator of the modality of rights, must necessarily reflect this economic dynamics and, for doing so, must have a jural and political structure different to the one that governs "family" societies. To ignore these forces or to attempt to eliminate them from the scene of society through an artificially imposed jural and political order means, according to Rosmini, going against the profound laws of historical evolution of civil society, since "the nature of things has indicated to the peoples the law shown by us: that the social administration be distributed proportionally to wealth" (Rosmini 1887, 213). It is clear, however, that civil society is not bound to accept just any factually existent economic situation, but only those within the framework of rational right, which society is always obliged to recognize.

[8] "Il peso che ha la ricchezza nell' Amministrazione sociale è un fatto independente dagli ingegni degli uomini" (Rosmini 1887, 213).

[9] "(. . .) bisognava dar tempo perchè le terre si divissero, perchè le famiglie parte assai moltiplicate, parte poco o nulla, od estinte, e gli altri accidenti producessero una notabile diseguaglianza fra i proprietarî (. . .)" (Rosmini 1887, 213).

8.1.6 Economy, Society and Happiness

Although the closest or proximate end of the political dimension of the economy consists in the regulation of the modality of economic rights with the purpose of attaining the greatest utility possible within a framework of justice – we will soon see what Rosmini understands by "justice" in the social sphere – in Rosmini's view the remote or ultimate end of such political dimension goes beyond this. In effect, the economy regulated by civil or political society must aim, in the last instance, for the ultimate ethical and eudaimonological end to which, according to Rosmini, every society is called, that is, "true human good, that is, contentment of spirit" (Rosmini 1994b, 210). We have already seen that, in the individual aspect, the human being does not only seek particular pleasures or utilities, but experiences the need for a general contentment of all his nature, which is only achieved by free adherence to objective good through virtue. In the same way, in the social aspect, the ultimate end of politics and of the economy regulated by politics cannot be solely the attainment of material goods or utilities through a just regulation of economic rights. The regulation of the modality of economic rights must also aim, according to Rosmini, for the ultimate end of virtue and the happiness of citizens.

This is owing to the fact that, according to him, the proximate end of civil society is never exclusive and determined, as it happens with commercial and other similar societies since "their remote end (contentment) lies outside society, and cannot be partly or totally the task of social administration; it can only be the private task of individuals as human beings, not as members." But the thing is completely different in civil society, "whose proximate end is *undetermined* and virtually universal." Hence it is that a political framework of the economy necessarily implies the moral and eudaimonological determination, not merely individual but social, of the economic means society considers most appropriate for the achievement of its ultimate end, that is, the attainment of the greatest possible virtue and happiness of persons. Therefore, for Rosmini, the political dimension of the economy cannot be limited to the multiplication of material means; the repercussion that these means will have on the moral and human fulfillment of people must be also taken into account:

> There are societies whose proximate end is undetermined and virtually universal in such a way that the end includes every human good obtainable by social means. An example is found in domestic and civil societies, where the remote end is both internal and external to the society. Social administration must keep its sights always fixed on this end, carrying out enactments which, far from harming the end, contribute as much as possible to its procurement. (Rosmini 1994b, n. 217)

Furthermore, Rosmini also rejects the opposite error of those who believe that the economy and politics have happiness and virtue not as their remote and ultimate end, but as their *close* or *proximate* end. For Rosmini, these are secularizations of the Christian religious ideal that endeavor to reach the ends by exclusively socio-economic means. This shows that, in Rosmini, the political dimension of the economy should aim at ethical realization without falling into moralism or economic communitarianism, which is the other extreme he fights against.

Thus, according to these two ends – the proximate one, which is the regulation of the modality of rights, and the remote one, which is to seek the greatest moral and eudaimonological good of citizens –, civil society has three fundamental duties, as follows: "(1) Protection of all the rights of the members and of the free exercise of their rights" (Rosmini 1996, n. 2132) which implies, at the same time, "not to obstruct the individuals composing the society so that they are prevented from or hampered in achieving *true human good*, the final and essential end of both individual and society" (Rosmini 1994b, n. 218); "(2) (. . .) to defend the right of each against any usurpation and oppression by others" (Rosmini 1994b, n. 218), and "(3) Amalgamation of private rights, when this is required to avoid a common evil or to obtain a common good" (Rosmini 1996, 2132), which implies no longer so much a predominantly negative and indirect action, as in the two previous functions, but the duty to "co-operate positively, using only the means proper to social government, so that individuals are encouraged and guided directly to the acquisition of true human good" (Rosmini 1994b, n. 218).

8.1.7 External and Internal Dimension of Society and Economy

In addition, the consideration of the two political ends of the economy implies, according to Rosmini, a twofold relationship between the two dimensions of society, which he calls "external" and "internal." According to him, society lies, in the first place, within the person's interior. The social relationship is, above all, an *internal bond* through which we join other persons in a spiritual communion in such a way that "the whole substance of society is internal and lies within the human spirit" (Rosmini 1994b, n. 152). Thus, Rosmini develops the concept of *internal society*. The social aspect is born in the person's interior rather than in external structures. It cannot be born from the outside but springs from the internal recognition of the other as a person, not as a thing. There is no "objective" society if we understand the term in the sense of a social being external to personal subjectivities. However, this by no means implies subjectivism or individualism since, according to Rosmini, full subjectivity is always, as we have seen, "objectified" in the light of the idea of being and "inobjectivized" on meeting others. To be precise, the social aspect is born at the very moment two subjectivities meet in the light of a common truth and a common good, in the presence of which two hearts are joined.

Rosmini states that internal society is, in certain way, an extension of the person's interiority expanded towards others by the dynamics of virtue, which is also, as we have seen, the dynamics founding society itself. Virtue is at the same time a personal good and a common good, the nucleus of personal interiority and social interiority. Thus, virtue, internal contentment and internal society are equivalent and make up the ultimate universal end of any society. As long as society grows in virtue and contentment, it necessarily grows in communion as well. Thus, Rosmini affirms that the end of society resides in reaching Man's maximum contentment, maximum virtue and maximum communion, since it is in "the internal, spiritual part" of society where "the human being exists, and where the delight and perfection of which he is susceptible resides. The final end of every society must therefore be found in this internal part" (Rosmini 1994b, n. 173).

Now, as well as an internal society, there also exists an "external" society. This external society is made up of all jural, political, economic and institutional means involved in a complex relationship with individual and social human interiority. There exists a complementary hierarchy between both societies. Therefore, according to Rosmini, the external and internal dimensions must be in constant communication. External society is called upon to be the expression and means of internal society. Then, external society must express the concerns of internal society and favor its development.

> Human beings, the basic element of society, are made up of two parts: one internal and invisible, the other external and visible. Similarly, there are two parts to every human society, the invisible and visible, the internal and the external part (Rosmini 1994b, n. 149). (...) The corporeal, external part of society must be considered the means for perfecting the internal, spiritual part, where, properly speaking, the human being exists (...) (Rosmini 1994b, n. 173)

Therefore, it may be said that, in Rosmini, the central problem of the socio-economic question lies in the relationship between these two dimensions. According to Rosmini, the mere unfolding or growth of means does not signify in itself a true development of society. Economic growth, unless actively lived as a moral good and a good of communion with others on the part of the person's interiority, may become something completely negative as much for the person as for the economy. The result of a purely exterior economy, void of interiority, is a pure fiction that cannot be maintained.

> If the external, material part of society does not reflect something internal and spiritual, the society's appearance is only a chimera; it cannot last. (Rosmini 1994b, n. 151)

Rosmini is therefore, like Saint Augustine, a harsh critic of "exteriorism," not because the external aspect is something bad, but because its value is lessened when it ceases to be a means at the service of the internal aspect. As long as the progress of external economic means does not express or help in the development of internal society, it becomes purely generic and impersonal, either in its liberal-individualist or socialist version, where the economy is reduced to a set of external means for the affirmation of an individual or collective subject, closed off from all interiority.

To Rosmini, external society must provide citizens with the politico-institutional means that will help them develop their economic capacities to the full, but always with the purpose of nourishing the framework of rights and virtues which make up the internal nucleus of social life. Even though a basic function of the government is to provide or encourage the provision of relative goods (we have already seen that economic goods are among them), more basic still is the function of promoting the internal disposition of citizens towards receiving these goods with a truly beneficial effect:

> Governmental wisdom has a responsibility for providing relative good for the societies it governs, but a much greater responsibility for procuring the appropriate dispositions of spirit for receiving the beneficial effect. (Rosmini 1994b, n. 663)

Now, according to Rosmini, the government's considering the existing moral dispositions for the economic action of civil society does not signify lack of care for the external means. On the contrary, it implies special care so that these means be the most appropriate for such moral dispositions. Although the external means economic policies may use never determine nor excuse individual moral decisions, they become, under certain circumstances, a strong conditioning, almost impossible to overcome. On certain occasions, Rosmini argues, the errors in the implementation of external institutional and political means are so enormous that they become an occasion and an incentive excessively strong to be resisted by the not too solid morality of the majority of persons. A serious politico-economic error, given its capacity for moral harm, is practically equivalent to a moral error. Therefore, in these cases it is no good lamenting morally about the evils that have occurred, blaming individual morality; one should discover the lack of morality in the political means which created an almost inevitable opportunity for those evils to become possible. According to Rosmini, in social life in general, mere individual morality is not enough: it is essential to measure the moral weight of external political and economic means.[10]

In addition, Rosmini develops this thesis challenging the utilitarian positions that deny the existence of this internal dimension of society and therefore, the necessity of subordinating the political dimension of the economy to moral ends. In this sense, Rosmini will perform an ample and keen criticism, above all, of three fundamental positions such as conservative utilitarianism, liberal utilitarianism and Statist or socialist utilitarianism, as we will see below.

[10]For example, when Rosmini refers to an opinion of an author who attributes to the mere existing moral vice the excesses committed by French revolutionaries (in this case, the plunder of goods,) he answers that in said case not only did pre-existent interiority and moral fail but also the political means used, which were not sufficiently adequate to counteract or at least not encourage such a poor morality. In the case of the French Revolution, the institution of a government of popular despotism was the almost irresistibly conditioning cause of the low morality. "Ella è una contraddizione quella di voler che il popolo metta le mani nel governo, e che poscia le raffreni dalle ricchezze dei privati: egli è un pretendere una virtù eccessiva e soprannaturale dagli uomini: voi date loro tutte le occasioni e gli incentivi di fare il male, e poi intimate loro la più severa morale. 'Oggi ricompaio come un' ombra di me stesso, dice il Sig. Raynal, non per avvertirvi di alcuni errori in politica, ma per rimproverarvi di molti delitti in morale.' Non è più il tempo di rimproverare i delitti di morale ad una nazione la quale ha precedentemente guastata la sua politica: gli errori in politica sono appunto quelli che tirano seco i più enormi delitti in morale: chi ha predicato quelli si è reso colpevole anche di questi (. . .) invece di riconoscere la causa di questi mali in un vizio intrinseco degli stessi principî politici, si contentarono di trasformarsi subitamente da politici in moralisti, e declamare contro l' umana perversità: contro questa perversità che essi stessi avevano suscitata" (Rosmini 1887, 246).

8.1.8 The Economy and the Historical Dimension

A complementary but no less important manner of understanding the political dimension of the economy is to trace the historical path, which Rosmini, following the footsteps of Vico, does not forget. In fact, according to Rosmini, philosophical truths are discovered in a speculative manner, but such discovery becomes more profound when calling upon history as the "vehicle" of philosophy.[11] Obviously, this does not mean falling into the error of reducing all philosophy to history or civil philosophy.[12] But what is clear is that, to the Roveretan, the great philosophic-economic intuitions can only be wholly understood in their historical development through the civil history of the peoples, which finally meet in the development of the history of humanity.[13]

Therefore, according to Rosmini, the historical dimension will strongly condition the exercise of economic rights and the kind of political action the State may undertake with regard to the economy. One thing is the ideally conceived civil society, where rights to ownership and jural economic freedom can be fully exercised, and another very different thing is a society which exists *de facto* (*fatto*). Although it is necessary to take the path towards the ideal of full economic freedom, in practice it is necessary to take into account historic-cultural limitations and, on the basis of this, to regulate the exercise of the modality of rights. Thus, Rosmini does not believe that theoretical principles are sufficient for economic policies: historical experience and political prudence are indispensable, which will determine how they will be applied according to the degree of culture and the conditions of each country. This turns Rosmini into a critic of rational abstractism in economic matters, which sustains that all problems depend on the application of a single absolute principle such as freedom or equality, and incorporates him into the tradition of those economists who consider it is indispensable to take into account the different relative situations proper to the historical dimension.

---

[11]"Senza la Filosofia la Storia è cieca, e farsi un noiosissimo andirivieni dello spirito umano, una successione d´opinione tutte di egual peso, o più tosto di egual leggerezza senza che vi si distingua giammai per entro la verità dall´errore . . . Senza la Storia la Filosofia diventa così secca, così lontana dalle forze di un ingegno ancor nuevo . . . La Storia dunque si può dire il veicolo della Filosofia . . . " (Rosmini 1994c, 292–294 in 2001, 566).

[12]"Errano però dannosamente coloro che di questa sola parte vorrebbero fare il tutto della filosofia" (Rosmini 1994c, 292–294).

[13]"Ma non basta aver veduta la *natura umana,* le sue *tendenze,* i *doveri*, i *diritti*, e aver considerato tutte queste cose ne´brevi ed angusti fatti dell´individuo; è necesario di più vederli, quasi riportati sopra scala maggiore, ne´fatti del genere umano: il che dà luogo ad una *Storia filosofica della Umanità.* Entra in questa parte anche ciò che oggidì si suol chiamare da alcuni la *Filosofia civile*" (Rosmini 1934, n. 22).

8.2 Critique of Conservative Utilitarianism

8.2.1 Appreciation of Conservatism and Critique of Patrimonialism

As it arises from his intellectual biography, Rosmini shares, in his youth, some of the theses of the Swiss political philosopher of the Restoration, Karl Ludwig von Haller, especially those which considered the historical root of society as strictly linked to the conservation and continuity of the ownership of land in the face of the revolutionary Jacobin abstractism. Hence, his youthful intuition of linking political power to that of the biggest landowners and reducing citizenry to the quasi-feudal relationship of subordination of the lesser landowners to the bigger ones. Together with Rosmini's youthful adherence to the Continental patrimonialism it should be mentioned his sympathy for English conservatism. He also seems to assimilate and follow the British tradition of real representation. Moreover, in a very "Burkean" manner, he always opposes the abstractism of the French Constitution to the practical and economical spirit of the "English Constitution" "enacted before being written (...) formed passage by passage, without a premeditated scheme, incessantly patched and mended according to counterpoising social forces and the urgency of instincts and popular needs" (Rosmini 2007, 1). And he even adds that "it would be desirable that Italians took greater interest I the study of the British politicians and economists. Some of them understood better than anyone else the function of ballast that property has in keeping the ship of the state balanced" (Rosmini 2007, 161).[14]

However, little by little, Rosmini will grow away from the patrimonialist conceptions of politics he espoused in his youth and, in his maturity, he will propose, as we have already seen, an ethical, jural and civil conception of political society, opposed to a "seigneurial," feudal and patrimonial conception of society, more appropriate to "family" societies. According to Rosmini, at a certain moment in history, the set of personal and economic forces are displayed with such amplitude and dynamism that they generate a complexity of relationships which largely outstrip family or merely inter-individual relationships and demand the formation of a new type of society, different to the patriarchal or family society: the civil society. Furthermore, while an element of subordination and dominion prevails in the former types of society, in civil society, social relationships are governed by a fundamentally new principle: the

---

[14]This phrase is almost literally the same as one of Burke's: "Let the great proprietors be what they may... at worst, they are the ballast of the vessel of the commonwealth" (Burke 1987, 45). In the *Naturale costituzione della società civile* Rosmini extensively explains the historical basis for real representation which originated in Rome and which continued throughout European history. Rosmini defends this class of political representation against the arguments of the "levelers," the "radicals" and other sympathizers of the French Revolution who attempted to prove that the English constitution was originally based on personal political representation, an argument which our author always considered historically false.

acknowledgement of right. Although, according to Rosmini, feudal society was also based on a kind of right, the latter was of a seigniorial kind, not entirely a right in the full sense of the term as there was no acknowledgement of the other as a fellow but as a subordinate. Thus, civil societies have progressively tended to eliminate this element of dominance and, although it cannot be completely erased, it has been replaced by a social right in the fullest of senses which gathers individuals, families, economic interests and the very State in a true society of citizens.

It is from this idea that Rosmini will conceive political power no longer as a mere exercise of the private right of ownership on the part of the Prince, nor as a summation of private dominions on the part of a series of proprietors, but as a truly common power which places under a jural and political tutelage the summation, also common, of the rights of all the members that associated individuals and families put into play. Therefore, although Rosmini does not set aside the monarchical and "vertical" principle of his Austrian background, he inserts into the monarchy "the principle of the Republic," by which the Prince enters into a sort of "social contract" that turns him into the minister and servant of rights rather than the owner of them. Here a certain contractualist dimension appears which will become the constitutionalist dimension of civil society. Rosmini always upholds his sympathy for the verticality and traditional origin of the monarchical principle which, modified in its sense, he sees as perfectly compatible with civil society. However, he will give great importance to the horizontal dimension in the origin and formation of civil societies. In this sense, he will clearly drift apart from Haller, for whom – according to Rosmini – the only possible form of civil society is "from top to bottom" by "a *unilateral* action, that is, from an act of the person assuming rule." Besides, in Rosmini's opinion, it is also fundamental to take into account the movement "from bottom to top" by "many acts of fathers" (Rosmini 1996, n. 1784–1785). From this it will derive, on the one hand, the reduction of patrimonialist theses to a single thesis of the need of "balance between political power and economic power" based on Parliamentary representation of the economic rights and interests of proprietors, although heavily compensated by the universal representation of all citizens by the Political Jury, as we will see later when referring to the role of institutions.

8.2.2 Ownership Is Not Mere Possession

Evidently, this remarkable reduction of the role of ownership in the political dimension is strongly linked to Rosmini's profound criticism of the conceptions of the right of ownership held by conservative utilitarianism. As we have already seen, according to Rosmini, one thing is ownership as "fact" and another one is ownership as "right" (Rosmini 1993b, n. 951–952). In fact, conservative utilitarianism bases all its arguments on a purely factual conception of ownership where the latter, being solely physical possession with no moral dimension, becomes absolute, perpetual and the source of all rights for its possessor. Thus, the very right of ownership remains subordinated to the "fact" of ownership and becomes a mere sub-product of the historical evolution of economic events. Hence the empiricist and historicist economist of the political constitutions proper to conservative utilitarianism.

Rosmini is, therefore, a critic of the traditionalist and conservative reduction of right – and especially of the right of ownership – to a purely historical product, its roots detached from natural and rational right. The Roveretan does not share the jural scepticism of conservatives such as Josef De Maistre, who affirmed that "the rights of the people can never be written" or that "freedom is a gift from kings" (De Maistre 1980, 211). Neither does he agree with Burke's affirmations about the absurdity of the possibility of natural rights concerning human beings.[15] Contrary to Burke, Rosmini forcefully affirms that "the best thing that was done in '89 was certainly the *Declaration of the Rights of Man and the* Citizen, proposed by Lafayette to imitate the American constitution" (Rosmini 2007, 29). In fact, Rosmini's most important idea in the field of political philosophy has probably been the vindication of natural and rational rights as the ultimate base of social order: "it conforms to the dignity of a constitutional statute that such a statute begins by proclaiming as inviolable the law of nature and of reason" (Rosmini 2007, 27). It is true that Rosmini agrees with conservatives and traditionalists that governments cannot consider every right as though it were a natural and absolute right. As we have already seen, many rights are also a product of the relativity of individual and social history, and they cannot be exercised by invoking "human nature" alone. This is the case of many economic rights that are partly the result of a complex historic process on which one cannot easily "go back." Rosmini rejects "radical" conceptions of the right of ownership that ignore the factual weight of its historic dimension. But even in this case, one cannot neglect their ultimate foundation on natural and rational right. Thus, Rosmini is in complete disagreement with the conservative idea that natural right has nothing to do with politics and not even with economics.[16]

8.2.3 *"The Unfair Aristocracy"*

The conservative utilitarian conception of the right of ownership leads, according to Rosmini, to political and economic despotism on the part of the classes that were historically the owners of wealth. It is the model of what Rosmini calls "unfair aristocracy," characterized by "the arrogance of the rich who would like to perpetually tie wealth to their families" (Rosmini 2007, 55). In complete opposition

[15]"In the gross and complicated mass of human passions and concerns, the primitive rights of men undergo such a variety of refractions and reflections that it becomes absurd to talk of them as if they continued in their simplicity of their original direction" (Burke 1987, 54).

[16]This can be seen, for example, in Burke's affirmation that "the pretended rights of these theorists are all extremes; and in proportion as they are metaphysically true, they are morally and politically false" (Burke 1987, 54).

to what Rosmini calls the French "unfair democracy," the Roveretan sees this utilitarian-conservative model incarnated especially in the England of his time and adheres, in this sense, to the criticism that the very English Liberals themselves were making with regard to this unjust conservatism:

> (. . .) England (. . .) has a Constitution (. . .) which certainly has shortcomings arising from the opposite tendencies (. . .) English politicians who do not belong to the aristocracy or who rise above its egotistical passions, attempt to cure optimally the wounds of that State. (Rosmini 2007, 67)

The English model represented, according to Rosmini, the replacement of the true idea of Parliament as the representative of ownership rights by an instrument for the profit of the wealthiest:

> Landlords wrote legislation which was to their exclusive advantage. (Rosmini 2007, 62)

As a matter of fact, Rosmini believes that both the apparently opposite French democratism and English aristocratism have in common the denial of natural right and its reduction to mere social right,[17] which Rosmini always sees as linked to "a philosophy that is utilitarian and based on the senses" (Rosmini 2007, 10), a philosophy that denies the light of right and reason and reduces the latter to a mere calculation of advantages and disadvantages.[18] Rosmini has always considered that utilitarianism, as a denial of right, leads to despotism, be it either modern democratic despotism or traditional aristocratic despotism. Furthermore, Rosmini will also make several critical references to the Spanish model and the pre-revolutionary French absolutism, as more statist versions of this same economic aristocratism.

8.2.4 Concentration, Populism, Corporativism, Immobilism

Rosmini maintains that society's juro-political system cannot be limited to protect forever the *status quo* of economic interests coming from the past, blocking the way to the legitimate right to development of those who have not been historically owners of property. This represents, above all, an injustice and a violation of rational right: in the first place, it does not take into account the limits to the right of ownership; in the second place, it neglects the right to jural freedom all citizens have to compete for the access to ownership and, in the third place, it ignores the

[17]This characteristic common to both models is explained by Rosmini especially in his *Philosophy of Politics*.

[18]Rosmini rejects the reduction of politics to the utilitarian calculation that is as characteristic of "radical" utilitarianism as it is of conservative utilitarianism. See Burke: "The rights of men in governments are their advantages; and these are often in balances between differences of good, in compromises between good and evil, and sometimes between evil and evil. Political reason is a computing principle: adding, subtracting, multiplying and dividing, morally not metaphysically or mathematically . . . " (Burke 1987, 54).

nature of civil society, the function of which can never be to obstruct these rights but to protect them and seek their greatest expansion. Moreover, this type of conception leads, according to Rosmini, to a moral degradation of society, where those who unlawfully retain an absolute dominion over wealth become either indifferent to the fortunes of their fellows – slaves to their own egotism and greed – or despots who make use of others as simple means towards their own ends.[19] In turn, those who are forcibly denied the right to have access to ownership and economic prosperity, or are strictly limited in the enjoyment of such right, remain in a state of infantile dependence which Rosmini calls "servile spirit," the source of the phenomenon of the alienating proletarization of a whole class of persons (Rosmini 1993b, n. 1597 and f.).[20]

Finally, such conservative utilitarianism inevitably derives, on the one hand, in an unproductive concentration of wealth in few hands, the creation of a whole class of poor people dependent not on their productive work but on the sole gifts of the rich, and on the other, in the fact that jurally just economic relationships among citizens are replaced by paternalistic and "patronizing" relationships of an anti-economic distributionism:

> However, there would soon be almost no occasion for the application of the rules of commutative justice. As I said, relationships between such an owner and his fellows (...) would shortly have to be regulated by humanity and benevolence on his part, and submission and gratitude on theirs. (Rosmini 1993b, n. 1237)

8.3 The Problems of Liberal Utilitarianism

8.3.1 Reduction of the Ends of Society

Although Rosmini agrees with the liberal criticism of the family and feudal conception of civil or political society and appreciates the liberal vindication of the economic dimension, he does not agree with the merely "mercantile" or "bourgeois"

[19]"Questo è quell'accumulamento, che reca l'ozio e l'inerzia, questo appare in quei lati fondi, che furono una delle rovine d'Italia; questo reca con sè delle disposizioni dure e contro natura a intendimento di retenere fisse nelle famiglie e quasi per forza quelle facoltà, che di natura loro si sentono sfuggevoli perchè non congiunte a un corrispondente potere, di cui nacquero ciò che ebbero di male i feudi e fidecommessi, e ciò che ebbe di male lo spirito particolare di famiglia, il cui peccato fu nell'eccesso, e che si riuscì crudele e barbaro non solo cogli estranei alla famiglia, ma coi membri della famiglia, ed è a cui i padri sacrificarono i figliouli: questo però contiene germe di risse e di guerre, e intrude nella monarchia uno spirito simulato, artificioso e disumano. Nutre questo i vizi dei potenti colle lagrime e col sangue dei miserabili; poichè il traboccamento della ricchezza dalla parte dei potenti adduce l'estremità della miseria dalla parte della classe minore, non essendo il traboccamento se non relativo a questo impoverimento" (Rosmini 1923, 145).

[20]Here Rosmini deals with the subject of the difference between dependence with dignity and the alienating servilism to which a whole class of persons is subjected.

conception of political society, which reduces the scope of its end to the achievement of purely external material prosperity:

> [...] the authors under discussion, instead of considering civil society in all its extension, stop at external, material prosperity, which they consider the only end of civil society -as if it were a society limited to business or something similar. (Rosmini 1994b, n. 215)

As we have seen, Rosmini believes that, within the economic environment, civil society must guarantee the safeguarding of the economic rights of individuals – especially the right of ownership, the right to the freedom to compete and the right to free trade, which can never be violated. However, he does not mean that the end of civil society is limited, as in individualist liberalism, to the protection of these rights – the celebrated "juridical security" that authors such as John Locke or Adam Smith maintain.[21] In Rosmini's opinion, these authors wrongly restrict the political dimension of the economy, which actually goes beyond the protection of the rights to ownership or economic freedom in order to acquire that ownership. In fact, according to Rosmini, this is barely a partial and external dimension of economic politics, the function of which should be that of regulating the modality of these rights in view of the common good, which is much more than the mere sum of individual rights to external ownership over material goods:

> Some writers limit the end of civil societies to safeguarding rights; others extend it to the acquisition of external prosperity (...) These authors excessively limit the end of civil society. (Rosmini 1994b, n. 215, footnote 67)[22]

Rosmini harshly criticizes the economicist and extrinsic conception of political society that reduces its functions to the jural protection of wealth, taking it as an end in itself for its mere accumulation or enjoyment, or as a source of hedonism or subjective utility. It is precisely this kind of chrematistic, individualistic and hedonistic concept of ownership and wealth present in the liberal utilitarianism of his time which Rosmini permanently battles against.[23] On the contrary, to the Roveretan, the wealth and ownership which civil society should encourage are only mediating goods that make possible the social generation of all other superior spiritual and moral goods (Rosmini 2007, 125)[24] and can even prevent moral

[21]"Civil government, so far as it is instituted for the security of ownership, is in reality instituted for the defense of the rich against the poor, or of those who have some ownership, against those who have none at all" (Smith 1976, II, 236).

[22]Furthermore, on this subject, as in so many others, Rosmini evolved greatly, since in his early writings, he agreed with the thesis that the end of society is the protection of ownership: "Lo scopo adunque della società a cui tutta si debbe rivolgere si è l' assicuramento delle proprietà" (Rosmini 1933, 105).

[23]We have already seen the development of Rosmini's criticism of the subjectivist and individualist concept of wealth in *Saggio sulla definizione della ricchezza,* as well as the same criticism, but referred to the concept of ownership, which he carries forward especially in his *Philosophy of Right.*

[24]"... influire sulle proprietà è il medesimo che influire su tutti gli altri beni che alla proprietà sono legati e condizionati. Tutti gl' interessi adunque anche i più cari e i più nobili si riducono a quello della proprietà come alla condizione ed alla causa di tutti" (Rosmini 1952a, 198).

evils.[25] In this sense, liberal utilitarianism reduces economic policy to an ethically neutral and purely chrematistic technique, erroneously banishing its moral and eudaimonological dimension to the sole sphere of what is private:

> They claim that whatever leads to contentment of spirit must be the work of individuals alone. In other words it is an extra-social end (. . .) In this society, the remote end (contentment of spirit) lies entirely outside the society and is left to the prudence and morality of individual members who seek contentment as human beings but not as members of the society. (Rosmini 1994b, n. 215)

8.3.2 Appreciation of Spontaneous Self-Regulation

Rosmini agrees with the liberal tradition regarding the importance of the *role of spontaneous order* arising from the framework of markets' inter-individual actions in the formation of economic order. In his opinion, an important role is played in this sense by the instinctive knowledge of his own interests each individual has, which produces unintentional social or collective benefits.[26] Thus, Rosmini maintains that:

> The masses are guided by a practical reason, a social instinct (. . .) [D]ifficulties arise when we try to indicate the precise reasons leading the masses to operate socially (. . .) (Rosmini 1994a, n. 52–54). The people act socially to strengthen and maintain their society if, in their eyes, the immediate good which constitutes the stimulus and motive of their activity is one with the good itself of the society. . . At this point, the action of the masses appears to possess great foresight and wisdom because it brings in its wake highly beneficial, long-term and universal effects. These, however, are not the effects of foresight and calculation on the part of the people because the very nature itself of the situation has led and forced them to act in that way. In this case the present, particular good, at which the people are aiming, is per accidens the self same good forming the support of society and containing the seed of its development (Rosmini 1994a, n. 54).

[25]For example, according to Rosmini, political representation of economic interests is essential for reducing corruption. Even though this last is an intrinsically moral and interior phenomenon and there is no incentive or external social organization which can avoid it completely, an economically honest administration which allows interests to take place, can be a more efficient dissuasive factor than a moralistic demand for moral integrity and virtue which can only be achieved by very few: "Invano si grida alla corruzione: quando anche l' influenza delle ricchezze si potesse chiamar corruzione; ella non resterebbe per questo d' esser meno un fatto che i ricchi facciano per diritto ciò che prima facevano per influenza illegittima; non mettete gli uomini in una situazione dove la tentazione è massima, pretendendo poi che essi conservino la più severa virtù (. . .) D' altra parte non è punto vero che ogni influenza che esercita nelle cose pubbliche la ricchezza sia una corruzione. La ricchezza è un bene, come è un bene il poter ottenere che la deliberazione pubblica sia fatta secondo la propia volontà o secondo i proprî interessi . . . " (Rosmini 1887, 209, n.1).

[26]". . . non è l' uomo solamente ragionevole, è anche sensitivo: egli non opera secondo la sola guida della ragione, soggiace agli istinti, dietro ai quali si muove spontaneo, e gli istinti sono sucitati dalle cose esteriori, dalle quali l' uomo patisce. . . La società umana è adunque naturale quando è ben ordinata secondo quello che esige la natura degli umani istinti, quand' ella ordina convenientemente le cose esteriori che gli suscitano" (Rosmini 1887, 667).

Therefore, Rosmini considers it absurdly impossible to expect to replace this order by a plan calculated by one or more individuals. Actually, to him, this would be like comparing the human mind to the divine mind, in the sense that the former would thus become endowed with the capacity to foresee all the possible direct and indirect consequences derived from the interrelated actions of millions of individuals. This is why Rosmini emphasizes the great importance freedom – as a general principle – has for the economy.

> I agree with Adam Smith and with so many other economists – argues Rosmini – that the most useful distribution of wealth is the one performed by the nature of things. This distribution and direction of wealth is all the more perfect when the place and time in which it is considered are vaster. It occurs thus with all natural laws, the regularity of which is not discovered until they are considered over an ample period of space and time. (Rosmini 1923, 137)

Despite these coincidences, there are important differences between Rosmini and Adam Smith's thought based on the diverse valuation they do with regard to the relationship between economy and the historical-cultural dimension; the right to competition as a principle and activity, and the relationship of economic freedom with the whole of human freedom.

8.3.3 Market Freedom and the Historical-Economic Context

In fact, in the first place, there is the historical and cultural factor: the spontaneous order of individual interests does not have the same efficiency at all times and in all cultures. Rosmini sustains that there are times when the spontaneous order of individuals coincides with the good of society; these are the foundational epochs of societies where, in general, the interests of individuals are altruistic and coincide with those of society. In effect, "... the infancy of a society is always an eminently *patriotic* epoch, as it were. The good of each person, considered as a member of the social unit, is equivalent to the elementary good itself of society" (Rosmini 1994a, n. 56). This is owing to the fact that in the abovementioned case, society's members are very aware that their survival depends on the survival of the society. Thus, "in the beginning, the very existence of the society is the good seen immediately and vividly by all ..." (Rosmini 1994a, n. 56). Therefore, as the interest in individual survival coincides with the survival of society, the spontaneous order of interests coincides perfectly with the common good.

On the contrary, in more advanced and sophisticated times, when the urgency of survival has been overcome, and even after society has been able to develop significant economic power upon the basis of sacrifice and productive discipline (stage of productive accumulation), the tendency of the individuals is to apply themselves to enjoy the benefits obtained and to abandon the rigorous economic ethics of earlier times. "This is the period of luxury and enjoyment, which now become the *immediate* good to which the masses tend and according to which they operate" (Rosmini 1994a, n. 58). According to Rosmini, these are times of economic decadence, when the spontaneous order of individual interests, transformed into a competition for the autistic search for one's own pleasure obviously does not lead to the good of all the society and even destroys the true good of the individuals. In such times, society "is blind to every good proper to the country and devotes its attention to individual good alone, around which it girates briefly before its final collapse" (Rosmini 1994a, n. 58). Thus, "the deficiency and incapacities of this new state of civilization will be found to consist, in my well-considered opinion, in the fact that peoples had arrived at conditions in which the immediate good for which they were working was no longer existence or the glory of their country or even something accessory to the social good, but the good of the individual" (Rosmini 1994a, n. 60).

Furthermore, the good or bad results that the spontaneous order may generate also vary according to the place and type of culture of the society in question. According to Rosmini, the individual economic interests of a nation's inhabitants are not natural forces that always tend to favor the society in which they are rooted, as Adam Smith suggests, for instance, when he maintains that the commercial aperture of a country can never bring harm to it because the economic interests of that country will tend, as by a gravitational force of their own, to favor themselves and, in doing so, they will benefit their own country.[27] In Rosmini's opinion, the liberation of individual economic interests is not always economically productive for a country but it depends on the degree of culture to which this country has arrived:

> In my opinion – Rosmini sustains – one cannot agree with [Adam] Smith and his followers in this: that private interest is perfectly educated and makes no mistakes, not even considered in an entire nation. The truth is certainly the opposite, since this depends on the degree of culture of the people. (Rosmini 1923, 139)

8.3.4 A Mistaken Conception of Rationality and Freedom

Still, according to Rosmini's thinking, the fallibility of spontaneous order is ultimately based on a different anthropological conception of rationality and freedom. As we have seen, Rosmini values enormously what we could call the "rational" aspect of action, that is to say, the capacity of the human being to abstract the means from the ends and combine these means so that they can be assigned in a more efficient manner to certain ends. In his opinion, such rational assignation depends

[27] "Every individual continually exerts himself to discover the most advantageous employment for whatever capital he can command. It is his own advantage, indeed, and not that of society which he has in view. But the study of his own advantage naturally, or rather necessarily, leads him to prefer that employment which is most advantageous to the society . . . therefore every individual naturally inclines to employ his capital in a manner in which it is likely to afford the greatest support to domestic industry, and to give revenue and employment to the greatest number of people of his own country" (Smith 1976, 475–477).

on the faculty of "abstraction," as he calls it, which is in turn intimately associated to the interactions existing amongst individuals. The more an individual takes part in exchanges, the more he develops his capacity for abstraction and instrumental reason, which would otherwise remain dormant. However, according to Rosmini, the sole increase in people of the capacity for an abstract conceptualization capable of distinguishing means from ends facilitates up to a certain point a "factual" display of means, but it neither guarantees the discovery or good choice of ends (ethics of action) nor a consistent correlation between the ends that may be attained and the means discovered or vice-versa (logic and efficiency of action.) The reason for this is, according to the Roveretan, that the development of the faculty of abstraction allows us to know the ends and means, but does not guarantee *per se* their appropriate valuation. Without a proper valuation, not only can ethically evil ends be chosen; also a logically false (irrational) and, consequently, inefficient interrelation between ends and means can be established.

This is the underlying ethical-anthropological reason why it is not possible to maintain that, to Rosmini's thinking, there exists the idea that the mere spontaneous interchange between individuals will generate *per se* a knowledge that will allow them, sooner or later, to compete with others in equal terms. On the contrary, the pure factual exchange can indefinitely deploy the faculty of abstraction without this ever leading to the development of what Rosmini calls "the faculty of thought." This last faculty has knowledge of the ends and is intimately linked to the capacity human beings have for valuing things from their internal freedom. The exchange only helps to display what is internal but not to create it. Hence the importance Rosmini gives to culture and ethics as the internal growth which is the foundation of and condition for social or economic exchange rather than its consequence. As a result, the sole fact that an economy is a "market economy" does not guarantee its morality nor the most efficient correlation between ends and means. The capacity to create economic value does not arise only from interpersonal interaction and the experimental knowledge resulting from it, but from the degree of culture and internal freedom as well.

Besides, liberal utilitarianism claims that the degree of freedom is generally measured by the number of possibilities of external action an individual has. According to Rosmini, however, the degree of freedom has its ultimate root in the capacity to act with the least number of internal and external conditionings. In this sense, the opening up of external possibilities does not always mean an increase in freedom. On the contrary, Rosmini maintains that a society which enables a kind of freedom and competition that provoke an exaggerated multiplication of economic desires and needs may generate unreachable expectations and may condition the individual to the extreme of adopting negative and even violent courses of action, which not only become a danger to the freedom of others, but go directly against his own freedom:

> Desires increase as competition for all social classes and responsibilities becomes more universal. Sometimes this competition is open to all equally by laws and custom. In fact, it is then impeded by the great numbers who trample one another down in the rush to fame and fortune. In this case, only a few manage to satisfy the desires and activity they share with the many. The majority look upon their fortunate rivals, with whom they

> have compared themselves so often, and see themselves at the bottom of the heap. Such numerous, frustrated desires and painful comparisons are normally the source of great harm to public morality and cause immense evils in society. (Rosmini 1994b, n. 851)

On this point, Rosmini, who is a fervent admirer of Adam Smith – an unusual case amongst Catholic philosophers – challenges Smith's thesis of the invisible hand considering it not as an exaltation of freedom but, on the contrary, as a negation of it (Rosmini 1994b, 414).

8.3.5 *Resignifying the Spontaneous Order*

According to Rosmini, this deficiency of the order of spontaneous interests is owing to the simple reason that it is not a completely natural mechanism, but one which depends on freedom, and freedom, in turn, depends on its greater or lesser adaptation to objective ethical values. In this sense, this order does not always function correctly because, to determine the good or bad orientation, it depends on the degree of lucidity and moral virtue possessed by individuals and on the conditionings imposed by the times and culture they live in. Although the base of the economy is the right of free competition, according to Rosmini, the concrete conditions of its exercise are equally important. These conditions are related to the material, intellectual, psychological, cultural and moral difficulties and limits of both individuals and societies to achieve such a capability that will enable them to exercise truly their right of free competition.

The market conception proposed by Rosmini contains, in our view, an original attempt to integrate the great discovery and assessment of the spontaneous order of passions and economic interests present in the market that comes from the Anglo-Saxon tradition, with the ethical and jural principles for their regulation and guidance that come from his personalist anthropology. This integration does not mean a rational or a priori construction but neither a mere release of spontaneous interests and passions. It implies, instead, as in all the classical tradition, to find the most *natural* and most *rational* order that often conflicts with its immediate and visible manifestations:

> I looked for what was supposed to be the best constitution of such a society. I said to me that the best had to be the one that which was more natural (. . .)Natural for man is to be reasonable, therefore natural has to be called that society of men which is made up according to reason. (Rosmini 1887, 666–667)

Sharply differing from empiricist or rationalist liberal conceptions of the spontaneous order, Rosmini rejects the naturalist idea of society and the market that reduces them to an exchange network between selfish and utilitarian interests and tries to discover its deeper rationality:

> A civil society formed under the requirement of pure reason and on that of human instincts is grounded in the nature of things, and therefore it is said aptly to be natural (. . .) Instincts underlie the human will which, being an internal reality, does not belong directly to external

> society (...) Therefore the constitution of civil society in relation to instinctive man has to be ordered in such a way to be able, at the same time, to satisfy human instincts with the increase of external goods and with the decrease of evils, and to apart itself as possible from all the occasions that men may have to abuse of these goods for their own misfortune and misery. (Rosmini 1887, 666–667)

8.3.6 Competition Also Produces Evils

Rosmini criticizes the thesis of liberal utilitarianism that limits the role of the State in the economy to simply "open up to possibilities" and to encourage an unrestricted free competition. According to Rosmini, economic freedom is subordinated to moral and jural freedom. The free multiplication of possibilities of consumption through a market economy can be terribly harmful to many people who, even when they live in a developed society, are deprived of the sufficient abilities to derive any advantage from this economic freedom:

> We must note that there is no nation, no matter how civilized and cultured, that does not contain deep within itself, 1. people entirely or partly deficient in foresight, 2. people who because of age or character have very childish, unpredictable tastes, 3. immoral people. (Rosmini 1994b, n. 679)

Now, Rosmini asks himself, do these people benefit from an indiscriminate opening-up to economic competition or are they harmed by it?

> Too many people crowding into restricted space obstruct each another, and the few for whom room is available can only enter more slowly and more difficulty. Moreover, saying that he way is equally open to all is not the same as claiming that all need take it, even when they lack the energy. It is always a good thing to find a mountain path open, provided I am free to climb to the peak or not. But it is an intolerable burden if I am forced to ascend in unsuitable conditions, or need to ascend without being able to reach the top. In this case, I am simply risking my life uselessly. In fact, it is the neediest who get hurt when many people compete in the way we have described. (Rosmini 1994b, 696–697)

Rosmini quotes the case of the American Indians to whom the competition with Europeans, given their disadvantage in abilities and resources, was not an occasion for progress but for ruin and destruction:

> As we saw, the American Indians perished in their poverty because they could not compete with the rich when their desires had increased their needs. Rich people can satisfy their needs with what is superfluous, but the poor only with what is necessary. The Europeans exchanged their abundance for things indispensable to the subsistence of the Indians who, when they had satisfied their artificial needs, had nothing even to live on. (Rosmini 1994b, n. 697)

Thus, Rosmini criticizes the utilitarian liberalism's position, by which free economic competition is always beneficial amongst all peoples. To him, it is clear that excessive competition amongst peoples of different levels of development is in the detriment of the underdeveloped ones:

> When competing with fully civilized nations, primitive nations are destroyed; those at the second level lose the means and will to progress along the road of civilization; decadent nations are impoverished and break up. (Rosmini 1994b, n. 669)

However, Rosmini's criticism of the concept of unrestricted free competition does not solely include the relations between nations but also each country's domestic economy:

> What has been said about competition between nations at different stages of progress towards civilization must also be said about classes of people who make up a nation. If we supposed the needs aroused in different classes of people to be equal, they would require equal expenditure to satisfy them. But equal pressure to spend is certainly not an equal burden for people with different means; it is a greater, more harmful burden for those with lesser means. For the hard-pressed families of artisans and peasants, ten pounds wasted on carousing can be much more disastrous than a thousand pounds wasted by a rich family on a banquet. Competition is not always the best thing for a nation, as some think; very often it profits only the rich, especially the industrially rich. (Rosmini 1994b, n. 701)

It is clear to Rosmini that this is "the effect of competition, always fatal to the poorest" (Rosmini 1994b, n. 699) based on "a universal fact put briefly (. . .) in a competition, 'the prize goes to the strongest' " (Rosmini 1994b, n. 698).

8.3.7 Fallacy of Consumerism as Redistributive Factor

In this context, Rosmini also disagrees with the thesis of liberal utilitarianism that states that the dynamics of consumerist competition leads to a fairer distribution of wealth, as affirmed by Gioia – to whom "fashion scatters the extraordinary wealth of the rich and distributes it with less disproportion among the majority" (Rosmini 1977a, 113). On the contrary, Rosmini states, quoting Say, that consumerism generated within the rich also infects the poor, whom it harms more deeply than the former, and thus inequalities not only do not diminish but increase:

> (. . .) if it were maintained that the system that encourages prodigality, favoring that of the rich, tends to produce a good such as the reduction in patrimonial inequalities, it would be easy for me to prove that the squandering by the rich sweeps up behind it the same squandering by the middle classes and the poor, these two being the first to reach the limits of their income. Thus, general wastefulness does increase patrimonial inequalities rather than decrease them. (Rosmini 1977a, 113)

Rosmini also criticizes the thesis claiming that the free play of the market necessarily brings about social harmony. In fact, in the liberal conception, the increase and multiplication of the affections and pleasures proper to an economy of abundance such as the market economy would make them "less common," that is to say, less concentrated on a single thing over which everyone fights – as it used to happen in feudal times – and would spread desires harmoniously over different objects. According to Rosmini, the mere increase and multiplication of the number of pleasures does not necessarily imply that these are spread over different objects proper to each individual. On the contrary, "the general increase in desires is followed by a general increase in envy and in the quarrels over beloved objects (. . .) Hence the increase in desires will be equivalent to the increase in jealousy and the breaking of trust" (Rosmini 1977a, 129). Furthermore, "the greater the desires, the more necessary and also the more difficult it will be to obey a rule and an order in them" (Rosmini 1977a, 130). In this sense, the increase or multiplication of desires and needs of an economy does not in itself bring harmonious distribution; in accordance with Rosmini, "a moral force" and "mutual attention and vigilance" are required. All this shows that such an economy is dominated by "a constant envy," which "is a painful and defective incentive" (Rosmini 1977a, 130) since "constant vigilance is impossible," as "the heart cannot be controlled." Therefore, in an economy where "people desire not what they have but what they lack," "mistrust and anguish can never be eliminated" (Rosmini 1977a, 130).

8.3.8 Rosmini Against Burke

Rosmini also criticizes the jural historicism and evolutionism of liberal utilitarianism, which reduces the jural order governing the economy to a "spontaneous" social calculation performed all throughout history.[28] Rosmini certainly values the *historical and evolutive* factor in morals and right and its relationship with the economy. In effect, as we have already seen, a great part of his philosophy of economic science is based on a philosophy of history closely linked to economic history. However, as we have mentioned, right is founded – in Rosmini's opinion – on a metaphysical nucleus that expresses itself in history but is never reduced to it.[29] In fact, Rosmini sums up his criticism of moral and jural traditionalism and historicism in his critical re-elaboration of the concept of common sense (the great communicator of which was the French traditionalist De Bonald) and in his metaphysical opinion on the value of historical traditions and social beliefs. According to Rosmini, social consensus and common beliefs are valuable but cannot

[28]Some current Italian scholars have shown the relationships between the evolutive and historical idea of morals and economy of Hayek, under the influence of German historicism and psychologism (probably from sources in Lessing, Romanticism, etc.), Scottish and English economic thinking, influenced by the psychologism and historicism of Hume or Burke, and the Italian economic thinking of Romagnosi, Genovesi and others, influenced by Vico. In this sense, Rosmini, although being a follower of Vico, clearly removes himself from historicism and psychologism. It is a mistake then to consider Rosmini, despite his sympathy towards British economic and political thinking, as an unconditional follower of this economic philosophy.

[29]In this sense, one can also see the essential difference between Rosmini and French traditionalist thinking, from which Rosmini gradually removes himself as his thinking matures.

be taken as the ultimate authority in the case of morals and right. Indeed, mere social or historical *consensus* is not equivalent to human common sense nor does it make an idea true or acceptable.

> Common sense should not be confused with true and false traditions (even error has its own tradition) that are sent and received from generation to generation on the faith and on the authority of the fathers who hand it down. (Rosmini 1987, n. 1148)

Social consensus becomes *common sense* provided it is the result of a truth which always has its objective measure in the personal intellect illuminated by the light of the idea of being. Anyhow, even in this case, common sense is only *extrinsic and reflexive* proof of the truth. Rosmini thinks that people's agreement on a common opinion – even through history – is of little value if this opinion is the fruit of pure social inertia or conformism. Common sense or agreement on values and beliefs has worth as long as these beliefs have been previously formed individually in each human being and there is agreement on them on the part of others who have travelled the same personal road. In other words, Rosmini values a socially accepted belief provided it derives from a former personal belief.

In this sense, Rosmini is a critic of the British liberals' historicist conception of right, and will follow a path similar to that of Vico, running between metaphysics and history, but giving the former clear pre-eminence. This has extremely significant consequences on the conception of Rosmini's social and political philosophy in relation to the economy.

8.4 Critique of the Statist and Socialist Utilitarianism

8.4.1 Public and Secret Happiness

The third economic-political model which Rosmini challenges is that of statism, utopian socialism and social utilitarianism. One of Rosmini's greatest tasks was his permanent criticism not only of the excesses of the French Revolution but also of utilitarianism's constructivist projects, utopian socialism and communism. In this matter, his *Philosophy of Politics* his *Philosophy of Right* – where he especially attacks social rationalism by antonomasia, which he sees incarnate in the work of Jeremy Bentham – are fundamental works, together with his *Essays on Socialism and Communism*, where he harshly criticizes the technocratic conceptions of thinkers such as Saint-Simon, Owen and Fourier. The same may be said of his criticism of what he calls "*statolatry*" (idolatry of the state) of Rousseau and of Hegel.

Rosmini considers that the central problem of social utilitarianism lies especially in its understanding of the concept of happiness as social end. Just as we have seen upon analyzing his criticism of liberal utilitarianism, Rosmini certainly agrees with social utilitarians in that economic policies cannot be indifferent to the ethical question by freely leaving up to individual discretion the setting of limits to the desires of enrichment or individual pleasure that market competition may bring about. The politician must influence the economy in some way so as to favor the development of economic actions compatible with the ethical development and true happiness of persons. In other words, civil society is responsible for somehow regulating economic activities so that they not only generate the greatest possible amount of wealth but said wealth is distributed amongst people in a manner compatible with the highest ethics and the greatest possible happiness of all citizens. However, despite agreeing with this premise, Rosmini differs with regard to the manner in which social utilitarianism understands this "happiness" and its just distribution.

Rosmini criticizes social utilitarianism's idea that happiness within society should be reduced to a sort of "objective catalogue" of unsatisfied needs and desires that the State can establish *a priori*:

> Who is able to compile this catalogue of pleasures? Who can foresee them all? What are public pleasures? Are they perhaps pleasures enjoyed by a certain real entity called the public? Isn't it rather a collection of private pleasures? (Rosmini 1976, 150)

To Rosmini, such an "objective" and "public" definition of pleasures is impossible, since these – as we already know from his anthropological theory – cannot be measured from outside each person nor – even if their measurement were possible – would it be correct to think that total of happiness in a society is equivalent to the sole sum of the satisfaction of those pleasures or needs. On the contrary, as we know, happiness is for him a different phenomenon, far more complex than satisfied pleasures or needs, varying enormously from one individual to another.

> We have seen that the end of civil society is ultimately the contentment of spirit of the individuals who compose it. Consequently, when a politician wishes to explain public happiness, that is, all the happiness present in reality in the people, he must take into account private, individual contentment whatever its source (. . .) Do the political evaluators consider themselves not bound to take account of these degrees of happiness simply because they are hidden and unseen by the public and not reflected in others? Happiness is not less real because hidden. We should not be looking for it in market places, theatres, trading banks and on the bloody battlefields but in the depth of the human spirit where alone it can be found. The public are only a collection of individuals and, if each individual were immensely happy in spirit without knowing how others feel, a body of happy people must surely be the result. Although our personal happiness is unknown to others and not reflected in them, we cannot consider our happiness is nothing (. . .) The opinion of politicians who think that we can rejoice in the happiness of a human being only when the happiness is visible and sought by others, is clearly blind, vain and of no value whatsoever. (Rosmini 1994b, 245)

Hence, Rosmini's criticism on a purely quantitative and extrinsic concept of public happiness. "I do not know how public happiness can exist unless it results from the happiness of individual persons" (Rosmini 1933, 22); "it is contradictory to say that something is useful to society and it is not useful to individuals" (Rosmini 1933, 22) he states. Thus – Rosmini maintains – "as long as politicians remain outside Man in their reasoning and fail to enter his interiority, they cannot even begin to talk of any source of happiness, no matter how many castles in the air they wish to build" (Rosmini 1933, 22).

8.4.2 *The State, a Guarantor of Happiness?*

In Rosmini's view, starting from this purely external sensist concept, social utilitarianism ends by turning the happiness at which any economic policy should aim into a happiness socially established and planned by the State. In fact, according to this state conception of happiness, the state does not only have the authority to defend the rights of individuals or to encourage and help them so that they may achieve their own happiness by themselves, but it has the jural responsibility of *ensuring* this happiness for all citizens. This implies, on the one hand, the affirmation of a right to happiness on the part of every individual, which would oblige all others to a jurally obligatory unlimited beneficence through the state apparatus, without the possibility of demanding any merit or service whatsoever in return. According to Rosmini, this constitutes an undue juralization of love for our fellows, which may be demanded from human beings upon the basis of ethical and religious reasons, but can never be the outcome of juro-political concerns. Therefore, in his opinion, the utilitarian conception of the welfare state is a monstrous secularization of the religious Christian ideal and contains a new form of despotism:

> We know that charity and beneficence can be commanded by God, but we contradict the proper notion of the duties of humanity and charity if we have the right to demand the practice of beneficence and to regulate it by law as we please (...) If individuals themselves cannot require from their equals, as a right of justice, what pertains to beneficence, much less can a government, which is principally instituted to defend and preserve the right of all the individuals that compose the society. If I am harmed by someone attempting to force a benefit from me, my right is violated, and the government must help me against those who violently attack me in this way. Clearly, a government which protects unjust and violent people is forcefully obliging me to do what in fact depends totally on my will and on the extent of my inclination to be beneficent. Not even civil society as a whole can change the natural duties of charity into duties of justice (...) How beneficence would be limited if society constrained the equal citizens that form it to be mutually beneficent? (Rosmini 1994b, n. 243–244)

8.4.3 *Against Democratic Despotism and Top-Down Nivelation*

Rosmini also criticizes the purely quantitative ideas of distribution of economic goods derived from this external and statalist conception of happiness taught by social utilitarianism. He points out several ways in which it understands distributive justice. On one hand, there is what Rosmini calls "democratic despotism," which consists in conceiving that the fairest distribution is one where the greatest number of goods accumulates in the majority of individuals conforming society. This presupposes the quantitative idea that there will always be a greater amount of happiness in a society if the majority is happy and only a minority suffers. But this conception of distributive justice is, for Rosmini, sheer despotism on the part of the majority over the rights of the minorities and individuals. In his *Politica Seconda*, Rosmini criticizes this interpretation of the concept of "public utility." To him, "if it [public utility] means the utility of the majority, the minority is completely sacrificed and the weak irredeemably offered in holocaust to the strong, to Moloch; everyone is at war with everyone else" (Rosmini 1994b, n. 241). Rosmini rejects the reduction of distributive justice to the "utility of the majority," "the greatest happiness for the greatest number," all formulas aimed, in his opinion, at the destruction of right:

> But it is totally false, impossible, unjust and immoral in the extreme that this modification should be conceived as what is useful for the majority. On the contrary, right exists without any relationship whatsoever to the majority; it exists between two persons alone where there is neither majority nor plurality. Moreover, right, whether it belongs to the majority or minority, or even to a single individual, can never be sacrificed for the good of the majority, whatever the size of the majority. Otherwise, the majority would be jurally the worst possible tyrant over the minority; it would be the sole depository of right; the minority would be deprived of all its rights and excluded from society and law. (Rosmini 1996, n. 1738)

In this same way, Rosmini will make similar criticisms of other utilitarian forms of conceiving economic justice, such as egalitarianism, which considers that material goods should be distributed within society according to mere physical needs or desires, allegedly similar in all persons. Given that utilitarianism does not admit the idea of contentment or internal happiness, and that happiness is converted into a purely social or state matter, distributive justice becomes reduced either to a strict arithmetic quantitative egalitarianism where goods are distributed in equal parts, or to a distribution based on purely physical needs or desires conveniently established by the use of the statistical method.

Rosmini questions this thesis from its root, appealing to his criticism of happiness as a material or physical phenomenon that is, therefore, equal in all persons according to purely arithmetical criteria. Given that, for him, happiness is a personal phenomenon, it is the fruit of internal psychological conditions and, above all, of cultural, jural and ethical conditions, which vary enormously from person to person. Thus, a state action aimed at equally distributing material goods would completely pass over the fact that each individual internally experiences identical material goods and the lack of them in completely different manners, because "it is certain and clear that an individual of the human species can differ infinitely from another individual of the same species in respect of the quantity of good and evil he possesses" (Rosmini 1994b, n. 559). Thus, the consequences of an egalitarian distribution would be, on one hand, the decrease of the total happiness existing in society as a consequence of the "leveling down" of the possibilities for development of those who are more deserving and, on the other hand, an unjust distribution of that happiness as goods are denied to those who have moral merits and given to others who lack such merits.

Now, according to Rosmini, egalitarianism maintains "false ideas regarding equity, justice and right" owing to the fact that its defenders are imbued with a "sensist philosophy" by which "human rights are rooted totally the human tendency to pleasure," from whence they deduce that "all have an equal right to good" and so "a government must not allow good to be accumulated in a single individual but strive to distribute it evenly so that no one has more than another" (Rosmini 1994b,

n. 612). In Rosmini's view, this "equality understood in this material way" arises from an "abstract conception" of Man reduced to his purely physical dimension which, if applied, would not lead to distributive justice but, on the contrary, to "an interminable succession of injustices, violations and enormous inequalities" (Rosmini 1994b, n. 623).[30]

8.4.4 Utopia and Irrationality of Planning

Furthermore, the last consequence of social utilitarianism consists in its expectation of carrying this planning of happiness to its ultimate consequences, that is, of achieving the elimination of pain and the maximization of happiness, understood as foreseeable and measurable pleasure, through sophisticated State engineering. The utilitarian idea of completely planning happiness as from the State is, according to Rosmini, not only immoral but also impossible. Thus, the egalitarianism that leads to social utilitarianism is not only unjust but terribly anti-economical. In Rosmini's view, it destroys all incentive for progress because it kills the moral nucleus of the economy that lies in each person's freedom and search for happiness.

The principle of utilitarian and consequentialist planning applied to the economy leads to the absurdity that the probabilities of obtaining a final positive or negative result are equally infinite, which turns planning into an essentially irrational action:

> Where are the limits of the utility system? There are none. Its action is as infinite as an arbitrary will: it assumes that it is possible to indefinitely make one reform in society after another; but it will never be known with certainty if there has been progress or regression. (Rosmini 1887, 151)

That is why Rosmini emphasizes the great importance of freedom as a general principle for society and the economy. In his opinion, the idea that the government, through a social planner or engineer, can completely foresee the results of the economy represents the death of both the economy and of society.

8.4.5 Utilitarianism, Totalitarianism and Hegelian Metaphysics

According to Rosmini, this idea of "happiness or public utility" maintained by utilitarianism implicitly involves the conception of utility as the "happiness of an abstract entity without any other existence than a mental one" (Rosmini 1933, 22), reduced to "the multiplicity of relationships between human beings" (Rosmini 1933, 29) and to "relationships with external objects" (Rosmini 1933, 31). That

[30]In Rosmini's view, it is evident that the sensist reduction of right to the tendency to pleasure would lead to an arbitrary and generalized claim by everyone for the satisfaction of their needs, whether by the force of the state or by the way of private violence.

is synthesized in the tendency to deify civil or political society, a thesis which will be the core of all Rosmini's criticism of what we could call "civil or political immanentism." In his opinion, the central error incurred into by supporters of social utilitarianism may be summed up in their reducing all rights to social right and to conceive civil or political society as the only source of right. When civil society does not recognize a natural and rational right previous to society itself but expects to become the very source of right, we arrive at the despotism of politics that today is many times the same, under democratic forms, to the one that existed in times of monarchical absolutism:

> Every despotism has at its root the negation of the rights of nature and reason (. . .) When the aversion of the people to the absolutism of princes exploded in modern times, instead of combating the absolutism itself, only one of its special forms was fought – and thus this radical vice of societies simply changed its form. (Rosmini 2007, 27)

Very early in his intellectual career, Rosmini perceives the totalitarianism implicit in the social utilitarian concept of "public happiness." In fact, Rosmini sees in radical social utilitarianisms such as socialism, the specter of an "objectivism" that denies the concrete person in favor of a purely generic social entity. In his celebrated *Saggio sul Comunismo e il Socialismo,* Rosmini describes utilitarianism's idea of society as "a pure mechanism of universal prosperity" (Rosmini 1978c, 92) in which "the individual is no longer anything" (Rosmini 1978c, 99) and it is society or the State, having become a universal subject, who "associates or dissociates men," because "what reason would men have for conforming a society if they no longer have interests of their own, the procuring of these being in the hands of the State?" (Rosmini 1978c, 101). Towards the end of his life, in *Le Principali Questioni politico-religiose della giornata*, Rosmini explicitly shows what had matured in his thinking over the years. To the Roveretan, social utilitarianism would be no other thing than idealistic metaphysics of ultimately sensist origin expressed in political terms. In this sense, Hegel's metaphysics, which necessarily leads to what Rosmini calls "statolatry," that is, a conception of the State as "a great organized God" (Rosmini 1978b, 135) does not essentially differ from the absolutization of "social utility" carried forward by the utopian socialists, the communists and Bentham.[31]

[31] To Hegel, individual life is ruled by "pure *subjective individual interest*," understood as "personal caprice;" access to objectivity is only achieved through the State: "the individual possesses objectivity, truth and ethicity only as a member of the State, since the State is objective Spirit" (Hegel 1944, 220–221).

Chapter 9
Paths Towards Social Recognition

9.1 Social Justice

9.1.1 A Word of Success

Rosmini assures that the main road through which political economy should run in order to break with the auto referential autism of the different forms of utilitarianism and create an economy of recognition is the one of "social justice." Together with Luigi Taparelli D'Azeglio, Rosmini was one of the first philosophers to use this expression, which would become the banner of the vindication – on the part of the Catholic social movement in the nineteenth century – of the rights of society's poorest and most exploited members, and would reach universal diffusion in the twentieth century with the same meaning. However, to Rosmini's way of thinking, the expression "social justice" has a much less affective sense and bears only a partial connection with the rights of the dispossessed. In fact, he sees social justice as society's architectonic principle, in the same fashion as all those of the classical period – from Plato and Aristotle onwards – had used it. In fact, to him "justice is the first element to enter the construction of every human society" since "in the last analysis, a society cannot be anything except an accumulation of rights and duties. Society is a complex of agreements which themselves are acts of justice" (Rosmini 1993a, 26). "The theory of justice, therefore, is part of the theory of society. Vice versa, the theory of society is, in another aspect, part of the theory of justice." In consequence, "the politician, that is to say, the person who is responsible for governing society, must be aware before all else of the theory of justice"(Rosmini 1993a, n. 26).

Thus, every economic policy, as subordinated to the ends of Politics, has justice as its ruling principle. We have already mentioned that there may be no utility without justice; likewise, there cannot be true economic growth within society unless it takes place within the framework of social justice, which – to the Roveretan – implies a "just regulation of the modality of rights." Therefore, to

C. Hoevel, *The Economy of Recognition: Person, Market and Society in Antonio Rosmini*, Ethical Economy 42, DOI 10.1007/978-94-007-6058-5_9,

Rosmini's way of thinking, this requisite of justice makes no room for an economic policy that overrides any right with the pretext of obtaining a greater utility; at the same time – as we have seen above – it demands, on the part of the civil society, the protection, defense and union of all individual and social economic rights.

However, the justice that Rosmini deems necessary in any economic policy is of a special kind: it is essentially different from other forms of justice since it is "that part of justice which binds individuals and joins them in society" (Rosmini 1993a, n. 26). By virtue of this trait, social justice goes beyond that which would suffice, for example, for commutative justice amongst persons, where the jural nature of the relationship is exclusively determined by mutual respect for the rights of each individual. Although social justice certainly includes within its foundation the requirement of respect for the individual rights of the members of society, its specific end must seek their coordination with a view to their maximum potentiating and enlargement in the shape of common good of society as a whole according to what political prudence may prescribe for each society at a concrete time and place.

> When we say that the natural constitution of civil society must be deducted from social justice, we are not referring to any kind of justice, but to justice applied to the determination of the forms and laws of society. (Rosmini 1887, 669)

9.1.2 Jural-Social and Politico-Social Laws

Within the basic jural structure necessary for any economic policy governed by social justice, Rosmini distinguishes two types of laws: on the one hand, the ones he calls "jural-social" laws, the aim of which is that of "the precise determination of rights according to jural reason" (Rosmini 1995a, n. 417); these are laws where "jural reason" is applied to the protection of the economic rights of individuals beyond their belonging to society (Rosmini 1996, n. 2479). They are the basic "floor" of any economic policy governed by social justice. On the other hand, and also necessary, there are the laws Rosmini calls "socio-political laws," where "jural reason is applied to determine social organization and the obligations of officials and single members of society, with the aim of enhancing cooperation for the attainment of the social end" (Rosmini 1996, 2479).

This second type of laws is aimed at obtaining the greatest benefit for the whole of society. For this reason, they are not limited to the mere protection of individual rights but give rise to "modification of individual rights, and to totally new, social rights" (Rosmini 1996, n. 2480). In this sense, according to Rosmini, the "legislator can act as follows as a consequence of the end of society, for the sake of which all are obliged to co-operate." In doing so, he can "suspend or prohibit members from exercising any activity proper to rights possessed independently of society," as well as "determine the rights which, according to simply individual Right, remain doubtful either absolutely or in relationship to the limited capacity of the human mind, a limitation which prevents [private] agreement about the solution of some specific case," and even "render [jurally] obligatory (provided this is necessary or useful for the social end) that which, according to individual jural-law, would be only morally or fittingly obligatory" (Rosmini 1996, n. 2481–2482).

9.1.3 The Risk of Regulations

These statements regarding the possibilities of socio-political laws certainly sound strong, especially when we take into account how harshly Rosmini criticizes the different forms of statist and socialist utilitarianism, which – with the pretext of the pursuit of society's good or utility – overrun individual rights and subject spontaneous acts of competition and even cooperation, agreements, and mutual assistance amongst individuals to the coercion of strict jural obligations. The answer to this apparent contradiction is that Rosmini is exactly the opposite of a thinker who attempts to replace the spontaneity of society and economy with utilitarian control over them through a legislative apparatus. In this sense, even if positive legislation, as a guarantor of social justice within economy, plays a central role in its healthy growth and evolution, it runs the risk of falling into an excess of generalization and abstractism – as it happens, in his opinion, with modern legislation. This excess, with the excuse of favoring general utility, ends up trampling over particular groups and individuals. He points out: "this century embraced as true the principle that every improvement consists in generalizing things" (Rosmini 1923, 75). And so, "the vice of modern generality consists in sacrificing particulars against what Nature demands: that we found the general upon the particulars" (Rosmini 1923, 76–77).

As a result, legislative abstractism places unnecessary hindrances in the path of possibilities of economic growth, which could otherwise materialize if attempts were not made to solve *a priori* those conflicts amongst interests that can often be solved by the initiative or agreement of the individuals involved, who know better than anyone else the conditions of their particular situation. In effect, Rosmini adds: "The government of any society whatsoever normally applies general enactments, and in most cases cannot do otherwise – But this is precisely why they can easily err. When a government draws up a general law or enactment, it believes it need consider only the general effects of the law or enactment, without descending to the anomalies of particular individuals. The intended law and the human nature to which the law is applied are considered solely in the abstract. This is not sufficient (. . .) rights are unjustly sacrificed to the inexorable generality of law (. . .)" (Rosmini1994b, n. 228). Thus, because of these enactments, governments frequently squander economic resources which, actually, belong to the individual (Rosmini 1994b, n. 229). So, in Rosmini's opinion, true social and distributive justice in economic matters is not achieved by a rationalist legislation that establishes,*a priori*, the outcome of matters. On the contrary, all good legislation should leave a door open for the expression of the possibilities contained in the concrete reality where particular individuals act. "Therefore, the more we observe the particular, the closer we are to distributive justice" (Rosmini 1923, 68–69).

Thus, Rosmini opposes economic legalism, which seeks to foresee and control all conflicts through an omni-comprehensive legislation accompanied by judicial coercion. He is critical of the French-style statist legalism, heavily founding his criticism on the English and Scottish juridical thinking of historical inspiration (Hume, Blackstone, Robertson, Young) as well as on many aspects of the British Constitution. In effect, according to Rosmini, French juridical rationalism tends to be the product of "the improvisation of audacious and imaginative minds, too much infatuated with too general and too imperfect theories . . . daughters of a philosophy that wanted to break with the past" (Rosmini 2007, 2), and which is usually, therefore, full of "vain abstractions" and of "theories that are inapplicable to social reality" (Rosmini 2007, 10). Besides, he considers that, in this sense, the British juridical tradition has been "formed passage by passage, without a premeditated scheme, incessantly patched and mended according to counter-veiling social forces and the urgency of instincts and popular need" (Rosmini 2007, 1).

9.1.4 The Prudential Dimension

Furthermore, in addition to the jural basis, any just economic policy evidently requires a prudential dimension, that is to say, a set of actions which can make the most useful application possible of economic laws for the different particular cases. This prudential aspect of economic policies has for Rosmini the specific function of obtaining the greatest possible utility within the framework of the laws mentioned, keeping the closest contact with concrete reality. In this sense, laws, even the just ones, do not have a single form of application. In fact, according to Rosmini, "civil society can be just in many ways, not in one alone. We have to search, therefore, amongst all the cases free from injustice in civil society, for that particular one which best protects justice from disturbance and facilitates the progress of human happiness. This case, this determination of society, which we call its *regular state*, is indicated only by civil prudence" (Rosmini 1996, n. 2580).

Furthermore, in line with Burke or Smith, Rosmini believes that even economic policies and legislation conceived in this latter fashion should not aspire to span it all. On the contrary, both should be conceived as aids and incentives making ample room for the initiative and ethics of individuals as the primary instrument for finding a just solution to conflicts of interests: "only morality can teach this good faith and moderation in the use of one's own right" (Rosmini 1994b, n. 144).

9.1.5 Regulation of the Modality of Rights

If we take this context into account, we will see that on defining politico-social laws or the administrative functions of economic policies, Rosmini never exceeds the maximum limit civil society has in relation with individual economic rights, such limit being that of the "regulation of their modality," which never includes the modification or elimination of the content of rights, but just a change in the way they are exercised. For this reason, even if "it can sometimes happen that these laws (...) modify the rights which jural reason would establish" (Rosmini 1995a, n. 419) this does not mean that they become unjust because "even civil-political laws are truly *jural*" (Rosmini 1996, n. 2478). In fact, according to Rosmini, politico-social laws do not lose their jural character "if the modification [of individual rights] is carried out with the express or presumed consent of all the members, or with some obligatory consent dependent upon another jural reason" (Rosmini 1995a, n. 419). In other words, it is not a question of eliminating the jural reason that proceeds from the individual right to replace it for a pure reason of social utility, as it occurs in utilitarianism, but a question of modifying the first individual jural reason by virtue of another stronger social jural reason. To Rosmini's way of thinking, this implies that in certain cases of "evident [social] necessity" (Rosmini 1996, n. 423), the best manner of exercising an individual economic right is by restricting or even prohibiting the exercise of it by means of the laws of civil society, as – on account of social right – the latter sometimes has the function of replacing the individual not with the purpose of diminishing his right or good but with that of increasing said right and good in the form of common good. In this way, even if a legislation restricting individual economic rights often represents an apparent loss for certain individuals in the short term, a just legislation must create the conditions so that this loss is not substantial but just accidental, in the sense that it is compensated and even gradually overcome by the indirect consequences forthcoming to individuals thanks to the benefits that their sacrifices brought to society as a whole:

> The law alters individual rights without cause for complaint by the members, who have to cede their right for the sake of the common good which is the end of society. These accidental losses or changes of rights, which gradually adjust themselves, are social burdens and obligations precisely because they are necessary for the end that society has in view, and because each member is compensated to his own advantage by the good he gains from society itself. In fact, there is no real loss, but a highly useful change of modality. (Rosmini 1996, n. 2482)

In addition, Rosmini maintains: "I will never tire of affirming that in my opinion legislations which show greater respect for individual rights are more moral and liberal; legislations are more perfect when they conserve individual rights as far as possible, sacrificing only the smallest part of them in order to avoid evidently greater inconveniences" (Rosmini 1995a, n. 424). However, contrary to the liberal thinking of Locke or Smith, Rosmini believes that the protection of individual rights is insufficient to achieve a prosperous and just economy. To the Roveretan, there is no greater encouragement for economy than when it is ruled by social justice, that is to say, when it occurs within the framework of the widest possible respect for Right as a whole, which includes individual rights as well as social rights within the framework of a legislation and political prudence aimed at the common good. In this way, "true and complete utility – Rosmini adds – is born out of justice rigorously applied to its ultimate consequences" (Rosmini 1887, 669).

9.2 The Common Good

9.2.1 The Rosminian Conception of the Common Good

Yet, it is already evident that, according to Rosmini, common good is not opposed to individual rights or goods: "*the common good is the good of all the individuals* who make up the social body and are subjects of rights" (Rosmini 1996, n. 1644). In another similar formulation, Rosmini adds that "because civil society (granted its universality) extends such protection to *all* rights, its end is the *common good*" (Rosmini 1996, n. 1643). Thus, given that "society is instituted for the good of the individuals who compose it (. . .) the good of civil society therefore can only be the common good of its members" (Rosmini 1996, 1679). In this sense, Rosmini makes it clear that the common good can never imply the denial of individual rights – not even a single one – on account of any reason alleged to be for the good of society. To him, invoking the good of society as the reason for denying any individual right whatsoever is an absurdity, a contradiction in terms, since common good, if established at the expense of the right of any individual, automatically ceases to be common and becomes, at the most, the good of a majority. In Rosmini's view, common good, in order to be such, must be a good for all, since society has been instituted by all and for all.

Furthermore, it is necessary to explain the difference between Rosmini's concept of common good and that of the individualistic liberalism which reduces it to the summation of individual goods. According to Rosmini, individual goods may certainly contribute towards the common good. However, he points out that not any individual good necessarily leads to the common good, but only those which tend towards social good (Rosmini 1994b, n. 196). In fact, we have already seen Rosmini's criticism of Adam Smith's idea that individual goods necessarily and always lead to the common good. Nonetheless, even in the case of individual goods which may contribute to the common good, the latter includes other goods which are not only the result of individual or inter-individual action, but of a common social action. According to Rosmini, this common social action is "the regulation of the modality of individual rights," which modifies individual rights and goods in such a way that a type of good which could never be obtained by the sole action of separate individuals is produced. Instead, individualistic liberalism holds that common action regulatory of rights and the common good which results from it no longer exist, because "social" action is limited to the mere protection of individual rights, and there is no modalization whatsoever.

Furthermore, according to Rosmini, the common good is not only the result of common regulatory action, but of a second, additional process. Although the sum of some isolated individual rights – provided their modality is regulated in common – is part of the common good, there are also some rights which, in order to generate common good, must experience a change. This change is what he calls "amalgamation of rights." In other words, some rights not only change their form but they also amalgamate by virtue of what Rosmini calls "social dynamics" – functions exercised by the State, which replace functions exercised by individuals – so as to obtain common goods which individuals could never achieve by themselves:

> The end of civil society can also be promoted by placing some rights in common. This amalgamation of rights would seem basically to be the same as a change in the form of rights (...) because rights may be associated only if their owners suffer no harm or are compensated for all losses, either by the avoidance of a greater evil or by the acquisition of a greater good. The third function, however, is concerned with change in the form of single rights without amalgamation, while our present function concerns the placing of rights in common, in society. (Rosmini 1996, n. 2146)

9.2.2 Public and Private Goods

In accordance to Rosmini, this "placing in common" by the government of civil society generates a new type of good which Rosmini calls "public good." The latter is different from common good, although it does not necessarily contradict it. Indeed, he defines public good as "*the good of the social body*, taken as a whole, or according to some opinions, taken in its organization" (Rosmini 1996, n. 1644). In addition, to make this definition more precise, he describes it as "the good of the social body, not of its single parts" (Rosmini 1996, n. 1657), specifically, of the "principal part of the body which is always formed by those citizens who control social authority" (Rosmini 1996, n. 1658). In a few words, public good is no longer the good of all individuals and societies that make up the political society, but the good of the State as the ruling and constituting part of such society:

> This is natural. The good of that part of the social body on which the constitution, life and movement of the body depend is undoubtedly more important for the general good of the social body; and it is this part which possesses social authority. (Rosmini 1996, n. 1658)

To Rosmini, it is then certain that a just and beneficial economic development demands an efficient administration of public goods, as these goods have a direct repercussion on the good of society taken as a whole, which is an indispensable requisite for achieving common good:

> These must be administered by the government with just economy, and their product applied to cover expenses necessary for the good of government and for the proportional benefit of member families. (Rosmini 1996, n. 2157)

However, Rosmini warns of the danger of confusing public good with common good, a confusion present – as we have seen – in social utilitarianism of a statist type:

> The common good should be distinguished from the public good. These two matters are confused with consequent serious harm to the science of public Right and to humanity which, because of this confusion of concepts, searches in vain for a suitable social constitution. (Rosmini 1996, n. 1644)

In this way, "civil society can in some way have *public good* as its end" "on condition that *public good* is subordinated as a means to *common good*, which is its sole proximate end" (Rosmini 1996, n. 1660). Now, if we consider that the common good is the aggregate of individual rights that are regulated in common and "amalgamated", it is evident that no public good will be attained by sacrificing these rights:

> Not a single right of individual citizens (the complex of these rights is the common good) can be sacrificed for the sake of the public good. (Rosmini 1996, n. 1661)

However, according to Rosmini, it is also evident that sacrifice of individual rights for the sake of the public good is unjust only when a right is "destroyed or damaged without recompense, when the right or its worth could otherwise be saved" (Rosmini 1996, n. 1661). Nevertheless, beyond these cases, provided the principle stating that individual rights must remain intact in their worth (not in their modality) is respected, Rosmini is categorical when affirming the hierarchical priority of public good over private good, as the former is a more direct means for the attainment of common good then the latter:

> Public good must be preferred to private good once the rights of individuals have been safeguarded. In this case, public good will undoubtedly further common good. (Rosmini 1996, n. 1661)

9.2.3 *A Complex Relationship Amongst Goods*

Therefore, Rosmini believes that a just order amongst these three goods would give priority to the common good – understood as the maximum good possible of all individuals – the public good – understood as good of the State – would follow in second place, while individual or private good would take the third place. However, this hierarchy should not be interpreted in a statist or socializing sense. On the contrary, once the common good and the public good have been guaranteed, the private good becomes a fundamental element for the growth of the common good. Private good is only opposed to common good and to public good when it becomes an exclusive or privileged good belonging to a single individual or group. As long as the private good begins to circulate and to be distributed alternately among different members of society, it becomes a generator of common good:

> In addition, when first the common good and then the public good have been safeguarded, the private good of individuals and families can and must be pursued, provided one condition is observed: the opportunity for obtaining private good through the action of society must be open equally to all families and all individuals. It must not be restricted to particular individuals or families or bodies. When this condition has been verified, all citizens have equality of opportunity and private good itself becomes part of the common good. The good that one family or individual gains today from civil society is gained tomorrow by another individual or family when they are placed in the same circumstances with the same opportunities. Private good, alternating between families and distributing itself evenly over a certain period of time, is absorbed and changed into true common good. (Rosmini 1996, n. 1662–1663)

9.3 The Two Main Regulations: Ownership and Freedom

9.3.1 How Is the Right of Ownership Regulated?

Both objectives of social justice and common good as ends proper to political society will give a special framework to the exercise of the basic economic rights we analyzed in Chap. 7 of this book, that is, the natural rights to ownership and of free competition. In fact, even though to Rosmini's thinking both rights have – already at the level of pre-social right – characteristics which clearly differentiate them from the liberal and socialist conceptions, at the socio-political level they will acquire further differences with reference to these interpretations. Taking into account all we have mentioned with regard to the right of ownership, the first thing we should say is that, according to Rosmini, the defense of the right of ownership is one of the central functions of the political or civil society and, therefore, of every economic policy:

> Generally speaking, the defense of private ownership is always present when civil society has been constituted. If the private owner himself is incapable of defending what he owns, society itself undertakes this responsibility. (Rosmini 1993b, n. 887)

In this sense, as we have already seen, Rosmini is a harsh critic of all statist, socialist and communist systems which tend to overrule the right of ownership. To him, the development of the economy demands from the State the fullest possible protection of the exercise of the right of ownership. However, he claims that civil society evidently does not have the sole function of protecting the right of ownership; it should also prevent its limits from being trespassed. These limits, as we have also seen, are a fundamental issue to consider when dealing with this right. In this sense, the laws and political ordinances of the government of civil society do nothing but transfer, to the field of positive law, the implications contained in rational law regarding the right of ownership. These implications allow civil society to "regulate the modality" of the right of ownership without diminishing its worth, with the purpose of achieving greater common good. Thus, it is clear to Rosmini that civil society has the power to "make ordinances about the *ownership* belonging to individuals when the end is their own greater good" or "when the aim is the common or public good"(Rosmini 1996, n. 1667).

Rosmini mentions numerous possible ordinances referred to the regulation of the modality of the right of ownership by the political society. These include those protecting the right to the just acquisition, preservation and transfer of ownership, and those which prevent ownership's exclusive accumulation in the hands of a few (Rosmini 2007, 55–56), as well as its unproductive possession. This is the basis of natural Right which allows, as we have already mentioned, "for the rest of the community to appeal" to an owner "in favor of minors or the public, or even the private good" and the writing of "laws with which civil society places wastrels under supervision" (Rosmini 1993b, n. 885). Rosmini even contemplates the possibility of expropriation in case public good or common good demands so, as long as due compensation is awarded:

> All properties are inviolable. Forced expropriation is not violation of property when a legally ascertained public good demands it, and through a fair indemnity which conforms to the laws. (Rosmini 2007, 13)

Furthermore, there is also the extreme case of forced confiscation by the State, when the conditions required by every right of ownership have disappeared.[1] In this sense, the role of the civil society is always that of protecting and encouraging the exercise of the right of ownership to the maximum, but always within its jural limits and in subordination to the demands posed by the common good.

9.3.2 *The "True and Healthy Liberalism"*

With regard to the key issue of the right of free competition, we have referred in Chap. 7 to the concept and limits of "jural economic freedom." Indeed, according to Rosmini, the right of free competition is based on competitiveness, that is to say, on the capabilities to obtain the benefits of the market, developed through intelligent and laborious efforts. In fact, no economic policy jurally enclosed within the framework of social justice can replace the right to free competition – which, in Rosmini's view, is natural and inviolable – by an act of force or governmental will:

> No one can prevent another person from earning except by occupying beforehand, through competition, what the other would have earned. Such pre-occupancy, as we call it, comes about through expeditious effort and greater industry (Rosmini 1993b, n. 1676). To limit, by an act of will alone, other's freedom to earn and in general their freedom to acquire some other good or occupancy, is an infringement of Right even if the limitation is supported with force. A private individual could not do this; the government, therefore, cannot do it in favor of an individual. Generally speaking freedom of trade is founded in natural Right and is therefore inviolable. (Rosmini 1993b, n. 1676)

We have seen how Rosmini stands out amongst modern Catholic thinkers for his understanding and admiration of freedom of trade which he sees as the most efficient form of distribution of economic resources. According to him, it is therefore very dangerous to attempt to replace the spontaneous order of market exchanges, seeking to artificially plan the economy. This would imply the assumption that it is possible to know the infinite motivations and reasons leading the multiple market agents to make decisions that are finally reflected in prices. As knowing such thing is impossible, the effect achieved is just the opposite: prices become distorted,

[1] Rosmini 1993b, n. 855–858.

decisions are made upon the basis of an unreal situation and, consequently, the wealth the economy could have otherwise achieved decreases:

> [The artificial direction of wealth in (large) markets] is, to say the least, very dangerous because it cannot be directed without knowing all the laws of its circulation, without calculating the mutual influence of the infinite number of agents related amongst themselves and the irregularities and particularities of their behavior. In this way, in the belief that one is doing something to increase wealth, one disturbs it and prevents its growth. (Rosmini 1923, 137)

Now, according to Rosmini, this affirmation of the free market as the fundamental basis of economy, both from the point of view of justice as of utility, does not imply the idea that the free market is an infallible mechanism nor that its absolute freedom may be sustained, as we have already seen in Chap. 7 when we considered his criticism of individualist liberalism. On the contrary, to him, it is clear that the distribution of wealth carried out by the markets – even by those that are extensive and free – does not always result in the benefit of all its participants, nor is it in agreement with social justice and Right. The principles of market freedom and competitiveness are necessary – though not sufficient – conditions for every economic policy. Therefore, Rosmini states with great emphasis that free economic competition can be by no means the sole ruling principle of economic order, but should always be subordinated to social justice and the common good:

> I fully support free competition for every kind of good, provided we do not misunderstand "competition", an undetermined and equivocal word. I do not espouse competition as the sole source and principle of justice, but as the effect, not the cause of justice, that is, as the effect of justice which is anterior to and therefore determines the right of competition. If this important distinction is ignored, the meaning of the word remains uncertain and opens the field to many unfortunate sophisms. (Rosmini 1994b, n. 695)

Now, what criterion should be applied for an economic policy to encourage fair free competition? Although Rosmini believes the right of free competition to be inviolable, he thinks a political orientation in the *modality* of its exercise is required:

> I think it is possible to find a simple formula that would express the unique principle of universal means which, applied correctly, renders civil society immune from every injustice. I would propose the following: "if civil society maintains inviolate the principle of universal free concurrence, according to rational Right, it will avoid every injustice." The formula can be explained in this way: rational Right allows all individual and collective persons to acquire equally any right, provided the means of acquisition are just. Granted that politico-positive Right does not use arbitrary ordinances to reduce the sphere of a jural person's freedom, the concurrence under discussion is preserved. I say "arbitrary ordinances" because there is in Right itself a mode of limiting another's freedom (...) (Rosmini 1996, n. 2271–2273)

Rosmini points out, on the one hand, that civil society "may establish ordinances regarding *inoffensive freedom* according to the following reasons: for the good of the individuals who make up society; for the public good as long as individuals do not experience any jural injury; for the common good." On the contrary, "offends individuals if it disposes of their freedom beyond these three aims and without the conditions which we have indicated" (Rosmini 1996, n. 1667).[2] But which are these legitimate methods of regulating and limiting free economic concurrence on the part of civil society? According to Rosmini, a first kind of intervention in the market on the part of the government should consist in generating incentives to guide those who are more active and to strengthen those who are less active. These incentives may range from the removal of obstacles to training or the awarding of prizes and subsidies:

> From which it will be the concern of the government to remove ignorance, prejudice, habits harmful to production, and, with prizes and other incentives, to guide those most active and encourage those less active (...) (Rosmini 1923, 138)

Furthermore, a second kind of intervention, more extreme and exceptional, would imply specific actions aimed at limiting or curbing market freedom. This will be possible as long as there does not exist an insoluble material incapacity regarding resources, geographical location, or natural talents for concurrence but only a temporary situation owing to exclusively cultural or educational reasons concerning training that may be remedied by limiting market freedom for a reasonable period of time:

> From which it is deduced that the greater the inertia and ignorance of the people, the greater the governmental action that limits the activity of commerce and industry must be (...) Regarding market, we see the application of what has been previously described in regard to the freedom which the government must grant to its people, and which must be as great as the science and will that people possess to use it. (Rosmini 1923, 139)

Thus, free economic competition, taken not as an unlimited and absolute freedom but as a jural and relative freedom subordinated to Right and the common good and regulated in its modality by the government, constitutes to Rosmini a formidable driving force for the human economic progress of all members of society:

> If government regulates only the modality of rights without disposing of their value, all citizens enjoy concurrence for all social and extra-social goods, because their right of relative freedom is maintained and guaranteed in all its extension (...) Relative freedom for all must be recognized as an intangible right which allows everyone complete free competition for all types of work (...) When these conditions are guaranteed, it is clear that the result will inevitably be the most natural and extensive development of all good initiative, business, branch of knowledge and talent (...) The result of this universal free concurrence for every unoccupied good, in conformity with activity and merit, is the best possible economic-moral situation at least for the greatest number if not all of the citizens. (Rosmini 1996, n. 2072–2075–2076)

In a word, according to Rosmini, free economic competition signifies not an unlimited exaltation of freedom but a "harmonious conciliation between private freedoms and the authority of the government, so that under the firmest authority,

---

[2]"Hence, it (civil society) injures the *rights of freedom* of particular individuals: (a) every time it impedes their occupying *actions* and *things*, without lawfully occupying them itself; or (b) restricts in any other way the activity of individuals to a greater degree than required by its own need" (Rosmini 1996, n. 1668).

each one retains the exercise of greatest possible jural freedom. Such is true and healthy liberalism (. . .)" (Rosmini 1978c, 96).

9.4 Distributive Justice, Economic Equity and Equal Opportunities

9.4.1 The Need of Changing the Perspective

Distributive justice is, according to Rosmini, an essential dimension of social justice – that is to say, the just distribution amongst the members of society of all the total benefits and costs that life in common implies – which is also one of the ends that every economic policy must keep in mind. Furthermore, although distributive justice implies a great complexity of elements, according to Rosmini, it is possible to discover a general criterion for the distribution of goods and evils or of costs and benefits in an economy. This criterion consists in adopting a *jural perspective* of the problem, the political or economic perspective remaining in second place. The mistake of all types of utilitarianism, whether conservative, statist or liberal, has been precisely that of inverting this order or priorities:

> They do not consider the distribution of responsibilities a jural but a political or economical problem. We may well ask: "Which distribution of social responsibilities helps a government most in its administration, or makes the responsibilities felt less by the majority of the citizens, or by the most powerful citizens, so that no one complains? Which distribution is more conducive to the production of wealth?" But before all these questions, we should ask another which is certainly more humble, but much more profound, sacred and helpful to society: "Which distribution of social responsibilities is more just?" (Rosmini 1996, n. 2163)

In this sense, a jural vision of the distributive problem implies considering, as the foundation of all just distribution, the acknowledgement of the human being as person, not as a purely passive and material being who may be the object of paternalistic protection by a feudal lord who grants gifts, by a benefactor State which turns him into an object of assistance or physical well-being, or by a market which induces needs and desires that suffocate true freedom. According to Rosmini, distributive justice begins when the laws and measures of political society allow human beings to unfold their moral and jural freedom and, through it, achieve by themselves the economic goods they need for their development. Thus, the nucleus of distributive justice on the part of political society and, in our case, of economic policy, does not consist in distributing economic goods in a direct manner but in seeking that the greatest possible display of the moral and economic capacities of the citizens may perform this distribution for itself.

9.4.2 Recognizing Diversity

Now, on referring to the principle which Rosmini calls "derivation of rights," we have seen that although those rights have their universal source in the equal personal dignity of all human beings by the mere fact of their belonging to human nature, it "is unjust and false to claim that the person alone is the *principle of the derivation or determination of rights*" (Rosmini 1993b, n. 350). If this were so, given the equal dignity of all human beings as persons, distributive justice would be equivalent to absolute equality. However, as we have already mentioned, economic rights do not derive directly from the equality of all men in human nature, but from the free moral acts on which they are founded. In this sense, according to Rosmini, it is clear that distributive justice must be based, in the first place, on the acknowledgement of the inequality of rights derived from the unequal merit of moral acts performed by different persons. Thus, to the Roveretan, the key criterion a government must adopt to perform a just economic distribution is, in the first place, to acknowledge the diversity of the moral merits of persons, because they are the foundation of the rights over economic goods and even of the economic capacities necessary to acquire them.

Therefore, distributive justice implies the generation of the maximum economic good possible in proportion to every person's rights, moral merits and economic capacities. As expressed from a negative point of view, according to Rosmini, it would not be legitimate for the government to apply any measure aimed at distributing income in a more egalitarian manner amongst more citizens at the cost of overriding a person's acquired rights and merits. A procedure of this kind would not be true distributive *justice* but unjust egalitarianism based on purely material criteria.

We can quite easily accept the principle that just distribution implies unequal distribution, given that the merits on which rights are based are – in general – unequal. However, beyond inequality of merits, it is not so easy to admit inequality in the abilities each person is endowed with and which do not depend on their freedom or effort. Indeed, economic goods are not the result of merit alone but of innumerable accidents and circumstances such as natural talents, levels of education and inherited economic goods, which have clearly been distributed in a very unequal manner amongst human beings. Now, according to Rosmini, it is also part of distributive justice to accept – in principle – this inequality as a necessary and inevitable reality due to the fact that human nature is subjected, in every person, to the circumstances proper to their incarnate and historical condition. To this, we should add the consequences of the state of fallen nature that determine, according to Rosmini, an inevitable inequality amongst human beings, not with reference to their dignity but to goods and capacities.

9.4.3 Critique of Egalitarianism and Social Perfectism

Rosmini's position is summarized in his celebrated criticism of what he calls "social perfectism," which consists in believing that society can completely remedy all the imperfections and evils inherent to the human condition. According to him, this social perfectism, aiming at suppressing these imperfections and evils, ends up losing and squandering many goods associated with the evils of inequality. It is true that Rosmini expresses his desire for a greater equality in distribution, so that "it may be possible to distribute this maximum among many rather than a few individuals," and also that "this maximum quantity of net good could be divided in equal proportions among all human beings" (Rosmini 1994b, n. 604). But this cannot be done at the cost of squandering goods since if "the distribution were not possible without diminishing the maximum quantity of net good enjoyed by humanity, supporting the distribution would mean that human nature had lost a part of its goods, and this would clearly be an offence against the virtue of humanity" (Rosmini 1994b, n. 604).

Thus, in clear opposition to any kind of perfectist or materialistic egalitarianism, Rosmini lays down the basic principle that all distributive justice is founded on the admission of the inevitable fact of inequality, which is in part the fruit of a hopeless randomness, and in part the result of effort and merit. In fact, Rosmini affirms, "if government arbitrarily preferred some individuals to others, it could be seen as sinning against distributive justice. But if it depends solely on external circumstances, on the nature of things, and often on the varying merits of the individuals themselves, it cannot be said to act with injustice and favoritism simply because some individuals are so placed in society that they inevitably share more widely in the good which the government, without respect or favoritism for any individual, is promoting with all its force" (Rosmini 1994b, n. 625). Thus, to him, an economically just distribution of goods within a society is, in principle, the outcome of competition amongst individuals and "it is never the task of government" (Rosmini 1994b, n. 628).

9.4.4 The Rosminian Conception of Equity

In this sense, it is clear that Rosmini's concept of distributive justice includes, in a first approach, not only the acceptance of inequality in the results of competition amongst persons but also of the inequality in the starting-point of pre-existing capacities. In fact Rosmini will define the distributive justice civil society must reach almost in the same terms as those of a commercial society. Indeed, in his opinion, the central principle of distributive justice in a society should imply that its members "receive earnings proportionate to their contributions." Thus, Rosmini will define distributive justice, at which any economic policy should aim, as a kind of "equity," understood as a constant process of search for equalization, not in the egalitarian fashion according to which "two citizens, one of whom has contributed the equivalent of one hundred units to a society, and the other, a single unit, would have to receive equal earnings." In Rosmini's view, distributive justice should be understood as a search to equalize or establish the best balance possible between what a person obtains from the distributive process and his contribution to the process:

> The object of civil society, therefore, in regulating the modality of the rights of the members, must be to equalize the SHARE-QUOTA of utility which members can derive from the institution and management of society; it does not consist in equalizing utility itself among the members. This is the equable distribution of common good to which legislative thought and the government of civil society should constantly tend if it wishes to walk in the way of Right. (Rosmini 1996, n. 1653)

Now, the Roveretan is not unaware that this definition of equity and distributive justice must be made clear so that it is not confused with some kind of "cosmic Toryism," which considers that all the factual and historic conditions into which human beings are born and with which they enter the process of economic competition are always inevitable and proper to a natural order that cannot be modified. As a matter of fact, Rosmini displays a high moral indignation over the extreme inequality proper to the developing industrial society of his time, which he seems not to consider as the effect of an inevitable and, therefore, just distribution, but rather as the result of a true distributive injustice in society:

> In our magnificent capitals, of which we are proud, extreme misery is seen alongside excessive wealth, the most monstrous immorality alongside social virtues. (Rosmini 1994b, n. 681)

From a historical point of view, according to Rosmini, the attempt to remedy an original *excessive inequality* is precisely amongst the accidental causes that gave birth to civil or political society, differentiating it from family or feudal society. Thus the constitution of civil society would not have merely implied "distributing according to contribution," but "making a better distribution of ownership" (Rosmini 1887, 220), so that the starting-point of each person's contribution can be gradually remedied and so, later on, more is obtained in the final distribution.

9.4.5 Two Forms of Distribution

Rosmini points out that, throughout European history, two forms of distribution of wealth took place. On the one hand, we find "unjust" distribution based either on the resistance to change at any cost on the part of the most powerful and wealthiest, or on the violent attempt to rapidly achieve distribution on the part of revolutionaries and reformists. On the other hand, we find "just" distribution, consisting in the establishment of jural and economically fruitful institutions that would gradually make it possible. As an example of unjust distribution, Rosmini mentions the English system – which he calls "of the unfair aristocracy" – where there was insufficient political regulation of the struggle between the economic interests of the nobility (territorial wealth) and the economic interests of the new industrial capitals, not much acknowledged in that country (Rosmini 1887, 241). This was a typical "resistance system," based on the rejection of any reform or change whatsoever with regard to a jural and political system based upon prerogatives, privileges and special protections which prevented the circulation of ownership as well as jural free competition. The same situation occurred in Italy with the proliferation of *latifundium* (large landed estates) and unjust protection of wealth accumulation.

Furthermore, as a reaction to these "resistance systems," Rosmini gives the examples of "movement systems" or "social perfectionisms" proper to the French Revolution and egalitarian reformists of all kinds (Benthamists, socialists and communists) that infringe the law of balance between ownership and power by depriving economic interest of political representation – which, according to him, is essential for their social regulation and, consequently, their just distribution – and derive in a fierce and irrational war of interests with no institutional regulation whatsoever (Rosmini 1887, 221).

It is true that Rosmini agrees in several aspects with another kind of reformism or "movement system" such as British liberalism, not so much based on State action but on the extension of market concurrence. In fact, Rosmini states that he agrees "with Adam Smith in that the most useful distribution of wealth is the one performed by the very nature of things" (Rosmini 1923, 136–137). Nevertheless, it is clear that to him such liberalism also fails to contribute an adequate conception of distributive justice. In effect, we have already mentioned that Rosmini differs largely with Smith and liberalism in general over the meaning of this "natural distribution." He does not believe that this natural distribution of wealth may be immediately identified with the results produced by the exchanges between individual interests that take place in the market. Rosmini certainly thinks that "the private interest, generally speaking, exercises a considerable degree of influence on the shaping of the public good," but he rejects the idea that "this should occur always and without exception." To affirm such thing is, according to Rosmini, "the excess of the true proposition, and it is this excess what is false about Adam Smith's doctrine" (Rosmini 1994a, 379–380).

9.4.6 Recognizing Rights, Capacities and Needs

Thus, beyond conservatism and statist or liberal perfectionism, Rosmini aims at a kind of society and economy which may head towards a gradual improvement in distribution, based on the *perfectibility* of human beings and society.[3] In this

[3]"These observations, however, are not intended to deny the perfectibility of human beings and of society. It is an important truth and a dogma of Christianity that human beings are continually perfectible. What we completely deny is that their *attainment of perfection* is necessary and fixed (. . .)" (Rosmini 1994b, 314).

way, Rosmini makes a distinction between natural inequality, which cannot and must not be modified but rather respected by every government, and inequality which can be remedied or at least reduced by appropriate action on the part of civil society. But what kind of action should it be? Rosmini is sure that society cannot completely modify historically inherited situations of economic inequality by, for example, massively redistributing ownership, without committing grave injustice. Neither can inequality be remedied by totally overlooking the results derived from free competition amongst existing capabilities or talents. Nevertheless, a wide field for action remains.

Rosmini assures that the solution to distributive justice is not to be found in conservatism and its attempts to defend the economic *status quo* of a privileged class, nor in egalitarianism and its attempts of quick distribution through the State, or in liberalism – which proposes an indiscriminate opening to massive concurrence. Rosmini agrees with the conception of distributive justice which, in his opinion, results from the long historic process started in the Middle Ages and continued during the Modern Ages until his time, characterized by the gradual and increasing rise of small owners (Rosmini 1887, 229), the elimination of privileges and laws oriented to the accumulation of ownership in the hands of a few, the establishment of institutions such as free labor regulated by jural contract, commercial franchises bestowed on cities, the development of a tax system aimed at encouraging or forcing the circulation of ownership, the progressive granting of proportional shares of political power to new economic interests (those of wage-earning workers, men of industry and businessmen) following the principle of the "law of balance of ownership and power",[4] and the provision of temporary assistance to the poor and marginal by means of beneficence by the Church, civil associations and, later on, even the State. It consists therefore in an organic and complex conception that includes numerous elements rather than a sole abstract generalizing factor or principle. Rosmini's economic policy is permeated with precisely this kind of gradual and predominantly indirect distribution of wealth aimed at creating a society of extended middle classes (Rosmini 1994b, n. 693).

However, distributive justice does not end in the acknowledgement and gradual redistribution of goods and rights but of *capacities* as well. In fact, Rosmini will give great importance to the problem of ignorance and the lack of education in relation with the economy, and to the need for promotion, incentive and education of capacities existing also in many people, though in a purely embryonic or potential state given the circumstances of their origin. In his opinion, the main cause of

[4]"Un più comodo riparto delle proprietà non si potea far che in due modi: il primo con violenza e con ingiustizia; e questo era celere, se pur non avesse incontrato una reazione che lo rendesse impossibile: il secondo colle instituzioni, e questo era lento verso all' impazienza dei francesi; ma poteva esser giusto. Egli è appunto quel modo, di cui, come abbiamo detto, si servì Luigi il Grosso (...) cercò di porvi remedio col promovuere una nuova distribuzione della proprietà in un modo giusto, qual fu quello della francazione delle città appartenenti ai dominî della corona, promovendo e creando in tal modo i piccoli proprietarî, e dando l' esistenza così ad un terzo stato, che allargasse la base del potere." (Rosmini 1887, 220).

distributive injustice has always been the "heavy burden of ignorance and inability that weighed on the great majority of nations" which has resulted in "their own rights (being left) undefended" and "the road to oppression was open to those whose education made them more powerful, more astute and more united" (Rosmini 1994b, n. 693).

By virtue of this thesis, governments should not only acknowledge and respect the capacities already developed within a group of citizens but strongly promote those capacities which are not developed yet within another. In this way, the government must take measures that seek the distribution of goods according to existing capacities, as well as measures aimed at the distribution and promotion of capacities yet not developed, especially in the case of less favored citizens:

> This kind of politics really wants to increase in the lower class knowledge of their own interests and the resolve to apply themselves to these interests with foresight and activity (Rosmini 1994b, n. 693). Hence it will be the task of the government to remove ignorance, prejudice, those habits which are harmful to production, and -through prizes and other incentives- to encourage those who are more active and motivate those who are less active (. . .) In a word, the government must increase the three forces from which the acceleration of production is born: knowledge, ambition and power, by eliminating ignorance and inertia, seeking the formation of trade organizations through which individuals may join forces. (Rosmini 1923, 138–139)

Furthermore, according to Rosmini, the equality in opportunities implied by a true economic distributive justice includes, in cases of extreme poverty, direct assistance to the most needy in the form of economic goods as well. In this way, the government must take measures against "the serious evils inevitably associated with inequality. The first of these is the extreme misery found at the lower end of the social scale." Therefore, to him, the obligation to "care of poor families by society" – a subject which, in his opinion, "has still not been considered sufficiently" – should also be part of distributive justice (Rosmini 1996, n. 2630).

9.4.7 The Meaning of "Equal Opportunities"

Rosmini strongly maintains the need for the government to ensure that economic concurrence be the result of the greatest possible equality of circumstances and opportunities:

> The word "competition" has been much abused. Free competition for what is good is a human right, but equal competition can only take place when individuals are in the same circumstances. (Rosmini 1994b, n. 628, footnote 286)

Then, according to Rosmini, for just concurrence to exist, there should be equal opportunities based on the government's generating the necessary circumstances so that "*all* [receive] *an equal right to compete*." This does not mean that the government should guarantee the result of said concurrence to anyone since "it is the individuals' responsibility to prepare themselves to share in the good." For this reason, "certainly, the government does admit any members' right *in rem*." However, the government "does admit an equal right *ad rem*," (Rosmini 1994b, n. 625–628) that is to say, equality in opportunities as the basis of competition. This is achieved by "protecting the rights and good already possessed by individuals" and by "promoting the greatest quantity of social good" (Rosmini 1994b, n. 628) through the promotion and encouragement of capabilities we already mentioned, especially through human, moral and – in some cases – material promotion of the less favored people.

9.5 The Art of Balances: Wealth, Population, Power, Culture, Virtue and Happiness

9.5.1 Complexity, Strategy and Statistics

Rosmini has always believed that the economic system is not an autonomous system or mechanism working according to an independent logic. On the contrary, the economy is just one of the various systems of balance making up a society. In fact, in his *doctrine of balances*, Rosmini explains how the creation of wealth at which economics aims must be performed by taking into account its balance with other factors. In this way, according to Rosmini, the economic wealth of a country must be in balance with five other fundamental factors: population, civil authority, (material) military power, knowledge or culture and, above all, virtue (Rosmini 1996, n. 2596–2618).

Hence, even if Rosmini believes in the existence of a "natural" dynamics of economy, it is necessary that the "civil philosopher" and the governor consider and calculate the forces at play so as to find their point of equilibrium in relation with the other goods society needs. This task of prudent intervention aimed at solving points of conflict with the purpose of achieving a final order (Rosmini 1923, 177) is the specific task of politics, in which economic policy is also inserted. This by no means implies the existence, in Rosmini, of any rationalism, or political or economic constructivism whatsoever – a way of thinking that, as we have seen, he rejects explicitly and emphatically throughout his work. Still, it is clear that he does not share the idea of economy's complete self-regulation. Although the spontaneous order of individual economic interests is a fundamental dimension of social life, the fact that it is not infallible and, therefore, not always oriented towards the common good, implies the need for prudent orientation on the part of the different instances of the government of political society. Nevertheless, despite the fact that he believes that enormous care should be taken when assigning politico-economic functions to the government, and that such functions should be predominantly negative, the role of strategic orientation in economic matters seems to be more relevant in him than in the liberal Anglo-Saxon tradition. according to Rosmini, the spontaneous order of individual interests must always be complemented by the vision and orientation of individuals who represent the common good of society: this is the role high politics must play in the estimation of the quality of the different interests and the evaluation of the strategic action of the State, so as to mitigate the effects of destructive tendencies as much as possible and encourage constructive ones.[5]

In this sense, Rosmini believes it is fundamental to adopt statistical tools to provide governors with information regarding the real situation of the economy at every moment, in order to give economy a certain framework of orientation based on a prudential judgment of facts and not on abstract principles. As we have already pointed out in Chap. 2, Rosmini differs on this point with Adam Smith, as the latter rejects the use of statistics and the subsequent possibility of a prudential and preventive strategy in the economic field on the part of the government, while according to the former, "the very end of statistics is the improvement of human society through a government" (Rosmini 1978b, 74) and by means of them it is possible "to foresee future needs and prepare in time for the evils which unexpectedly occur to nations" (Rosmini 1978b, 76).

9.5.2 Ethics as the Center of Gravity of Economic Policy

In this matter, Rosmini adopts the point of view of Italian civil economics, but adds to this concern for statistics an element which – in his opinion – is not so clear in the Italian economists: the moral element. In fact, according to Rosmini, the different factors (wealth, population, civil authority, military power, and even knowledge and culture) that the civil philosopher and the politician must consider in their mutual inter-relationships are in some way external with regard to the human spirit, where they acquire their final shape and orientation through moral free action. In fact, according to Rosmini, the moral factor is the "touch-stone" of the whole social body or – resorting to a metaphor taken from physics, which Rosmini likes to use – the point where the "center of gravity" is found and around which all the other social balances develop. In effect, Rosmini maintains that the key for social order, and within this, for economic order, is in the degree of moral power that may exist in a society in relation with all other social factors:

> [...] other kinds of goods can usefully increase, in proportion to the increase of moral virtue amongst human beings, provided they are commanded by this first sovereign good. The other kinds must not, however, exceed the moral power that human beings have for dominating and directing them. (Rosmini 1996, n. 2645)

[5]In this sense, Rosmini praises the thinking of Alexander Hamilton and quotes the following passage from *The Federalist* to support his thesis that politics must often correct individual desires and seek to orient them towards their *true interests*: "Generally, it is true that the people desire only the public good. However, they are often mistaken in their search for it... When the people's *real* interests are in opposition to their desires, those responsible for these interests have the duty to combat the error of which the people are the victim..." (Rosmini 1994b, n. 195).

Thus, echoing the thoughts of thinkers of the classical era and of other modern authors such as Montesquieu, Hamilton or de Tocqueville, Rosmini places himself within the tradition of virtue as the nucleus of political and economic life, and rejects those conceptions which consider that the economy depends solely on good external organization or on a good institutional system. To him, an economic policy solely based on the criterion of "organizing a good system" is doomed to failure because all systems are impotent unless animated by virtue:

> [G]ood faith, uprightness, the morality on which the tranquility and the very existence of humankind rest, seem fragile and accidental. However, it is all we have and we must be content with that. No mechanical expedient, no external organization of society can render it useless, and it is a ridiculous hope – I will not get tired of saying this – that of material politicians who think they can find a political order which does not have morality as its mainstay, in which no type of virtue is necessary (. . .) (Rosmini 1887, 685–686)

9.5.3 Economizing Virtues

Now, although moral virtue is the fruit – as we know – of personal freedom and as such it is capable of growing and developing beyond all social influence, freedom is also limited and susceptible to influences. In fact, Rosmini says that economic goods exert an enormous pressure upon freedom to the point that they frequently divert it even from a good original direction. For this reason, political society will have a fundamental role, not in producing but certainly in protecting the development of virtue. Failing to check, in every situation and place, the moral and psychological condition of people would imply assuming the existence of a freedom in them that is always good, infallible and immune to any external influence. Furthermore, in general, for the sake of *prevention*, no economic policy should assume the existence of a maximally virtuous freedom in an aggregate of persons, but of a minimum of values and virtues (Rosmini 1994a, n. 100):

> Instincts are subject to human will which, as an internal thing, does not directly belong to the external society of men: it can preserve its rectitude, whatever the disposition of external things may be. However, these perceptible goods and evils tempt its constancy and, in this sense, the dispositions of civil society, if well-ordered, may diminish these temptations while, in the opposite case, they may increase them. (Rosmini 1887, 667–668)

9.5.4 Economy and Happiness

Furthermore, according to Rosmini, at this point it is clear "the error of governments who only want to materialize society, positing all social progress in the continuing increase of external goods." Whether through market or State utilitarianism, these governments forget the ultimate end of society, which is happiness, and cannot be achieved – as we have already seen – by the sole multiplication of goods or the mere satisfaction of external needs, but by the inner contentment or "*appagamento*" of the spirit, which is the fruit of the virtuous use of external goods. "Consequently, while they think they are satisfying the people by increasing the quantity of material enjoyment, they are in fact only causing disquiet and discontent. An increase in material pleasures in no way affects an increase in contentment of spirit, in which alone we find rest; rather, the contrary often happens" (Rosmini 1994b, n. 214).

Therefore, according to Rosmini, the question of happiness, understood as the "true human good" and fruit of inner contentment derived from a virtuous use of material goods, must occupy a central position in every economic policy. Thus, to him, economic policies should take into account the quality, volume, speed and type of production, consumption and trade of an economy so that "with the increase of external goods and with the decrease of evils, the occasions on which citizens may abuse their freedom to the cost of their own misfortune and happiness are avoided" (Rosmini 1887, 668). In this sense, according to Rosmini, every economic policy (which has as its specific end the search for the increase in wealth) should be governed by the principle of the relationship between such increase and the degree of virtue and happiness (*appagamento*) existing in society. In fact, the protection of this principle on the part of the government is essential not only for the ultimate end of every policy – which consists in achieving the virtue and happiness of people – but for the prosperity of the economy as well, because the latter always ends up destroying itself if it neglects its intimate relationship with ethics:

> Economists, for example, will tell us how to augment private and public wealth which, however, is only one element of true social prosperity. People can be wicked and unhappy even when wealth abounds. Wealth, moreover, is quite capable of destroying itself. (Rosmini 1994a, n. 7, Preface)

Now, the design of a complex economic strategy centered in the moral-eudaimonological factor on the part of the government cannot be based on mere "high-flown declarations and vague, incomplete considerations," but on the accurate analysis "of the moral, intellectual and physical state of peoples" (Rosmini 1994a, n. 121). To achieve such a goal, Rosmini proposes the adoption, on the part of the government, not only of economic statistics but of what he calls "politico-moral statistics" (Rosmini 1994b, n. 853–854).

> [...] the wise government of a nation necessarily requires knowledge of the state of the spirit of the people who make up the nation. This shows the insufficiency of economic statistics, and the necessity of comprehensive and philosophical statistics (...). Politico-moral statistics form part of comprehensive philosophical statistics, and present a vast, almost untouched field for learned investigation and research. (Rosmini 1994b, n. 853–854)

Rosmini's proposal of such "statistics of happiness" may be surprising at first sight, because we have described him as a great defender of the personal nature of happiness and a critic of every attempt to reduce it to an external quantitative measure. However, although for him happiness is certainly not an external fact completely measurable from the outside, it should not be considered a purely subjective fact dependent on the arbitrary desires of the individual, of which he alone can possess knowledge. On the contrary, though inscribed within the demands of an objective human nature common to all human beings, happiness is certainly the fruit of a personal process. Furthermore, in spite of the fact that contentment or *appagamento* is a fundamentally internal phenomenon by virtue of the incarnate nature of the human being, it presents external symptoms by which it may become known in an indirect manner. Although knowledge of happiness is never perfect, it is possible to make a certain external objective evaluation of the eudaimonological state of the members of society taken individually and, consequently, to establish a certain "measure" of "public" happiness, understood not as a quantitative sum of pleasures, but as the "state of contentment" of society as a whole.

In this sense, politico-moral statistics would have the characteristic of providing measurable quantitative data regarding "the *proportions* of nations' physical goods as a whole and separately, of their mutual interaction, in their action in what regards social life as a whole," but would also include an interpretation of said data as "*physical symptoms* of the intellectual state and moral conditions of nations" (Rosmini 1994a, n. 121, 1994b, n. 854). Thus, the auscultation of such moral state behind the quantitative data of the economy on the part of the government of civil society would not only fulfill the principle stating that "the spirit, as the seat of *appagamento*, is the aim of politics," but also achieve a fuller economic development, since all "external development has a need for internal morality" (Rosmini 1978b, 72).

9.5.5 Relational Goods

Furthermore, according to Rosmini, this kind of statistics would not only have the function of verifying the state of people's virtue and private happiness: they should also contribute to reveal the moral and psychological state of their mutual inter-individual relationships and of their relationship with society as a whole, so that they would enable the "discovery of the degree of social life which is the real inner power which allows society's subsistence, which is totally different from a simple 'economic description of nations' " (Rosmini 1994a, n. 121). This "inner power" of society includes, according to Rosmini, the different social virtues that join people to each other, such as trust,[6] the sense of reciprocity (Rosmini 1994b, n. 223) or benevolence, and also those strictly public virtues which join people to the social whole, such as "collective spirit" (Rosmini 1994a, n. 93) "public spirit," friendship or social love, and patriotism, amongst others. To him, these virtues are essential for the functioning of the economy. In this sense, statistics capable of accounting for this moral and internal dimension of economy would become, in Rosmini's opinion, "truly political or, as Romagnosi would call them, civil statistics" (Rosmini 1994a, n. 121).

[6]"We add the opinion of an economist" – Rosmini tells us, quoting Gioia this time, in a surprisingly eulogistic tone- "when Numa Pompilio raised an altar to Good Faith, that is to say, a moral code, he understood the sense of the economy better than modern economists." (Rosmini 1994a, n. 15, footnote 15, Preface). See also Rosmini (1994b, n. 148).

Upon the basis of these, it would be possible for the government – in relation with economic goods – a "political theory, accompanied no doubt by moral science" that could teach "how these objects are to be employed to benefit rather than harm society" (Rosmini 1994a, n. 102). Anyway, it is clear that Rosmini's thesis about the supremacy of the moral issue in economy does not mean that he supports a moralist position. On the contrary, although the moral issue is the most important one, it is closely related to the other material and external factors. Thus, the key to every economic policy resides not only in the moral issue but in the "unending problem about balance" (Rosmini 1994a, n. 120) amongst all these factors. But given that "matter is subject to division; the spirit on the contrary reduces all things to unity," the main end of an economic policy would be to find this unit "in which alone resides the force which constitutes true social power" (Rosmini 1994a, n. 134).

9.6 Personal Responsibility and the Subsidiarity Principle

9.6.1 Each Person, the Primary Judge

Although, according to Rosmini, the State must concern itself with measuring and supervising not only the level of growth and economic production but the degree of social happiness or contentment behind this level as well, the responsibility of achieving this happiness rests primarily on the individual rather than on the State:

> Every social administration must carefully reflect therefore that individual happiness is not, properly speaking, its task but only and always the task of individuals themselves. (Rosmini 1994b, n. 225)

In this way, in clear opposition to every social or statist utilitarianism and in agreement with some valuable elements of liberal philosophy, Rosmini believes that the primary judge regarding the need for means – in this case, economic ones – to achieve one's own happiness is always the individual person. In fact, even in the case of economic means, which – theoretically speaking – are not *absolutely necessary* for a person's development, it is the individual alone who must determine if they are necessary to him concretely and according to his individual circumstances, that is, if such means are necessary in relation to him (*relative necessity*.) This position is founded on Rosmini's conception of happiness as an eminently personal phenomenon. Thus, to him, the individual's right of jural concurrence to acquire legitimate ownership of economic means is always an inviolable right of the person, which the State cannot injure.[7] To conclude, Rosmini maintains that "those

[7]"Here we must note that the means for moral contentment which are not absolutely necessary, speculative considered, can be *relatively necessary* (...) The publicist who attempts to indicate the just limits of governmental power and determine the moral duties which bind this power, must not limit himself to the theoretical consideration of the *absolute necessity* of the means

enactments are illicit and unjust which limit the use of the right of all human beings to use the best and most perfect means to procure virtue and moral contentment for themselves" (Rosmini 1994b, 97).

9.6.2 A Dangerous Confusion

In this sense, Rosmini is a harsh critic of modern statism and its tendency to overrun private individuals' priority and ignore the exclusively subsidiary nature of State action in economy, seeking economic progress through exaggerated State centralization. Furthermore, in Rosmini's opinion, this passion for centralization has its origin in a substantial confusion: to believe that the priority of the common good and public good have over private good that we have mentioned before is tantamount to priority of State action over private individual action. The mistake consists in confusing priority of *goods* with priority of *actors*. According to Rosmini, the priority of common good or public good over private good means that, in case of conflict with an individual's private good which is just, the common good of all or the public good of society, provided they are jurally and morally just, have a hierarchical priority over the former as long as it is duly compensated. However, according to Rosmini, both common good and public good are, in the first place, the result of the private goods obtained by the activity individuals perform on their own; only in the second place are they the result of supplementary actions performed by the State. Then, when Rosmini explains the priority of common good and public good over private good, he is not giving priority to the action of the State over the action of individuals, but to the good of all over the exclusive good of one or some individuals. This good of all – be it either common or public – is the fruit of State action only in a secondary manner, since the sum of individual goods achieved by private individuals is the main base of the production of social good. Therefore, this confusion has generated a dangerous tendency to sacrifice the interest of private individuals in the name of a purely generic and abstract concept of common good and public good:

> This century embraced as true the principle that every improvement consists in generalizing things (Rosmini 1923, 75). Because the vice of modern generality consists in sacrificing

---

conductive to human perfection. Theoretically, it is certain that no external means is absolutely necessary. This would easily lead to the false conclusion that means of this kind do not form the matter of inalienable rights relative to individuals, and that all means are therefore equally within governmental power; consequently government can dispose of them as it thinks fit (...) On the contrary, it is most important to pay close attention to the *relative necessity* of these means. This necessity is not revealed simply by ideal speculations but by the study of the facts and by careful observation of the different states and conditions of *individual freedom* as it is variously limited in different individuals. Clearly, therefore, the means which are *relatively necessary* for the individual's moral perfection constitute a right as *inalienable* as his right to be virtuous and happy" (Rosmini 1994b, 94–96).

particulars against what Nature demands: that we found the general upon the particulars. (Rosmini 1923, 76–77)

On the contrary, according to Rosmini, true distributive justice on which common good is founded has its main base in the fruitful activity of private individuals:

Therefore, the more the particular is observed, the closer we come to distributive justice. (Rosmini 1923, 68–69)

9.6.3 Subsidiarity as the Remedy to Statism

All this does not imply that the path from private good to common good is easy or that there exists an automatic identification between them that would make any State action unnecessary. Such a belief would place Rosmini in a position of individualistic thought. On the contrary, to him, the error opposed to statism consists in believing that the sole sum of private good achieved by individual action is sufficient to achieve common good and public good. In his view, such belief fatally leads to particularism, since the absolute and simultaneous exercise of all economic rights by all individuals without sufficient State regulation aimed at moderating, limiting or replacing them in some cases in the exercise of such rights, would imply the triumph of some at the expense of others, as it would mean the triumph of private good over common and public good. Hence, according to Rosmini, the priority of individual action does not suppress the need for the role of the State as a regulator and moderator of the economy:

[T]his cannot be done in excess. Later, we will establish the limits of this particularization in public things. (Rosmini 1923, 68–69)

Consequently, although the government should, in principle, respect the right of the individual to judge and choose for himself, it also has the right to evaluate the suitability of the individual's judgment, and produce its own judgment. This is based on what we have just explained: happiness is neither an external fact completely measurable from the outside nor a purely subjective fact which the individual alone is entitled to judge or which depends on his arbitrary desires. In fact, even though the person is the primary judge of his own needs and interests, if these judgments are wrong and it is clearly ascertained that they may endanger the economic order of society as a whole, the State is entitled to replace the individual's erroneous judgment with its own corrective judgment and, therefore, has the moral obligation to restrict the use of the individual's economic rights.[8]

---

[8]"Our initial solution deserves further clarification. We did not mean that the individual has the right to all those means which according to him possess the aptitude mentioned above [that is to say that they are relatively necessary for his moral development]. This would destroy social administration or would make it impossible. We are talking only about those means which are actually best and most perfect. Consequently, if the means under consideration are not such, our

Anyhow, in general, the State has the task to correct or replace the individual only in very exceptional cases. Its function is predominantly negative: to protect the individual efforts of persons, to remove the obstacles they may encounter and to assist them in the most indirect way possible so that they may have a wide field for free development:

> Government can only safeguard this task: it can and must defend the free effort continually made by every member of society to attain so great an end; it can and must remove any obstacles and help each individual. But because government cannot do more than this, its action must be mostly negative, and its treatment of the members very cautious and reserved – more supervisory than directly involved. (Rosmini 1994b, n. 225)

Thus, according to Rosmini, every economic policy must be respectful of the central role of personal responsibility, and all the activities a person is capable of carrying out on its own must be left to him. All the superior social instances – the highest being that of the government of civil or political society – should solely act in a subsidiary way. Furthermore, this principle does not only answer to ethical and jural reasons, but to economic reasons as well, since "what citizens do by themselves is always more economical than what they do through others, and principally through the government" (Rosmini 1923, 64). This is so because, in Rosmini's opinion, an individual is generally capable of knowing the concrete circumstances of his economic activity (needs to be satisfied, available means, time factors, etc.) much more accurately than the government, which is usually acquainted with only the most general aspects of the case. This grants the individual the possibility of finding the most appropriate and efficient solutions. Besides, the individual has an additional incentive to carry out such activity successfully: the utility or own interest resulting from an efficiently performed economic activity.[9]

Evidently, these last theses prove that Rosmini is in an interesting position which balances the liberal elements of his criticism of the excessively intervening State with a prudent distance from any anti-State or "minimal State" thesis. Thus, in his view, within strictly jural and politico-economic limits that clearly indicate the leading role of the initiative of individuals and private enterprises, the State - certainly not only the national one but the regional and communal as well- also has an active role that expresses itself in its economic policy.

---

principle cannot be applied. It is true that an individual's real or apparent judgment about the suitability of these means can easily collide with that of the government (. . .). Furthermore, when we affirm that an administration 'cannot licitly or justly limit the use of the right of the individual to use the best means for procuring virtue and moral contentment for himself', we simply mean that it is illicit for a government to do so without moral necessity. Such a necessity would result from the government's obligation to defend an equal right in all individuals, by preventing a particular individual from using his right to obstruct an equal use of the right in others (. . .) The government is the natural judge and defender of all these limits (. . .)" (Rosmini 1994b, n. 231–232).

[9]Evidently, this does not mean that, to Rosmini, self-interest is the only or principal motive for action, since, as we have already seen in another chapter of this work, all useful or interested action must be, to him, within the framework of a fair or moral valuation. All of which does not stand in the way for Rosmini to appreciate individual interest as a very important driving force of economic action.

Chapter 10
Instruments of Economic Policy Under the Light

10.1 Production, Business and Industrial Policies

10.1.1 A Free Economy Without Privileges

In matters of industrial policy, Rosmini supports the principle of "not directing the general course of wealth, but only of accelerating it"(Rosmini 1923, 137):

> The government, as said principle states, is in danger of disturbing the legitimate order of wealth if it seeks to give it a direction, but not when it seeks to increase the movement and activity of citizens in general, mainly towards everything that activity is oriented to. (Rosmini 1923, 138)

In fact, the task of the government in this field is to encourage "not so much this or that branch of industry in particular, but industrial activity in general" (Rosmini 1923, 138). Rosmini is indeed a harsh critic of industrial policies based on regimes of privilege, monopolies and special subsidies. While, on the one hand, he states that the regime of "patents granted to inventors of something useful" could never be called "privilege" or "favor," on the other hand he claims: "I cannot see, however, that the same comments could be applied to those true privileges which are sometimes granted to a person who is allowed the exclusive exercise of a trade or craft that he has not invented. If such a privilege is granted, the natural freedom of all other persons is restricted by their exclusion from the exercise of that trade or craft; if public authority favors some person or family, or provides them with some advantage; all other individuals are injured in their rights" (Rosmini 1993b, n. 1675). Rosmini shows how the outright rejection people feel with regard to monopolies and privileges, whose sole foundation is in pure power exercised by the government, is a symptom of the essential injustice in them:

> This explains why a government which makes some means of income exclusive to a person or family is usually the object of animosity. The people's good sense wants to know why the freedom of many craftsmen should be restricted for the sake of a single worker, who might be worthy of the privilege but would have had no need of it if his own predominance had

C. Hoevel, *The Economy of Recognition: Person, Market and Society in Antonio Rosmini*, Ethical Economy 42, DOI 10.1007/978-94-007-6058-5_10,

> enabled him to capture business from others. The people's first feeling, and this is especially true of the other craftsmen, finds such privileges offensive. It seems to them that they have been unjustly restricted in their rights, not by prior occupancy, which is the only lawful way of restricting others' freedom, but by mere words supported by governmental force. (Rosmini 1993b, n. 1675)

This way, "industry and commerce must certainly be protected and encouraged – but not through injustice, which never brings to the state any true and solid good" (Rosmini 2007, 82). Thus, according to Rosmini, "each man has the right to use his abilities to his advantage. Therefore, enterprise must be free, as it constitutes part of *juridical freedom*" (Rosmini 2007, 98). All this "demonstrates the freedom of industry and internal commerce through an argument coming from the principles of right. These principles exclude any form of monopoly" (Rosmini 2007, 98).

Furthermore, Rosmini contemplates curbing the exercise of the principle of the right of freedom of industry, as he admits the possibility of subsidies and special protections for certain sectors of the economy under special circumstances by virtue of the principle of common good that should govern every economic policy. However, these exceptions cannot be based solely on the government's isolated decision, but require either previous consensus by those sectors which might be directly injured or the granting of due compensation to said sectors:

> Relative to individuals and different classes of persons within a nation, government can impede the universal right to exercise the same branch of trade or industry, by favoring certain individuals or classes if this is helpful to the public good. This, however, depends either upon the willingness of individuals and classes to give their assent to laws which prevent their competing in these activities or on due compensation. Otherwise, their right of freedom would seem to have been violated. (Rosmini 1993b, n. 1676)

10.1.2 Priority of Private Initiative and Critique of the Entrepreneurial State

Rosmini is a harsh critic of a statist conception of economy where the State was entitled to undertake any kind of economic and business activity without limitation. In his criterion, this goes directly against the very nature of civil society, which has the regulation of the modality of the citizens' rights as its end. Because of this, the right to economic initiative on the part of the citizens should prevail, and the state should avoid any attempt to hinder, replace or absorb them by competing with them or by monopolizing for itself particular activities or sectors of the economy:

> Civil society was not instituted to undertake some particular utility but, as we said, to regulate the modality of rights. The protection and facilitation of all the enterprises of the citizens and of other societies are directed to this end. Hence civil government acts contrary to its mandate when it competes with its citizens or with the societies they form to procure some particular utility and even more when it reserves to itself the monopoly of enterprises which it forbids to individuals or their societies. (Rosmini 1996, n. 2166–2167)

Rosmini rejects the idea of the "entrepreneurial State" because it does not regulate, but directly violates the right to free jural competition:

> The government of a civil society must not convert into a mercantile or industrial agency. This goes directly against the purpose of its institution which is that of protecting the liberty and competitiveness of the citizens for profit and never to invade this, or enter into competition with it. (Rosmini 2007, 78)

Furthermore, the taking over of business enterprises on the part of the State is generally anti-economical and goes against distributive justice and common good:

> Rarely can the government realize from those enterprises the same profit that is realized by the private sector, which exercises vigilance over those enterprises because of its own interests. Thus, monopolies or even simply profitable enterprises that the state takes over bring two great evils to the nation: They take away branches of industry from the citizens and they make them less productive and sometimes even non-productive or passive. And even in the case when they would yield a considerable income to the state, such income would benefit some but not all citizens, nor would it be distributed in function of individual income. (Rosmini 2007, 78)

Consequently, according to Rosmini, the State should divest itself as much as possible of commercial and industrial activities to leave them in the hands of the private sector, protecting and promoting private spontaneous undertakings. This is, furthermore, the best way to encourage not only the common good and the private good, but also the public good of the state itself, which is primarily founded not on the enlargement of state-owned companies, but on the growth of the private sector:

> [. . .] the more civil societies relinquish enterprises and leave them to private activity, which they must protect and encourage, the more closely they approach their ideal. We can safely assert that in this matter at least, greater progress in civilization is made by a government that procures more public good through the spontaneous action of individuals and of the private societies it protects, and distances itself from leadership in such enterprises. (Rosmini 1996, n. 2168)

10.1.3 Cases of Subsidiarious Interventions

However, and despite these clear definitions that bring Rosmini closer to liberal economic thought, his conception also points to a clear subsidiary role of the State in all those economic activities private individuals cannot undertake:

> [. . .] civil society has the authority to undertake of itself the useful enterprises which could not in any way be successfully attempted by individuals or private societies. This is the only case where civil society can properly undertake such enterprises without exceeding the sphere of the modality of rights. In doing so, it is not removing or obstructing the freedom of individuals and the possibility of concurrence, that is, it is not depriving them of any valuable right. Citizens, who have instituted civil society as a necessity, not superfluity, want government to do only what they themselves cannot do. (Rosmini 1996, n. 2169)

Contrary to authors such as Adam Smith, who only agree on the existence of state-owned enterprises when the activity to be performed is by *nature* impracticable by private individuals, Rosmini widens the field of possible public undertakings. In fact, following his thesis of the fallibility of the spontaneous order of the market based on the possible problems of education, capacity or initiative of those who take part in it, Rosmini admits to the possibility that the state takes charge of the necessary training while it *provisionally* takes over certain enterprises, even if their nature is essentially private, until the private sector can take care of them:

> A hope that individuals and private societies undertake certain useful enterprises may be vain, not because the nature of said enterprises makes said undertaking impossible, but because individuals and private societies do not attain the level of ideas, ability and activity necessary for these enterprises. If this is true, civil society (the government) will take care to increase in the citizens the abilities they still lack. It can provisionally initiate some private enterprises, for example, provided they cede them as soon as should themselves be ready to undertake them. (Rosmini 1996, n. 2170)

10.1.4 Public Spending: Economy's Driving Force?

Furthermore, in his early writings, Rosmini hints at a thesis which seems to precede Keynes, by maintaining the possibility that, only in the exceptional cases of economic depression and high unemployment, could the State drive the economy forward by increasing expenditure, not in unproductive activities but in public works and even other enterprises capable of generating employment and collaborating in restoring the cycle of reproduction of wealth:

> Such a reason would not be forceless in a single case. If the population were so numerous as to outnumber all the positions which they could occupy (. . .) When there was no longer any way to employ them in an industry that obtains its profits through exports abroad, active trade or the perfecting of products necessary in the domestic market; then it would be the case in which the Prince could make expenses in order to give work to those people. But we would prefer that he choose to spend, rather than on the luxury of the Court which voraciously consumes production, on those activities that provide useful and stable things to the state, such as roads, buildings and all public and private ornament (. . .) Let us say that, above all, that state expenses should not be superfluous, nor wasteful nor unproductive. (Rosmini 1923, 323)

However, in matters of public finance, Rosmini always recommends a prudent use of expenditure and criticizes every excess in this regard, upon the basis of the very principle of the State's function only as regulator of the modality of rights:

> Hence it follows that all partial expenses that the Government makes (. . .) should not be more costly than if had they been made by the citizens themselves: when the Government takes over these expenses, it is simply acting as the citizens' vicar or procurator. (. . .) (Rosmini 1923, 328)

Rosmini certainly admits that "expenses by the hand of the Government increase and are doomed to increase because what citizens do for themselves is always more economical than what they do through others, especially the Government (. . .)" However, it is necessary that "to this inevitable increase in expenses, the

Government should not add another arbitrary expense so that, instead of playing the role of the citizens' trustee, it plays the role of the speculator" (Rosmini 1923, 328).

10.1.5 Maintaining the Balance Between Production and Consumption

Probably following Sismondi, Rosmini also notices the need to maintain a proportionate ratio between the level and pace of production and consumption on the part of the individuals or societies that are part of the markets, and their level of net income:

> Finally, from all these reflections we can form a most important principle for determining 1. the level of needs which does not prejudice the well-being of families and the State, and 2. the point where the harmful excess of needs begins. The principle is: "Artificial needs must never exceed the quantity of means proffered by net income from possessions or work." (Rosmini 1994b, n. 702)

This balance has to be well studied by measuring not only the value of the wealth produced and consumed in a certain moment, but also the possible variations on the value of wealth accumulation according to the relative situation of societies and businesses:

> Wealth has a different value in different nations according to whether they are richer or poorer and according to whether the wealth is more or less necessary for them. Thus, the value of the wealth consumed in a particular company should be compared with the value of the good which is expected from the company, multiplied by the probability of achieving it. (Rosmini 1923, 56)

Furthermore, according to Rosmini, behind this imbalance between income and expenses taking place in a free market, there is another problem that we have seen before: the disordered and sometimes exacerbated display and liberation of fictitious needs that exceed the means or capabilities required to satisfy them, thwarting true human contentment or "*appagamento*" and hampering the development of true economic freedom. Thus, the government's actions could not be limited to open the possibilities for every kind of desire, but should count with proper indirect actions that promote the display of economic means in accordance with a proper economic and moral evaluation of them since "if passions and desires increase, it is necessary that virtue or moral strength also grow for pleasures to become less common and more private" (Rosmini 1977a, 130).[1]

Therefore, it is not a question of attempting to encourage an unlimited expansion of consumption, trusting that it will generate production – as Gioia says – or expecting that the expansion of production will generate demand – as Says proposes.

---

[1]"[...] it is virtue or moral strength alone growing together with desires what ennobles them, regulates them and makes them proper, focusing them on a single object" (Rosmini 1977a, 130).

On the contrary, according to Rosmini, the government of civil society must seek to orient, through the various instruments of political economy such as fiscal, monetary, commercial, industrial and labor policies – which we will consider next – the expansion of consumption and production in fair and economic proportion to the income of persons at different moments and places:

> The Prince can encourage this honest order of expenses for public utility. And to do so, he must distinguish those places where opulent and sluggish owners excessively practice the art of accumulation in relation with that of spending, from those territories where, on the contrary, the vivacious and agile inhabitants, lovers of the fine arts, are inclined towards profusion and negligence in the cultivation of the land and the productive industries (. . .) The Prince must encourage honest spending only in the regions where the people are inclined towards avarice but he must repress consumption in other places. (Rosmini 1923, 160)

Moreover, this orientation of production and consumption in balance with income, as proposed by Rosmini, shows the intrinsic link between economic balance and ethical balance:

> This proves why no intelligent and wise government promotes vices on the pretext of increasing public wealth but prefers to promote virtues. (Rosmini 1923, 157)

10.1.6 Acknowledging and Empowering Capacities

However, although Rosmini establishes industrial freedom as a general principle, he also believes it should be encouraged, especially by means of general incentives which he calls, after Gioia and other authors of the Italian civil economic tradition, "knowledge, will and power," that is to say, training in knowledge, initiative, and the power of action of business enterprises. Furthermore, Rosmini includes, amongst the actions of governmental industrial policy, the encouragement of associationism and cooperativism amongst small and medium-size producers – also very typical of Italy – who may allow for a fairer competition with the larger producers in the market:

> In a word, the government will be able to increase the three forces from which production growth is born: knowledge, will and power, by removing ignorance and inertia, encouraging the formation of trade organizations, achieve a stronger union of forces. (Rosmini 1923, 138)

10.2 Labor Policy

10.2.1 Freedom to Work

As well as to policies regarding business enterprises, production and industry, Rosmini pays special attention to the problem of labor policies, that is, policies directly concerned with the worker as a key actor within the economy. According to Rosmini, the right to labor is placed within the same framework as all the other economic freedoms, alike which it finds support in the obligation not to place obstacles in the path of the exercise of competitive capabilities, and to protect and encourage such exercise. Thus, the government must seek, in the first place, a legislation that may guarantee the possibility of the free exercise of labor to all people on the sole condition that they possess some kind of competitive capabilities. In Rosmini's view, the main jural instrument for such purpose is the contract of free labor, which allows both the employee and the employer to enjoy great flexibility in the establishment of labor relationships, while it creates the framework of essential commutative justice that must govern said relationships, avoiding alienating relationships that would enslave the worker by submitting him to some kind of servitude. Therefore, the government must guarantee that labor be "an entirely free service determined by contract and compensated by a proportionate, agreed payment" (Rosmini 1993b, n. 1613).

10.2.2 Which Should Be the Limit of Work Flexibility?

In any case, Rosmini sees that freedom of contract alone is insufficient for the appropriate exercise of the right to labor. In fact, such freedom, when excessive and unlimited, generates great conditionings that may prove to be a serious obstacle to the exercise of the right of labor. Rosmini crudely describes the numerous conditionings that may affect the capacity – no longer purely legal but real – of the worker to exercise the right to labor in a market economy characterized by excessive competition. Such competition ends up by pushing, especially the working classes, to various abuses of the right to labor, which are partly ascribable to them and partly induced. Rosmini mentions, as an example, the problem of excessive work resulting from the pressure exerted by the economy in order to satisfy ever-increasing needs and desires, even at the expense of sacrificing all values and, in the last instance, also all the capabilities and forces sustaining labor itself. The results are hatred towards labor, poverty, and an inclination towards crime:

> Peasants, artisans and manufacturers, therefore, who have been used to labor, respond to new needs with increased effort. Is this increase in effort good or evil? – Clearly, if the families of peasants and wage-earners are obliged to make an excessive effort to supply their needs, they become subject to a heavier burden and greater poverty. Excessive work, necessary for supplying their needs, finally becomes oppressive and unbecoming to human nature. Dissatisfaction with work itself sets in, and bodily strength is no longer conserved but dissipated. (...) In other words, the more tired this class of people becomes, the more tempted they are to abandon the work in order to look for some means which can offer an immediate way to satisfaction without such oppression. (Rosmini 1994b, n. 683)

Rosmini is in fact a critic of excessive labor flexibility and mobility. In his opinion, there certainly exists, in principle, a "natural" labor mobility deriving from fluctuations in the supply and demand of labor, which take place as a response to the logical variation in real needs occurring in society:

> If peasants and artisans abandon their employment because their numbers exceed society's needs, no evil is done. (Rosmini 1994b, n. 687)

However, excessive labor mobility – which is that generated by fictitious needs – is terribly negative since "those who abandon their own profession to learn a more lucrative trade expose themselves and the nation to inevitable loss." Amongst the losses caused by this excess of labor mobility Rosmini mentions "a loss of both time and ability": "the worker who abandons the profession in which, as it were, he was born, and takes on another, abandons a known skill to learn an unknown skill." All this will imply such worker should "pay for his course of studies and compete with other keen students while contending with adverse circumstances and the unfamiliarity of a state whose customs and practices he does not know. He lacks experience in dealing with concomitant dangers, and finds himself amongst colleagues who are already experts" (Rosmini 1994b, n. 689).

10.2.3 The Counterproductive Effect of Interventionism

Besides, although the field of labor – like all the other fields of economy – admits a certain degree of intervention that curbs the general principle of freedom, in Rosmini's opinion, an excessive intervention on the part of the State with the purpose of ensuring employment or its presumably more just or useful distribution, generally distorts labor markets.

> It is a problem that we do not believe can be totally solved through dispositions, which create an artificial economic environment (. . .) (Rosmini 2007, 83)

In fact, an exaggerated rise in the price of labor within certain markets due to the lack of labor supply or to high labor costs, the result of which is a decrease in the country's competitiveness with regard to other countries:

> The work deteriorates because of the reduction of workers, with consequent economic harm to industry and to the nation in general. A nation in which the employee's will to work is lacking and the price of labor is excessive faces a huge obstacle, which makes its progress in industry and trade, that is, in its enrichment, difficult or even impossible. Such a people trails behind in the competition it faces from other nations. (Rosmini 1994b, n. 688)

Although Rosmini defends the right of labor and the obligation on the part of the State to provide all the means possible for this right to be realized, he considers it would be a "major and supreme imprudence" to attribute "to the unemployed workers the right to obtain employment from the state" (Rosmini 1952b, 271) either under in the form of direct employment or through impositions on the private sector aimed at maintaining positions beyond supply and demand in the labor market:

> Someone may wonder whether civil society is under the obligation to constantly maintain a fixed number of workers. To this, [the answer] is "no": the number of workers can never be stable; it must grow or decrease according to the demand by capitalists. (Rosmini 1887, 102)

10.2.4 Subsidiary Interventions in Labor

Therefore, although some measures of direct intervention may be exceptionally admitted, in the field of labor, it seems more appropriate "to protect the natural course of property" (Rosmini 2007, 83) through indirect measures -especially, as we will see, related to taxation- aimed at increasing the circulation of wealth by generating investment and wide competition, and creating the greatest possible number of jobs. This does not prevent Rosmini from maintaining that it also necessary "the simultaneous help of moral means" (Rosmini 2007, 83). With regard to this type of assistance in the search for the solution to the problem of employment, Rosmini includes the possibility that the State performs the task of connecting capitalists with potential candidates for a job, providing extra information or a recommendation regarding said candidates, which is something market actors, often ill-informed or in a rut, generally lack:

> On the other hand, if an excellent craftsman or manufacturer is left high and dry as a result of people's ignorance of what is good for them and of their blind attachment to custom, the government may bring this craftsman and manufacturer to the people's attention by informing them of the available advantages. (Rosmini 1993b, n. 1675)

In *Della naturale Costituzione della società civile* (1887), Rosmini even seems to hint at the need for the creation of a collective social security system for workers:

> Civil society, therefore, as much by the principle of utility as of justice, must consider the body of workers as endowed with a right to sustenance, and must ensure that provision of such sustentation is firmly secured by a stable fund (. . .) (Rosmini 1887, 102)

Finally, as one contribution to the solution of the labor problem, Rosmini envisions the possibility that "the government itself may come to employ these workers" (Rosmini 1993b, n. 1675), even though this should be done within the framework of qualification requirements in the case of positions within the public sector, and should not be indefinitely extended in time or in the number of workers thus employed. To the creation of private employment as the fundamental way to fight poverty, the labor possibilities offered by the State should be added; however, the State must not save public positions for a certain social *élite* but it should "call all abilities, without distinction, to public service, In this way, it opens the way even to those who own nothing to improve their economic condition." Naturally, this cannot be done in the fashion of a handing out of privileges, but according to the principle of the "free competition for employment according to the merits of each (. . .)" (Rosmini 2007, 98–99).

10.3 Tax and Fiscal Policy

10.3.1 Criteria for Taxes' Legitimating

The long pages which Rosmini devotes to the tax question in *Politica Prima, The Philosophy of Right* and *Costituzione secondo la giustizia sociale* show that, in his opinion, the tax policy is one of the most important tools the State has to influence the economy, both in its productive and competitive dimension and in its distributive aspect. The tax scheme somehow becomes the backbone of economic policies since all the principles governing said policy will come into action according to the way in which the nature, applicability, distribution and collection of taxes are conceived.

Here, we will just enunciate some points of Rosmini's extensive analysis concerning taxes, which would certainly deserve a separate study. It should be first pointed out that, in Rosmini's view, taxes have an economic dimension but also a jural dimension (Rosmini 1996, n. 2163) from whence "distributive justice and public utility are the two principles which should regulate taxes" (Rosmini 1923, 325). From the jural point of view, taxes arise from the very nature of civil society. In fact, the legitimacy of taxes is based on "society's right to use for its own ends a part of the goods of private individuals" (Rosmini 1996, n. 2160).

> Civil society regulates the modality of all the rights of its members (. . .) Every member therefore of civil society receives an advantage proportioned to the quantity of the rights he places under the protection of the society. It follows that he must contribute to the society a share-quota of the external means necessary for its existence and administration. This quota will be in proportion to the quantity of rights, whose modality is regulated. Such is the only principle suitable for directing the equal distribution of taxes. (Rosmini 1996, n. 1686)

In this sense, Rosmini maintains that the right of society can never imply an absolute or arbitrary dominion. On the contrary, the government is "simply the collector and administrator of the common *contributions* for the end of society" (Rosmini 1996, n. 2160). Rosmini thus rejects a paternalistic or feudal conception of taxes that sees them as a forced extraction of funds on the part of a lord from his vassals, as well as a Statist conception that considers them as a simple means of financing an omnipresent state, with no other limit than the unrestricted needs of expenses it may wish to establish upon the basis of an "egalitarian" estimate of alleged social utility. Furthermore, Rosmini also rejects a completely liberal position regarding the question of taxes, as for him taxes are not simply inevitable evils that should disturb the operation of the markets as little as possible, but a formidable means of jural-economic regulation of the web of duties and rights of society and individuals, by means of which it is possible to attain a significant portion of the common good and distributive justice in an economy.

Furthermore, in order for a tax to be just, it should be paid by whom benefits from it, which implies avoiding the error of "unduly making some citizens pay a tax from which they will never benefit" or "making all pay for a few" (Rosmini 1923, 329). Besides, people should be aware of the benefit a certain tax means to them, and there should also exist an assumed willingness on their part to finance such benefit through their contribution (Rosmini 1923, 326–327). In this sense, Rosmini closely links the payment of taxes to people's knowledge and free decision to form part of society and also to afford the cost of maintaining it.

Besides, from the point of view of a jurally framed utility, taxes should always stay within two fundamental limits, as follows: "1) the contributions must not exceed the need of the social end, and 2) they must be equally distributed in proportion to the citizens' abilities" (Rosmini 1996, n. 2160). Rosmini suggests straining the eye from the economic viewpoint, so that taxes are not anti-productive, but encourage investment and the creation of wealth in the private sector, while providing sufficient funds for public expenses. In order to achieve this, it is necessary to evaluate as accurately as possible the consequences of the imposition of a certain tax on each economic activity, taking into account the costs, possible profits, and characteristics of each market at a certain time and place. Furthermore, even though Rosmini maintains that there may be accidental situations such as unemployment or economic fluctuations that demand an increase in public expenditure and therefore high taxes (Rosmini 1923, 322, 324), these last generally mean "consumption and destruction of wealth" (Rosmini 1923, 320). Because of this, they "should be as moderate as possible", and attempts should be made at finding a point of equilibrium with the purpose of establishing "the maximum possible decrease in taxes" so that production growth is encouraged and the "State revenues do not drop but increase" (Rosmini 1923, 325).

In a word, the State cannot demand taxes in an unrestricted way by invoking its right to impose them or alleging unlimited needs on its part. On the contrary, in Rosmini's opinion, the State's right to spend should be circumscribed to a set of needs to be ascertained, in each case, in a dynamic but relatively objective way. Furthermore, if the State spends beyond its needs, it not only departs from the basic jural architecture of the economy, but exposes itself and the whole of society to serious financial problems.

10.3.2 Income Taxes

Upon these jural-economic principles, Rosmini believes that taxes should be levied on capital assets, as these are increased not only because of the effort and competitiveness of their owners, but also by virtue of the protection given by the public goods resulting from State expenditure. However it is also essential that taxes be levied not only on capital but on "capital multiplied by labor," which is to say on the citizens' net income (Rosmini 1923, 340). This is due to the fact that, although society has the right to collect taxes from individuals in proportion to their assets, the latter "can be estimated only through the income they yield." This obviously brings about the need for an estimation of the earnings of tax-payers, which implies evaluating the varying possible yield of taxable goods as well as the greater or lesser precariousness and brevity of the feasible revenue obtainable from them (Rosmini 1923, 340). Rosmini recognizes "the extremely difficulty experienced in distributing the tax burden in such an equal way as to get it to hit all property incomes with the right proportion" (Rosmini 2007, 72) but believes that this is the only solution possible if a criterion of true distributive justice is to be respected. He regrets, furthermore, how little confidence economists have on the actual applicability of this just conception of taxes. In Rosmini's opinion, those who conceive taxes must be convinced that the fairest system, no matter how difficult it may be, is also the most useful and the most necessary:

> This difficulty seems to be so great in the eyes of certain economists, they declared the hope of overcoming it a utopian idea – so little was their faith in justice! We are firmly convinced that whatever is just is also possible, and possible to the extent it is useful and necessary. (Rosmini 2007, 72)

Thus, he concludes that it is appropriate to levy taxes on the following:

> 1. Lands and houses (...) II. Mortgage capital (...) III. State obligations -the state which pays interest to the creditors must retain the percentage established by the law on any income. IV. Public banks, insurance companies, and any other enterprise of public interest which is managed by private individuals (...) V. Personal credits (...) VI. Private bankers, wholesale merchants, and heads of factories (...) VII. (...) retail merchants and the heads of stores (...) VIII. Each mechanical art must have its license taxed on an approximate calculation of the art's income (...) IX. (...) all the pay checks issued by the State to its officers. (Rosmini 2007, 82–83)

10.3.3 The Problem of the Taxes on Consumption

According to Rosmini, an immediate consequence of this conception of taxes is that they should not be levied on consumption. In fact, "the tax should be levied on what comes in and not on what goes out, and consumption is what goes out and not what comes in. Nor is it valuable to state that those who consume must have something to consume and also have income, because this supremely general principle does not answer the question in the slightest" (Rosmini 2007, 73). While a tax levied on income as the fruit of labor and production is in some way what a citizen pays to the State for the public goods and the protection of private goods the State provides, consumption does not bear such relationship with public services and expenditure, because it is not always in relation to each person's income. In fact, "a part of consumption is necessary – such as what is necessary for survival – and that is determined by need, and not by income. Other consumption is determined by the will of consumers and since that is arbitrary, the consumption is not all proportional to the income" (Rosmini 2007, 73). Thus, there may be a case of identical consumption by two different individuals with completely different income levels. In such case, a tax on consumption will imply that the person who earns more and benefits more from public expenditure must pay the same amount as the person who takes little or no advantage of said expenditure:

> A poor family with many children may consume and thus pay to the state more than a stingy grand seigneur who lives alone. Two families with the same number of members and

> the same means end up contributing to the state very different amounts, uniquely for the circumstance that in one of them the head of the family is generous and in the other, he is stingy. (Rosmini 2007, 73)

Taxes on consumption also carry the great defect of falling "indifferently on both what is necessary for living and on what is superfluous:"

> So, the tax on consumption can never be equally distributed; but when it falls on first necessity goods such as bread, salt, etc., then not only is it unjust, but I think it is also barbarian and inhuman! (Rosmini 2007, 74)

Furthermore, taxes on basic consumption are also anti-economical since they place pressure on the salaries of workers and therefore on labor costs. By eliminating this type of tax it would be possible to reduce labor costs without affecting workers' life-style:

> We must reflect upon the fact that, since there is no longer tax on first necessity merchandise –neither directly nor as customs duties (because they have been abolished) – that decreases the price of manpower, which comes as an advantage for the nation's commerce and industry, which can produce with less expenditure and be more competitive on the universal market. This is a just and wise way to favor national industry. Since in this way the consumption of things that are necessary to life is facilitated, a greater number of citizens get a benefit from being catered to, and the difficulty posed by the great problem of employing people decreases. (Rosmini 2007, 83)

10.3.4 Taxes and Social Morality

However, within his general criticism of taxes on consumption, Rosmini makes an important exception: the case of consumptions whose abuse can be morally harmful to citizens. In this case, taxes on consumption of certain items (though they are not taxes strictly speaking, because they are not levied on income) become important tools of indirect market regulation aimed at orienting it according to the principles of the common good, happiness and the moral good of individuals and society as a whole:

> Taxation over consumption should be abolished generally speaking (. . .). I say generally since an exception should be made for those goods that, when abused, are detrimental to the state. For example, in China, where opium is abused, there would be nothing unjust with a tax on this good. In countries where alcoholism dominates, a tax on inebriant liquors would be commendable. And what is stated for merchandise also applies to related arts and professions (. . .). Such tax weighs, so to speak, on the vice, and it is an indirect penalty used in the attempt to hit and diminish it. (Rosmini 2007, 74)

Rosmini states the same with regard to luxury goods, which aroused so many debates during his time. To him, the fiscal tool is the key to achieving an improvement in the morality of the markets without affecting their operation:

> If consumption of luxury items threatens the morality of the people either for their excess or for their quality, in this case the government is authorized to charge people with a tax

> that becomes some sort of a fine – the ability that government has in such a case does not proceed uniquely from the right it has to impose taxes, but much more from the right it has to improve public morality and prevent its corruption. These measures are useful to the whole nation, but especially to those who are taxed; therefore there is no injustice to them. (Rosmini 2007, 74)

However, this type of tax on morally risky consumption "should be municipal or provincial, as it is clear that they should be higher in some places and lower in some others – and not universal" (Rosmini 2007, 74) because the cultural and moral problems are not the same in all places nor in all situations. However, in the case reasonably luxurious articles – which Rosmini calls "innocent" – are moderately consumed in a certain region, such a tax becomes unjust and a strong factor of distortion of the economy:

> But if we are talking about an innocent luxury in a country where luxury is held within certain limits, it would be unjust to impose taxes on luxury items, firstly because these contributions would not be equally distributed and would deprive some citizens of those innocent satisfactions that they are entitled to. Furthermore, such taxes would fall in the end on the poorer classes, such as that of the workers, since the manufacturers would have to sell at a higher price and thus try to decrease the cost of manpower or to restrict the number of the workers – and that would imply a wound to industry. (Rosmini 2007, 74)

10.3.5 Taxes on Work, Gambling, Public Goods and Foreign Trade

Furthermore, following the same line of reasoning, not only taxes on consumption should be rejected: income taxes "must only be levied on the income that exceeds the needs of survival, since neither justice nor humanity allows that the government taxes the governed on what they need to survive" (Rosmini 2007, 73). For this same reason, Rosmini generally opposes the imposition of taxes on a person who lives only on his salary and lacks property. Inspired by the theory of the Italian civil economist Broggia, Rosmini maintains that "whoever had the labor of his own hands alone, lacked capital and worked within the capital of others, should pay nothing" (Rosmini 1923, 345). This last criterion, furthermore, brings economic benefits to the area of labor costs, which increase when taxes are applied to the earnings of workers.[2]

Rosmini also rejects what he qualifies more specifically as "immoral taxes", such as those collected via the lottery and gambling: "The lottery is immoral because it

[2]"D'altra parte ed anzi in conseguenza di questo principio qualora si volesse imporre una tassa sui guadagni degli operai dovrebbe necessariamente crescere il valore della mano d'opera e così quella tassa sarebbe dunque un obbligare la proprietà a fare un giro inutile; e dare un moto artificiale alla proprietà è sempre incomodo e nocevole appunto perchè contro natura" (Rosmini 1952a, 140).

betrays poor ignorant people and deprives families of the indispensable by raising empty hopes that very often change into most disgraceful passions, fermenting irresponsibility and disinclination to work by promoting superstition and empty observances." Besides, it is unjust because it implies a "contract between uneven parts" (Rosmini 2007, 75).

According to Rosmini, it is also unfair that the State should collect taxes so that a profit is made on the maintenance of public goods since "it is just that those who make use of these public commodities pay the expenses that the State sustains in their favor. But it is not just that the price becomes inflated because of profit-making on those services, services which the public is obliged to make use of." Furthermore, "[g]etting a net profit out of public commodities maintained at the expense of the State is something that contains within it yet another injustice, which is that of depriving many citizens of the use of those services – all the citizens, that is, who cannot sustain the higher cost. That is directly opposed to the purpose of instituting public commodities. It offends the jural equality of the citizens, and has the taste of unjust aristocracy" (Rosmini 2007, 76).

Moreover, Rosmini criticizes the establishment of "import and export duties" as a tax, since "they can never be distributed in a mode that is proportional to the income of all citizens, which is the principle of justice that is to govern taxation." Thus, "all customs duties established as a tax are unjust" and they also "harm commerce and national industry because they deprive both of the necessary liberties" (Rosmini 2007, 77). However, as we shall see, Rosmini admits the legitimacy of the imposition of duties for reasons other than the fiscal ones.

10.3.6 Collection Methods

Upon these jural-economic principles, Rosmini also derives the principles that should rule, in his opinion, the manner in which taxes are collected. He places this subject in a historical context and maintains that, while in pre-modern times, there was a tendency towards "particularism," which generated "too many taxes, uncertainties, irregularities and chances to escape payment" (Rosmini 1923, 351) in modern times the opposite tendency prevails. In fact, according to Rosmini, the modern method attempts to solve problems through excessive generalization – the so-called "spirit of the system" – which, in the case of taxes, translates into ideas Rosmini refuses to adhere to, such as those of single tax or indirect taxes. In his view, such taxes make collection simpler and more certain, but are essentially unjust because they do not tax what and whom they should. Even if, according to Rosmini, modern generalization served for partially remedying the excesses of particularism, a just and truly economic tax policy should be oriented not to excessive generalization but to a precise identification of the private individuals who will bear the burden of taxation, while keeping track of the consequences such fiscal policy has in relation to the needs of the State.[3]

Furthermore, Rosmini disagrees with those who maintain that, as taxes levied directly on incomes weigh more heavily on the citizens, "it is therefore convenient to make them swallow the bitter drink without realizing it" (Rosmini 2007, 80). For him, this would simply be "covering the injustices" and keeping "the people in ignorance of their interests as well as finding indirect ways to tax without the people realizing it" (Rosmini 2007, 80). Therefore, indirect taxes "must be either abolished or greatly modified if we want to reform public finances according to the principles of justice, which is the only basis considered indisputable by society." Instead, direct taxes "generally speaking, are susceptible to a fair distribution, that is, a distribution which approximates as much as possible the exact ratio of the income of the citizens" (Rosmini 2007, 79). Furthermore, "a person, well instructed about its interests, would not want further indirect taxation, because it would at least want to know whether taxation were equably distributed, which indirect taxation would never allow. On the other hand, the people would not refuse to contribute directly what they saw was necessary and obviously distributed according to strict justice" (Rosmini 1996, n. 2164). In this way the State will gain simplicity and celerity in the collection of taxes, along with an increase in its credit and economic and moral esteem (Rosmini 1923, 359).

In a word, by virtue of the principles ruling every economic policy, Rosmini will defend the requirement of "savings, political prudence and morality" (Rosmini 1923, 352) for taxes to be as least costly as possible, to affect the mood of tax-payers to the least extent and to imply the least harm to their moral and eudaimonological state, meeting the two goals of "harming the tax-payer as little as possible, providing the State with the greatest possible utility" (Rosmini 1923, 352).

10.4 Policies on Poverty and Social Assistance

10.4.1 Between Malthus and Romagnosi

Probably one of Rosmini's most original and modern contributions to the treatment of the question of poverty consists in his approaching it as a complex problem

[3]"... bisogna avvertire dal savio ministro della finanza le cagioni influenti sì sullo stato che sui particolari, ossia gli oggetti che s' impongono, conoscere la storia degli effetti dell' imposta quanto alle mutazioni, che produce nei particolari, distinguere la diversità delle merci, o derrate, altre necessarie, il cui scemamento scema l' industria, altre estere, altre interne; notare i punti diversi, ove si trova la merce quando è colpita o nella stessa sua origine... ecc. E su tutti questi punti accozzare insieme quelle idee giuste, che debbono dirigere al bene comune i tributi, e che non sono mai fatte da chi omette qualche relazione, ma si affissa troppo in qualche particolare idea senza considerarla nella relazione con tutte" (Rosmini 1923, 122–123).

derived from lack of capabilities rather than a matter of a lack of material goods, which shows the degree of sophistication of his thinking in this regard, which overcomes simplistically materialistic conceptions. Then, in Rosmini's opinion, the real solutions to poverty are not to be found in a set of particular measures of mere material distributionism, but in the confluence of all the above mentioned tools of economic policies that are aimed at establishing a dynamic balance and proportion amongst not only material factors, but cultural, psychical and moral ones as well.

Nevertheless, Rosmini does not discard the need to develop specific policies to alleviate the problem of poverty, as a complement of the other general policies. In fact, even though economic growth regulated by an economic policy oriented towards the common good and distributive justice may gradually tend to improve the condition of the poor through an increasingly better distribution of property and the unfolding of the means and capabilities necessary to acquire it, this process does not occur from one day to the next. Rosmini does not share, for example, the position of Romagnosi, who believes that the problem of poverty has no other solution than the complete balance of the whole economy. Neither does he believe in the theological explanations by Malthus – quoted by Romagnosi – which justifies extreme poverty as an inevitable evil desired by God. Although Rosmini believes that from a theological point of view the poor will always exist, it is inadmissible to resignedly accept extreme and degrading poverty without taking any action, relying on gestures of private generosity on the part of the wealthier: it is necessary to adopt immediate social policies that may alleviate the problem of extreme poverty and attempt to put an end to it, although they may never fully achieve such goal:

> In addition, he (Romagnosi) says: 'If Malthus and his school show me that the social commandment of the divine Kingdom and its justice has taken effect there (in Ireland and England), we can indeed discuss whether the sufferings of so many unfortunate people should be ended.' Frankly, these words are ill-considered and out of place. No matter how oppressive the rich may be, or how unfairly possessions divided, do we have to wait until the rich are more sympathetic and possession better shared on earth before we try to remedy the sufferings of the poor?. It is utterly pointless to declaim against the rich and the estate owners. What we need to know, granted that at the moment no one has the power to abolish poverty, is whether he number of poor is excessive. My opinion is this: there are poor people precisely because the kingdom of God is not yet perfect and universal on earth. And while the poor are among us, we must think of alleviating, if not ending, their suffering. (Rosmini 1994a, n. 35, App. 1)

10.4.2 Social Assistance in Extraordinary and Extreme Situations

Now, the problem Rosmini faces is how to implement this special assistance. In fact, in Rosmini's view, the State must intervene in several instances in order to directly assist the poor. The first of these instances refers to the "maintenance of public security and tranquility." In extreme cases of popular rebellion owing to an economic crisis, direct and immediate assistance must be opted for without hesitation, leaving aside any violent repression, a usual method at the beginnings of the industrial era:

> There is no doubt that the civil government is authorized to perform acts of beneficence when these are seen as necessary or useful in order to prevent or calm a tumult provoked by unemployed workers or by starving indigents in times of scarcity. Thus, in such circumstances, these beneficial and generous means must absolutely be preferred to other means, more violent and contrary to the spirit of humanity, even though with these last, it would be possible to repress and contain the mob. These are exceptional and accidental cases which do not consist in mere beneficence but in a good means to attain an end commissioned to the government, that is to say, the end of the security of citizens and public order. (Rosmini 1952b, 265–266)

The second case of social assistance is based on "the right Man has to make use of what he has at hand in times of extreme need" (Rosmini 1952b, 266). We have seen in Chap. 6 the limits to economic freedom and private ownership affecting all those who take part in the market, which result from the rights generated by extreme need and oblige to provide the assistance owed to the neediest (Rosmini 1993b, n. 1236). Here, however, we are specifically dealing not with the obligation of the private citizen, but with the obligation of the very State to assist the needy in extreme indigence. It is not a matter of a mere act of charity but of the acknowledgement of a strict right:

> Society must acknowledge this right and it is generally acknowledge by all legislations, for which reason no court would condemn as guilty of theft anyone who managed to prove that he has escaped death by eating another person's bread. This right presupposes a corresponding jural duty, by which every person is obliged to allow a fellow the faculty of using, with the purpose of preserving his very existence, the goods which he possesses and which are not necessary for the preservation of his own life. Here it is not a question of spontaneous beneficence, but of the right of one party and the jural duty of another. Thus, it is inarguable that civil government has, because of its own nature, the faculty or rather the obligation to provide for the citizens' extreme necessities, whoever the citizens are, given that it has been instituted for this purpose: to protect and regulate all rights. (Rosmini 1952b, 266)

In this sense, Rosmini agrees with Romagnosi in opposing the opinion of "those who censure governments that help the poor" (Rosmini 1994a, n. 32, footnote 18) and affirms the possibility that civil society undertakes the jural obligation of helping the poor in cases of real indigence. Resorting to the celebrated case of the "Poor Laws" as an example, Rosmini mentions "the case in England (...) where a poor-tax is imposed" (Rosmini 1996, n. 1896). This is, in his opinion, a case of true remunerative justice as there "the laws themselves make the workers' condition burdensome" and "the government must therefore compensate with the poor tax." Thus, in these cases of social injustice, the poor tax, "considered as a form of governmental restitution, becomes a necessary remedy and a kind of satisfaction" (Rosmini 1994a, n. 32, footnote 18).

However, even in this case, where assistance is a matter of strict justice to which the poor are entitled, there exists the risk of trickery, and therefore it is necessary to provide said assistance in such a way that persons who do not need it do not receive it, which, apart from being unjust, would mean the introduction of discouraging stimuli for the economy. This was the problem that social assistance brought about precisely in England: despite it was just, as it did not demanded anything in return, it was requested by people who did not actually needed it and ended up by discouraging labor and creating further poverty:

> England ended up crushed by the Poor Laws, which instead of curing the sickness, made it worse. (Rosmini 1952b, 268)

Thus, it is a right to demand that a service is provided in exchange for this type of assistance, as this allows verifying who is in a situation of true extreme poverty:

> It is clear that through this assistance and through the indigent who accept it, society gains a right to require work from the poor as a strictly jural obligation. Without such an obligation, it would be impossible to verify amongst the indigent those who had the right to assistance; the idle must be considered thieves under such a system. (Rosmini 1993b, n. 1896)

10.4.3 The Debate on the Welfare State

Finally, in the third place, Rosmini mentions the type of assistance that goes beyond the cases of extreme necessity, which he calls "beneficence". Here, Rosmini opens an interesting and keen debate that anticipates in many years the arguments set out by the modern Welfare State. In fact, according to Rosmini, the acts of beneficence differ essentially from acts of strict justice. By quoting Aquinas, Rosmini defines the former as simple free transfers so that "if a person simply transfers what is his to another without incurring any debt, as in donation, it is an act of liberality, not of justice" (S.T., II-II, q. 61, art. 3). Thus, "donations are not measured or equated against any debt but solely against benevolence and liberality, which are freely chosen and therefore not susceptible of any assignable measure, except that of the donor's large-heartedness represented in the gift itself" (Rosmini 1993b, n. 1210).

In that sense, according to Rosmini, whenever public security or extreme necessity are not involved, direct assistance to the poor is not the object of strictly jural obligation but of beneficence. In his view, beneficence is not a matter of a jurally obligatory act, that is to say, it is not subject to jural duty and consequently does not give birth to a right proper. It is rather a *morally* obligatory act subject not to jural duty but to *moral duty*. Yet, precisely because it is an essentially moral duty and not a strictly jural one, it cannot be vindicated as a "perfect" right by those benefited from said act:

> For example, if I refuse to do good to another, I am not thereby violating the sphere of rights (...) It is not true that I have the right to be inhuman to other people, although it is true that I have the right not to be disturbed or damaged in what I am doing if I refuse to do to others the good to which I am held by a higher moral law. (Rosmini 1993a, n. 261)

So, according to Rosmini, it is necessary "to re-establish the distinction between perfect and imperfect rights, between the duty to help humanity and the duty of respect for each other's ownership (...)" (Rosmini 1994b, n. 623). This last point, in Rosmini's opinion, is essential to correctly approach the question of what the State is entitled to demand in matters of social assistance. In fact, Rosmini strongly warns that terrible evils may fall upon society due to the confusion – generated by statist utilitarianism – between the duty of beneficence and strictly jural justice regarding social assistance:

> To confuse what pertains to beneficence with what pertains to justice, to impose on the obligation of beneficence the rigorous and harshness of what is due, to equate the precept to do good with the precept forbidding theft: all this is to abolish the division between two virtues always considered distinct. Such action necessarily leads society to destruction unless it turns back at the sight of the terrible consequences. (Rosmini 1994b, n. 619)

According to Rosmini, the most evident consequence of this serious mistake would be violence: if beneficence generates a "perfect right," this would include the use of force, by which "anyone who has perfect right can, whenever defense requires it, violently repel the person inflicting violence:"

> Thus, if the right of each individual to the same portion of good is perfect and absolute, the result is obvious: each time a government fails to equalize all the good, all those with a smaller quantity of the good can violently force the government to effect the equality. This can only occasion an open ceaseless war between the majority of the associated members and the government because those who have less good are always the majority. (Rosmini 1994b, n. 619)

However, Rosmini wonders if the State should limit itself to protect and regulate rights, or if it should also undertake part of the duty of spontaneous beneficence (Rosmini 1952b, 265). Rosmini certainly does not refer here to whether the government may undertake the responsibility for an extraordinary and momentary beneficence (which is jurally obligatory and required by force of law in the two cases we have mentioned above), but to whether the government should undertake responsibility for an "ordinary and continuous" beneficence (Rosmini 1952b, 266). On the other hand, this does not refer either to a question such as "(that) of knowing whether the civil government may advise and exhort citizens to beneficence" since there "cannot be any doubt" (Rosmini 1952b, 266) about this. The specific question here is whether "the government can use the goods from the state Treasury for purely beneficial works, whether it can tax citizens and thus oblige them to contribute to the works of beneficence which it considers appropriate to perform" (Rosmini 1952b, 266). Moreover, another question related with the latter is "if in said case, the beneficence performed by the government loses its spontaneous nature" (Rosmini 1952b, 267). According to Rosmini, "it will be difficult to avoid dealing with this question" which is no other than "the great question of the workers and also the great question of poverty [pauperism]", as this is not a matter of mere private morality, but an issue which must be considered from the social point of view since it is a problem that must be solved "according to justice" (Rosmini 1952b, 265).

10.4.4 A Middle Road Between Two Extremes

In this sense, Rosmini states that the functions of the government in matters of beneficence are generally approached from two different viewpoints. On the one hand, "some maintain that civil government, instituted for the protection and regulation of the modality of rights, has no authority of any kind to perform acts which are of mere beneficence" (Rosmini 1952b, 265). According to Rosmini, this attitude is limited to "severe reason" (Rosmini 1952b, 265) since it fails to consider the wide field of generous donation to which individuals are also called. On the other hand, there is the position of those who "have a vague and indeterminate conception of civil government as having a kind of mysterious authority coming from superior spheres which is omnipotent, may dispose of everything, and may take from one place to put into another (. . .)" According to Rosmini, this attitude is "inspired solely by sentiment, does not take into account interest and even goes against self-interest" although – as he ironically points out – "many other times, it is moved by interest, finding in or expecting from said beneficence some self-advantage" (Rosmini 1952b, 265). Faced to these two diverging positions, Rosmini maintains:

> My opinion falls between two extremes. (. . .) I believe that the middle road is that which should be taken to find the true solution. (Rosmini 1952b, 265–266)

Indeed, in his opinion, it is not about rejecting all the actions performed by the State as a benefactor, or of indiscriminately affirming such dimension. The challenge is to find the way in which the State can prudently perform this function without overstepping its limits as regulator of the modality of rights and without destroying the spontaneous nature of acts of beneficence. In this sense, according to Rosmini, the solution to the problem of the legitimacy of the Welfare State lies in the fact that those who make decisions about beneficence should not be beneficiaries themselves, as would occur in an excessively democratic form of government that would allow a poor majority to unrestrictedly use the power of the state to oblige owners of wealth to re-distribute it permanently among the poorest people. This "democratic despotism" is, in Rosmini's opinion, a true "organized theft" (Rosmini 2007, 54) which ends up by causing a "grave harm not only to the nation but to the very indigent class whom it is aimed at benefiting." When funds are compulsorily extracted from owners, without their consent, a negative disposition is generated in them. This "dries up the sources of private beneficence," "diminishes the joy of charity, which is less experienced when the benefactor does not wipe away the tears of the poor with his own hands" and "destroys the bond of affection which joins the rich class to the poor," replacing the "gratitude" of the latter with the "arrogant pretension of a presumed right, sowing envy and hostility towards the rich." Consequently, it "upsets the mutual concord and benevolence between social classes which is civil society's most precious good, the guarantee of its duration and the very noble cause of popular and social morality" (Rosmini 1952b, 272).

Rosmini thus believes that the spontaneous nature of beneficence actions on the part of the state essentially depends on a matter of institutional design where it is "the owners themselves who establish the taxes to be paid for public beneficence and so it will be owners themselves who establish which part of their goods will they assign to the public good, without anyone obliging them to do so by force" (Rosmini 1952b, 267). Besides, if this institutional design were not possible, then Rosmini believes that "it would be convenient that all beneficence were to be ceded by the government to the liberality of individual citizens and private associations which could freely be formed or dissolved outside the government" (Rosmini 1952b, 267). In that sense, he considers of vital importance the associations of civil society and above all, of the Church, not only because of their greater effectiveness in many cases owing to their closeness to concrete needs, but also because of the possibility they have of enriching moral and social bonds along with their capacity to provide material assistance. For this reason, although the government may take charge or it, in Rosmini's opinion, "by its very nature, beneficence is not a governmental affair" but rather "a right of the heart which no one can usurp (. . .)" (Rosmini 1952b, 271).

10.5 Foreign Trade

10.5.1 In Principle an Evident Benefit

Foreign trade is another field of economic policy Rosmini deals with. According to him, this is a highly controversial aspect of economic policy:

> [. . .] Everyone knows that freedom of trade is a question which splits economic theorists irreconcilably. (Rosmini 1993b, n. 1676)

Such a controversy arises, according to Rosmini, because the question has two different aspects and the arguing parties generally consider them as isolated from each other, absolutizing them. In fact, on the one hand, there is the aspect of general principles and, on the other, that of their concrete application in certain historic-cultural contexts. Thus, from the point of view of principles, Rosmini maintains that "the advantages from these liberties seem today beyond any controversy" (Rosmini 2007, 77), if we consider the ideal of international trade amongst individuals forming part of one and the same global society, who relate amongst themselves in equal terms, without obstacles or conditionings:

> If we abstract from the special circumstances of nations and particular States and consider only human beings in one and the same family, free trade is obviously beneficial and moral; restrictions on free trade are a disaster for the human race. (Rosmini 1993b, n. 1676)

In fact, Rosmini argues, trade with other countries is, in principle, beneficial. Since it provides the country itself with the products and services it cannot produce unless at a much higher cost or with poorer results regarding quality, this exchange becomes the most natural way for nations and regions to distribute production among themselves according to their different competitive advantages. Besides, the introduction of foreign goods can also be a powerful incentive for improving the quality of domestic production since, if a nation "embraces or imitates the customs of another because of their merit, it adopts a reasonable attitude" and "only a false policy or a disordered national pride could preach the contrary" (Rosmini 1923, 474, footnote 62).

10.5.2 Prudential Limitation to Foreign Trade According to Historical and Cultural Context

However, Rosmini's enthusiasm for foreign free trade has clear limits which appear when the principles of freedom are put into practice within the concrete historical and cultural dimension of countries. Given the particular circumstances and concrete relationships of each country or region, Rosmini admits the possibility and usefulness of establishing restrictions to said freedom, as long as they are provisional and for a limited period of time:

> But we still have to see if such curbs could be advantageous when considered in relation to the particular good of a nation or a region, at a determined time and in determined circumstances and external relationships. Here I have no hesitation in accepting the opinion of those who maintain that customs and other curbs of this kind can be advantageous for the special regions for which they are established, provided they are moderate and used for exceptional cases -in other words, they are simply provisional, temporary laws. (Rosmini 1993b, n. 1676)

This way, Rosmini places the question of free trade amongst nations in the sphere of prudence and not only of pure principles. The task of determining how, when and up to which extent these restrictions should be established will be the art of prudence of economic policies:

> The question of curbs placed on trade is in many ways more difficult. If the government decides to impose curbs for the sake of public utility, it will be the responsibility primarily of political economy to whether such utility will result from the particular fact in question. (Rosmini 1993b, n. 1676)

10.5.3 Cases of Gradual Liberalization and Temporary Protectionism

According to the Roveretan, "a just and wise government could be authorized to temporarily raise some duties" in two exceptional cases: in the first place, in agreement with Adam Smith, when a country had been subject to a protectionist system, as it is advisable that the opening should be gradual and not sudden:

> In a State where the prohibition system has prevailed and thus industry and commerce have taken an exceptional course and shape, we cannot – without damaging many – all of a

sudden destroy that status quo which is against nature by suddenly allowing a full liberty of industry and commerce. It is wise to allow time for industry and commerce to back out of their false direction and return to their natural and free ways. It is therefore appropriate that customs duties be gradually decreased until the natural state of full liberty is reached. (Rosmini 2007, 77)[4]

The second case refers to a country where, despite the productive and competitive potential, there is still an insufficient development of capital, capabilities or initiative to put it into practice:

> The condition of a people could be such as to benefit from some ramification of commerce and industry that cannot flourish in that nation – and that for several reasons: because the first investments need capital that cannot immediately yield sufficient profits because of the competition from foreign merchandise coming from countries where the businesses are already organized, for the incompetence of those who start a new industry for the nation, and because of the lack of initiative of the capitalists. (Rosmini 2007, 77–78)

In such circumstance, the abrupt opening up of the economy would have most unfortunate consequences, because the economic culture needed for competition cannot be acquired from 1 day to the other and demands protection during the learning period:

> In this last case, industry, crafts and ways of increasing wealth are not learnt instantly by the uneducated for whose education time must be set aside. During the period which must be dedicated to learning, any contact with cultured people is usually fatal. The products of cultured peoples are inevitably better and less expensive than those produced by less educated peoples whose industry is still young and equipment primitive. This kind of unequal competition endangers their nascent industry to some extent, because people will not work hard unless there is some hope of gain for themselves. (Rosmini 1994b, n. 704)

In such cases, Rosmini fully justifies the introduction of protective measures, even though they should be very well-studied, publicly discussed in Parliament, and established not as permanent taxes at the service of the voracity of the State, but as temporary laws exclusively aimed at promoting the development of the local industry and labor:

> In this case, a customs duty that protects against foreign merchandise, and an export duty on raw material that is imposed judiciously and moderately, could encourage the whole

[4]"Qui entra l'Economia politica, la quale dimostra che la libertà del commercio è utile reciprocamente a tutte le nazioni, qualora però non sia avvenuto in alcuna di esse una distribuzione ed un accumulamento di ricchezze artificiali, siccome accade quando una nazione soggiacque lungamente all'azione di un sistema proibitivo. E questo più o meno è avvenuto in tutte le nazioni d'Europa, dove l'arte fu dalla presunzione de'Governi sostituita alla natura, e si credette poter far derivare ogni bene da quella mettendo questa in ceppi e sciupandola. Tale essendo la condizione de' diversi Stati d'Europa, egli è forza di ricondurli alla libertà del commercio gradatamente, lasciando tempo alle ricchezze di riprendere il loro corso naturale, il che se si volesse fare istantaneamente e violentemente, cagionerebbe degli sconcerti gravissimi alle private fortune. Ma egli è necessario che nella Costituzione venga dichiarato che si vuole arrivare a questo, rimettendo alla sapienza governativa il modo di farlo, graduato secondo la varia condizione economica della nazione" (Rosmini 1952a, 167).

> industry by allowing the birth in the nation of workshops and factories which, once they have been well started, could sustain themselves and maintain competition with foreign products. At that time, any protective customs duties should cease so that those very enterprises do not grow unnaturally in opposition to the free course of industry.
>
> These customs duties that cannot be justified as tax can be perfectly justified instead as being in the interests of national common utility. But considering how easily state financial authorities could perpetrate abuses in this case, it is appropriate that each case of their application be discussed in great depth by the legislative chambers, and be recognized by law. (Rosmini 2007, 78)

However, it is clear that Rosmini does not support protectionist measures of a Colbertist style, which he considers harmful in principle. However, in certain cases, he approves of such type of measures provided they prove to be more useful for the economy than the liberal ones and are oriented at protecting a rising industry during its learning period. These measures, besides, should be aimed at the achievement of competitiveness and not at perpetuating protection of a local industry that would be unprofitable if let to compete in the international market, although it is very difficult to establish the boundary in this respect:

> Thus in the Colbertist system, the prohibition of exporting raw materials is, in general and in itself, certainly harmful, because as these are retained within the country, owners are prevented from selling and obtaining the profits they would make if said prohibition did not exist. But if this were to lead to building factories in the country that could contribute greater profits, it would certainly be useful. But this will not happen unless it can be shown with all certainty that these factories are lacking at present because of inertia or ignorance, and not because the profits that established entrepreneurs can make there are always necessarily scarce, which is something difficult to ascertain. (Rosmini 1923, 369)

The different forms of protection and regulation of foreign trade will vary thus according to the different states of evolution of each people regarding their economic and commercial capacity:

> It is not surprising that Peter the Great should have had to take charge of promoting industry and commerce in Moscow with greater action and with many more numerous regulations than those necessary in England. Nor am I amazed that Mr. Huskisson should have put forward a plan aimed at opening England's ports to all natural and industrial foreign products with such low Customs duty that contraband disappeared. This shows the superiority of English trade, the activity and knowledge of the private persons who develop it, and the interests that move them; they are sufficiently enlightened to act not against themselves but in their own favor to the highest degree, and this is why they have need of only minimal governmental action. (Rosmini 1923, 370)

10.5.4 The Principle of Justice Above All

Furthermore, according to Rosmini, economic policies in matters of foreign trade must be directed, above all, by principles of justice (Rosmini 1993b, n. 1676). Thus, it is always necessary to wonder about the consequences that measures aimed at curbing trade may have on the right of all the actors involved. In that sense, restrictions on foreign trade are always negative for humanity as a whole, because they prevent mankind from achieving the ideal of a free inter-relationship among all its members, which would grant them full exercise of their right to compete upon the basis of their greatest talents with the purpose of attaining a constant quantitative and qualitative improvement in the production of manufactures and services. However, even if we acknowledge the justice contained in a temporary measure that, with the purpose of favoring local industry, restricts this universal freedom, which is based on the right each country has to trade with others and on the freedom of deciding whether to do so or not (Rosmini 1952a, 167), we should ask ourselves whether such measure is really beneficial to all the nation or only some of its members:

> But are such curbs fair in relationship to other peoples even when it is agreed that they are harmful to mankind as a whole? Are they just relative to all the individuals of the society for which they are established when the immediate advantage of such provisions is enjoyed only by certain determinate classes of persons, owners, traders or manufacturers? (Rosmini 1993b, n. 1676)

It will be essential to weigh all these consequences in order to adopt such measures in full conscience and with full care for the various rights affected. This does not invalidate the possible legitimacy of said restrictions, but demands that the need for possible rewards or compensations be considered.

10.5.5 The Complex Road Towards a Global Market

In a word, in Rosmini's view, the question of economic policies in the field of foreign trade must aim at progressively abandoning protectionism and at opening up the economy through commercial treaties drawn up with each country in particular. By means of these treaties, it would be possible to start leaving aside reciprocal protection policies in order to gradually consolidate freedom of trade. Freedom of trade should not be restored all of a sudden or in a generalized and indiscriminate manner, but following a careful criterion of reciprocal compensation. Such compensation means that whenever the opening to free trade of a sector implies a benefit for one country, there should follow an opening to free trade of another sector that is beneficial to the other.

According to Rosmini, by applying this criterion, the right to free economic competition and the interest of individuals would be saved, along with the right of ownership and the interest each nation has over its own territory. Nevertheless, this does not prevent one country from exercising the right to impose curbs on trade in case the other country refuses to enter into a free trade agreement, as such exercise would be legitimated by the right to legitimate defense each nation has:

> Relative to nations, it seems to me that it is always possible (when nations are agreed in recognizing the obligation) to make just agreements or trade treaties which would not be intended to balance materially the burdens variously imposed on the import and export of products and manufactured goods, but to maintain intact freedom of trade by allowing reciprocal compensation and recompense in so far as free trade benefited one or other of the parties. The compensation and recompense could be derived from the right of ownership

that each nation has over the territory of the land it inhabits. One consequence of this would be the exclusion of foreigners whose trade would thus be impeded indirectly. If such agreements are possible, they are also obligatory as a means of safeguarding simultaneously the freedom of private individuals and the national interest. Hence, if one of the nations refuses to enter into such agreements based on freedom of trade, the other acquires, by the very refusal, the right to curb the trade of this nation. Tariffs and curbs are thus legitimated by being brought into the Right of self-defence. (Rosmini 1993b, n. 1676)

Chapter 11
State Institutions, Civil Society, Family and Religion

11.1 The Political and Economic Institutions *as Means for Social Recognition*

Rosmini believes neither in the abstract freedom of economic interests as forces capable of ordering themselves nor in an artificial and totalitarian order imposed from above. To him, in either the liberal or the statist form of social utilitarianism, interests are reduced to purely "factual" forces, which – as such – are blind and essentially amoral. It could be alleged that these individual interests, integrated by elevated individual morality, are in themselves sufficient for achieving common good and distributive economic justice. However, true social justice does not depend solely on individual morality but on how society's institutions are organized. Rosmini maintains that individual morality alone is therefore insufficient for regulating economic interests: a *social* morality or prudence is required. However, this social or moral prudence is exercised by persons through the institutions of society and the government. According to him, a good economic policy finds support "on moral principles and on institutions" (Rosmini 1977a, 133, footnote 1) as its two foundations.

> [B]ecause despotism is not only in persons, it may be in the form of government, it may be within the government itself and, finally, it may be within civil society itself, when the latter is wrongly conceived and defined (. . .) (Rosmini 1887, 670)

Thus, in the Roveretan's opinion, social and economic justice becomes possible only through an institutional order that recognizes and reflects society's complexity. Rosmini thinks that the State is an expression of society as a whole under a representative form. Its function is to make visible, transparent and – therefore – susceptible of regulation, the complexity of relationships, interests and rights interacting in the complex fabric of social reality. This transparency or visibility does not mean rational control or exhaustive knowledge. The Roveretan entrusts a good part of the social order – what we might call the body or basis of society – to society's spontaneous, "instinctive" dimension. To him, the function of the State is

C. Hoevel, *The Economy of Recognition: Person, Market and Society in Antonio Rosmini*, Ethical Economy 42, DOI 10.1007/978-94-007-6058-5_11,

to regulate this spontaneous order, after having recognized its principal components and integrated them into the unity of the common good.

In fact, according to Rosmini, the historical evolution of civil society reveals that, in its beginnings, economic interests were only regulated by custom or by laws handed down by tradition, which varied widely within each country and along time. The final result, purely factual to a great extent, was adequate for a pre-civil age, but imperfect for civil times, since many interests and needs remained unsatisfied, either because they stayed hidden, were absorbed or overrun by others more powerful, or because they were simply ignored. Rosmini believes that, in modern societies, exist a generalized tendency for interests and rights to be recognized, expressed and openly discussed, confronted in a moral and rational discussion with others through the political institutions. According to Rosmini, this expression of interests via the visible platform of political institutions progressively reveals society an increasingly larger scope with reference to the ends which it must commonly reach and, therefore, a growing complexity in the political means necessary to achieve them, if compared with those of former societies, still poor in their structure of representation and political organization.

> A time will certainly come when what has up to the present been tacitly and factually determined will be expressly determined by the will of interested parties; dependent on their interests and needs, the end of civil association and the offices entrusted to its government will be restricted or expanded. (Rosmini 1994b, n. 215, footnote 67)

11.1.1 Critique of the "French System"

Rosmini is an acerbic critic of institutional systems inspired by what he calls "the French system." In fact, like other critics of his time, he considers typical of the French system those Constitutions which are "created altogether, emerging complete as theory from the mind, like Minerva from the head of Jupiter," and "written before being enacted." These Constitutions are, according to Rosmini, a product of "the improvisation of audacious and imaginative minds, too much infatuated with too general and too imperfect theories (. . .) daughters of a philosophy that wanted to break with the past" (Rosmini 2007, 1–2). Consequently, they are full of "vain abstractions" and of "theories that are inapplicable to social realities" (Rosmini 2007, 10). Rosmini admires, instead, institutional designs such as the "Constitution of the Venetian Republic" and especially that of the "English Constitution," both of which have been "enacted before they were written," "passage by passage, without a premeditated scheme, incessantly patched and mended according to counter-veiling social forces and the urgency of instincts and popular need" (Rosmini 2007, 1).

According to the Roveretan, the French system reveals an extremist concept of freedom and of political representation, which deifies the political majority personified by the Legislative Power to the detriment of the rights of individual citizens, families, private associations, minorities and the Church, apart from conditioning the economy in a very negative manner. In fact, by reducing the election of the government to universal suffrage, it puts all the power of the State exclusively in the hands of an anonymous electoral mass of equal votes without any kind of connection to the varying weight of their economic interests and rights.[1] As a logical consequence of such disproportionate exaltation of popular power, these constitutions "promote in all citizens a limitless ambition to ascend to ever greater degrees in society," and they "open the way to corruption in the election of deputies and, especially, of the president if the form is republican." Such constitutions give "such preponderance to the Chamber of Deputies, even for their comparatively excessive number, that the state is kept in the danger of revolution" at the expense of the economic rights of groups and individuals which have been rightfully acquired in a competitive market.

Political representation based exclusively on universal suffrage does not "guarantee sufficiently and in all fullness of law the freedom of the citizens," nor can it "guarantee the distribution of properties" (Rosmini 2007, 6) since its constant redistributionism completely deforms the finances and economic policies of the government,[2] and obscures the possibility of a transparent and just fiscal policy; finally, it destroys all kinds of incentive for authentic and sustainable economic development and eventually becomes, in Rosmini's own words, "organized theft."

11.1.2 The Parliament as the Representative and Regulative Institution of the Modality of Economic Rights

Thus, Rosmini affirms that the solution to the problem of political representation is vitally important in order to give economy an appropriate institutional framework. This representation must be, in his opinion, closely related to economic interests and rights. This is particularly true in what he calls the current "historical era

[1]"What is, then, the universal franchise in this assumption, and what does it involve? It is, and it involves, an equal amount of power in the writing of the laws granted to all citizens regardless of the major or minor groups of rights that each citizen possesses or represents" (Rosmini 2007, 58).

[2]"We can expect economy from men who spend their own, but how can we expect it when they spend somebody else's money, which they dispose of by law, with which they can buy the glory of doing great and beautiful things? For those who have little or nothing, it is of very little importance whether the finances of the state are administered with economy or not" (Rosmini 2007, 66). "These legislators are inclined to let the Government into all those enterprises that should be freely left to private industry, and often inclined to reserve to the government itself the monopoly, because they care very little about the damage that is caused to private entrepreneurs and to capitalists" (Rosmini 2007, 66). Finally, Rosmini carries his argument to an extreme by maintaining that universal suffrage necessarily leads to economic socialism: "an equal vote in the election of deputies eventually results in socialism; and that this system tends to convert the whole nation into one gigantic work house, into one immense manufacturing plant where the only entrepreneurs is the Government" (Rosmini 2007, 67). In this sense, he was praising the English tradition: "only England so far has understood well that it is convenient for the government not to substitute itself for private industry" (Rosmini 2007, 67).

of civil society" (very different from the historically previous era of "family society"), where the economic factor is essential not only for progress but also for the basic functioning of society.[3] According to Rosmini, it is a great mistake to ignore the economic dimension of Man and society. In fact, the right of ownership and the principle of freedom are the foundations of society's entire institutional organization.

In a civil society, economic matters have an enormous weight both on the preservation of political power and on the equitable distribution of goods and opportunities which allow society and its members to be led to their social end. In Rosmini's opinion, it is essential to separate the "moral dimension" of the government from what he calls its "economic-administrative" dimension. In civil society, when economic interests are not recognized and lack political weight, they end up "buying" this weight in a corrupt manner and deforming the functions of the government, be they either moral or strictly economic. This is why Rosmini rejects the idea that the government should be constituted only by "personal representation" (one person, one vote) and is convinced that there should also be an institution where economic interests are exclusively represented – "real representation" (based on *res*, that is, property) – as "the function of ballast that property has in keeping the ship of the state balanced" (Rosmini 2007, 161)[4] is undeniable.

In this sense, the institution of the Legislature or Parliament is, according to Rosmini, the place where the economic interests at stake in society must be represented, so that they can be regulated according to political means ruled by ethics and the law. It is within them that the laws governing potential actions and interventions in the economy on the part of the State should emerge. According to Rosmini, these actions may be more or less far-reaching, depending on the prudence and vision of the governor; they are never the result of the governor's sole individual decision but the outcome of a previous open rational discussion amongst all the owners of wealth. Therefore, in Parliament, the "electoral vote must be considered as an appendix, a portion of property rights" (Rosmini 2007, 53), so that "the majority of taxes are approved by those who pay them" (Rosmini 2007, 64) and there may be "economy in finances" and a "political and economic administration" of the "citizens' properties, the complexities of which form the wealth of the nation." (Rosmini 2007, 7) In fact, Rosmini says that within the environment of

[3]"Civil society cannot exist without money; with it, it pays the bureaucrats and the military (...) it performs public works and so on. Nothing is done without money" (Rosmini 2007, 126).

[4]This phrase is almost literally the same as Edmund Burke's: "Let those large proprietors be what they will...they are, at the very worst, the ballast in the vessel of the Commonwealth" (Burke 1987, 45). In the *Naturale costituzione della società civile*, Rosmini explains at great length the historic basis of real representation, the origin of which took place in Rome and later continued during the entirety of European history. The Roveretan defends the historic interpretation against the arguments of the "levelers," "radicals" and other sympathizers of the French Revolution, who attempted to prove that the English institutional system was originally based on personal representation, which argument Rosmini considered historically untrue.

parliamentary representation, whoever does not own property should not participate in political society as an active citizen, but as a passive citizen.[5]

All things considered, the fact that Rosmini gives great importance to the economic dimension of the government, especially represented in Parliament, by no means signify that such dimension is *amoral:* to the Roveretan, every human action, even economic actions, are ruled by morality.[6] Given the social character of the economy's moral question, to which we have referred above, the economic administration of society as carried out by Parliament cannot remain *aseptic* when facing the moral question: its actions necessarily demand that the technical-economic means also point towards that dimension.[7]

11.1.3 Constitutional Measures Against the "Unfair Aristocracy"

Although Rosmini considers that one of the risks of the Legislative Power is that of becoming an "unfair democracy" like the French Revolution, characterized by "the arrogance of the non-rich who would like to steal wealth from the rich," it also runs the risk of becoming "an unfair aristocracy" characterized by "the arrogance of the rich who would like to perpetually tie wealth to their families" (Rosmini 2007, 55). In fact, the English parliamentary system of real representation of his times, admired by Rosmini in certain aspects, errs in the opposite direction (Rosmini 2007, 67) of the French system, in the sense that it has deformed the idea of Parliament as the representative of rights to ownership, turning it into a mere instrument for the excessive profits of the wealthier. Thus, "Landlords wrote legislation which was to their exclusive advantage" (Rosmini 2007, 62). In this way, Rosmini's proposal that members of Parliament should represent economic interests does not mean

[5]"(...) che quelli che nulla pagano al tesoro dello Stato rimangano privi di voto elettorale è un corollario del principio incontroverso, che la società civile ha la sua esistenza e il suo esercizio dai contribuenti... Che la società civile riconosca per suoi propri membri anche quelli che nulla contribuiscono al fondo sociale onde ella trae l' esistenza e l'attività, non viene prescritto dal diritto di natura e di ragione, ma insinuato dallo spirito del Vangelo che esclude dal mondo la schiavitù. Tutti gli uomini redenti da Gesù Cristo sono liberi, sono fratelli: la società civile cristiana riconosce come tali anche i poveri, e gli ammette gratuitamente nel suo seno tutelandoli con giustizia, beneficandoli con carità: il che però non importa la necessità che ella attribuisca loro altresì un potere politico..." (Rosmini 1952a, 199–200).

[6]"E non è già che io escluda nell´amministrazione la moralità: questa è necessaria in tutto..." (Rosmini 1887, 306).

[7]"Tale costituzione organizzata in un modo al tutto amministrativo non curerebbe di sua natura che gl' interessi, e ciò che è morale sarebbe straniero alla medesima, cioè a dire apparterrebbe alle persone singole, ma non alla Amministrazione stessa presa in astratto..." (Rosmini 1887, 303–304).

that they can be independent of law and justice.[8] On the contrary, the function of Parliament is to put these interests under an objective light by which they may be openly recognized, clearly measured in their true dimension, and conducted to their subordination to justice and natural law. In fact, Rosmini believes precisely that, in a Parliament where economic interests are openly discussed, these will be more easily subjected to ethics and to the law than in those presumably moralistic governments that end up falling into a hidden savage economicism.[9]

This is the reason why Rosmini also designs an electoral system that does not tend towards the accumulation of power, whether in the hands of a few big owners who oppress the smaller owners, or in those of a great mass of small owners who oppress the big ones. In this sense, we understand, for example, Rosmini's rejection of a system having only one Legislative Chamber and his proposal of two separate Chambers, respectively representing the big and the small owners as an attempt to save his institutional design from being purely a defense of the *status quo* of the wealthiest. Rosmini's institutional design aims at protecting the legitimate rights of the actual owners from the possible excessive ambitions of the smaller owners and non-owners, while it also protects the right of the latter to acquire or increase wealth from the excessive avarice of the former, who wish to conserve it and may abuse their right to do so. In this way, Rosmini grants the new social classes' participation in Parliament, making room for the promotion of not only industrialists, tradesmen and workers (including non-owner workers) not as voters, but as people eligible as representatives to both Chambers.[10] In Rosmini's times, this meant a significant step, considering the exclusive power which the landowning nobility had wielded for centuries.

[8]"La lotta delle parti che sostiene, anche presentemente, il governo d' Inghilterra non è parimenti che una lotta d' interessi, la ricchezza industriale che combatte colla ricchezza territoriale. Dovunque le forze della natura hanno libera azione, questa lotta si debbe manifestare, e non può finire se non allorquando tutti i membri della società sieno convenuti nell' equità dell' Amministrazione da noi proposta, nella quale ciascuno si appaghi di avere un voto corrispondente alla sua ricchezza di qualunque genere questa sia, o territoriale o mobiliare" (Rosmini 1887, 241).

[9]"Si ha dunque ragione di gridare contro al materialismo che corrompe i governi de' nostri tempi, dando loro la forma di un negozio mercantile, ma si farebbe ancor meglio nell' insegnare come si possa dividere l' amministrativo da ciò che è morale . . . " (Rosmini 1887, 306).

[10]Contrary to all that has been said regarding the elitism of Rosmini, it should be said that in his *Della naturale Costituzione della società civile* he makes a long exposition of the arguments of those who in their time rejected political representation for workers to reject them with arguments which rested on the idea of social and distributive justice stated here. See "Articolo IX. Stato della terza classe di persone nella Società civile cioè dei mercenarî" (Rosmini 1887, 94–103).

11.1.4 The Political Tribunal

Now, as Parliament personifies, above all, the utilitarian dimension of Man, Rosmini also designs a special institution to specifically represent Man's moral dimension he will call the "Political Tribunal."[11] The Political Tribunal is the Supreme State Tribunal. In Rosmini's concept, it differs from a regular tribunal of justice, because it is not in charge of enforcing the law passed by the Legislative Power but, on the contrary, it has the crucial mission of "holding the natural and rational right against all other powers of the states" (Rosmini 2007, 29). The Political Tribunal is the institution by which all citizens may claim the acknowledgment of and respect for their own economic rights, which might have not taken place within Parliament. The project for this institution – Rosmini considers it the most important one within the State – was inspired by his reading of the civil philosopher Giammaria Ortes and other authors, such as the Abbé de Saint Pierre and Leibniz.[12] Especially thanks to the latter, Rosmini probably discovered, amongst other things, the need for an instance different and superior to that of economic administration in order to protect the two functions of government, that is, the jural-moral function and the economic one, by separating and giving them hierarchy at the same time.[13]

In fact, Rosmini's criticism of the French Revolution does not point to its Declaration of the Rights of Man and of the Citizen – as in the case, for example, of Burke – but to the lack of "a corresponding tribunal that would enforce it" (Rosmini 2007, 29), which led to a tyranny of the alleged "government of the people." Who can defend the citizen from a power which presents itself as the ultimate incarnation of the law unless a "judicial branch be above the legislative branch in order to judge the justice of the acts of legislation?" (Rosmini 2007, 25). Thus, the Political Tribunal is the instance to which any citizen of the State may appeal in case his natural rights have been violated, especially by what has become the nightmare of modern politics: "the specter of an omnipotent civil society" (Rosmini 2007, 29) or, in other words, "the omnipotence of the law – that is, of the omnipotence of the legislators through the laws" (Rosmini 2007, 53).

The introduction by Rosmini of a Political Tribunal for the defense of rights does not only have consequences on the control of those laws which Rosmini calls "jural" or of "pure justice" (Rosmini 2007, 129) and relate to basic natural rights, but also on the so-called "laws of utility" created by Parliament – which the Roveretan also calls of "politic-economic administration." The latter also fall within the Political

---

[11]"L' esistenza morale dell' uomo riguardo alle cose esterne che possono essere oggetto della civile società, viene conservata nella sua integrità mediante la giustizia, e per ciò mediante un Tribunale politico che a questa presiede; l' esistenza sensibile dell' uomo viene conservata e migliorata da una saggia amministrazione dei suoi beni . . . " (Rosmini 1887, 118).

[12]Carlo Gray believes that Rosmini did not take into account American's Supreme Court.

[13]"L' amministrazione perfetta dunque non si può ottenere se non si divide da essa tutto ciò che nel governo c' è di morale; cioè se non lo si porta tutto nei tribunali e specialmente nel Tribunale Politico" (Rosmini 1887, 306).

Tribunal's regulation because "a power that is turned to utility must be accountable to another power that oversees the preservation of justice, so that the utilitarian instincts that naturally move the parliaments do not damage justice" (Rosmini 2007, 129–130). Thus, amongst the rights protected by the Political Tribunal, Rosmini points out the importance not only of innumerable connatural rights such as the right to life, to a fair trial, to travel freely throughout the interior of the country and abroad, and to profess one's own religion freely, but also of a series of economic rights or rights very much related to economy, such as the right of ownership, the right to association, and the right to freely practice an economic activity or profession.

Furthermore, the role of the Political Tribunal being that of watching over the connatural rights of citizens – which are equal for all by the sole fact of their participation in human nature – the qualification of those who choose its members must not be related to their social or economic position, as it happens in the Parliament conceived by Rosmini. Thus, while Rosmini rejects personal representation and universal suffrage with regard to the Legislative Power, in the case of the Political Tribunal, he believes that its members should be elected by the equal vote of all citizens:

> We have established a proportional vote, but we have not excluded the universal and equal vote. The proportional vote we have kept for the election of the parliaments representing the material interests – and those interests are not equal in all men. The universal vote we have adopted for the election of the Political Tribunal, representing the interests and the personal rights, which are and must be equal for all. (Rosmini 2007, 163)

Thus, Rosmini introduces the democratic principle of the universal vote into the very heart of his institutional system, which in his time had "an extension that is greater than all those that have admitted it so far" (Rosmini 2007, 163).

In this sense, according to Rosmini, nor the design of the main State institutions neither the division of powers should be focused solely on the problem of the balance of powers amongst themselves, as Montesquieu taught, but on the problem of the balance between power and wealth, which the Roveretan sees as the great institutional question of the future. Foreseeing the grave class conflicts of his time, Rosmini designs State institutions that differentiate him from socialism – which proposes complete political control of economic interests in favor of equalization – conservatism – which tends towards the protection of older or more powerful interests – and extreme liberalism – which defends a general liberation of interests. He promotes, instead, a combination of institutions capable of satisfying the legitimate demands of such positions, which surpass them by virtue of the originality of his stand.

11.2 Civil Society

11.2.1 The Rosminian Conception of Civil Society

Rosmini is an unyielding critic of any political society established by a State which severs spontaneous pre-existent bonds between persons,[14] and of the attempt of the modern State to create artificial bonds in their place, since such bonds are doomed to be felt as chains and, in the end, dissolve.[15] The Roveretan rejects an abstract and absolutist conception of civil society, creator of all rights and freedoms and repressive of all forms of spontaneous association.[16] As it has been signaled by many specialists of Rosmini's thinking – like for example Giorgio Campanini – the political society which Rosmini is thinking of as a "regulator of the modality of rights" is not the statist civil society which arose especially in France, first in a monarchic form and then as a liberal State promoted by the Chapellier law.[17] From this historical perspective, the Roveretan thinks of feudalism and State absolutism – be it either monarchical or democratic – as imperfect forms of society under a process of evolution towards the most perfect form of society, that he calls, like most of the authors of his time, "civil society," an expression equivalent to "political society." While in the former ones a component of subordination and dominion prevails, in civil society social relationships are governed by the principle of the acknowledgement of the right of the other, which aims at benevolence and friendship towards the other.

Thus, in his conception of civil society, Rosmini appeals to the rich Italian experience which he himself had through his participation in different types of intermediate religious, economic and cultural associations and organizations (the *sorerias*, trade unions, and Academies and *amicitiae*, respectively), and in the association of associations represented by the Communes (*comune*), as the highest expression of political life in Italian *città.* In fact, Rosmini has in mind societies such as those civil associations of mutual assistance of the medieval communes,

---

[14]"Questo genere di corruzione o imperfezione fu specialmente proprio dei nostri tempi, nei quali apparì uno sforzo di cotale spirito averso alla specie umana di rompere tutti i vincoli sociali (. . .) e si vide riposta l'umana felicità o nell' individuo solitario o selvaggio (. . .)." (Rosmini 1923, 222).

[15]"L' uman genere sentivasi nel secolo XVII e seguente troppo legato perchè male legato. Non è meraviglia se si abbia fatto sentire una volontà comune di disvincolarsi (. . .)." (Rosmini 1923, 224, n. 1).

[16]"Quelli improvidi legisti i quali vogliono derivati tutti i diritti dalla società civile, la rendono essenzialmente dispotica . . . Né solo il diritto individuale è anteriore alla società civile . . . ; ma vi ha anche delle società anteriori ad essa, quali sono la società teocratica e la domestica, come pure tutte quelle che scaturiscono dal diritto d' associazione che è uno dei diritti individuali . . . "(Rosmini 1887, 670).

[17]"Questa dottrina fondatrice e giustificatrice della tirannia civile cominciò ad essere fabbricata sistematicamente sotto Luigi XI e andò perfezionandosi in Europa sotto tutta la lunga serie dei despoti che a quello successero fino che ricevette una prima sconfitta dalla rivoluzione francese, la quale cangiò forma al dispotismo, non l' estinse perciò (. . .)" (Rosmini 1887, 670).

which are against the non-civil power of the *seigneur.* Their spirit was fundamentally a corporate, non-individualistic spirit, to the point that in their struggles, they presented themselves as a compact team, frequently violent, against the old nobility (Rosmini 1887, 235–241). So, even though Rosmini's "liberalism" contains a strong component of defense of individual rights, it also contains much of the defense of the "associationism" of the rights of the multiple forms of lesser societies which may spontaneously spring up under the protection of the more ample and universal form of society, that is, civil society. So, Rosmini's civic liberalism is also cooperativism, since it does not defend freedoms resulting from the liberation of "individuals" taken in an *abstract* sense, but freedoms protected by the capacity of association, common bonds and mutual assistance amongst individuals.

In a word, to a great extent, the Roveretan sees civil or political society as the result of a sort of sum of intermediate societies, "small scale" models of the former. So, although civil society finds its ultimate representation and order in the "unique mind" of the State government,[18] it contains within itself a sort of enlargement of the intermediate associations to the most universal possible degree. Through these unions, the associates establish a series of common rights with the aim of defending and potentiating them much better than if they were to exercise them separately. In this sense, Rosmini is not thinking of civil society in the liberal French fashion, that is, as the product of a State that irrupts into the *civitas* or the medieval commune in order to *create* rights and freedoms. Rosmini does think of a liberal society which arises from that *civitas,* composed of an endless number of associative forms and aimed at checking the exaggerated leading role of the State.

11.2.2 Its Economic Importance

Understood in this sense of association of associations, civil society is essential to Rosmini's thought as a framework for economic life. In this sense, he agrees with the Italian civil economist philosophers, who, as from Vico and Doria, consider that economic interests do not self-regulate by the mere *invisible hand of the market*, but that they require regulation by civil society. In effect, according to Rosmini the way to achieve larger production and a fairer distribution of wealth is certainly that of a market where the interchange between individual interests plays a leading role, although always within the rules of ethics and the law. In fact, according to Rosmini, civil associations are necessary for the economy as long as the market

[18]"Lo Stato è certamente prima di tutto un certo numero di famiglie e d'uomini, uniti insieme al fine di dare un ordine pacifico alle loro reciproce relazioni, per così fatta maniera, che tutti i diritti di ciascun individuo e di ciascuna famiglia sieno tutelati e regolati, e così possano coesistere ed essere da chi li possedono, esercitati senza collisioni; il che non potendosi ottenere, se non ci sia nel mezzo di tutti questi uomini una mente sola, o individua o collettiva, che produca quest'ordine, questa tutela e questo regolamento; perciò si dà autorità di ciò fare ad una o a più persone, e così si istituisce quella potestà che si chiama *governo civile*" (Rosmini 1978d, 126).

does not manage to distribute in the fairest manner all wealth, since there always exists an accumulated surplus in certain persons while there are others whose basic needs remain unsatisfied.

Certainly, Rosmini believes that, in some cases, the fair economic order may demand the direct intervention of the State in order to obligatorily redistribute part of this surplus. The remainder of this surplus may also be re-distributed, owing no longer to an obligation but as beneficence, that is to say, not because of a strict jural duty but because of the duty of moral generosity which leads people to freely give part of their profits, without expecting anything in return, by means of works of beneficence or human promotion. In this way, distribution is fully completed – something which the sole dynamics of the market or of the State fails to achieve. As a precondition for this to occur, there must exist not only an ethical order of the market which allows overabundant resources not to be wasted on unnecessary consumption, but people blessed with special civil virtues who, through associations and works of civil beneficence, may channel goods and efforts to the needy along paths which are beyond the market:

> Turn the man most virtuous and, without the need to incite him to turn to the vanity of fashion and senseless luxury, you will make him liberal and beneficent. He will use his profits, but wisely. He will not purchase hats or shawls but will establish prizes for virtuous works; he will not fill his house with trinkets but will make tears of joy well up in the eyes of the poor; he will encourage the Arts, build public works, improve agriculture and, as well as an immortal legacy, he will leave his sons an inheritance with which they can imitate and perpetuate his examples, an even better legacy than the inheritance itself. (Rosmini 1977a, 112)

11.2.3 Civil and Social Dimension of Businesses

However, even the activities of the market require forms of associationism in order to take place. This is the case of what Rosmini calls "commercial" or "industrial societies." Even though the constitution of these societies is significantly motivated by individual interests and by the search for profit by their members and do not have a specifically moral end in themselves,[19] they imply – according to Rosmini – a basic moral link, indispensable for the existence of any association. Besides, as in every society, the moral link joining together the members of a business organization should not be closed but called upon to grow wider.

On the other hand, Rosmini admits the possibility of the existence of industrial or commercial firms that, without losing sight of their own objectives – that is, to obtain

[19]"Let us imagine a society formed for the specific end of commercial speculation. The gain intended by the members through their association is obviously the object or immediate end of the association. In this society, the remote end (contentment of spirit) lies entirely outside the society and is left to prudence and morality of individual members who seek contentment as human beings but not as members of the society. In a word, the remote end in this example can be called entirely extra-social (Rosmini 1994b, 88).

a particular good and profit – seek the greatest reach and participation possible with reference to the individual interests that conform them. Rosmini believes that the company will operate more and more balanced in so far as it becomes more "civil," that is, to the extent that it incorporates or "co-interests" not just a group of partners or directors but all its workers. All this is possible only in proportion to the growth in education and skills upgrading of workers:

> That balance will come when all workers are co- interested in the job and this co-interest is clear to each worker. It is evident that this participation will be proportional to the degree of the workers' culture.[20]

Thus, the quality of firms in an economy depends not only on the initiative and ability of individuals or on the protection of their rights, but also on the increasingly complex and rich forms of association or civil existent in society.

11.2.4 Centralism and Regionalism

Now, for this process of association, benevolent cooperation and, finally, civil friendship to flourish, the government of civil society must be sufficiently careful not to sever and suffocate, through excessive centralization, these initiatives of free associationism:

> Here, it is sufficient for us to see how, because of the love of uniformity and generality, it happens that from the goods of many private beneficence organizations a single mass is formed and the variety of particular organizations is destroyed, while new ones are created, as it seems better to unite them and give them a common administration. (Rosmini 1923, 76)

It is also very important to respect the forms in which civil society is organized according to particular regions and places, because their strength derives from the bonds of local friendship:

> If the father's love is fair, if the son's piety, the tenderness of spouses, the affection of brothers are fair, and if all the antiquity and the voice of Nature do not lie, it is therefore reasonable that the citizen loves better his own city than others, and the place where his life develops or the people from whom he received his education (. . .). (Rosmini 1923, 76)

In this sense, Rosmini also gives great importance to the relative autonomy of regions and cities with regard to the central State (Rosmini 1978d, 218). Thus, to him, a basic principle of "civil economy" is always to consider private societies neither as an "accident" of general society, nor as something to be overcome by an

---

[20]Rosmini believes that businesses function as long as not only the interests of the partners are satisfied but also those of the workers: "E questo equilibrio vi sarà quando ogni uomo lavoratore sarà *cointeressato* nel lavoro e questo cointeressamento risulti *chiaro* all'occhio del lavoratore, chiarezza che debbe essere proporzionata alla maggiore o minore cultura de'lavoratori" (Rosmini 1923, 369).

abstract universalization or uniformization on the part of the State or the market, but as the shape adopted by the universal society to realize itself in a concrete sense:

> Because of this, the more we observe the particular, the closer we come to distributive justice. However, it saddens me to hear not a few people discard anything showing some kind of difficulty which has not been solved yet just because the art of government has not reached perfection. (Rosmini 1923, 68–69)

Besides, even though the Roveretan detects an evil in the spirit of the system, and in the tendency to generalize and pass over the particular, he is also a strong critic of family, corporate or business particularism which fails to understand that the ends of particular societies must be in harmony with the common good of all society. This distances Rosmini from an anti-universalist or anti-State particularistic position, which some interpretations of his thought seem to insinuate:

> We are certainly not keen on centralization, but neither do we maintain that the Government should dissolve into an endless number of tiny republics as happened during medieval times. Central government should be strong and, at the same time, those governed must enjoy the greatest of freedom. To distinguish between what belongs to the strength of the Government, and not to the freedom of those governed, from what belongs to the freedom of those governed, and not to the strength of the Government: not to surrender any of this and not to usurp any of that: this is one of the main and most difficult issues of political wisdom. (Rosmini 1978d, 218)

The government must, then, respect the particular characteristics and ends of regional and local civil associations, but must also know how to regulate them with the common good in mind.

> Thus, the government may supervise those private institutions and see if, according to the manner in which they were founded, they are well and wisely conducted. And when it uses this caution and seriousness (. . .) it may regulate them again regarding their methods, while maintaining the founding spirit and substance, if it is good. And while allowing these institutions to subsist, each with their own particularities, it could establish a general system for their supervision, which will be very useful for the generality. Because the vice of modern generality consists in sacrificing the particulars against the rulings of Nature, which desires that we found the general on the particulars. (Rosmini 1923, 76–77)

In fact, many of these ideas materialized in Rosmini's federalist project presented mainly in his constitutional works. The project provided an early Italian federation embracing together the kingdoms of Rome, Florence and Turin in the form of a "Political League." This League was to be "as the core cooperator of Italian nationality," open at the beginning to other members wishing to join it in the future. The League was conceived as a perpetual confederation of the first three states, under the honorary and perpetual presidency of the Pope. Rosmini's desire was to bring together all the organizations present in the Italy of his time within a single frame and federal state. In this spirit of "unity in diversity," Rosmini looked to the United States of America and, paraphrasing Alexis de Tocqueville, wrote: "Unity in diversity is the definition of beauty. Now beauty is for Italy. The closest possible unity in its natural variety: this seems to be the formula of Italian organization" (Muratore 2011).

11.2.5 Civil Society and Virtue

To Rosmini, though, civil life is good for Man provided it is at the same time moral life, virtuous life and inner culture. Rosmini rejects the idea of civil life or civil society as a diffuse force exercised by "the whole" or the simple "interaction" or "relationality" of its members without these being previously shaped by a personal ethical virtue. The sole horizontal interaction, the sole community, does not produce society. This is based on a previous inner moral acknowledgement of truth as we have seen in Chap. 4. This is perhaps Rosmini's essential difference with the civil philosophies of the eighteenth century, such as those of Rousseau and of Genovesi and his disciples, Gioia and Romagnosi, who, in Rosmini's view, over-praise the positive effects of civility *per se* without paying enough attention to its ethical basis. In an argument with Gioia, Rosmini challenges his amoral idea of civility.[21]

According to Rosmini, the sole system of civil institutions does not guarantee justice or morality in the economy. In fact, it should be considered the "example of Athens – found in all its historians –, which, together with civility and culture, established dissoluteness, and, in times of Pericles, there was no more cultured city nor a more dissolute one" (Rosmini 1977a, 134). Rosmini criticizes the Illuminist idea that corruption is basically a phenomenon of primitive countries where there is insufficient institutional control. Taking over the classical positions of Aristotle and Plutarch with regards to the different types of corruption existing in Athens and Sparta, Rosmini arrives at the conclusion that corruption in more advanced countries, although apparently less visible on account of its being strongly controlled by external institutional mechanisms, is nevertheless deeper, because it is rooted in individual subjectivity, while corruption in primitive countries is more a product of their rusticity and imperfection than of their lack of morality (Rosmini 1977a, 134–139). Besides, there is also the case of primitive peoples who, because of an overly rapid contact with civilization, have become corrupt (Rosmini 1977a, 138).

> The characteristic of the primitive nation is that of ignorance; the character of the corrupt nation is vice. Ignorance is of virtues and vices. Ignorance of virtues is the evil suffered by young nations; ignorance of vice is its good, because vices should be known in order to be practiced. Therefore, wherever there is knowledge, greater vices also exist, and wherever ignorance prevails, such as within peoples who are primitive but not already damaged, there are less virtues but also less vices and, with the latter, less corruption." (Rosmini 1977a, 139)

In this sense, Rosmini clearly places himself within the republican Roman tradition of civic *virtues* followed by Machiavelli, Montesquieu and a part of

[21]"Il dimostrar poi una speranza inesausta, indefinita, confusa nelle forze della civiltà, e nello stesso tempo uno scoraggiamento e una diffidenza estrema nelle forze della virtù, dà pur segno di un uomo superficiale, che trae dietro all' apparenza delle cose e non ne tocca il profondo: perché la civiltà così scompagnata dalla virtù è un liscio disteso sulla putredine dei vermini, un artificiale bagliore che trae ed incanta le luci de' fanciulli, ma che nessun solido bene racchiude e mantiene. La virtù all' incontro è l' interno, il solido della civiltà: essa è la *civiltà* stessa" (Rosmini 2001, 1, 415–416).

American liberalism before the modern liberal idea of social progress by the sole effect of institutional and civic forces. Indeed, to the Roveretan, civil virtue is not mere "mutual utility," "reciprocity," "benevolence" or other "moral sentiments" – although it includes them but it mainly implies, as we have seen before, the acknowledgement of the other as a partner not as a means but as an end in himself.

11.3 The Family

11.3.1 Center of the Economic Balance

In the origin of civil society, Rosmini sees a conflict with what he calls the "domestic society," characterized by particularism and closure over itself. In some sense, this conflict between the domestic area and the civil area is always latent:

> The major obstacle preventing humanity from associating perfectly and peacefully in civil commonalties is "family selfishness". This selfishness is the great evil proper of domestic society. (Rosmini 1996, n. 1963–1964)

In this sense, Rosmini is evidently not a traditionalist thinker: he believes that the conservative element contained in the family must be permanently compensated by the renovating element of those individuals who, at some point, drift apart from it and, in doing so, give dynamism to society and economy. However, this does not mean that Rosmini agrees with an individualistic position. The Roveretan believes that the economic system is a phenomenon that comes after the family, as "domestic society is previous to civil society" (Rosmini 1994b, n. 406). For this reason, the family should not be at the service of economy and civil society, but the opposite. Furthermore, the incorporation of families into society must never mean they should witness their rights being reduced. On the contrary, the sense of that incorporation is the enhancement of their rights and goods:

> [T]he families did not deprive themselves of their own goods when they entered civil society, but only of the trouble of regulating the modality of their rights (. . .) Moreover, families, in ceding such a burden to civil society, have not in any way ceded the right to abuse modality, but only the faculty of regulating it advantageously or, at least, with more advantage than they could have achieved by themselves. (Rosmini 1996, n. 1695)

In fact, since Rosmini sees the family as a "natural society," it becomes an essential institution to maintain social balance as a whole. Following his thesis on social balance, Rosmini always considers that the economic wealth of a society must be in equal balance with the force of its families:

> When proportional balance between family force and wealth is lacking, the social constitution (. . .) can be just but irregular. In other words, it is not constituted according to the natural laws which provide it with security and tranquility. (Rosmini 1996, n. 2597–2599)

Rosmini links, to a certain extent, the origin of poverty and the proletariat to the break-up of the family and the consequent isolation of the individual.[22] In a very realistic way, he presents the situation of the destruction of values, abilities and relational good that may occur within this family matrix when – both in society in general and within the family itself – the ethical-economic balance is broken between the needs and the means to satisfy them, especially within poor families:

> Those who have observed the events of daily life will understand this immediately. A family is composed of a weak part (the women and children) and a strong part (the fathers and adult sons). If the needs to be satisfied are many, the result will inevitably be domestic tyranny or the oppression of the weak part by the strong. Heads of family who have many urgent artificial needs will leave their wives and children languishing in misery, while they find contentment for their demanding appetites by squandering their earnings in taverns and places of riotous, dissolute living. The adult sons quarrel with their fathers, and war breaks out between the two strong parties. Usually the sons win, either because paternal love mitigates the fathers' fury, or because the elder, stronger sons, challenge the older father who works and earns less than they and whose disorderly conduct has never inspired respect. Amongst the adult men there are vices and discord; amongst the women, drudgery, deprivation and affliction. Education is abandoned, and joyless families left without anyone to govern them. (Rosmini 1994b, n. 684)

11.3.2 Need of Specific Policies in Relation to the Family

In this way, according to Rosmini, for economy to be truly just and oriented towards the common good, it is essential to encourage not only the autonomous development of individual capacities taken in isolation, but the relative autonomy of families, as they are the matrix where all the rest of social and economic relationships take shape. Rosmini therefore proposes a political action to provide, first, some kind of universal income that enables a minimum support:

> If the family lacks what is necessary, penury and misery arise (...) Therefore, it is necessary that common families have a greater ease of living, less urgency to subsist and thus they may enjoy a sweeter family repose. (...) For this reason, every free family will want to have fixed and free sustenance (...). (Rosmini 1923, 373)

In order to achieve this, State policies should not exclusively aim at a general balance of economy, but they should closely observe the internal ethical-economic balance of families. The conditions for this balance cannot be reduced to a single formula, but will vary according to each family's situation:

> Within the family, the wealth necessary for it to be a free body in itself and equal in relation to all the other families in the State will also vary. (Rosmini 1923, 373)

[22] "This explains the natural origin of the *poor* and the *proletariat*. The isolated individual is weak and abandoned" (Rosmini 1994b, 189, footnote 158).

Hence, economic policies must include a family policy which studies the conditions of the internal balance of families according to the different social classes:

> Constant facts prove the truth of these teachings, which can be summarized as follows:
>
> 1° In classes or, more accurately, in families where effort and activity are in increasing movement, artificial needs can increase without causing any notable and obvious economic harm.
>
> 2° In classes and families where effort and activity are stationary, needs must also be stationary; any increase would be harmful.
>
> 3° In classes and families where effort and activity diminish, economic deterioration follows inevitably unless needs are simultaneously reduced.
>
> 4° Finally, if effort and products increase in different ratios in different classes and families, that is, progression is faster in some than others, but needs develop equally in all with maximum progression, the class where effort has maximum movement will rise above all others, who will rapidly deteriorate.
>
> These are the guidelines which wise government should use to calculate the remotest effects of its enactments. (Rosmini 1994b, n. 705)

Besides, the State should reward the family "for the indirect benefit which domestic virtue provides to the whole of society" (Rosmini 1923, 485).

11.4 The Role of Universal Society and the Church

11.4.1 Fraternal Universal Society and the Global Economy

Rosmini sustains that neither politics nor civil society are enough to realize all the possibilities attaining to the economic. Politics realizes the moral dimension of economy, by limiting and integrating the right of ownership and to economic freedom into its ethical and jural ends, preventing their deformation by an unquenchable thirst for possession or competition. But beyond this, political power can do no more than persuade, or create an appropriate atmosphere for other uses of economic goods, such as productive investment or simple donation. But, which are the social institutions that make up the framework of this dimension of economic life and carry it beyond the logic of the market, and of political and civil society?

Rosmini defines two classes of superior societies where human beings are inserted beyond the economy and the State to which they may belong. These two societies are the universal society of mankind, which the Roveretan also calls the theocratic society of the natural or first gender and the theocratic society of the supernatural or second gender. The former is the one all human beings form amongst themselves owing to their own nature and to the fact that they share God as common good in the form of common truth, moral good and happiness, to which every person is metaphysically and morally summoned. Then, according to Rosmini, the universal society of mankind is the first rudiment of every society, and no other society can destroy or obstruct this society; instead, its ultimate end is to perfect the society of mankind and carry it to its realization. In fact, while the other societies have a limited number of members, this one embraces all human beings within itself; while those are cemented by a special love of family, city or public affairs, this has as its cement the universal love of mankind.

In this sense, a global economy based on a universal society that goes beyond the interests of the different nations would naturally be, according to Rosmini, an economy of gift that would permit an equal development of all. On the contrary, when a global economy is based on the particular interests of the different countries without this universal basis, it carries within itself the kernel of antagonisms and untrammeled economic competition which ends up in a real war waged by economic means:

> If we assume that this art of wealth is exercised by a mankind organized into a single society, or by a man who, through a spirit of love, makes the interests of his fellows his own, this art of wealth will be the external expression of the most perfect beneficence. But if we assume it is exercised by each individual on his own, economic science becomes an art of disputing the possession of wealth; economic science in this case is nothing but war between civil nations, the refinement and the perfection of this universal war. In this sense, I said that the perfecting of economic science, assuming that it does not come across men well-disposed by Morality, produces only the increase in mutual hostilities. (Rosmini 1901, 5)

Therefore, to the Roveretan, it is necessary that national societies and economies should be regulated in some way by a universal society. In fact, in his political projects for Italy, Rosmini does not only conceive the idea of the Italian union, but he dreams of an European union and even of a universal union, which he believes possible through the federative articulation of different national and regional unions. Rosmini believes that complete freedom of international trade is only possible upon the basis of a union of this type.

11.4.2 The Role of Christianity and the Church in the Constitution of a Universal Society

Besides, Rosmini reinterprets the universalist and cosmopolitan ideal of the Enlightenment in a theological and ecclesiastical key. Indeed, in his opinion, the union of mankind is not possible upon the basis of a merely generic and secular fraternity: it demands the effective and supernatural love towards the concrete fellow brought by Christianity. In this way, even though the global institutions slowly constructed by the acts of civil societies are fundamental means for the achievement of this universal society, Rosmini does not consider them possible or fecund without the supernatural action of religion incarnated in the form of ecclesial communion.

Certainly, in Rosmini's time the political role of the Church is projected with great force in the European horizon because of the historical circumstance of the counter-revolutionary processes and, in the case of Italy, because of the absence of an actor in order to conduce the country towards its political union. However, Rosmini rejects this political role – sustained especially by French traditionalism that attempted to identify the Church with the State – and interprets the social role of the Church only as a moral and spiritual influence. As it is reflected in his great work *Delle cinque piaghe della Santa Chiesa,* according to Rosmini, Christianity and the Church should not act directly as factors of power in the political and social scene, but indirectly through the spiritual, moral and cultural transformation.

11.4.3 Free Labor, Modern Wealth and Gift as Fruits of Christianity

Rosmini presents a series of concrete historical arguments to prove the transforming power of Christianity and the Church over society in general and economy in particular, not as the fruit of direct political action, but rather of their indirect moral and spiritual influence. In *Della naturale Costituzione della società civile,* Rosmini quotes Sismondi to contradict his idea that the working class came up during Medieval times when the lords saw the maximum economic capacity that free labor could provide. Rosmini maintains that utility was not the cause of the liberation of slaves, but the consequence of a previous act of moral conscience about the workers' dignity, encouraged by Christianity. To illustrate this, Rosmini affirms that in Ancient times, before the Christian revelation, free labor already existed since there were cases of hired labor and, thus, it was possible to measure its maximum economic capacity. Nonetheless, this did not result in the liberation of slaves due to the fact that in those times the workers' human dignity was unconceivable: this lack of moral acknowledgement shattered any possibility to explore the maximum productivity of free labor. It was not before the advent of Christianity that the notion of human dignity in labor was spread and the underlying concept of utility recognized:

> I have already demonstrated that slavery in Europe could not cease without the intervention of religion, which revealed to men their own dignity to restore it, without its power to reconcile men endowing them with equality, melting the cold hearts of the lords. However, its most exquisite act was not upon the lords, but upon the slaves themselves. It gave them the power of freedom which resulted in the development of the intelligence and virtue, by means of which, as free men, they could carry out their work and provide society with a more useful service. Hence, the lords' interest itself could persuade them to set the slaves free as far as the influence of religion had dictated that the latter were more useful as free men... [Sismondi] is wrong... to attribute de merit of the abolition of slavery to the lords' interest and not to religion/because he thinks that the abolition of slavery was a merit of the lords' interest and not of religion, since there is still no explanation why the lords realized so late which their interests were and why the gentile lords, who certainly did not lack the avidity to obtain more benefits, did not see the utility of hired labor, which, according to Sismondi's principles, is so clear. He assumes that free labor only began during the barbarian times, but it also took place at the height of the Roman Empire and the Republic, just as described by Cicero (...) Religion made it possible for slaves to work as free men. Working as free men made them more useful for society than working as slaves. Later on, the lords' interest speeded up the liberation of men from the chains of slavery. (Rosmini 1887, n. 1)

Another example Rosmini gives about the process of moral recognition brought by Christianity is the modern conception of wealth and capital accumulation. To the Roveretan, such a productive and, therefore, moral conception of wealth would not have been embraced out of mere intra-historical forces; on the contrary, it has a purely Christian nucleus.[23] In effect, Rosmini states that, in Ancient times, wealth was always conceived as the product of avarice or simple plundering. Besides, according to Rosmini, as people in those times were not acquainted with the Christian promises, they were unable to consider a long-term process and were inclined to quickly ruin their economy due to their tendency to immediate consumption or fearful saving. With the advent of Christianity, societies, moved by the promise of happiness by eternal life together with God, expanded their horizon.[24]

> The primitive and immediate use of wealth lies in the pleasures it provides. Yet a second degree or step in the human industry consists in spending wealth not only on pleasures, but on the increment of strength and power as well. This use of wealth was unknown in Ancient times – when the only use of wealth considered was that of pleasures – and was thought to be suitable only to weaken the State, rather than support it... As I have already mentioned, this is the degree of culture brought by Christianity for those who have a wider view of reality and are willing to be fair. Christianity got rid of the danger entailed in wealth as the use of pleasures, and infused humanity with a greater spirit, by which wealth could provide another use such as, for instance, to calculate wealth instead of gaining strength. This use is proper to Christian nations. (Rosmini 1923, 140–141)

On the other hand, in Rosmini's words, Christianity introduced a novel teaching, unknown in Ancient times, about the use and consumption of goods by means of the 'evangelical poverty' concept as a possible lifestyle when it is a freely chosen calling,[25] without excluding other callings that comprise a wider use of the economic goods, as long as both of them are moved by love:

---

[23]See Rosmini (1977a, 112): "In somma, se ne'nostri tempi prevale l'economia e prevale insieme la ricchezza; se non si rinnovano più quegli obbrobî degli Apicj e dei Luculli, e quelle stolte magnificenze di Seramide e di Cleopatra: è perchè la ragione umana si è riformata pel corso di duemil'anni; perchè il Cristianesimo ha portato la luce nel mondo; e perchè i predicatori del Vangelo, declamando costantemente contro tutte le pazze pompe, la moda ed il lusso, come contro tutte le altre umane follie, hanno eccitata l'industria di pari passo che hanno aumentata l'intelligenza, e per mezzo della virtù hanno condotte le umane ricchezze (...)."

[24]"The same considerations explain all the progress of modern industry and trade. Nations now become fearlessly proud because of their progress; ancient nations greatly suspected such increase, and their more perspicacious politicians railed against it. The sense of courage (I exclude rash pride) of modern nations is as reasonable as the sense of fear proper to ancient nations. Modern nations feel powerful and capable of combating material corruption without perishing. The pagans were very much aware that their existence could not last when assailed by the softness which accompanies luxury. We must not think, however, that luxury causes no harm in modern nations, and that corruption does not have the same consequences as in ancient nations. The difference is that the harm done by luxury to modern nations is compensated by the great healing action of Christianity..." (Rosmini 1994b, 578–579).

[25]"It is a divine man who, out of love for his fellows, tolerates the cruelties of poverty: he is a hero whose virtue is likely to be better understood by God than by men" (Rosmini 1923, 154).

> Christianity (. . .) passed on teachings for all the aspects that have to do with the use of external goods, which range from sublime poverty to the teachings on the magnificence. (. . .) (Rosmini 1933, 16)

Finally, the Roveretan also claims that Christianity has made possible the opening up of the State and the economy to the dimension of common good and the fair distributive justice, which would have never been attained by the sole forces of the market or the State, and not even through the spontaneous action of the civil society. Despite the obligations that political society might impose to fulfill the duties deriving from social and extra-social rights, the State finally becomes impotent to force people to share what they can only give out of love. Hence, the capacity to give or the beneficence of a society or State are only possible, according to Rosmini, through the indirect influence of the ecclesiastical society as a love communion:

> If beneficence is not something of a State nature, but a right of the heart which cannot be usurped or imposed either by external law or by force, it is therefore, by nature, an eminently ecclesial thing. Yes, the solution to this great problem must be sought in Jesus Christ. He has instituted the Church and charged Her to succor all human misery. (Rosmini 1952b, 271)

11.4.4 Christianity as the Driving Force of a Non-exclusive Globalization

Rosmini believes that the history of society has a meaning and he illustrates it by the interpretations of Condorcet (history as progress), Vico (corsi e ricorsi) and Fichte (movement in a spiral) (Rosmini 1994b, 541). In agreement with Vico, according to Rosmini there is no rectilinear, unique history which evolves in a straight line. Nevertheless, Rosmini dissents in other aspects; he thinks that the great Napolitan philosopher does not see clearly the powerful influence exerted by a force which transcends history and penetrates its logic: Christianity.

> We will limit ourselves therefore to the movement of humanity within the sphere of intellective development of the ancient nations and to the corresponding external forms of society.
>
> Vico's system is founded on too narrow an observation. He limits himself to the development of the ancient nations. Such an exclusive study of the Latin classics kept him unaware of the social omnipotence of Christianity. (Rosmini 1994b, 542)

According to Rosmini, although the supernatural history of salvation cannot be indentified – in a Hegelian way – to ordinary history, it exerts a powerful indirect influence over mundane realities, and it modifies Vico's *corsi e ricorsi* by giving it a sense of "an upward movement in spiral." Therefore, the Gospel pervades and modifies the natural evolution of the peoples towards an ever greater unity aiming to gather all men in a perfect universal society through the power of love.[26] Certainly,

[26]This is, in effect, the thesis maintained by Francesco Traniello in his *Società religiosa e società civile,* where the historian from Torino maintains that the Roveretan's social philosophy only

though, in this life, this kind of society can never be completely and immediately attained, it can always be reached in a gradual and incomplete way:

> My opinion is that human society, supported by Christianity, moves, (regarding social and intellectual progress) 'in a spiral whose curves become wider and wider; the movement begins near the centre and continues in ever greater spirals, without our being able to assign any necessary limit to their size.' (Rosmini 1994b, 542)

It is through this progressive expansion of Christianity and ecclesiastical communion that Rosmini sees the true possibility of a universal society of humankind, capable of making explicit the tendencies to mutual acknowledgement and self-donation existing within the human being, on which even the economy finds support.

reaches its full significance within the brotherhood of men in Christ. "...il Rosmini è riuscito a sottrarsi finché ha intravisto nella dimensione ecclesiale della religione il massimo compimento della naturale sociabilità umana..." (Traniello 1997, 55).

Chapter 12
Conclusion: Towards a New Economic Science

12.1 The Problems of Economic Science

12.1.1 Fragmentation

Rosmini frames his debate about economic science by verifying the crisis in which modern science is found. One of the most serious problems he points out is the fragmentation of knowledge. Indeed, he argues, "the harm done to science and morality by the fragmentation of knowledge is incredible" (Rosmini 1991, n. 7, Appendix N1):

> In industry, experience has shown that the division of work is very helpful, because each part can stand on its own. For example, a person who works in a factory producing sewing accessories and is employed in putting the points on needles, does not need to know how to make the eye; this can be done by someone else. We become more skilled and attentive in proportion to the simplicity of the task assigned to us. Contemporary society, occupied in mind and spirit by material things, thinks that sciences follow the same law as industry, and so divides the sciences into tiny parts. (Rosmini 1991, n. 7, Appendix N1)

The Roveretan alludes to different cases of fragmentation of knowledge. For example, in the field of Law:

> People who attend German universities can testify to the harm done to the behavior of the young by the separation of natural law from ethics in teaching, without any regard to the intimate connection between the two. The last century, for example, was spent in discussing human rights but forgot human duties. Such presumption greatly furthered the division of law from ethics, which enabled the human being to receive from everyone and give to nobody. (Rosmini 1991, n 7, Appendix N1)

This fragmentation also took place in Medicine, in Theology and also in special Political Sciences, amongst which Rosmini includes Political Economy (Rosmini 1991, n 7, Appendix N1). Rosmini certainly appreciates the analytical dimension of sciences and considers that their great specialization has had great importance for their development. However, at the same time, this specialization has produced oblivion of ends and blurred the synthetic dimension of sciences.

C. Hoevel, *The Economy of Recognition: Person, Market and Society in Antonio Rosmini*, Ethical Economy 42, DOI 10.1007/978-94-007-6058-5_12,

12.1.2 Excess of Abstraction

Besides, Rosmini claims that this fragmentation is the result of a second serious problem affecting modern sciences -amongst these, economics- which is that of excess of abstraction. Certainly, Rosmini gives great importance to what he calls "the faculty of abstraction," which allows "relationships and qualities to be seen in isolation from things" and enables him "to find distinctions, which are extremely useful to right judgment about things and their right use" (Rosmini 1994b, n. 833). In fact, being economics an art "rendering the use of external things more comfortable, less costly (. . .)," and "devoted to showing how several benefits can be drawn from a single object," it requires precisely a "continual, increasing development of the faculty of abstraction" (Rosmini 1994b, n. 834):

> Considerable use of the faculty of abstraction is a necessity in a certain kind of industry[1] where so many means have to be coordinated, and even subordinated to one another in a chain of distribution where each is conditioned and ordered to moving another. As we have said repeatedly, every means requires some abstraction on the part of the mind; and a long series of concatenated means requires a series of elevated and complicated abstractions (Rosmini 1994b, n. 365).

However, most sciences – amongst which Rosmini places economics – "cannot be classified amongst those sciences which limit themselves to a quality abstracted from a total complex, as pure mathematics does when it reasons about quantity as conceived solely in the mind by virtue of abstraction, although such a quantity does not exist in reality." Still, even those "abstract sciences are commendable in that they prepare us, although remotely, for practical conclusions. But as long as they are treated in isolation, they have no effective use" (Rosmini 1991, n. 4). In fact, these sciences are fixed to an abstract and ideal moment which, according to Rosmini, should merely be an intermediate stage on the way to the real praxis the human being ultimately tends to, explains the lack of interest in them on the part of the majority of the people:

> In my opinion, this explains why abstract sciences are studied by so few: they do not directly arouse the interest and universal study of human beings. In the last analysis, human beings seek what is of real, practical use, and only when they have obtained it, do they feel they have complete effective knowledge (. . .) Nature is not aroused to action by abstract ideas; it must be dealt with effectively and its forces acted upon (Rosmini 1991, n. 4).

12.1.3 Rationalist Reductionism

The defect of excessive abstraction results, especially in the field of social and human sciences, in a rationalist reductionism by which human behavior is deduced

---

[1] Rosmini uses the word "industry," but he does so in the broad sense of the word which allows us, in our criterion, to understand it as "economy."

a priori from a series of principles, without any relationship with the concrete reality of the human being:

> Many writers fall into this curious error. They claim that the most important things concerning human beings, namely, how to be virtuous and happy, must be deduced a priori by reason. To do this, they use an unreal rationalism which never descends to the level of human needs. (Rosmini 1991, n. 4)

The strangest thing about this rationalism that presents itself as "scientific objectivity" is that it not only separates science from reality but also deforms it. In fact, as long as scientists are allowed to select the part of reality which best suits their method of study, they end up subordinating it to their merest whim:

> (...) after dividing knowledge into so many parts, [they] choose the parts which suit their taste, condemning the remainder as useless because unsuited to their palate, and opposing its use. (Rosmini 1991, n. 7)

As a result of these arbitrary dissections, certain principles remain absolutized and finally invade other sciences, attempting their total assimilation.

12.1.4 An "Intrinsic Evil" Aggravated by Utilitarianism

Certainly, from the methodological point of view, economics performs an abstraction of reality and establishes as its specific subject the study of wealth or utility. In this sense, Rosmini accepts the need to distinguish economics from the rest of sciences:

> Because every science has to deal with a single object, scientific method requires economy to deal solely with wealth. (Rosmini 1994b, n. 191, app. 4)
>
> [Hence we give] a definition of political economy as the science which has wealth as its subject matter and teaches how to acquire it through the optimal method of producing, distributing and consuming it. (Rosmini 1901, 3)

Nevertheless, according to Rosmini, political economy shares the defect proper to every special political science, which is that of the abstract consideration of means:

> The so-called special political sciences deal with these means, but only by considering them separately, without showing how the means must be used to bring about the intended complex effect. Economists, for example, will tell us how to augment private and public wealth, which, however, is only one element of true social prosperity (...) (Rosmini 1994a, n. 7)[2]

---

[2]"Another reason why moral, eudaimonological philosophical teachings (for example those concerned with the common end of societies) are excluded from political treatises is the self-imposed duty of many authors to follow abstract methods. As a result, what ought to be strictly unified is divided into different treatises (...)" (Rosmini 1994b, 88).

In fact, it is precisely at this point where the "intrinsic evil" of economic science arises. According to Rosmini, this "intrinsic evil" consists in having been conceived by its founders fundamentally as an analytical science, dedicated to the study of means for the increase of wealth and obtaining profits but isolated from the ends and more general aims of the human person, especially its moral or ethical ends:

> But what is this intrinsic evil of economic science? ... it is profit itself where the intrinsic and essential evil of that science lies, an evil, which as I have already said, cannot be avoided except through Morality. Economic science, by teaching to acquire wealth, increases, by its very nature, generally speaking, Man's ambition (...) (Rosmini 1901, 5)

As we have tried to demonstrate in this book, the Roveretan states that this problem is rooted not in economics as a science – which to a certain point is obliged to specialize in its own subject that is wealth or utility – but in a utilitarian philosophy a-critically assumed by some economists:

> The defect therefore lies not in the science but in the scientists who, obsessed by wealth as the sole object, reduce the entire State to wealth alone and make all society tend exclusively to it. (Rosmini 1994b, n. 191, app. 4)

12.2 Economics, Eudaimonology and Ethics

12.2.1 Critique of the Conception of Economics as the Science of Happiness

As it has been shown throughout this book, Rosmini identifies the problems of "isolating" economics with the "Anglosaxon" version of utilitarianism (the Scottish and English classical economists, as well as Say, in France), mainly dominated by the fear of scarcity, and obsessed with the creation and accumulation of wealth (actually, he used to call them "economisti avari"! [avaricious economists]). Yet, as we have also pointed out, there also exists a second risk, proper to the representatives of the "Continental" version (the French and Italian utilitarians, as well as Bentham, in England), who advocate for a conception of economics as integrated to ethics and the "eudaimonological" sciences or the science of happiness.

In effect, Rosmini mostly agrees with this integration attempt. Moreover, he mentions that Romagnosi – who supported that "the method followed by the Italians is different from the English´s, since the former analyze science in regard of all its relationships and do not reduce it to wealth (...)" – (Romagnosi 1845, 78–79) "takes a more complex view than his predecessors" (Rosmini 1994a, 140, n. 1). However, according to Rosmini, both Romagnosi and Gioia, as well as the "subjectivist" economists in general, trying not to isolate economics from the rest of sciences, end up making the opposite mistake, that of "invading" the former with the latter. This phenomenon takes places, Rosmini states, because they tend to confuse the concepts informed by their sensist and utilitarian philosophy. As far as they are concerned, economics and ethics as well would be nothing but two parts of the same great "science of happiness," without them showing substantial differences.

12.2.2 Economics Does Not Explain All Human Needs

As we have seen in Chap. 3, Rosmini gives as an example of this position Gioia's definition of economic wealth, that afterwards will be re-elaborated in another language, but with the same meaning, by many representatives of the neoclassical school of economics such as Stanley Jevons, Lionel Robbins and, in recent years, by the Chicago economist Gary Becker. In fact, according to Gioia (quoted here by Rosmini) "the word 'wealth' is applied to anything capable of satisfying a need, or providing comfort or pleasure" (Rosmini 1978a, 15). According to Rosmini, this definition is a typical example of an invasive conception of the integration of economics with other sciences. In his view, the problem of this definition is that it lacks precision with regard to what type of needs or pleasures economic wealth can satisfy. In fact, formulated in this manner, the definition implies, in Rosmini's view, that economic wealth can satisfy all kinds of material and spiritual needs and therefore can convert economics into a sort of general science of satisfaction or human happiness. Here certainly there is, according to him, an "integration" of economics with eudaimonology, but through the absorption of the latter into the former:

> When, in Economics, one wishes to speak of everything that is suitable for satisfying a need or providing pleasure, it would be convenient to clearly define what "everything" is about: otherwise, Economics would turn into a confusing mix of a variety of ideas and would destroy, by absorbing them, all the other branches of knowledge. (Rosmini 1978a, 16, footnote)

However, this pretension to explaining "economically" all human needs would not be the fruit, according to Rosmini, of a truly scientific economic analysis, but of a utilitarianism hidden behind scientific knowledge which reduces Man to his purely material and subjective needs:

> Gioia, who is not free from this defect when approaching the economic science, owes this defect to his low and material philosophy. This reduces Man to his body and, therefore, human knowledge to economic speculations. (Rosmini 1978a, 16, footnote)

Clearly opposed to this position, Rosmini affirms that "there are also intellectual and moral needs." Therefore, "what satisfies this kind of needs cannot be called *wealth* as it is the object of Economics. In fact, there are cultured, poor and virtuous people deprived of all material support. Likewise, a nation could surpass the others in culture and ethics without surpassing them in *wealth* in the proper sense of the word" (Rosmini 1978a, 16, footnote). So, according to Rosmini, intellectual and moral goods, and the needs satisfied by them, although greatly important, as we shall see, because of the indirect influence they exert on the economy, are goods much more elevated than economic ones. Therefore, they can by no means be a specific object of economic science, but of other sciences with their own autonomy:

> So, knowledge, truth and virtue are certainly much more than material wealth and they form part of the object of study of Economics as long as they influence material wealth or because they aid in their production, or because they may effectively be exchanged for material wealth. However, owing to their own nature, these goods belong to other sciences. (Rosmini 1978a, 16, footnote)

Hence, according to Rosmini, it is not possible to speak of the satisfaction studied by economics as an equivalent to happiness without further precisions:

> In the quoted passage, Gioia completely departs from the economic issue in which it is not analyzed how Man becomes happier but how he can increase his wealth: the idea of happiness must not be confused with the idea of wealth: the richest man may very well be the unhappiest. (Rosmini 1978a, 27)

Certainly, according to Rosmini, every economic good is, in a way, a "mixed" good: on the one hand, it provides satisfaction of a physical need and on the other hand, it enters into a close relationship with other kinds of pleasures, not only physical but also psychological and affective (Rosmini 1923, 35–38). Nevertheless, according to Rosmini, it is vital to clearly state that economics aims at the study of the satisfaction of a special kind of needs which he describes as "subjective," especially those of survival and material well-being, as relatively necessary means to achieve happiness. Thus, according to Rosmini, economics is not in charge of explaining all the complexities of the phenomenon of happiness and it cannot therefore be understood merely as the science of happiness. Instead, economics should be deemed a "eudaimonological" science which is certainly open and integrated to the other eudaimonological sciences (ethics, political sciences, etc.), yet preserving its "subordinated" and "special" character.

12.2.3 How Economics Helps Ethics

In a long letter Rosmini sends to his great friend Alessandro Manzoni, the Roveretan deals with the question of the relationship between ethics and economics, attempting to answer the question about whether "progress in economic science gives Man a better disposition towards moral improvement" (Rosmini 1901, 3). To this question, Rosmini will answer that with reference to "evil actions which men perform in order to achieve profit – such as slave trade, and so on – it can be proved that many of these are based on a false premise, since men could have gained more profit and satisfied their interests in a better way without performing them." In fact, when it comes to what Rosmini calls "accidental" moral evils – that is, occurring not as a result of a moral cause strictly speaking but because of a wrong economic reasoning, economic science can help to diminish or even suppress this evil:

> With the progress of economic science, all these immoral actions should gradually cease. These evils which I have called accidental and which occur due to a lack of knowledge should end as this knowledge grows. (Rosmini 1901, 3)

There are even some moral goods which may be obtained by the mere action of economic science, without any need to appeal to moral science. For example, according to Rosmini, the augmentation of wealth is always a good in itself in cases of extreme misery, as it provides appropriate means to diminish the moral degradation that is always associated with such cases:

> Finally, I give to economic science the merit of contributing a good when, speeding up the increase of production, it universally expands well-being. By suppressing misery, it also eliminates many of the vices associated with it. (Rosmini 1901, 6)

Furthermore, Rosmini also believes that, even though the typical defect of economic science may be that of encouraging an unlimited accumulation of wealth which may result in great immorality, this negative effect is usually possible in practice only for a minority. Indeed, to the great majority, the availability of greater wealth usually grants more possibilities for an ethical life and not the contrary:

> So as not to omit anything that may be said in favor of Economics, I finally add that, since many men seek wealth to live, others do so in order to enjoy life and only a small number seek wealth for itself, Economics – by showing men a larger number of ways by which they may live independently from others – increases the number of honest means of subsistence. Now, when men have honest means, they often do not seek dishonest means. (Rosmini 1901, 6–7)

12.2.4 Ethics and Economics: Two Fundamental Differences

However, according to Rosmini, the capacity of economic science to favor the moral good of humanity stops here. Our philosopher only partly shares the "doux commerce" theories of the eighteenth century, which exalted the moralizing power of economic knowledge. In fact, to the Roveretan, there are two fundamental differences between economics and ethics. In the first place, economic science lacks the key element of all moral knowledge since "it does not attribute *guilt* regarding actions: if the human being does not abide by moral rules, he does nothing but harm himself, and no one exonerates oneself. The obligation to be held accountable for one self's actions does not include any of the elements that common sense attributes to accounting for one's own actions before a superior and truly legislative authority. Morals, on the contrary, impose laws which contain in themselves an *obligation* in a true and vigorous sense" (Rosmini 1976, 134, footnote 4).

Furthermore, "secondly, (. . .) economic science neither forbids nor prescribes actions unless they increase in great quantity; so that there can be innumerable *individual* actions that may not mean any monetary damage (. . .) which, however, are strictly forbidden by a healthy morality. In fact, it is rather a case of a series of immoral acts what harms economy (. . .) A particular immoral act, repeated just a few times in judiciously selected times and places, could contribute to wealth rather than harm it (. . .) and still be immoral" (Rosmini 1976, 134, footnote 4).

In addition, according to Rosmini, "one may wonder whether, with the progress of economics, it could not be able to demonstrate that all evil actions are contrary to *wealth*" (Rosmini 1901, 4–5). However, he thinks that there are certainly "evil actions carried out with the purpose of obtaining profits which cannot be proved contrary to the increase of wealth: these actions cannot be suppressed by the progress of economic science, but by the progress of *moral science* alone. Furthermore: it might be said that, with economic science, such evils should increase rather than diminish" (Rosmini 1901, 3).

Thus, economic science cannot be understood simply as a "moral science" or as a special part of morality. On the contrary, it requires moral principles extrinsic to economic science itself. These last come from moral science, superior to any economic calculation. In this sense, Rosmini argues that certain economic principles, such as the optimization of the distribution of economic goods do not spring from the sole logic of economic science, but are based on the level of moral conscience that economics finds in a given society:

> (...) let's suppose (...) that apart from teaching men how to be rich, one wished them to become aware of the moral principle that maintains that it is better if everyone has what is necessary than if they seek wealth at the expense of other's misery. By following this principle, each man will temper his own desires and set aside his immoderate ambition of self-enrichment, even when he may have needs. Now, I maintain that this is not an economic principle but a moral one, which has not been introduced into the world by Economics but has been found by Economics, and thanks to the moral principle, it has found well-disposed men. (Rosmini 1901, 4)

12.2.5 The Tree and the Branches

Thus, according to Rosmini, economic science requires principles coming from individual and social ethics, right, politics and religion. Indeed, only in the hypothetical case – certainly not desirable – that economic activities were regulated by a unique government which applied the same jural, political and economic principles to all peoples, economic science could have a perspective sufficiently universal and social to compare it with morality. Yet the truth is that such a multidimensional globalization does not exist:

> [...] supposing that the whole of humanity were under a single government, whose objective was to protect universal good. Economic science could be exercised by that government with maximum perfection and would be identified with Morality due to its own nature. But this is not so, because economic science is exercised by each individual, by each nation or even by any part of the body of humankind. (Rosmini 1901, 4–5)

Even leaving aside the ideal of a universal ethical-jural regulation, and the fact that virtuous men could lead the government of humanity, it would still be impossible for economics to be completely autonomous: it will have to be articulated with principles and values which are beyond its specific epistemological sphere:

> On the other hand, if the man who exercises it identifies himself with the body of humankind without this body being organized and without him being the one who governs it, this

> identification will not occur by virtue of a principle belonging to economic science, but rather a principle which belongs to moral science and that is completely independent of economic science: this is the principle of universal benevolence, that is, the principle capable of diminishing the evil proper to economic science. (Rosmini 1901, 4–5)

Thus, Rosmini believes that the only way to establish a good relationship between economic science and ethics is to maintain the distinction between the former and the latter, and the subordination of economic science to ethics, instead of attempting a false integration such as the one proposed by those who try to "insert ethics like a branch into the trunk of political economics." Indeed, according to the Roveretan, "what differentiates the way of thinking of those who truly reckons morals from those who acknowledge it in theory but deny it in practice, is that the former conceive morals as the *trunk*, and economics and the arts of pleasure as the *branches* that must be inserted into that trunk, while the latter conceive *economics* or any art of pleasure as the *trunk* and wish to convert *morals* into a branch of that *trunk*" (Rosmini 1870, 183, footnote 23). But the consequences of this inversion in the hierarchy of the sciences are, according to Rosmini, just as destructive for moral science as for economic science itself. Instead, the subordination of economics to morals results for the benefit of both:

> When morality is converted into a branch of economics, the former is destroyed. On the other hand, when economics is inserted into morality and becomes one of its branches, it is not destroyed but both morality and economics are preserved at the same time. Moreover, economics thus acquires a new dignity; it is, we might say, sanctified. (Rosmini 1870, 183, footnote 23)

Rosmini keenly sees in this question the starting-point of the proverbial and endless controversies between moralists and economists:

> When you seek to insert morality within economics, turning it into nothing but one of its branches, you will provoke the wrath of the moralist, you provoke him to make war against economics for being a usurping science. If, on the contrary, you insert economics within morality, the moralist becomes a preacher of economics as a good and beneficial science. (Rosmini 1870, 183)

Thus, the best way of favoring the progress of economic science, or any other science, is, according to Rosmini, to promote its development within its limits, rejecting any program of excessive expansionism:

> One may ask the same question when it comes to all the other sciences, all the useful arts, all the pleasures in life: do you wish to save them? Compel them to fit within their limits, to order themselves, and not to fight against morality. (Rosmini 1870, 183, footnote 23)

12.2.6 An Indirect Influence

In this sense, Rosmini defends the idea of a not invasive integration of economic science, by which the latter takes into account the subjects of other sciences not in order to absorb them but for their indirect influence over its own subject. Hence, economic science is not directly concerned with the study of the satisfaction of psychological or spiritual needs, or of moral and jural duties, upon which, in principle, it does not pronounce itself. This would be the specific task of moral science and of eudaimonological political sciences. However, economic science takes on account the *indirect influence* of these questions on the formation of wealth or economic value that is the direct and proper subject of economics:

> If the miser is unhappy, this does not mean that he does not possess great wealth: his avarice or his exclusive love placed on a material good such as wealth will be immoral; for this reason, the moralist or also the eudaimonologist (allow me to call a master in the art of being happy by its Greek name) will correct him. But in the eyes of the economist, the miser will be guilty only in so far as he contemplates wealth lying in the vault instead of multiplying and producing further wealth by the spreading of commerce, the enlargement of factories and the improvement of land. Only after this, the economist will find reasons to condemn him, not because of his being unhappy or immoral, upon which the economist will not pronounce himself, but because his unhappiness and immorality always have more or less remote consequences which end up harming wealth itself. (Rosmini 1978a, 27)

As we have seen in Chaps. 4 and 5, every economic good, being the good of a human person, is in some way a "mixed" good, that is, a good that has an external material component related to the spontaneous-instinctive dimension of the human being and an internal component related to the degree of interior content or satisfaction obtained as a fruit of moral recognition. The utilitarian mistake has been the reduction of economic utility to its material dimension, whether by explaining it as a mere organic satisfaction, or as a purely extra-subjective psychological or rational satisfaction. According to Rosmini, economic science, like medicine, is a mixed science: although it is primarily focused on obtaining material benefits, it must certainly deal with the subjective and moral dimension as long as the latter has an indirect influence upon the former:

> Honesty, virtuous moderation, truth are always useful to Man's happiness: to prove this in its particularities is also a convenient argument for the wise economist who does not forget that he is a moral being, and recognizes that the sanction of the law, by means of which the author of Nature demands being ordered and virtuous, also manifests itself in material things, as well as in wealth. (Rosmini 1978a, 22, footnote 11)

12.3 Experience, Praxis and Wisdom

12.3.1 Importance of the Empirical and Practical Dimension

This integration of economics to Ethics, Right and Politics as taught by Rosmini could lead to thinking that he aims at carrying out a merely deductive work, that is to say, to subordinate economic science to a set of principles deduced *a priori* from philosophy. It is necessary to avoid the tendency to abstraction proper to particular sciences, as much as it is necessary to avoid the one philosophy could impose on economics. The abstract subordination of economics in the "epistemological tree" of sciences is necessary, but does not guarantee the opening up of the former to other sciences. In that sense, Rosmini believes that such integration can be reached especially in the field of experience and praxis. Therefore, it is necessary to proceed by applying a partly deductive and partly inductive method that combines what he calls "method of reason" and "method of history."[3]

> [. . .] in order to insert these sciences into the order of realities, all the omitted qualities of the case must be included. Thus, surveyor (. . .) must first identify and assemble all the data about the real bodies on which he intends to work. These facts are neglected in general, abstract theory (. . .) This cannot be done unless positive knowledge with its applications and modifications is added to the general theories. Thus, sciences (. . .) that have a complex object, and aim at complete finite knowledge, cannot and must not limit themselves solely to details obtained by pure speculation. They must make use of every opportunity to enrich themselves through reason or history. (Rosmini 1991, n. 4)

In that sense, Rosmini develops an interesting analysis of the importance of statistical sciences as auxiliaries of economic science:

> A public administrator, for example, urgently required to make a piece of land productive or to establish some industry or trade, cannot be satisfied with a general theory of economy. He has to apply the economic rules, and obtain the most detailed information about the local climate, soil, population, customs, prejudices, and level of skills available, that is, he needs practical information. (Rosmini 1991, n. 4)

Rosmini will make a criticism of the quantitativist tendency that set in since the eighteenth century, which takes into account only the measurable material aspects and leaves aside the spiritual dimension of social and economic problems:

> Everything connected with quantity was the object of incredibly intense study; mathematics, the mechanical arts and everything concerned with the professions, commerce and industry certainly made swift and marvelous progress. But this is only an accident relative to peoples' happiness. Matter is subject to division; the spirit on the contrary reduces all things to unity, in which alone resides the force which constitutes true, social power. (Rosmini 1994a, n. 134)

Thus, the Roveretan maintains that it is necessary to elaborate a richer and more complex "new theory" of statistics, which will provide a wider framework to such a useful auxiliary science of economics (Rosmini 1978b, 72). Foreseeing much of what is taking place nowadays in relation to the so-called statistics of happiness, Rosmini proposes, then, a new type of statistics for economics that he will call "politico-moral statistics," which "form part of comprehensive, philosophical statistics, and present a vast and almost untouched field for learned investigation and research" (Rosmini 1994b, n. 854). Arguing with Charles Dupin, who maintained that statistics should reflect "the number and the measure of

[3]Rosmini considers that "to follow a particular or general method depends on the nature of the objects." (Rosmini 1923, 105).

productive and commercial forces," Rosmini considers that statistics should evolve from a purely material primary age to an "intellectual" or "moral" age:

> At the first step, the governing principle of statistics is the calculation of the prevalent force, that is, of the force consisting in physical forces (population, armed forces, and so on); at the second, the governing principle is found at a higher level where it calculates intellectual forces, especially the forces of production and commerce, in addition to physical forces. Finally, the statistics of the third and last step are raised to the dignity of moral statistics. Their governing principle is far more sublime and broad than those of the two preceding steps. Calculation is now made of all other forces in relationship to the force of the principles which move human beings and things. In these statistics everything is complete and unified. And these are the statistics which must be compiled in our days. (Rosmini 1994a, n. 140, footnote 44)

12.3.2 A Wisdom for Economic Science

This book has been intended to show how Rosmini, through his debate with the utilitarians of his times, refused the attempt to reduce the entire human and social reality to the cannons of economics understood as a science of wealth or happiness, just like many critics of economic utilitarianism have done during our times. Thus he believes that it is necessary to have an integral vision of economic issues which, in the first place, certainly imply considering "the production, distribution and consumption of external goods" (material factor). However, there are another two key factors, such as "the activity of the human spirit" – that is, the moral and psychological factors – which have a powerful influence on the material factor and are in turn influenced by it; and the institutional and social factor which, as we have seen, "influences directly both the human spirit and the production, distribution and consumption of external goods" (Rosmini 1994b, n. 191, app.4). In this way, Rosmini criticizes all those who reduce the economic dimension either to "abundance of external goods" (material factor), "the increase of common pleasures", to the "contentment of spirit" (moral and psychological factor), or to the "social order" (social or institutional factor), without realizing that the three factors must be jointly considered.

The need for this integration of economics with the rest of human dimensions has its basis, according to Rosmini, on the metaphysical certainty: "[that] disorder in any part of the order of human things has a faster or slower repercussion on all the other parts of the same order," because "everything within the universe is connected, and there is no action against the law of honesty which does not unleash a terrible sanction, even if remote, on nature itself" (Rosmini 1978a, 27). Nevertheless, this theoretical certainty also needs to become a practical wisdom based on the concrete recognition of the human person that orients and guides the economy making it capable to convert wealth and prosperity into an authentic human good:

> We need a more elevated science than political economy; we need some kind of wisdom to guide economy itself and determine how and within what limits material wealth can be directed towards the true human good (. . .) (Rosmini 1994a, n. 7)

Bibliography

Akerlof, George, and Rachel E. Kranton. 2001. Economics and identity. *Quarterly Journal of Economics* CXV(3): 715–753.

Akerlof, George, and Janet Yellen. 1986. *Efficiency wage models of the labor market*. New York: Cambridge University Press.

Alessio, F. 1886. L. O. Boni e l'economia politica. La Sapienza, Rivista di Filosofia e di Lettere, Seconda Serie, Anno VIII, vol. XIII. 361–371.

Antiseri, Dario. 1995. *Cattolici a difesa del mercado*. Torino: Società Editrice Internazionale.

Antiseri, D., and M. Baldini (eds.). 1997. *Personalismo liberale*. Catanzaro: Rubbettino.

Barucci, Piero. 1965. *Il pensiero economico di Melchiorre Gioia*. Milano: Giuffrè Editore.

Barucci, Piero.1977. La 'cultura economica' di Alessandro Manzoni. *Rassegna economica*, Marzo-Aprile, 279–312.

Battaglia, Felice. 1987. *Economia, diritto, morale*. Bologna: Ed. Clueb.

Beccaria, Cesare. 1765. *Dei delitti e delle pene*. Lausanna: Venturi.

Beccaria, Cesare. 1804. Scrittori *classici italiani di economia politica: parte moderna*. Milano: Destefanis. Vols. 11–12.

Becker, Gary. 1978. *The economic approach to human behavior*. Chicago: The University of Chicago Press.

Becker, Gary. 1991. *A treatise on the family*. Cambridge: Harvard University Press.

Becker, Gary, and George Stigler. 1977. De Gustibus non est disputandum. *The American Economic Review* 67: 2.

Bergamaschi, Cirillo. 2001. *Grande dizionario antologico del pensiero di Antonio Rosmini*. Roma: Città nuova.

Blackstone, William. 1823. *Commentaires sur les lois angloises avec des notes de M. Ed. Christian*. Traduits de l'anglais. Paris: Bossange Père.

Bonola, Giulio. 1901. *Carteggio fra Alessandro Manzoni e Antonio Rosmini*. Milano: Cogliati.

Botto, Evandro. 1992. *Etica sociale e filosofia della politica in Rosmini*. Milano: Vita e pensiero.

Broggia, C.A. 1804. *Scrittori classici italiani di economia politica: parte moderna*, vols. IV–V. Milano: Destefanis, Gio. Giuseppe (tip).

Brunello, Bruno. 1974. Marco Minghetti economista e moralista. *Rivista Rosminiana di filosofia e di cultura*. Centro Internazionale di studi Rosminiani, Anno LXIII (Nuova Serie Anno VIII, Fasc. II, Aprile–Giugno): 137–154.

Bruni, Luigino. 2000. Ego facing alter: How economists have depicted human relations, *Annals of Public and Cooperative Economics* 71(2): 285–313.

Bruni, Luigino. 2002. Sul consumo, sui beni, sulla felicità. In *Economia come impegno civile*. A cura di L. Bruni and V. Pelligra. Roma: Città Nuova.

C. Hoevel, *The Economy of Recognition: Person, Market and Society in Antonio Rosmini*, Ethical Economy 42, DOI 10.1007/978-94-007-6058-5,

Bruni, Luigino, and Stefano Zamagni. 2007. *Civil economy: Efficiency, equity, public happiness*. Bern: Peter Lang.

Bulferetti, Luigi. 1942. *Antonio Rosmini nella Restaurazione*. Firenze: Le Monnier.

Bulferetti, Liugi. 1944. *Il Rosmini e il Sismondi nel pensiero politico della restaurazione*. Gubbio: Soc. Tipografica Oderisi.

Bulferetti, Luigi. 1949. *Socialismo risorgimentale*. Torino: Giulio Einaudi Editori.

Bulgakov, Sergei. 2000. *Philosophy of economy. The world as a household*. Trans. Catherine Evtuhov. New Haven: Yale University Press.

Burke, Edmund. 1987. *Reflections on the revolution in France*. Indianapolis: Hackett.

Campanini, Giorgio. 1983. *Antonio Rosmini e il problema dello Stato*. Brescia: Morcelliana.

Campanini, Giorgio. 1990. *Rosmini politico*. Milano: Giuffrè.

Campanini, G., and F. Traniello (eds.). 1993. *Filosofia e politica. Rosmini e la cultura della restaurazione. Atti del Convegno promosso dal Comune di Rovereto, dalla Provincia Autonoma di Trento e dall' Istituto di Scienze Religiose di Trento – Rovereto, 20–22 nov. 1991*. Brescia: Morcelliana.

Campanini, Giorgio. 2004. Tra globalizzazione e cosmopolitismo. Rosmini e la "Società universale del genere umano". *Rivista Rosminiana. F. II-III:* 129–138.

Cantilo, Giuseppe. 1991. Pietro Piovani interprete di Rosmini. In *Filosofia e Politica*. Rosmini e la cultura della Restaurazione, ed. Giorgio Campanini e Francesco Traniello, 379–415. Rovereto: Morcelliana.

Carli, Conte Gianrinaldo. 1784/1786. *Delle opere del Signor Commendatore*, vol. 12. Milano: Monastero de S. Ambrogio Maggiore.

Carli, Gianrinaldo. 1804. *Scrittori classici italiani di economia politica: Parte moderna,* vols. XIII–XIV. Milano: Destefanis, Gio. Giuseppe (tip).

Cassirer, Ernst. 1979. *The philosophy of the enlightenment*. Trans. Fritz C. A. Kollen and James P. Pattegrove. Princeton: Princeton University Press.

Chandler, S.B. 1974. *Alessandro Manzoni, the story of a spiritual quest*. Edinburgh: Edinburgh University Press.

Cioffi, Mario. 2005. *Persona e diritto in Rosmini*. Stresa: BSR 28.

Copertino, Luigi. 1997. *I paradossi del cattolicesimo liberale*. Roma: Pagina libere.

Crespo, Ricardo. 1997. *La Economía como Ciencia Moral*. Buenos Aires: Educa.

Croce, Benedetto. 1942. *Filosofía práctica en sus aspectos económico y ético*. Buenos Aires: Anaconda.

Cuccu, Mauricio. 1988. Le dottrine economiche nella cultura italiana. In *La cultura filosofica e scientifica*, ed. Paolo Aldo Rossi. Busto Arsizio: Bramante Editrice.

D'Addio, Mario. 1972. *Appunti di storia delle dottrine politiche*. Genova: Edizioni Culturali Internazionali.

D'Addio, Mario. 1991. *Concetto di filosofia politica in Antonio Rosmini. Filosofia e Politica, Rosmini e la cultura della Restaurazione*. Atti del convegno promosso dal Comune di Rovereto, dalla Provincia Autonoma di Trento e dall'Istituto di Scienze Religiose in Trento Rovereto.

D'Addio, Mario. 2000. *Libertà e appagamento. Politica e dinamica sociale in Rosmini*. Roma: Edizioni Studium.

Daros, William. 1992. Ética y derecho según Rosmini. *Rivista Rosminiana*. F. I.: 15–27.

Davis, John. 2003. *The theory of the individual in economics: Identity and value*. London: Routledge.

De Benedittis, Ornella. 2009. *Diritto e stato in Rosmini. Per una politica della persona*. Pavia: Bonomi Editore.

De Bortoli, Maurizio. 2010. *Una biografia: Antonio Rosmini*. Milano: Ragione & libertà.

De Giorgi, Fulvio. 2003. *Rosmini e il suo tempo. L' educazione dell´uomo moderno tra reforma della filosofia e rinnovamento della Chiesa (1797–1833)*. Brescia: Morcelliana.

De Lucia, Paolo. 1995. Uomo ed economia in Rosmini. *Rivista di Filosofia neo-scolastica* Anno LXXXVII(aprile–giugno): 220–248.

De Mably, L'Abbé. 1776. *Le droit public de l'Europe fondé sur les traités*, Geneve: Compagnie des libraires.

De Mably, L'Abbé. 1789. *Des droits et des devoirs du citoyen*, Paris: Kell.

De Maistre, Josef. 1980. *Ensayo sobre el principio generador de las Constituciones políticas y de las demás instituciones humanas*. Buenos Aires: Dictio.

De Melon, Jean-Francois. 1754. *Essai politique sur le commerce*. Amsterdam: F. Changuion.

De Simone, Joseph Francis. 1946. *Alessandro Manzoni, aesthetics and literary criticism*. New York: S. F. Vanni.

Derla, Luigi. 1969. *Manzoni e l'economia politica*, 506–531. Roma: Nuova Antologia.

Dickinson, H.T. 1981. *Libertad y Propiedad. Ideología política británica del siglo XVIII*. Buenos Aires: Eudeba.

Donà, Massimo. 2001. *L' uno, i molti: Rosmini-Hegel un dialogo filosofico*. Roma: Città Nuova.

Donati, Benvenuto. 1949. *Rosmini e Gioia*. Firenze: Sansoni editore.

Donohue-White, Patricia, et al. 2002. *Human nature and the discipline of economics. Personalist anthropology and economic methodology*. Lanham: Lexington Books.

Dossi, Michele. 2007. *Il santo proibito. La vita e il pensiero di Antonio Rosmini*. Trento: Il Margine.

Droz, Giuseppe. 1826. *La morale applicata alla politica*. Firenze: Vieusseux.

Droz, Giuseppe. 1854. *Economia politica o Principii della scienza delle ricchezze*. Torino: Biblioteca dell'Economista, diretta da Francesco Ferrara, Cugini Pomba e comp.

Dutot, Charles. 1754. *Réflexions politiques sur les finances et le commerce*, vol. 2. La Haye: Vaillant & Prevost.

Easterlin, Richard. 1974. Does economic growth improve the human lot? In *Nations and households in economic growth: Essays in honor of Moses Abramovitz*, ed. Paul David and Melvin Reder. New York: Academic.

Elster, Jon. 1987. *The multiple self: Studies in rationality and social change*. New York: Cambridge University Press.

Etzioni, Amitai. 1988. *The moral dimension: Toward a new economics*. London: Collier Macmillan.

Fehr, Ernst, and Simon Gächter. 2000. Fairness and retaliation – The economics of reciprocity. *Journal of Economic Perspectives* 14: 159–181.

Ferguson, Adamo. 1791/1792. *Saggio sopra la storia della società civile*, Opera tradotta dall'Inglese dal Sig. Bergier, ed ora dal Francese in Italiano da Tomaso Cerato, Avvocato Vicentino, 2 vols. Vincenza: Stamperia Turra.

Ferrari, Anton Filippo. 1954. Diritto ed economia socondo il Rosmini. In *La problematica politico-sociale nel pensiero di Antonio Rosmini*, 229–302. Roma: Fratelli Bocca Editori.

Ferroni, Lorenzo. 1987. *La critica di Rosmini a Hegel nella "Teosofia"*, 7. Stresa: Biblioteca di Studi Rosminiani.

Filangieri, Gaetano. 1807. *La scienza della legislazione*. 5 vols. Livorno: Stamperia delle Provincie Unite.

Franck, Juan F. 2006. *From the nature of the mind to personal dignity: The significance of Rosmini's philosophy*. Washington, DC: CUA Press.

Frank, Robert. 2000. *Luxury fever: Money and happiness in an era of excess*. Princeton: Princeton University Press.

Franklin, Beniamino. 1783. *Opere politiche. Tradotte dall'inglese Padora*. G. Venezia: Manfré.

Franklin, Beniamino. 1826. *Filosofia della statistica*, Tomi 2 in uno solo. Milano: Pirotta.

Fraser, Nancy, and Axel Honneth. 2003. *Redistribution or recognition? A political-philosophical exchange*. London: Verso.

Frey, Bruno. 1997. *Not just for the money: An economic theory of personal motivation*. New York: Edward Elgar.

Frey, Bruno. 2006. How influential is economics? Notes and communications. *De Economist* 154: 2. doi:10.1007/s10645-006-9005-2.

Fullbrook, Edward, ed. 2000. Open letter from economic students to professors and others responsible for the teaching of this discipline. Post-autistic economic newsletter 2. http://www.paecon.net/PAEReview/wholeissues/issue2.htm.

Galiani, Ferdinando. 1750. *Della moneta*. Napoli: Raimondi.

Galiani, Ferdinando. 1803. *Scrittori classici italiani di economia politica: parte moderna*. Vols. 3–6. Milano: Destefanis, Gio. Giuseppe (tip).

Genovesi, Antonio. 1768. *Delle lezioni di commercio, o sia, d' economia civile da leggersi*. Milano: Agnelli.

Genovesi, Antonio. 1827. *Opuscoli e Lettere familiari (Ragionamento intorno all' Agricoltura)*. Venezia: De Alvisopoli.

Gentile, Giovanni. 1958. *Rosmini e Gioberti, Saggio storico sulla filosofia italiana del Risorgimento*. Firenze: Sansoni.

Gerdil, Giacinto Sigismondo. 1768. *Discours de la Nature et des effets du luxe*. Turin: Frères Reycends.

Gioia, Melchiorre. 1850. *Nuovo Galateo*. Torino: Presso i fratelli Canfari Tipografi-editori.

Gioja, Melchiorre. 1815–1819. *Nuovo prospetto delle scienze economiche*, vol. 8. Milano: Pirotta.

Gioja, Melchiorre. 1819. *Sulle Manifatture Nazionali e Tariffe Daziarie*. Milano: Pirotta.

Gioja, Melchiorre. 1841. *Teoria civile e penale del divorzio*. Lugano: Presso gli editori.

Giordano, Antonio. 1976. *Le polemiche giovanili di Antonio Rosmini*. Stresa: CISR.

Giordano, Antonio. 1985. *La politica tra logica e storia. Il pensiero filosofico-politico di Antonio Rosmini*. Palermo: Ed. I.L.A. Palma.

Goisis, Giuseppe. 2009. Il pensiero politico di Antonio Rosmini e altri saggi fra critica ed Evangelo. S. Pietro in Cariano (VR): Gabrielli Editori.

Gray, Carlo. 1952. Introduzione. In *Progetti di costituzione, Saggi editi e inediti sullo stato*, a cura di Carlo Gray, Opere edite e inedite, vol. XXIV. Milano: Fratelli Bocca Editori.

Graziani, Augusto. 1972. Le idee economiche del Manzoni e del Rosmini. In *Economia e Storia*, Verona, Gennaio/Marzo, 49–58.

Greenfield, Kent Roberts. 1934. *Economics and liberalism in the Risorgimento. A study of nationalism in Lombardy*. Baltimore: The John Hopkins Press.

Gregg, Samuel. 2001. *Economic thinking for the theologically minded*. Lanham: University Press of America.

Guidi, Marco. 2000. Terenzio Maccabelli and Erica Morato. Neo-Smithian political economy in Italy. In *History of Economics Society Annual Meeting*, Vancouver.

Hahn, Frank, and Martin Hollis (eds.). 1986. *Filosofía y teoría económica*. México: FCE (Philosophy and Economic Theory, Oxford University Press, 1979).

Halévy, Elie. 1972. *The growth of philosophical radicalism*. London: Faber.

Haller, C.L. 1963. *La restaurazione della scienza politica*. Torino: Unione tip. editrice torinese.

Hargreaves Heap, Shaun. 2001. Expressive rationality. Is self-worth another preference? In *The economic world view: Studies in the ontology of economics*, ed. Uskali Maki, 98–113. New York: Cambridge University Press.

Harrington, G. 1802. *Aforismi politici*. Brescia: Dalla tipografia Dispart.

Hausman, Daniel S. (ed.). 1994. *The philosophy of economics. An anthology*. Cambridge: Cambridge University Press.

Hazard, Paul. 1967. *European thought in the eighteenth century, from Montesquieu to Lessing*. Cleveland: Meridian Books.

Hazard, Paul. 1998. *La crisis de la conciencia europea (1680–1715). Versión española de Julián Marías*. Madrid: Alianza Editorial.

Hegel, Georg. 1944. *Filosofía del Derecho*. Trans. A. Mendoza de Montero. Buenos Aires: Claridad.

Helvetius, M. 1784. *Oeuvres completes*, vol. 7. Sanson: Deux-Ponts.

Hirsch, Fred. 1978. *Social limits to growth*. New York: Routledge.

Hirschman, Albert O. 1977. *The passions and the interests. Political arguments for capitalism before its triumph*. Princeton: Princeton University Press.

Hirschman, Albert O. 1992. *Rival views of market society and other recent essays*. Cambridge: Harvard University Press.

Hodgson, Geoffrey. 1998. The approach of institutional economics. *Journal of Economic Literature* 36(1): 166–92.

Hoevel, Carlos. 2005a. *Economía e instituciones en el pensamiento de Antonio Rosmini: coincidencias y diferencias con la tradición liberal*, 5–35. Eseade: Libertas.
Hoevel, Carlos. 2005b. *Rosmini como filósofo social. La filosofía cristiana de Antonio Rosmini*. Buenos Aires: Educa.
Hoevel, Carlos. 2006. *Beyond democratism and conservatism: The original approach of Rosmini's 'Costituzione'. The constitution under social justice, by Antonio Rosmini, studies in ethics and economics*, xi–xxviii. Lanham: Lexington Books.
Hoevel, Carlos. 2007. The fiscal and tributary philosophy of Antonio Rosmini. *Journal of Markets & Morality* 10(1): 67–84.
Hoevel, Carlos. 2008. Rosmini y los economistas civiles italianos. *Archivio Storico Lombardo, Giornale della Società Storica Lombarda*. Anno CXXXIV: 147–180.
Hoevel, Carlos. 2009. Rosmini's socio-economic personalism and the soul of Europe. In *Imagine Europe – The search for European identity and spirituality*, ed. L. Bouckaert and J. Eynikel, 35–47. Apeldoorn: Garant Antwerpen.
Hoevel, Carlos. 2011a. A Rosminian vision for the post-crisis global economy. *Revista de Instituciones, Ideas y Mercados (RIIM)* Año XXVIII(55): 235–258.
Hoevel, Carlos. 2011b. La teoría de la justicia de Amartya Sen y los orígenes del concepto católico de justicia social en Antonio Rosmini. *Revista Cultura Económica* Año XXIX(81–82): 38–53.
Hoevel, Carlos. 2012. Rosmini's Risorgimental Reinterpretation of the Classical Economic School. In *Rosmini, Gioberti e Cavour. Cristianesimo, filosofia e politica nel Risorgimento*, ed. Silvio Spiri Brianza: Limina Mentis Editore.
Honneth, Axel. 1996. *The struggle for recognition: The moral grammar of social conflicts*. Cambridge: MIT Press.
Hume, David. 1767. *Saggi politici sopra il commercio, Traduzione dell'Inglese di Matteo Dandolo*. Venezia: G. M. Bassaglia.
Hume, David. 1825. *Storia d' Inghilterra*. Milano: Bettoni.
Kirchgässner, Gebhard. 2008. *Homo oeconomicus: The economic model of individual behavior and its applications in economics and other social sciences. The European heritage in economics and the social sciences*, vol. 6. New York: Springer.
Komar, Emilio. 1983. El progreso ilimitado y su posible filosofía. *Revista Valores en la sociedad industrial*. Año N° 1: 38–43.
Koslowski, Peter F. (ed.). 1985. *Economics and philosophy*. Tubinga: J. C. B. Mohr (Paul Siebeck).
Krienke, Markus (ed.). 2008a. *Sulla ragione. Rosmini e la filosofia tedesca*. Soveria Mannelli: Rubbettino.
Krienke, Markus. 2008b. *Antonio Rosmini. Ein Philosoph zwischen Tradition und Moderne*, 238. Freiburg/München: Karl Alber.
Krienke, Markus. ed. 2008c. *Sulla ragione. Rosmini e la filosofia tedesca*. Atti del convegno 'Rosmini e la fi losofi a tedesca', Catanzaro: Rubbettino
Layard, Richard. 2005. *Happiness: Lessons from a new science*. London: Penguin Press.
Leocata, Francisco. 1979. *Del iluminismo a nuestros días. Panorama de las ideas filosóficas en relación con el Cristianismo*. Buenos Aires: Ediciones Don Bosco Argentina.
Li Vigni, Ida. 1988. L'età dell'illuminismo. In *La cultura filosofica e scientifica*, ed. Paolo Aldo Rossi, 539–584. Busto Arsizio: Bramante Editrice.
Liberatore, P. Matteo. 1889. *Principii di Economia Politica*. Roma: Tipografia A. Befani.
Liermann, Christiane. 2004. *Rosminis politische Philosophie der zivilen Gesellschaft*. Paderborn: Schöningh.
Maffei, Scipione. 1744. *Dell'impiego del danaro*. Verona: Tumermani.
Malthus, Thomas. 1985. *An essay on the principle of population*. London: Penguin.
Manzoni, Alessandro. 1885. *Opere inedite o rare*. Milano: Fratelli Rechiedei.
Marangon, Paolo. 2000. *Il Risorgimento della Chiesa. Genesi e ricezione delle "Cinque piaghe" di Antonio Rosmini*. Roma: Herder.
Maritati, Gianni. 1988. *Manzoni L'esigenza di una 'cultura económica' cristianamente ispirata*. Nuova Umanità, Nov/Dic: 65–82.

Mattheu, Vittorio. 1988. L'idea dell illuminismo in Kant e in Rosmini. In *Rosmini e l'Illuminismo. Atti del XXI Corso della "Catedra Rosmini"*, ed. Pepino Pellegrino, 81–96. Stresa: Centro Internazionale di studi Rosminiani.

Mengotti, Francesco. 1787. *Del commercio de romani*. Milano: Pandora.

Mengotti, Francesco. 1803. *Scrittori classici italiani, parte moderna*, vol. 36. Milano: Destefanis, Gio. Giuseppe (tip).

Mercadante, Francesco. 1981. *Il regolamento della modalità dei diritti*. Roma: Multa Paucis.

Minghetti, Marco. 1868. *Della economia pubblica e delle sue attinenze colla morale e col diritto*. Firenze: Succesori Le Monier.

Muratore, Umberto. 1988. *Antonio Rosmini. Vida y Pensamiento*. Madrid: BAC.

Muratore, Umberto. 2008. *Conoscere Rosmini. Vita, pensiero, spiritualità*, nuova edizione aggiornata, Stresa: Sodalitas.

Muratore, Umberto. 2011. *Rosmini per il Risorgimento. Tra unità e federalismo*. Stresa: Edizioni Rosminiane.

Muratori, Ludovico Antonio. 1735. *La filosofia morale esposta e proposta ai giovani*. Verona: Angelo Targa.

Muratori, Lodovico Antonio. 1749. *Della Pubblica Felicità*. Verona: Edic. Lucca.

Muscolino, Salvatore. 2003. *Il problema della legge naturale in san Tommaso e Rosmini*. Palermo: Ila Palma.

Muscolino, Salvatore. 2006. *Genesi e sviluppo del costituzionalismo rosminiano*. Palermo: Palumbo.

Muscolino, Salvatore. 2010a. *Persona e mercato I liberalismi di Rosmini e Hayek a confronto Prefazione di Flavio Felice Postfazione di Markus Krienke*. Soveria Mannelli: Rubbettino.

Muscolino, Salvatore. 2010b. *Persona e mercato. I liberalismi di Rosmini e Hayek a confronto*, Prefazione di F. Felice, Postfazione di M. Krienke. Soveria Mannelli: Rubbettino.

Necker, Jacques. 1781. *Compte rendu au roi*. Paris: de l' imprimerie du cabinet du roi.

Necker, Jacques. 1784. *De l'administration des finances de la France*. Paris: [S.n.].

Nicoletti, Michele and Michele Dossi (eds.). 2007. *Antonio Rosmini tra modernità e universalità*. Brescia: Morcelliana.

Nicoletti, Michele and Francesco Ghia (eds.). 2012. *Conservare l'intelligenza: lezioni rosminiane*. Trento: Università degli Studi di Trento.

North, Douglas. 1990. *Institutions, institutional change and economic performance*. New York: Cambridge University Press.

Ortes, G.M. 1804. *Scrittori classici italiani di economia politica: parte moderna*, vols. 21 to 27. Milano: Destefanis, Gio. Giuseppe (tip).

Ottonello, Pier Paolo. 1978. *L´attualità di Rosmini*. Genova: Studio editoriale di cultura.

Palmieri, Matteo. 1825. *Della vita civile, Biblioteca scelta di Opere Italiane antiche e moderne*. Milano: G. Silvestri.

Parisi Acquaviva, Daniela. 1984. *Il pensiero economico classico in Italia (1750–1860)*. Milano: Vita e Pensiero, Università Cattolica Milano.

Parisi Acquaviva, Daniela. 1999. Pre-classical economic thought profitable commerce and formal constraints in the economic studies of the young Pietro Verri. *Revista internazionale di scienze sociali* Anno CVII(Ottobre–Diciembre): 455–479.

Picenardi, Gianni (ed.). 2011. *Rosmini politico: Tra unità e federalismo. Atti del XIX Convegno Sacrense – Sacra di San Michele, 17–18 sett. 2010*. Stresa: Edizioni rosminiane.

Piovani, Pietro. 1951a. Ancora del 'socialismo' di Rosmini. *Rivista internazionale di Filosofia del Diritto* Anno XXVIII – Serie III (Aprile-Giugno, Fasc. II): 432–434.

Piovani, Pietro. 1951b. Rosmini e il socialismo risorgimentale. *Revista internazionale di Filosofia del Diritto* Anno XXVIII – Serie III (Gennaio-Marzo, Fasc. I): 76–93.

Piovani, Pietro. 1957. *La teodicea sociale di Rosmini*. Padova: Cedam.

Piovani, Pietro. 1961. Il liberalismo di Rosmini. In *Atti del XXXVII Congresso di Storia del Risorgimento Italiano*, 215–222. Roma: Istituto per la Storia del Risorgimento Italiano.

Pippin, Robert. 2000. What is the question for which Hegel's theory of recognition is the answer? *European Journal of Philosophy* 8(2): 155–172.

Putnam, Robert. 2000. *Bowling alone: The collapse and revival of American community*. New York: Simon & Schuster.
Quattrocchi, Pietro. 1988. Dal Risorgimento alla prima metà del Novecento. In *La cultura filosofica e scientifica*, ed. Paolo Aldo Rossi, 589–645. Busto Arsizio: Bramante Editrice.
Radice, Gianfranco. 1991. *Annali di Antonio Rosmini Serbati*. Milano: Marzorati Editore.
Raschini, María. 1961. *Il principio dialettico nella filosofia di A. Rosmini*. Milano: Marzorati Editore.
Raschini, María. 1986. *Rosmini e l'idea di progresso*. Genova: Sodalitas.
Raynal, Guill Th. 1776. *Histoire philosophique el politique des établissements & du commerce des Européens dans le deux Indes, A – La Haye*. Amsterdam: Gossefils.
Ricoeur, Paul. 2005. *Parcours de la reconnaissance*. Paris: Gallimard.
Riconda, Giuseppe. 2005. *Manzoni e Rosmini*, vol. 12. Roma: Fondazioni Capograssi.
Riva, Clemente. 1958. Economia, politica e exigenza morale. *Rivista Rosminiana* Anno LII (Gennaio-Marzo Fasc. I), 16–21.
Riva, Clemente. 1970. *Attualita' di Rosmini*. Roma: Editrici Studium.
Roberti, Conte Giambattista. 1785. *Opuscoli quattro sopra il Lusso*. Bassano: Remondini.
Robertson, William. 1774. *La storia del regno dell'imperatore Carlo – Quinto*. Colonia: D.D Publisher.
Robertson, William. 1778a. *L'histoire de l'Amerique*. Paris: Thou.
Robertson, William. 1778b. *Storia di America*. Firenze: Florentino.
Robertson, William. 1821. *Recherches historiques sur l'Inde ancienne, sur la connoissance que les anciens en avoient, et sur les progrès du commerce avec cette contrée avant la découverte du passage par le Cap. de Bonne Espérance*. Paris: Janet et Cotelle.
Romagnosi, G.D. 1805. *Introduzione alla studio del diritto pubblico universale*. Parma: Stamp. Imperiale.
Romagnosi, G.D. 1828. *Della suprema economia dell'umano sapere*. Milano: F. Rusconi.
Romagnosi, G.D. 1829. *Gioja, Melchiorre, Elogio dell' Autore*. Milano: Silvestri.
Romagnosi, G.D. 1832. *Dell' indole e dei fattori dell' incivilimento*. Milano: S. Ed. Annali Universali.
Romagnosi, G.D. 1833. *Genesi del diritto penale*. Firenze: Guasti.
Romagnosi, Giandomenico. 1839. *Sulla crescente popolazione*. Milano: Presso gli editori degli Annali universali delle scienze e dell'industria.
Romagnosi, G.D. 1845. *Opere, Riordinate ed illustrate da Alessandro de Giorgi*. Milano: Presso Perelli e Mariani Editori.
Rosmini, Antonio. 1855. *Logica: libri tre*. Torino: Cugini Pomba.
Rosmini, Antonio. 1870. Galateo de' letterati. Opere edite e inedite, Letteratura e arti belle, Parte prima. Opuscoli varj. Bertolotti.
Rosmini, Antonio. 1887. *Della naturale Costituzione della* società *civile. Filosofia della politica*. Rovereto: Tip. Giorgio Grigoletti.
Rosmini, Antonio. 1901. *Carteggio fra Alessandro Manzoni e Antonio Rosmini. Raccolto e annotatto da Giulio Bonola*. Milano: Cogliati Editrice.
Rosmini, Antonio. 1923. *Opere inedite di politica*. A cura del Prof. G. B. Nicola. Milano: Stab. Tipo. Lit. G. Tenconi.
Rosmini, Antonio. 1933. *Saggi di Scienza Politica, Scritti inediti*. A cura di G. B. Nicola. Torino-Milano: G. B. Paravia & C.
Rosmini, Antonio. 1934. Introduzione alla Filosofia. *Opere edite e inedite di Antonio Rosmini-Serbati*, vol. II. A cura di Ugo Redano. Roma: Anonima Romana Editoriale.
Rosmini, Antonio. 1938. *Teosofía*. A cura di Carlos Gray. Roma: Edizione nazionale delle opere edite e inedite di Antonio Rosmini.
Rosmini, Antonio. 1941. Storia comparativa e critica dei sistemi intorno al principio della morale. In *Principi della scienza morale e Storia comparativa e critica dei sistemi intorno al principio della morale*. A cura di Dante Morando, Opere edite e inedite, vol. XXI. Milano: Fratelli Bocca Editori.

Rosmini, Antonio. 1952a. La costituzione secondo la giustizia sociale. *Progetti di costituzione, Saggi editi e inediti sullo stato*, a cura di Carlo Gray, Opere edite e inedite, vol. XXIV. 65–239. Milano: Fratelli Bocca Editori.

Rosmini, Antonio. 1952b. La costituente del regno dell'alta Italia. *Progetti di costituzione, Saggi editi e inediti sullo stato*, a cura di Carlo Gray, Opere edite e inedite, vol. XXIV. 243–288. Milano: Fratelli Bocca Editori.

Rosmini, Antonio. 1976. Breve esposizione della filosofia di Melchiorre Gioja. *Studi critici su Ugo Foscolo e Melchiorre Gioja.* A cura di Rinaldo Orecchia, Opere edite e inedite, vol. XLVIII, 87–191. Padova: Cedam-Casa editrice Dott. Antonio Milani.

Rosmini, Antonio. 1977a. Esame delle opinioni di Melchiorre Gioja in favor della moda. In *Frammenti di una Storia della empietà e scritti vari.* A cura di Rinaldo Orecchia. Opere edite e inedite, vol. XLIX. Padova: CEDAM.

Rosmini, Antonio. 1977b. *Teodicea. Libri Tre.* A cura di Umberto Murature. Roma: Città Nuova Editrice, Centro Internazionale di Studi Rosminiani.

Rosmini, Antonio. 1978a. *Saggio sulla definizione della ricchezza.* Filosofia Della Politica, vol. IV. *Opuscoli Politici.* A cura di Gianfreda Marconi en Opere edite e inedite di Antonio Rosmini, Edizione critica promossa da Michele Federico Sciacca. 15–45. Roma: Centro Internazionale di Studi Rosminiani, Città Nuova Editrice.

Rosmini, Antonio. 1978b. *Sulla Statistica.* Filosofia Della Politica, vol. IV. *Opuscoli Politici.* A cura di Gianfreda Marconi en Opere edite e inedite di Antonio Rosmini, Edizione critica promossa da Michele Federico Sciacca. 65–80. Roma: Centro Internazionale di Studi Rosminiani, Città Nuova Editrice.

Rosmini, Antonio. 1978c. *Il Comunismo ed il Socialismo.* Filosofia della Politica, vol. IV. *Opuscoli Politici.* A cura di Gianfreda Marconi in Opere edite e inedite di Antonio Rosmini Edizione critica promossa da Michele Federico Sciacca. 81–121. Roma: Centro Internazionale di Studi Rosminiani: Città Nuova Editrice.

Rosmini, Antonio. 1978d. *Le Principali questioni politico-religiose della giornata.* Filosofia della Politica, vol. IV. *Opuscoli Politici.* A cura di Gianfreda Marconi in Opere edite e inedite di Antonio Rosmini Edizione critica promossa da Michele Federico Sciacca. 123–240. Roma: Centro Internazionale di Studi Rosminiani: Città Nuova Editrice.

Rosmini, Antonio. 1981. *Delle cinque piaghe della Santa Chiesa.* A cura di Alfeo Valle, Istituto di Studi Filosofici, Centro di Studi Rosminiani, Stresa. Roma: Città Nuova Editrice.

Rosmini, Antonio. 1987. *New essay concerning the origin of ideas.* Trans. by Denis Cleary and Terence Watson from the Nuovo Saggio sull'Origine delle Idee. Durham: Rosmini House.

Rosmini, Antonio. 1988a. *Principles of ethics.* Trans. by Denis Cleary and Terence Watson from Principi della Scienza Morale. Durham: Rosmini House.

Rosmini, Antonio. 1988b. *Psicologia. Libri Dieci*, vols. I, II. A cura di Vicenio Sala. Istituto di Studi Filosofici, Centro Internazionale di Studi Rosminiani, Roma: Città Nuova Editrice.

Rosmini, Antonio. 1991. *Anthropology as an aid to moral science.* Trans. Denis Cleary and Terence Watson. Durham: Rosmini House.

Rosmini, Antonio. 1993a. *The philosophy of right, vol. 1: The essence of right.* Trans. Denis Cleary and Terence Watson. Durham: Rosmini House.

Rosmini, Antonio. 1993b. *The philosophy of right, vol. 2: Rights of the individual.* Durham: Rosmini House.

Rosmini, Antonio. 1994a. *The philosophy of politics: The summary cause for the stability or downfall of human societies.* Trans. D. Cleary and Terence Watson. Durham: Rosmini House.

Rosmini, Antonio. 1994b. *The philosophy of politics, vol. 2: Society and its purpose.* Trans. Denis Cleary and Terence Watson. Durham: Rosmini House.

Rosmini, Antonio. 1994c. Sull'Unità dell'Educazione. *Dell' Educazione Cristiana- Sull'Unità dell'Educazione.* A cura di Lino Prenna, Opere edite e inedite di Antonio Rosmini, Edizione Nazionale promossa da Enrico Castelli. Roma: Città nuova.

Rosmini, Antonio. 1995a. *The Philosophy of Right, vol. 3: Universal Social Right.* Trans. Denis Cleary and Terence Watson. Durham: Rosmini House.

Rosmini, Antonio. 1995b. *The philosophy of right, vol. 5: Rights in the family*. Trans. Denis Cleary and Terence Watson. Durham: Rosmini House.
Rosmini, Antonio. 1996. *The philosophy of right, vol. 6: Rights in civil society*. Trans. Denis Cleary and Terence Watson. Durham: Rosmini House.
Rosmini, Antonio. 2001. *Grande dizionario antologico del pensiero di Antonio Rosmini*. A cura di Cirillo Bergamaschi. Roma, Centro Internazionale di Studi Rosminiani: Città Nuova, Edizioni Rosminiani.
Rosmini, Antonio. 2003. Politica Prima. *Apendice, Frammenti della Filosofia della Politica (1826–1827)*. A cura di Mario d´Addio. Roma, Istituto di Studi Filosofici, Centro Internazionale di Studi Rosminiani: Città Nuova Editrice.
Rosmini, Antonio. 2007. *The constitution under social justice*. Trans. Alberto Mingardi. London: Lexington Books.
Sancipriano, Mario. 1968. *Il pensiero politico di Haller e Rosmini*. Milano: Marzorati.
Santonastaso, Giuseppe. 1879. Rosmini e l'economia politica. In *Per Antonio Rosmini nel primo centenario della sua nascita – 24 marzo 1897*. Milano: Cogliati.
Say, Jean Baptiste. 1819. *Traité d' Economie politique*, vol. 2. Paris- Deterville: Quatrienne Edition.
Say, Jean Baptiste. 1854. *Trattato d'Economia Politica. Biblioteca dell'Economista, diretta da Francesco Ferrara*. Torino: Cugini Pomba e comp. Editori.
Sciacca, Michele Federico. 1954. *El pensamiento filosófico de Rosmini*. Barcelona: Luis Miracle.
Sciacca, Michele Federico, ed. 1957. *Atti del Congresso Internazionale di Filosofia Antonio Rosmini* (Stresa-Rovereto 20–26 luglio 1955). Firenze: Sansoni.
Sciacca, Michele Federico. 1958. El espiritualismo cristiano. In *Filosofía italiana del 900*. Buenos Aires: Asociación Dante Alighieri.
Sciacca, Michele Federico. 1962. *Il pensiero giuridico e politico di Antonio Rosmini*. Bologna: Sansoni-Firenze, Bologna.
Sciacca, Michele Federico. 1963a. *Interpretazioni Rosminiane*. Milano: Marzorati Editore.
Sciacca, Michele Federico. 1963b. *Metafisica, gnoseologia y moral. Ensayo sobre el pensamiento de Antonio Rosmini*. Madrid: Gredos.
Scitovsky, Tibor. 1976. *The joyless economy: The psychology of human satisfaction*. Oxford: Oxford University Press.
Screpanti, Ernesto, and Stefano Zamagni. 2005. *An outline of the history of economic thought*. Oxford: Oxford University Press.
Sen, Amartya. 1977. Rational fools: A critique of the behavioral foundations of economic theory. *Philosophy and Public Affairs* 6(4): 317–344.
Sen, Amartya. 1987. *On ethics and economics*. Oxford: Basil Blackwell.
Sen, Amartya. 1999. *Development as freedom*. Oxford: Oxford University Press.
Sidney, Algernon. 1702. *Discours sur le gouvernement, Traduits de l'Anglois par P. A. Samson*, vol. 3. La Haye: Van Dole.
Simon, Herbert. 1957. A behavioral model of rational choice. In *Models of man, social and rational: Mathematical essays on rational human behavior in a social setting*. New York: Wiley.
Sismondi, G.Carlo. 1809–1816. *Histoire des Républiques italiennes du moyen age*. Paris: Nicolle.
Sismondi, G. Carlo. 1819. *Nuovi principii di economia politica, o sia, della ricchezza posta in raffronto colla popolazione*, trad. Pref. Gaetan o Barbieri, Milano, Vismara.
Sismondi, G.Carlo. 1821–1822. *Storia dei francesi*. Milano: Trad. Perotti.
Sismondi, G.Carlo. 1974. *Nuovi Principi di economia politica o della ricchezza nei suoi rapporti con la popolazione, a cura di Piero Barucci*. Milano: IEDI.
Smith, Adam. 1976 [1843]. *An inquiry into the nature and causes of the wealth of nations*. Chicago: The University of Chicago Press.
Smith, Adam. 1782. *Théorie des sentiment moraux*, vol. 2. Paris: Chez Laporte.
Smith, Adam. 1790. *Richerche sulla natura e le cagioni delle ricchezza delle Nazioni. Tradotte per la prima volta in Italiano dall' ultima edizione Inglese*, vol. 5. Napoli: G. P. Merande.
Smith, Adam. 1797. *Essais philosophiques*, vol. 2. Paris: Chez Agasse.

Solari, Gioele. 1957. *Studi rosminiani*. Milano: Giuffrè.

Solari, Gioele. 2000. *Rosmini inedito. La formazione del pensiero politico*. A cura di Umberto Muratore. Stresa, Centro Internazionale di Studi Rosminiani: Presentazione.

Somervell, D.C. 1929. *English thought in the nineteenth century*. London: Methuen & Co. Ltd.

Sonnenfels, (de) Giuseppe. 1774. *Fondamenti della Scienza politica del Commercio e Finanze*. Coira: Giacomo Otto.

Spiri, Silvio. 2004. *Essere e sentimento. La persona nella filosofia di Antonio Rosmini*. Roma: Città Nuova.

Sully, Maximiliam de Bethure. 1662/1663. *Duc de Sully*. Rouen: Memoires ou economics royales d' Estat.

Tadini, Samuele. 2012. *La teosofia di Rosmini. Invito alla lettura*. Stresa: Sodalitas.

Taparelli D'Azeglio, Luigi. 1949. *Saggio teoretico di diritto naturale appoggiato sul fatto, ristampa della quarta edizione corretta e accresciuta*. Roma: Civiltà Cattolica.

Taylor, Charles. 1994. The politics of recognition. In *Multiculturalism. Examining the politics of recognition*, ed. Amy Gutmann. Princeton: Princeton University Press.

The Cambridge 27. 2001. Opening up economics. In *Post-autistic economics newsletter* 7, Article 1. http://www.btinternet.com/~pae_news/review/issue7.htm.

Theunissen, Michael. 1991. The repressed intersubjectivity in Hegel's philosophy of right. In *Hegel and legal theory*. London: Routledge.

Tommaseo Niccolò. 1999. *Antonio Rosmini*, a cura di Umberto Moratore. Stresa: Sodalitas.

Traniello, Francesco. 1970. Una fonte veneta del pensiero politico-religioso di Rosmini: Giammaria Ortes. In *Rosmini e il Rosminianesimo nel Veneto*, ed. Andrea Mario Moschetti, Alberto Vecchi, Dante Gallio, and Domenico Romani. Verona: Casa Editrice Mazziana.

Traniello, Francesco. 1997. *Società religiosa e società civile in Rosmini*. Brescia: Morcelliana.

Turiello, Lucia. 1982. *Persona e società civile nel pensiero di Rosmini*. Roma: Città Nuova.

Venturi, Franco. 1969. *Settecento riformatore. Da Muratori a Beccaria*. Torino: Giulio Einaudi editore.

Verondini, Enrico. 1967. *La filosofia morale di Antonio Rosmini*. Bologna: Cappelli Editore.

Verri, Pietro. 1804. *Scrittori classici italiani*, vol. 15–17. Milano: Destefanis.

Williams, Robert. 2000. *Hegel's ethics of recognition*. San Diego: University of California Press.

Young, Arturo. 1794. *L 'esempio della Francia avviso e specchio all' Inghilterra*. Pavia: B. Comino.

Zamagni, Stefano. 1982. *Saggi di filosofia della scienza economica*, F. Hahn et al. a cura di Stefano Zamagni. Roma: NIS.

Zamagni, Stefano. 2005. Happiness and individualism: A very difficult union. In *Economics and happiness: Framing the analysis*, ed. Luigino Bruni and Pierluigi Porta. Oxford: Oxford University Press.

Zolo, Danilo. 1963. *Il personalismo rosminiano*. Brescia: Morcelliana.

Zoppi, G.B. 1897. Antonio Rosmini e l'Economia politica. In *Antonio Rosmini nel Primo centenario dalla sua nascita*. Milano: Tipografia Editrice L. F. Cogliati.

Name Index

C. Hoevel, *The Economy of Recognition: Person, Market and Society in Antonio Rosmini*, Ethical Economy 42, DOI 10.1007/978-94-007-6058-5,

Subject Index

C. Hoevel, *The Economy of Recognition: Person, Market and Society in Antonio Rosmini*, Ethical Economy 42, DOI 10.1007/978-94-007-6058-5,

MIX
Papier aus verantwortungsvollen Quellen
Paper from responsible sources
FSC® C105338

If you have any concerns about our products,
you can contact us on
ProductSafety@springernature.com

In case Publisher is established outside the EU,
the EU authorized representative is:
Springer Nature Customer Service Center GmbH
Europaplatz 3, 69115 Heidelberg, Germany

Printed by Libri Plureos GmbH
in Hamburg, Germany